Occidentalism

Occidentalism

A Theory of Counter-Discourse in Post-Mao China

*Second Edition,
Revised and Expanded*

Xiaomei Chen

Foreword by Jinhua Dai

ROWMAN & LITTLEFIELD PUBLISHERS, INC.
Lanham • Boulder • New York • Oxford

ROWMAN & LITTLEFIELD PUBLISHERS, INC.

Published in the United States of America
by Rowman & Littlefield Publishers, Inc.
A Member of the Rowman & Littlefield Publishing Group
4720 Boston Way, Lanham, Maryland 20706
www.rowmanlittlefield.com

PO Box 317, Oxford, OX2 9RU, United Kingdom

Copyright © 2002 by Rowman & Littlefield Publishers, Inc.

First edition by Oxford University Press, 1995

British Library Cataloguing in Publication Information Available

Library of Congress Cataloging-in-Publication Data

Chen, Xiaomei, 1954–
    Occidentalism : a theory of counter-discourse in post-Mao China / Xiaomei Chen.—2nd ed.
    p. cm.
    Includes bibliographical references and index.
    1. China—Intellectual life—1976– 2. China—Politics and government—1976– 3. Chinese
literature—20th century—Western influences. I. Title: Theory of counter-discourse in
post-Mao China. II. Title.

DS779.23 .C443 2002
303.48'25101821—dc 21

2002021369

Printed in the United States of America

♾™ The paper used in this publication meets the minimum requirements of American
National Standard for Information Sciences—Permanence of Paper for Printed Library
Materials, ANSI/NISO Z39.48-1992.

In memory of

C. Clifford Flanigan

Contents

Contents

Foreword

At the turn of the century, China no longer appears to be a subaltern among nations. At the very least, China already has become a piece, albeit one difficult to position, in the mosaic of global capitalism. In the post–Cold War era, economic profit, global market share, and cultural differences have become even more important focal points as the Western world looks at China. It may seem possible now to discuss China's history and present situation only within the context of global postcolonialism, or as a developing Third World nation. But this would not be the entire story.

From one perspective, China is still a "subaltern." China's social transformation in the post-Mao era has always been tied and indebted to the Mao era and China's history of socialism. China's "modernization" (or, more accurately, the rebirth of capitalism within social praxis) must be viewed in reference to the positive and negative aspects of Mao's policies. To use one of my favorite phrases, since 1978, the Mao era has been "an enormous inheritance and debt" that society has found difficult to acknowledge. Until only recently, it was clearly recognized as an "alternative modernization" (to use this rather suspicious term). If China during this period was the "Oriental Other" sealed behind the bamboo curtain, then China has never truly been outside the history of global capitalism and its resistance. Emphasizing the significance of the Mao era as an alternative course of modernization, however, does not signify the elimination or replacement of the theoretical field of vision and historical reality of China and the socialist revolution.

We could recount China's turbulent twentieth century by focusing on the historical development of global capitalism. However, the Mao era provides us with a history difficult to delineate clearly within a single cultural logic, such as modernization, alternative modernization, or the Cold War. Moreover, this history is an inherent component in the construction of China's social reality and political and cultural praxis today. It is precisely the interweaving of its history with the rebirth of capitalism, labeled as "socialism with Chinese characteristics," that forms the complex social reality of China at the turn of the century. In my view "postsocialism" is a more apt and useful concept than "postcolonialism" for discussing China during the past twenty years. It is precisely in regard to this issue that Xiaomei Chen's *Occidentalism* offers an indispensable contribution.

OCCIDENTALISM VS. ORIENTALISM

The publication of Edward Said's *Orientalism* was certainly a momentous event in America, or at least in the Western academic community. As a work filled with penetrating insight, *Orientalism* brought to light the social and cultural difference and opposition between "East" and "West." According to Said, this difference, rather than a basic truth within the "history of human civilization," is a discursive structure produced by the Western capitalist world. This difference expresses itself as an Other that must exist as the West's Eurocentric mirror image. The discourse of difference is manifested in the institutions of the humanities and social sciences in the West. In the Western world and the modern, Eurocentric academic tradition, *Orientalism* provided a new critical space and path to self-cognizance and reflexivity. Undoubtedly it ranks as one of the most significant contributions to Western sociocultural critical theory. Yet as it challenges and subverts Eurocentric cultural institutions, *Orientalism*, with its foundations in Western social and cultural critical theory, remains confined in Eurocentric/Ethnocentric constraints. From one perspective, the work represents within the English-language world the increasingly prominent voice of Third World scholars. Therefore, when *Occidentalism*, written by a woman scholar from China, was first published, it was necessarily viewed as inspired by the scholarly ideas of *Orientalism*. At the same time, *Occidentalism* is bound to gain recognition for engaging and challenging *Orientalism*'s tendency to depict the oppositional intellectual traditions of "East" and "West" as static.

In this first comprehensive study of Occidentalism in post-Mao China, Xiaomei Chen offers an insightful account of the unremittingly favorable depiction of Western culture and the negative characterization of Chinese culture in early post-Mao China from 1978 to 1988. She examines the cultural and political interrelations between the East and West from a vantage point more complex than that furnished by most current theories of Western imperialism and colonialism. Going beyond Said's construction of cross-cultural appropriations as a defining facet of Western imperialism, Chen argues that the appropriation of Western discourse—what she calls "Occidentalism"—can actually have a politically and ideologically liberating effect on contemporary non-Western culture. She maintains that simplistic allegations of Orientalism frequently found in current critical discourses seriously underestimate the complexities of intercultural and multicultural relationships.

Similar to *Orientalism*, *Occidentalism* illustrates how the position of Third World native cultures can create subversive intellectual inquiries in the theoretical development of American academia and English-language scholarship. On this level, *Occidentalism* engages *Orientalism* while still being constructed within its legacy. Although *Occidentalism* might engage *Orientalism* on many common intellectual issues, the work is best not construed as a direct response to *Orientalism*. *Orientalism*'s subversive stance reveals that the "Orient," as a discursive construct of the Other within Western culture, is a capitalist/imperialist/colonialist by-product of the institution of social sciences, produced and reproduced by Orientology. *Occidentalism*, on the other hand, takes up the discursive significance of the "West" in politico-cultural practice in post-Mao China.

As illustrated by Chen, the cultural landscape of China in the late 1970s and 1980s, which recalled its early twentieth-century process of "Westernization," experienced a very real institutional transformation. The adoption of capitalism by the socialist state as a type of discursive practice manifested a profound and self-conscious cultural misreading, namely in its reliance upon Western (mainly eighteenth- and nineteenth-century) materials to construct an effective native Chinese counter-discourse. One of the major contributions of *Orientalism* stems from its insightful analysis both outside and inside the cultural traditions of the West. In contrast, *Occidentalism* adopts an "outside" position, revealing the intellectual trends during the transformation of China's society in the 1980s while being cautious to identify with the American (mainstream or leftist) academic tradition.

First, one must take up the cultural predicament deeply and urgently faced by intellectuals who are leftist, Marxist, or adopt a critical position toward socialism/capitalism, whether they live in China or overseas. In dealing with contemporary China, we cannot readily escape from our social positioning, theoretical resources, and discursive dilemma. We clearly realize the relentless course of global capitalism, the economic penetration and cultural invasion that accompanies transnational capitalism, and the exploitation of nascent capitalism. With the birth of capitalism in China, we also realize how China is being pigeonholed as a "Third World" nation. We also witness how in China the division between rich and poor is becoming more and more severe. At the same time, one still cannot ignore the violence, devastation, and depredation in China's socialist history, during certain periods (e.g., the Cultural Revolution) and within certain areas (e.g., the immense countryside).

Similarly, we cannot neglect the multiple roles played by the Chinese state during the post-Mao era. For example, China's political regime vigorously promotes the rebirth of capitalism with its "modernization" campaign. In this way, cooperation between the regime and the hegemonic influence of transnational capitalism grows stronger each day. At the same time, on issues of national and ethnic sovereignty, the regime offers a stance of opposition, even to the point of hostility, toward transnational capitalism and imperialism. We must also consider that as the "last great socialist power in the world," although unable to legitimately declare itself a socialist leader in the international and domestic political realms, China can only adopt ad hoc social measures to extend the life of the socialist system. Rather absurdly, the political regime has continued to depend on the apparatus of socialist ideological control to conceal severe inequalities in class and gender. In international politics, China has always attempted to participate in global capitalism but at the same time finds itself still positioned, without choice, within the Cold War–like politics of the post–Cold War era. Therefore, our sociocultural position, as intellectuals living in China or overseas, cannot adopt the rather simple, critical positioning and leftist tradition of the West. The task at hand is to self-consciously carry on the historical legacy of socialism, clearing the historical debt of the socialist era, and to directly combat the course of global capitalism while refusing to cede authority to the political regime. This task requires that we adopt a critical, but indigenous and concrete, oppositional position to history and China's present. This is far from being just a simple choice between "right" and "left." This critical position and its predicament do not originate from a different Western cultural resource (such as the theoretical resource of anti-essentialism provided by poststructuralism). Rather than a native critical positioning that naively challenges the cultural superiority of the West, it should emerge from directly confronting and taking responsibility for the social reality of contemporary China. It is from this perspective that I read Xiaomei Chen's discussion of Occidentalism in China as a type of complex social, political, and cultural practice.

Chen's discussion of Occidentalism in the late 1970s and 1980s brings to the forefront a very important aspect of China's many-sided cultural milieu. Occidentalism, as a self-conscious discursive construction and one of China's most important oppositional cultural practices in the 1980s, became complexly interwoven with China's "official stories" and national order. In the course of its development, Occidentalism was riddled with contradictions and conflicts. It has always drawn on materials constructed by the imperialistic hegemonies of politics, economics, and culture. Even if this very fact could be seen as testifying to the hegemony of cultural imperialism, Occidentalism is not a last-ditch measure imposed by the omnipresent hegemony. Rather, within different sociocultural practices in various Third World nations and regions, Occidentalism has always possessed the potential for expressing plural subjectivities according to different circumstances.

In reality, Occidentalism sometimes leads to self-Orientalization. Examples can be seen in the difficult task of creating native versions that fit into the logic of modernization. These discourses may take the guise of "traditional modernization," or when elites construct narratives of "uniqueness," "cultural difference," "ethnicity," and the "special characteristics of X country." Occidentalism may be adopted by developing countries as an effective method to affirm their ideological legitimacy or to construct a new regime and its structure of oppression. But these actions can also be leveraged to achieve a degree of "ethnic" resistance to imperialist political or military invasion, economic infiltration, or exploitation. Occidentalism may move beyond just a type of national order or discourse as it is drawn upon as a native oppositional force to oppose domestic political violence and the oppression of class, gender, and minorities. It may serve as armament for Third World native intellectuals in their politico-cultural guerrilla warfare and as a weapon for the people's resistance.

CHINA: PAST AND PRESENT

China is somewhat different, however, from the other Third World countries. The construction of Occidentalism in contemporary China draws from the history of colonialism and its resistance, but becomes more complicated by its ties with the history of socialism. First, the history of the socialist/communist movement and the experience of Chinese socialism have their historical roots in the West (as seen in the writings of Marx and Engels), although it was indeed subject to rewritings by Lenin, Stalin, and Mao Zedong. The banners of internationalism raised by communism/socialism (e.g.,"Let the proletariat around the world unite" and "world revolution") prevented Maoist ideology from expelling its Occidental characteristics. However, the establishment of the socialist system within China became the successful route for creating a powerful and modern nation-state. China had no choice but to adopt an international policy of "independent self-reliance," keeping all enemies outside its doors. This Cold War stance involved confronting the powerful camp of Western capitalism, realizing the chasm between "East" and "West," and sealing off the political economy. At the same time, China very quickly faced a rupture in its alliance with the Soviet Union. Therefore, the establishment of

China's socialist ideology has always more or less relied upon a type of self-Orientalism, emphasizing the "uniqueness" of China's history and current state to pronounce and establish a powerful, unyielding national order.

As astutely pointed out by Chen, from 1950 to 1970, and particularly since the 1960s, the expression of resistance to capitalism in socialist ideology has always proceeded with essentialist expressions of Occidentalism or an effective imagining of Self/West. We see this pattern in the rising invincible giant of the Orient pitted against the "imperialist bandits" from the feeble capitalist system, whose people struggle in great misery because of the degenerate Western culture and lifestyle. In the rhetorical representations of the Sinocentric imagination (e.g., "China is the heart of the world revolution," "source of the world's revolution," and "red heart"), we see the interweaving of the discourses of communism, internationalism, and world revolution. Therefore, while official Occidentalism adopts China—as a modern nation-state—to construct a discourse in opposition to global capitalism, it also functions as an important component of nationalism. Occidentalism helps conceal China's domestic political violence and obscures the mechanism of oppression in the socialist system. During the Mao era, therefore, the regime had already successfully employed the discourse of anti-imperialism to construct an external enemy, and thus Occidentalism was already part of China's sociopolitical, economic, and cultural structure.

As soon as the Cultural Revolution ended and the Deng Xiaoping era began in the late 1970s, a new essentialized version of Occidentalism took root. Intellectuals began to adopt the imagination of the West as an effective counter-discourse to oppose the political regime, as reflected in their critical debates on the post-Mao enlightenment, historical teleology, and the democratic and liberalist movements. This method of opposition took shape replete with an Orientalist historical narrative. In this story, "Oriental despotism," as an extension of lingering Chinese feudalism and the "super-stable, cyclical structure" of China's history, negated the development of socialism. Therefore, the debate whether socialism or capitalism should become the future orientation of China could only be accommodated by a shift in cultural metaphors. Occidentalism, rather than Orientalism, on this account, became a rather appropriate choice. Official Occidentalism helped the state ideology effectively avoid the inherent conflicts between communism, internationalism, and nationalism, and evade the crisis in the "official story," brought on by the harsh reality of the socialist camp's divisions. The new era's use of the terms "Occidentalism" and "Orientalism" as code words for "capitalism" and "socialism" eased political oppression and conflict. Of course, the Deng era's Occidentalism must conceal China's modernization during the past century and socialism's role in China's modernization. At the same time, this Occidentalism also necessarily masks the basic fact that the Occidental cultural resources used by the intellectuals in the late 1970s and 1980s actually derived from an existing structure within contemporary Chinese culture and socialism. As illustrated by Chen, Occidentalism, as expressed by the intellectuals as a counter-discourse, although directed at China's socialist system, cannot be classified as an open, direct initiative to promote transnational capitalism. Rather, this discourse sketched out a new and different ideal landscape and presented a "diagnosis" for contemporary Chinese culture. The establishment of Chinese socialist ideology, in part based on cultural resources from the Renaissance through nineteenth-century America and (primarily) Europe, and from twentieth-century, pre–World War II American and European texts, necessarily embraced a productive method of misreading. As such, for non- or anti-official intellectuals in the post-Mao era, the discursive construction of Occidentalism draws on the same cultural resources, but for a subversive function. Although it adopts a position of seeking to "correctly" understand the West, its construction as a counter-discourse to pursue an oppositional stance has gone far beyond the "original intention" of acquiring a "proper" grasp of liberal Western culture. Therefore, this counter-discourse once again had to become a "new" version of a misreading.

More interestingly, while this counter-discourse provided an ideal sociopolitical solution, it also drew largely from communism's representation of the ideal society. The counter-discourse excluded the realities of class, gender, and ethnicity in the era of global capitalism. With its prospect of shared plenty, social democracy was promoted as an implicit critique against the autocratic and oppressive characteristics of the Chinese socialist system. The demands for social democracy had nothing to do with political institutions or human rights issues, but rather were concerned with political participation and self-determination. This construction of a new counter-discourse immediately won the Chinese people's far-reaching and committed endorsement. As a reversal of the various official narratives of socialist ideology, the "enlightenment discourse," constructed by the new Occidentalism, highlighted the inherent connections and rupture between Marxist theory, the practice of socialism, and the history of capitalism.

The phenomenon of a distinct "intellectual time lag" needs mentioning. Occidentalism, in fact, also originated from within the cultural reserves of socialism. As required by the socialist ideological construction in the past, the "noise" and "impurities" of twentieth-century Western history were consciously filtered out. Therefore, it is precisely this effective "intellectual time lag" that ensured that any Marxist or non-Marxist intellectual

traditions that criticized capitalism and modernism in the twentieth century, and especially in post-war America and Europe, would become the
blind spots of Chinese culture in the new era. Because of these blind spots,
post-war Western intellectual developments did not play a part in the
construction and expression of the utopia espoused by the new Occidentalism.

The socialist history of sealing off enemies guaranteed that the contemporary Western world would remain distant and alien in the 1970s
and early 1980s. Despite the reopening under the Deng regime's banner
of reform (or more accurately, transnational capitalism) to the Western
world, China still completely operated in the socialist economic and cultural system. Imperialism and transnational capitalism had been demons
in the Mao era's official narratives, and an object of imagination and desire within the intellectuals' construction of new discourses, rather than
a tangible reality. Occidentalism not only advanced an imagined Other to
reflect China's Self but also provided intellectuals with a place to position themselves in their anti-official stance. Chinese intellectuals relied
upon the discourse of Occidentalism to establish their identity as representing the Chinese people in opposing the officials and subverting the
current political regime. However, as Chen observes, within the complicated practice of Chinese politics and culture, the official Occidentalism,
the intellectuals' anti-official Occidentalism, and the various forms of
non-official Occidentalism representing the masses were all interde-
pendent and mutually reinforcing. Although the specter of Eurocentric,
colonial culture still haunts these counter-discourses, they were to a
greater degree enmeshed in the history of Chinese socialism and the
strategic choices in the political struggles during the late 1970s and 1980s.
Yet one could not foresee that these counter-discourses would be used to
facilitate the rebirth of capitalism and China's deepening entanglement
with global capitalism.

THE PREDICAMENT AND POSITION OF THE SUBJECT

In addition to providing a detailed analysis of the post-Mao era and
China's Occidentalism, the author is an alert and introspective Third
World intellectual in American academia reflecting on the dilemma of
subjectivity. Since the publication of *Orientalism* and the subsequent discussion on post-colonialism, the intellectual critique of Western culture by
non-Western intellectuals has developed into a distinct cultural trend in
the West, especially within American academic institutions. If this critique
can be seen to extend and complement post-war Western intellectuals' effort to subvert the mainstream culture, then the intervention of the Third

World perspective has fashioned a new critical vantage point, even taking on critical theory itself. However, as critical intellectuals from non-Western countries speak about Western mainstream culture, their critical or subversive position presupposes having their prior inculcation into the mainstream academic system. In other words, if the true pursuit of émigré intellectuals finds them questioning the Western intellectual tradition and its standards, then they still must subject themselves to that tradition, or at the very least be intimately familiar with it. For intellectuals from the Third World to be heard, they must adopt the tradition of Western social and cultural criticism as their theoretical resources. Moreover, only by ways of reference to the Western mainstream academic institutions and cultural tradition can they acquire their positions of authority.

Therefore, academic intellectuals from the Third World face a challenging predicament. Although their awareness of the critical issues may stem from native cultural experience or concern over the native culture, they still must pose these issues in a way that conforms to the traditions of Western scholarship and intellectual history. After a passage through the academic system, very likely made at the juncture of the tradition of critical thought and the margins of the institution, their version will just become the tradition's new or different component. In some extreme cases of these identity transformations undertaken at certain cultural margins, the weak may seem to become strong, as they apply their blackface and perform in Western academia.

Mainland Chinese intellectuals in Western academia confront a crisis of subject position and representation over the extent to which the Western critical theory they use derived from Marxism. If China, and especially contemporary China, remains the object of their research, or the starting point for their examination of critical issues, then Chinese intellectuals invariably must reflect on China's socialist history. They have no way of skirting the historical fact and present reality of Marxist theory, which still in name constitutes Chinese mainstream ideology. Therefore, if their devotion to their native experience and concern over its present conditions prevent them from identifying with Western leftist intellectuals, then their cultural experience as an émigré intellectual also makes it difficult to truly identify with the Marxist mainstream critiques in Western universities. A position of double resistance and opposition puts them between a rock and a hard place.

Chen's awareness of this serious predicament makes her depiction of her subjective position all the more valuable. She does not opt for a perfect academic narrative that would sacrifice her analysis and representation of her native culture. This type of choice does not allow her to transcend this predicament of subjectivity, but rather, allows her work to illustrate this very predicament. She points out, regarding her own position or that of

For intellectuals to be heard they need a "western voice" or academic status. This demonstrates desire for the education intellectuals in American academia in general, the pitfalls of taking part in and benefiting from Western cultural hegemony or creating a revised ethnocentric narrative. In her analysis of Chinese socialist culture in the late 1970s and 1980s, Chen also expresses doubt at the ability of elite intellectuals to speak for the subalterns. Therefore, *Occidentalism*, perhaps rather unwittingly, becomes an interrogation of the role of intellectuals during the post-Mao period. Indeed, Chen's narrative and subjectivity themselves become subject to her introspection and clearing of the Maoist era's historical debt. As such, the Mao era and its cultural legacy can be said to be reflected in Chen's narrative style and subjective position. *Occidentalism* on many levels engages with *Orientalism* in a deeper and more implicit dialogue than what might appear on the surface. However, *Orientalism* is clearly not its only partner in dialogue, and not even the primary one.

COLLUSION AND ASPECTS OF COLLUSION

According to *Occidentalism*, in the late 1970s and 1980s, Occidentalism as a cultural strategy helped bid riddance to the Mao era. Although sometimes these anti-official or nonofficial expressions appear to conflict with the official version of Occidentalism, there are points of mutual reference and reliance. In the mid-1980s, as the Deng Xiaoping regime stabilized, "opening up and reform" and "modernization" became a major part of Chinese society. Therefore, in the course of expanding capitalism promoted by the Communist Party, the reform party began to draw upon the elite intellectuals' Occidentalism to legitimize the transformation of the Chinese socialist system. A rather absurd situation arises as we see the continuation of the intellectual community's tragic imagination of the 1970s and 1980s, positioning themselves in opposition to society as a community on the margins. On the other hand, we see the strengthening of a tie between the reform party and the elite intellectual community. When the Communist Party, within the socialist system, adopted the name of socialism while promoting the expansion of capitalism, this decision caused the post-Mao regime to face a dilemma in its ideological expression. Consequently, the Communist Party had to draw upon Occidentalism constructed by the intellectuals to evade its inherent structural ideological contradictions. Elite intellectuals, straddling both the official and anti-official positions, became Chinese society's "tribe" of cultural heroes in the late 1980s and acquired remarkable prestige. This collusion became a key feature of Chinese society and culture in the later 1980s and 1990s.

In shedding the Maoist legacy, the Deng regime downplayed and even eliminated the communist and internationalist ideology. The reliance upon the "new" world landscape as sketched by this official Occidentalism entailed a readjustment of China's position. No longer the "center of world revolution," China was now to be positioned as a developing country on the margins aspiring to a place at the center. This step indeed effectively shattered the Mao era, in terms of seeing China as the center of world revolution. Therefore, in the later 1980s and the 1990s, nationalism became one of the most important banners the political regime relied on to avoid institutional conflicts, reinforce its hegemonic legitimacy, successfully deflect social contradictions and crises, and create its social cohesion and vitality.

In drawing on the West, Occidentalism spawned a new disposition toward cosmopolitanism. For the Chinese intellectual community, this cosmopolitanism lies absurdly, yet harmoniously, situated within the native ethnic viewpoint and nationalistic sentiment. Although this stance appears to join the Occidentalist discourse, official nationalism and the global orientation of the intellectuals, it also projects what appears to be a rupture between the officials and intellectuals. If the official nationalism primarily seeks to conceal deep, domestic social conflicts while not jeopardizing its romance with transnational capitalism, then the cosmopolitanism of elite intellectuals, however it may serve as a weapon in domestic politics, has undoubtedly prevented them from directly facing China's predicament in the new international politico-economic order.

There is more to this. As a counter-discourse, Occidentalism opposed the Maoist socialist regime, at least its ideological controls and mechanisms of social oppression. Consequently, intellectuals partially relied on Deng's political regime, which inherited the authority of the Maoist ruling party. By relying on Occidentalism, and at times of even greater importance, on economic utilitarianism, Deng was able to circumvent the unavoidable contradictions within the ideological and socialist system. A profound conflict, however, existed: the perpetuation of the political regime and the legitimacy of the new leadership required repeated affirmations and tacit rewritings of the fundamental nature of Chinese socialism. On the other hand, the Chinese intellectual community during the 1980s, in their package of Occidentalism, sought to bid farewell to socialism. Throughout the 1980s, China's officials and elite intellectual community, in a type of tacit agreement, carried out an ideological about-face. They turned away from the Cold War mentality of "only socialism can save China" to the endless potentials of the capitalist system. Therefore, they rather successfully established a new cultural hegemony based on the all-encompassing imagination of a modernized future.

The choice here, however, appeared to be only one of different paths within an identical social program. Was the solution to transform the social system through systemic economic reform, promoted under the banner of economic utilitarianism? Or was it to first adopt political systemic reform and establish a Western social democratic polity (undoubtedly as the West imagined in monolithic, essentialized terms) to facilitate the course of capitalism in a logical manner that was true to its name? This choice led to a profound conflict within the reform party of the Chinese political regime during the 1980s. The majority of elite intellectuals who constructed the discourse of Occidentalism became primary supporters of the latter solution. Undoubtedly this approach threatened the stability of the domestic order and directly imperiled the leadership's collective interests. As Occidentalism became a universal narrative, it is precisely on this level that it continued to administer its critical sociopolitical function. At the same time, within the steady, compelling course of global capitalism, the discourse sought to realize its historical purpose. This conflict reached its flash point in spring 1989 and in the end brought about an absurd tragedy.

In the 1989 democracy movement, the elite intellectual community and the Chinese masses made their last joint effort of the twentieth century. They readily shared common goals and interests, and even displayed the strength of the newly constructed cultural hegemony consummated in the 1980s. The intellectuals' pursuit of Western democratic systems had already combined with the masses' self-interest. Subtle fissures, however, between intellectuals and masses began to appear as a result of their fight against the corruption and public graft in the new society.

CHINA'S PROSPECTS AFTER THE TURN OF THE CENTURY

The June Fourth Incident was not only a natural denouement to an era that touted "modernization." It also dashed the prospect of harmony and shared political views among the officials, the intellectual community, and the masses that had been quite successfully realized in the mid- and later 1980s. The 1990s would be marked by the dissolution of the Soviet Union, major changes in Eastern Europe, and the "battle-free victories" of capitalism around the globe. After successfully passing through the crisis of extreme political power, the policies adopted by Chinese officials were clear. They sought to continue strengthening socialist-style ideological controls and management while simultaneously promoting reform of the economic system. They were also attempting to instate "reform of the state-owned enterprises" while relying on transnational capitalism. The result of these political initiatives rooted China more securely in the process of global capitalism and fired the people's desires and imagination with a vision of economic takeoff. The political regime and leadership in this way effectively weathered a profound crisis.

The introduction of foreign capital, however, necessarily brought with it its cultural values and inevitably dissolved the socialist ideological system, which became an empty shell of an unmistakable political dictatorship. With its deepening entrenchment in global capitalism, the Chinese political regime sank more into the absurd predicament of political sovereignty faced by Third World nations, and China's role became even more contradictory and complicated.

Within this context, Occidentalism and nationalism were no longer just discourses or cultural metaphors of China's domestic politics. Rather, they became increasingly tangible and complex sociopolitical practices. If Occidentalism continued to provide the theoretical justifications of universalism and modernization for China's entrance into global capitalism and supplied a blueprint for China's future, then, the Other or "other place" was no longer forever unreachable: it had already become a social reality and part of daily life. Occidentalism not only used consumer culture to usher in the "completely new," or globally homogenized lifestyles, values, behavioral norms, and social structures, but also turned transnational capital into a transformative, intrusive, and contentious force in China's social, economic, political, and cultural life. If consumerism became an apolitical and nonideological style that successfully moved China away from the 1989 social crisis, then the flood of transnational capital, while giving China's regime a boost, also generated a series of nagging problems that required the government's attention. The discourse of nationalism, despite effectively concealing the present crisis, still puts China more and more clearly in a position of a Third World nation, prompting China to conform to international political and economic patterns.

When discussing China in the 1990s, one cannot ignore what I refer to as the "Cold War policies of the post–Cold War era." Since China is the "last socialist power" (at least in name), it still disconcerts and threatens the more reactionary forces in the West. At the same time, to affirm its legitimacy, China's regime must also to some degree secure its image as a "socialist power," which certainly was an extremely important factor in Chinese culture in the 1990s. The Cold War–style politics and cultural logic in China's international affairs in reality more often than not act as an effective rhetoric tool or lever to prod China into entering the machinery of global capitalism. Therefore, in China's foreign relations in the 1990s, we can identify as a distinct factor—the continuation of Cold War ideological conflict. On the other hand, the profits reaped by global capitalism also stay concealed within Cold War logic and rhetoric. In other words, in the developed countries of the West, an ideological opposition still resides between the system of global capitalism and national interests.

In this context, Occidentalism, cloaked in the garb of universalism and nationalism, hidden in the discourse of socialism, began to play an even more complex role in Chinese society and culture. At times Occidentalism or nationalism served as a critical weapon used by the masses or intellectuals, because these discourses seemed to offer a type of public discursive space. In most cases, however, these discourses construct, in a variety of ways, a socially oppressive force.

After 1989, elite intellectuals still relied on the discourse of Occidentalism to extend their politico-cultural position of the 1980s and to criticize official policies, creating rifts with the regime on the issue of social democracy. At this time, however, the discourse of Occidentalism, despite the wishes of its promoters, had to allow for the arrival of global capitalism and its manifest cultural and social functions. As intellectuals continued to pursue social democracy as they had in the 1980s, they still held a weak, marginal position in China's political arena. Yet they unquestionably stood on the side of the hegemonic culture, in a China that already had entered on the irreversible course of globalization. In a cultural environment that in several ways stood apart from that of the 1980s, many expressions of Occidentalism assumed extremely different positions and meanings.

China's modernization and reform of the economic system in the 1990s ushered in an even more important change: the transformation of state enterprises, bankruptcy of regional enterprises, and the introduction of transnational capital. These reforms led to crises of resource distribution, natural resources, and environment. Moreover, they created greater class divisions, along with growing problems of gender and age discrimination. The power structure was once again founded on the basis of money, between the "rich" and the "poor." In fact, this power structure is still linked to the history of socialism: the absolute power of the bureaucratic class and its extreme corruption, the relationship between power and money, and the previous residency system's divisions between urban and rural. These legacies of a socialist power structure became more evident by its generation of an army of urban proletariat composed of the farmers, workers, and the unemployed, resembling the era of primitive capital accumulation. These subalterns, subjected to social restructuring, became the sacrificial goods in China's modernization. From this perspective, the various alluring prospects promised by modernization and development can only but fade, although without question, these expectations are still a main factor in safeguarding Chinese society. Compared to the late 1970s and early 1980s, however, with the prospect of joining the narratives of socialism and communism with universal prosperity, the massive circulation of goods, and equally shared wealth, these hopes already became extremely faint and unclear. Not only did the relatively solid alliance between the masses, elite intellectuals, and reformist officials in the late 1970s and the early 1980s basically fall apart, but also the group of liberal intellectuals who had shared similar ideas began to splinter over different viewpoints. A debate between two groups who were mischaracterized as "liberals" and "new leftists" brought these deep divisions to the surface. The debate introduced a group of critical intellectuals who reflected on modernity, sorted out the legacy and debt of socialism, rethought issues of class, gender, and ethnicity in China, and reevaluated the potential contributions of Marxist thought.

The Occidentalism of the late 1970s and the 1980s, which offered a critical perspective or held out a promise for social cohesion, has fundamentally disappeared. Nationalism, or self-Orientalism, as an instrument of the officials, has become the only effective measure for social cohesion. This discourse can still be drawn on in different contexts and by different groups for oppositional purposes. Yet a portrait of China at the turn of the century can never again sketch a country sealed off from the rest of the world.

Jinhua Dai
Peking University

Translated by Jonathan Noble

Preface to the Second Edition

The main purpose of this second edition is to provide a substantive new chapter on the Chinese diaspora and to make a paperback available for scholars and students interested in the subject. I am grateful to Susan McEachern, executive editor of Rowman & Littlefield Publishers, Inc., for her wisdom, support, and patience in making it possible. I thank Jehanne Schweitzer, production editor, for her help and understanding in bringing this edition to conclusion.

Since much has happened since the first edition, I have not attempted to update the core of the study and its bibliographical information. Rather, I would like it to remain as a historical document of my consideration of Western theory and my examination of modern Chinese literature and culture in cross-cultural perspectives in the early 1990s. In this edition, I have corrected mistakes and typographical errors and refined some of the arguments throughout the text. In view of the recent materials on the history of *menglong* poetry that have been published in the PRC, I have updated chapter 3 and refined my argument.

Chapter 7, on reading stories of the Chinese diaspora, was written especially for this edition. Centering on a group of short stories, novels, reportage, and autobiographical writings in the 1920s, 1980s, and 1990s, I intend to illustrate that despite China's troubled position in the world in different historical periods, writings and readings of the Other are always initiated as a local activity, determined always at least partially by the exigencies of time and place. By contrasting stories of the 1920s with the 1980s and 1990s, I do not present them as narratives in a linear line of historical development or suggest that stories of Occidentalist writings about the diaspora can be interpreted within a single theoretical framework. In fact, I want to explore how the motivations of the students in post-Mao China resemble or differ from those in the 1920s. Like their predecessors, they can have a voice of their own in writing back against nationalist and imperialist conditions. Unlike their predecessors, however, post-Mao writers inherited and battled against even more complex cultural and ideological traditions, Confucian and Maoist, capitalist and postsocialist. Through studying the short story of Yan Li, an ex-*menglong* poet, for example, I want to demonstrate the spiritual trajectory of people who went from being Red Guards, to *menglong* poets, and finally to Chinese Americans. In doing so, I continue to challenge readers to think about China's interaction with the West in a way that offers a refreshing perspective of China as agent, not victim.

This chapter also engages with the current scholarship on Asian American Studies, especially that on Chinese American literary and cultural studies, which has seldom examined the Chinese side of immigration, by researching documents and writings in the Chinese language. I address three factors: (1) the Chinese cultural, ideological, and economic conditions in different historical periods that prompted emigration; (2) the Chinese imagining of the West as a better or alternative space; (3) postsocialist reflections, written in Chinese, by emigrant Chinese writers on the shortcomings of the capitalist West. By doing so, I intend to challenge the nationalist paradigms of both China and its foreign Others, especially the perspective that views Asian American experience as predominantly an American one. I thank my students in Chinese/Comparative Studies 678: Chinese American Literature and Culture at Ohio State University for their enthusiasm for this neglected aspect of Chinese American literature and their encouragement to teach and write about it. This chapter is therefore dedicated to my students of Asian American Studies.

Throughout this revising process, I benefited greatly from the support of my friends and colleagues. My first thanks go to Professor Jinhua Dai for her thoughtful Foreword and to Jonathan Noble for his meticulous English translation. I also want to express my thanks to Susan L. Glosser, Marie-Paule Ha, Michel Hockx, Barry Keenan, Barbara Rigney, Yingjin Zhang, and Yanfang Tang for their timely support for my effort to acquire a paperback edition. I am especially grateful to Kirk A. Denton, who carefully read through the draft of chapter 7 and offered invaluable suggestions for improvement. Patricia Seiber urged me on with her cheer and encouragement. Julia F. Andrews remains a constant source of inspiration.

Last but not least, I would like to thank Mark Halperin for his unwavering support, timely help, and constant supply of one-liners in proofreading the entire manuscript and clarifying my thoughts on certain issues in chapter 7.

Acknowledgments
(from the first edition)

Three chapters of this book were based on early works written under the supervision and guidance of Professor Eugene C. Eoyang, a brilliant teacher and a patient mentor, to whom I feel an immense intellectual debt. I am also indebted to C. Clifford Flanigan, Brian Caraha, Irving Lo, Claus Clüver, Marvin Carlson, Sumie Jones, and Marta Calinescu, whom I was privileged to have as inspiring teachers in the Program of Comparative Literature at Indiana University.

I am grateful to have received an Andrew W. Mellon Fellowship from Stanford Humanities Center for the 1990–91 academic year, during which a multicultural and interdisciplinary atmosphere provoked further thoughts on Occidentalism; a Seed Grant from Ohio State University and a Special Research Assignment Grant from the College of Humanities, which allowed me uninterrupted time for reading, thinking, and writing parts of this book; to my colleagues and friends at the Department of East Asian Languages and Literatures, where a nurturing environment and moral support made the writing of this book a pleasant experience; and in particular, to the chairpersons, Thomas Kasulis, Shigeru Miyagawa, and Frank Hsueh, for their belief in this project; to Sabra Webber, the chairperson, and my colleagues and friends at the Division of Comparative Studies for their intellectual companionship and their valuable suggestions during a group discussion on part of this book; to my invaluable friend Jiwei Ci for spending many hours reading different drafts and making important suggestions for improvement; to Arif Dirlik, who believed in my project at a crucial stage of its development; to William Tyler for helping me proofread the manuscript; to Kirk Denton, Galal Walker, Lindsay Jones, Shelley Quinn, and Nikki Bado for reading, or helping me with, different parts of the manuscript in its final stage of completion; to Chang Hao and Douwe Fokkema for talking to me about the concept of this book; and to Lydia H. Liu for her love and support. I am also grateful to two anonymous readers whose critiques were helpful in revising this book, and to Senior Editor Elizabeth Maguire, Copy Editor Ruth Sandweiss, and Managing Editor Ellen Fuchs at Oxford University Press for their patience and help throughout the process of producing this book.

I would like to thank my teachers at Beijing Foreign Languages Institute, where I first acquired knowledge of the English language; Edward Geary and Richard Poulsen at Brigham Young University, who guided me through my first two years in graduate school in the United States; and to my parents, Chen Yongjing and Ji Shuping, whose successful performing careers in Chinese spoken drama inspired my early interests in modern Chinese theater, and whose understanding, patience, and support for my years overseas are most precious.

This book is dedicated to the memory of Professor C. Clifford Flanigan, a brilliant teacher and an indispensable friend who gave every draft of this manuscript, in every stage of its development, as much attention and care as if it had been his own. To my greatest regret, Clifford did not live to see the publication of this book. This book, in a small measure, testifies to his legacy—his generosity in offering his time and energy to light the path for his students. His curiosity and eagerness to learn new things and to teach new classes made him a master teacher who had decisively molded the careers of many students all over the world.

X.C.
1995

Introduction

In the years since its introduction, Edward Said's celebrated study, *Orientalism*, has acquired a near paradigmatic status in the Western academic world as a model of the relationships between Western and non-Western cultures. Said seeks to show how Western imperialist images of their colonial Others—images that, of course, are inevitably and sharply at odds with the self-understanding of the indigenous non-Western cultures they purport to represent—not only govern the West's hegemonic policies, but were imported into the West's political and cultural colonies, where they affected native points of view and thus themselves served as instruments of domination. Said's focus is on the Near East, but his critics and supporters alike have extended his model far beyond the confines of that part of the world.

What are the implications of Said's model on early post-Maoist Chinese attempts to define China's self-image or the nature of Sino-Western social, cultural, and political relationships?[1] On first consideration, a neglect of Said's work seems justified. Throughout this century, and especially recently, the People's Republic of China (PRC) and its political forbears have emphasized their unique and "Chinese" ways of doing things. Yet, such talk can be deceptive. Indeed it seems clear that when Mao Zedong and Deng Xiaoping advocated a "particularly Chinese road to socialism and communism," their "Chineseness" was not merely the product of how the Chinese understood their unique political and cultural circumstances. Rather, just as Said's model suggests, the "pure Chinese" self-understanding advocated by such belated figures had already been historically "contaminated" and even constructed by cultural and cross-cultural appropriations that belong to the whole of Chinese-Western relationships, which to a marked degree have been determined—and overdetermined—by the way that the West has

1

understood itself and China. In early post-Mao China, for instance, in announcing its cultural uniqueness, the advocates of a culturally pure China have declared their nation "the last banner of socialism." Such claims seek to have hortatory as much as descriptive content, since they take as their priority the national campaign against "the foreign imperialists' dream of a peaceful transformation to capitalism in China," especially in view of the disintegration of the Soviet Union and other Eastern bloc socialist countries, which had "tragically regressed to the road of capitalism."

Indeed, as this remark suggests, nowhere is the phenomenon of pervasive Orientalism, or the Western construction of the Orient, more visible in modern China than in the history of the Chinese revolution. One might well argue that to a large extent all elite discourses of anti-traditionalism in modern China, from the May Fourth movement to the 1989 Tiananmen student demonstrations, have been extensively Orientalized. This at least partially self-imposed Orientalism is quintessentially reflected, for example, in Chinese appropriations of the idea of history as progress and teleology, notions derived from the Western Enlightenment and from various schools of Western utopian thinking that, of course, found their most potent expression in the ideas of Karl Marx. Indeed, as Arif Dirlik has succinctly pointed out, Chinese Marxism has been greatly influenced by a Marxist globalized historical consciousness, which takes unilinear European history as the model to represent China's past in order to attain China's admission into universal history.[2]

Yet for all of this it would not be accurate to say that Chinese political and intellectual culture is nothing more than an outpost of mindlessly replicated Western thought. However Western these "Chinese" ideas may be in their origins, it is undeniable that their mere utterance in a non-Western context inevitably creates a modification of their form and content. In such modifications of Western Marxist thought we see examples of the way that in China—and perhaps elsewhere—Orientalism has been accompanied by instances of what might be termed *Occidentalism*, a discursive practice that, by constructing its Western Other, has allowed the Orient to participate actively and with indigenous creativity in the process of self-appropriation, even after being appropriated and constructed by Western Others. As a result of constantly revising and manipulating imposed Western theories and practices, the Chinese Orient has produced a new discourse, marked by a particular combination of the Western construction of China with the Chinese construction of the West, with both of these components interacting and interpenetrating each other. This seemingly unified discursive practice of Occidentalism exists in a paradoxical relationship to the discursive practices of Orientalism, and in fact, shares with it many ideological techniques and strategies. Despite these similarities, however, Chinese Occidentalism has mainly served an ideological function quite different from that of Orientalism. Orientalism, in Said's account, is a strategy of Western world domination, whereas, as the rest of this study seeks to show, Chinese Occidentalism is primarily a discourse that has been evoked by various and competing groups within Chinese society for a variety of different ends, largely, though not exclusively, within domestic Chinese politics. As such, it has been both a discourse of oppression and a discourse of liberation.

Chinese Occidentalism, especially as it is reflected in the political and literary expressions of the post-Mao period—which is the focus of this study—might be regarded as two related, and in many instances, co-existing and even overlapping discursive practices, or perhaps, different appropriations of the same discourse for strikingly different political ends. In the first, which I term *official Occidentalism*, the Chinese government uses the essentialization of the West as a means for supporting a nationalism that suppresses its own people. In this process, the Western Other is construed by a Chinese imagination, not for the purpose of dominating the West, but in order to discipline, and ultimately to dominate, the Chinese Self at home. This variety of official Occidentalism perhaps found its best expression in Mao Zedong's theory of three worlds, in which Mao asserted that the First World superpowers—the Soviet Union and the United States—invariably exploit and oppress the Third World countries in Asia, Africa, and Latin America. This theory was to a great extent a product of the radical ideology of the Cultural Revolution, which, despite its expressed concern for the non-Chinese oppressed of the world, had as its chief interest the domestic legitimization of Mao as the "great leader" of the Third World. It thus was a strategy to consolidate Mao's shaky and increasingly problematic position within the Chinese Communisty Party. At the dawn of the Cultural Revolution in 1965, Lin Biao, Mao's chosen successor at the time, advocated the application of Mao Zedong's theory of "establishing revolutionary base areas in the rural districts and encircling the cities from the countryside"—a theory that was said to have brought about the victory of the Chinese revolution—to the international arena of the Third World countries in their struggle against "aggression and enslavement on a serious scale by the imperialists headed by the United States and their lackeys."[3] We can see these concerns in Lin Biao's long essay "Long Live the Victory of People's War," published in *People's Daily* on September 3, 1965, in commemoration of the twentieth anniversary of victory in the Chinese people's war of resistance against Japan:

> Taking the entire globe, if North America and Western Europe can be called "the cities of the world," then Asia, Africa and Latin America constitute "the rural areas of the world." Since World War II, the proletarian revolutionary

movement has for various reasons been temporarily held back in the North
American and West European capitalist countries, while the people's revolutionary movement in Asia, Africa and Latin America has been growing vigorously. In a sense, the contemporary world revolution also presents a picture of the encirclement of cities by the rural areas. In the final analysis, the
whole cause of world revolution hinges on the revolutionary struggles of the
Asian, African and Latin American peoples who make up the overwhelming
majority of the world's population. The socialist countries should regard it as
their internationalist duty to support the people's revolutionary struggles in
Asia, Africa and Latin America.[4]

As has subsequently become clear, Lin Biao's discourse, although seemingly directed to Third World countries against Western imperialist policies, was part and parcel of his radical anti-Western and antibourgeois
ideology advanced in an attempt to advocate the Cultural Revolution for
decidedly domestic political ends. The most direct impact of his work
was to initiate and promote a Maoist cult, which reached its peak at the
beginning of the Cultural Revolution, under the pretext of spreading
"Mao Zedong Thought" as the supreme principle and living gospel of
Marxism and Leninism. We seem to have here an Occidentalism wholly
Chinese in its content and purpose. This is not to deny, of course, that
China sought to compete with the Soviet Union as the sole leader of the
socialist camp.

   Yet matters are more complicated than they might at first appear. Even
the brief quotations given above suggest the complex relationship between Chinese Occidentalism and Western Orientalism. Lin Biao cleverly
elaborated Mao's supposedly Chinese theory of the dichotomy between
the town and the country—a dichotomy that had served a strategic function in the triumph of the Chinese revolution—into a larger context of
world revolution, in which the Third World "countryside" was expected
to surround and finally overcome the "cities" of the imperialist Western
superpowers. Beneath these claims lies a pervasive modern Chinese antiurbanism that, as Maurice Meisner has pointed out, reveals a key element
of Maoist thought, which was characterized by "a deep emotional attachment to the rural ideal of 'the unity of living and working'" and a profound distrust of the cities as sites of foreign dominators and their servants, urban intellectuals.[5] Mao presented these notions as products of a
specifically Chinese experience, as indigenous insights far removed from
Western thought. Yet obviously this supposedly uniquely Chinese Maoist
antiurbanism shares "certain similarities with a strain in the Western intellectual tradition, partly derived from Rousseau, which viewed the city
as the embodiment of all social evils and moral corruptions, as a monolith
threatening to crush the natural purity of the countryside."[6] In this regard
Maoist Occidentalism seems dependent on the very Western predecessors

with which it disavows any connection. Like its Orientalist counterpart, it seeks to construe its Other by asserting a distorted and ultimately anxious image of its own uniqueness. In addition, the apparent aim of its discourse seems, again like its Western counterpart, to be directed toward an imperialist strategy: it is China that will lead the rural Third World to its liberation, because it is China, at least after World War II, that seems uniquely suited for this task.[7] Yet it must be strongly emphasized that the ultimate aim of this Occidentalist practice was not primarily Chinese hegemony in the Third World, but the consolidation of a particular group within domestic politics. It is possible to overemphasize this point, of course. Concerns with domestic politics are seldom absent from the exercise of Western Orientalism. But if we historically compare Western Orientalism with Maoist Occidentalism, it seems clear that the primary aim of the Chinese discourse has been domestic oppression of political opponents rather than world domination, while the inverse has been true in the West. Such a difference, obviously, does not arise out of the moral superiority or even the ultimate political aims of the Chinese practitioners of Occidentalism; after all, China has a history of imperialist longings and practices far older than its counterparts in the West. Rather, this difference reflects the historical moment in which Western imperialism, aided in large measure by its Orientalist discourse, was at or near its apogee and in various ways presented a threat even to the prevailing Chinese political order. In this sense, Chinese Occidentalism is the product of Western Orientalism, even if its aims are largely and specifically Chinese.

This official Occidentalism—Chinese in purpose yet in paradoxical ways dependent upon Western ideas—is pervasive in contemporary Chinese culture and life. But Chinese Occidentalism is by no means confined to this official use. Alongside of it we can readily find examples of what we might term *anti-official Occidentalism*, since its purveyors are not the established government or party apparatus but the opponents of those institutions, especially among various groups of the intelligentsia with diverse and, more often than not, contradictory interests. As a result of the cultural and sociological specificities of contemporary Chinese society, such Occidentalism can be understood as a powerful anti-official discourse using the Western Other as a metaphor for a political liberation against ideological oppression within a totalitarian society. It is here that I distance my approach from that of Said and other postcolonialists inspired by Said's paradigm. I argue that what might rightly be considered as a global, "central" discourse of Occidentalism in their account can also sometimes be used as a locally marginal or peripheral discourse against the internal dominant power in a particular culture. Under these special circumstances, therefore, arguing absolutely against cultural imperialism in the international arena can be politically dangerous since it inevitably, if unintentionally, supports the status quo of a ruling ideology, such as the one in contemporary China, which sees in the Western Other a potentially powerful alliance with an anti-official force at home. By distinguishing official Occidentalism from anti-official Occidentalism, I do not mean to suggest an essentialist approach and separate them as binary opposites. In fact, due to a lack of existing counter-culture in the political sphere of the PRC, I emphasize instead the common phenomenon of a coexisting, interrelated, and, in many cases, collaborative nature of Chinese Occidentalism between various discourses, or official and anti-official discourses, simply defined for the sake of discussion. By examining the complex and multifaceted relationship between Orientalism and Occidentalism, I do not mean to suggest a dualist divide between China/West, or hegemonic/oppositional, but rather to demonstrate that Occidentalism takes many different forms, prompted by all kinds of motivations, sometimes of a contradictory nature.[8]

Post-Mao Chinese society presents us with a compelling example of Occidentalism, by which I mean a Chinese representation of the Occident as "its deepest and most recurring images of the Other."[9] Such Occidentalism may be considered as a counter-discourse, a counter-memory, and a counter-Other to Said's Orientalism. These terms, of course, readily evoke Michel Foucault's notion of "discourse," employed also by Said in his definition of Orientalism, as "a Western style for dominating, restructuring, and having authority over the Orient."[10] Yet a critical difference between Said and Foucault's conceptions, as noted by Uta Liebmann Schaub, resides in that "whereas Foucault allows for the emergence of counter-discourses beneath the official discourse of power, Said ignores Western discourses about the Orient that oppose Western expansionism and subvert, rather than support, Western domination."[11] The same claim, as we shall see, can be advanced from yet anther perspective: Said's claims do not provide for even the possibility of an anti-official discourse within "Oriental" societies that employs an Occidentalism to combat the official cultural hegemony dominating a given non-Western culture. In such cases, the Western Other at least theoretically can and often does become a metaphor for political liberation against indigenous forms of ideological oppression.

As the following chapters make abundantly clear, this has often been the case in contemporary China, though the appearance of this phenomenon is by no means limited to Chinese culture. But in China, the evocation of the West, as a counterpart of the indigenous culture, has more than once set in motion a kind of "dialogic imagination" that in turn has become a dynamic and dialectical force in the making of modern Chinese history, both literary and political. One difficulty in the ongoing debates concerning Third World and anti-colonial discourses is that some critics seem to have interpreted Said's book as asserting that any kind of indigenous cultural appropriation of the Other has necessarily negative effects, being either an act of imperialistic colonialization when performed by the "superior" culture, or one of self-colonialization when carried on by the "inferior" culture in the context of global domination. Such a charge, for example, has been brought against Peter Brook's production of the Indian epic *The Mahabharata*.[12] While not in total disagreement with Brook's intertextual reading, which relates *The Mahabharata* to various Shakespearean themes, Gautam Dasgupta believes that "one should not, under cover of universality of theme or character, undercut the intrinsic core of how *The Mahabharata*'s characters function within the world of which they are a part."[13] Here we see a privileging of the "intrinsic core" of an original text and the culture of which it is a part, understood from "the native's point of view," over the alien specificities of a receiving culture that necessitate cross-cultural communications in the first place.

My argument with Said in terms of the early post-Mao Chinese experience connects with some critiques of Said's Orientalism from what might well be termed post-Orientalist perspectives. In his review of Said's book *Culture and Imperialism,* Ernest Gellner asserts that Said's Orientalist discourse against imperialism and colonialism fundamentally neglects "that the industrial/agrarian and Western/Other distinctions cut across each other, and obscure each other's outline. . . ."[14] In Gellner's opinion the current spate of economic success stories from the Pacific Rim may now call for a critical reversal of the concept of power structure as defined by Said's Orientalism, since one might be able to argue that industrialism—one of the crucial yardsticks with which Said developed his binary categories of the Orientalist and Orientalized entities—might be better "run in a Confucian-collective spirit" in the non-Western societies.[15] From a different angle, moreover, Gellner argues that Said, while selectively criticizing some Europeans as Orientalists, privileges anti-colonialist critics such as Franz Fanon in a thoroughly unhistorical manner. Though Fanon was enormously influential in "the international literary-intellectual scene" in the West, Gellner claims, Fanon nevertheless "meant nothing to the Algerians themselves (whereas Ben Badis, unknown internationally, meant a very great deal)"[16] to his own people. Gellner continues to hold this view even after having been challenged by Eqbal Ahmad[17] and David Davies,[18] both of whom claimed that Franz Fanon was indeed influential in wartime Algeria. To this charge Gellner insisted that "vicarious populist romanticism means nothing to the average Algerian, who does not know Fanon's name," whereas Ben Badis's "influence was pervasive and persistent, and there could be no need to 'appropriate' him. He was there all the time. He more than anyone else had made modern Algeria."[19] In another review of Said's *Culture and Imperialism,* Fred Inglis also sees its theme as "nothing less than the monster claim that imperialism is the biggest fact of the 20th-century world, that it pervades and defines the structure of feeling . . . of the epoch, and that all culture and all art, high or low, must [*sic*] be read as a revelation of old imperialism and its colossal field of force."[20] Said's claim to this universal truth, however, finds its supports only in regional parts of the world in "strictly British, French and American provenance."[21]

Although I cannot endorse their entire political agendas, Gellner's and Inglis's critiques of Said's more recent reflections on Orientalism nevertheless have a certain cogency, because they point to the (ir)relevance of Western theory to the day-to-day life experience of those persons who are victims of ideological illusions in their indigenous cultures both in the Orient and the Occident. These reviews raise an important issue: many Western cultural critics created a system of values from which they criticized the Orientalism of their own culture, a critical act which I applaud since it was motivated by a desire to address problems in one's own social and political environment. But the events of the last half-decade have made it impossible for us to overlook what these thinkers betrayed in endorsing in an essentialist way the opponents of Orientalism. Indeed, Said's Orient is a half-Western Orient, and it is inevitable that "real" Orientals from China and Korea are likely to see how one-sided Said's arguments really are. Seen from this perspective they are valid, but they are not the whole story, as Said continues to claim even in his recent response to Gellner's review, whom he accuses of having, once again, expressed "the ways of Orientalism."[22]

The discourses of Orientalism and of Occidentalism are, of course, intricately related to the problems of Eurocentrism and ethnocentrism. Among the reams of material produced on these subjects, one of the most telling is Kwame Anthony Appiah's insightful essay "Europe Upside Down: Fallacies of the New Afrocentrism." Appiah analyzes two approaches toward African studies taken by scholars in the West: the first group is characterized by its attempt to promote a negative belief that everything produced on the part of Western and European scholars about Africa is highly Eurocentric; it either implies that Europe is the "ideal type," or describes its African Other as "sympathetic," thus presupposing that Africans themselves "have produced little of much cultural worth" with "sophistication" and "value."[23] The second group, according to Appiah, proposes an Afrocentric view as a positive alternative to negative Eurocentrism; it attempts to claim "African cultural creativity" as the origin of Western civilization, as typically shown, for example, in the works of Cheikh Anta Diop, who sees "the splendours of Egypt" "as a reason for contemporary African pride. . . ."[24] Appiah demonstrates how Afrocentrists such as these fall into the same trap as those they are attacking: similar to the Eurocentrists who are heavily influenced by nineteenth-century European thought, Afrocentrists are likewise preoccupied "with the ancient world."[25] More importantly, by claiming Egypt as the source of Greece and thus of the West, Afrocentrists admit, willy-nilly, that "the West too is a moral asset of contemporary blacks, and its legacy of ethnocentrism presumably one of our moral liabilities."[26] Afrocentrism is therefore seen by Appiah as "simply Eurocentrism turned upside-down." It functions merely as a reaction to Eurocentrism, Appiah implies, not as a possible refutation of or a real alternative to it. Appiah's concern is with contemporary Afrocentrism, its uses and misuses, while this book is concerned with a quite different part of the globe. Yet Appiah's essay is relevant to the discussion of Occidentalism that follows, since both warn against a dangerous tendency in contemporary American academic discourse. Some Africanists, especially American ones, have invented an Africa that has little to do with the African peoples and their experiences and forms of life. This academically sponsored Afrocentric discourse functions primarily, and seems so intended, as a tactic to advance interests and careers in the West. Even while claiming those interests as "African," their advocates, as Appiah shows, are often totally removed from African experience, no matter how great their sojourn in Africa has been. Indeed, while making antiracial claims and judgments, they often perpetuate a fundamental racism. In the studies that follow, I have attempted to avoid this pitfall by strongly rejecting binarist and universalist arguments based on the concept of an Orient constructed either by East or by West as its "true Other." Only in this way, as far as I can see, can scholarship remain responsible both to the theoretical insights from which it often and legitimately proceeds and to the concrete situations of the peoples it seeks to describe in their cultural and historical integrity.

In this regard, perhaps a parallel can be drawn between what Diana Fuss defines as the binarism between essential and constructive feminism and what I discuss as the antithesis of East and West. In her *Essentially Speaking*, Fuss criticizes "appeals to a pure or original femininity, a female essence, outside the boundaries of the social and thereby untainted (though perhaps repressed) by a patriarchal order."[27] The studies that follow make a similar critical move, arguing that it is also an essentialist claim to assume that the West is by nature or definition monolithically imperialistic, and therefore has subjugated all non-Western cultures throughout all historical periods. Of course, it would be just as mistaken to assume that "Oriental" cultures have never been imperialistic, or that they have only learned their "imperialism" from the West.

Despite the claims to the contrary, and the endless disputes among comparatists, theoreticians, and cultural critics over cultural imperialism, it seems clear that neither East nor West is an essential and empirical category.

Indeed, this study intends to demonstrate, among other things, that in many instances being politically "correct" in the West might be at the same time politically "incorrect" in the East where a totalitarian regime posits the West—or any form of Other—as antithetical to its dominant power. My ultimate aim, then, is to discuss particular cultural phenomena in light of their own historical exigencies and to explicitly avoid the totalizing strategies and universal claims that have all too often been part of even those interpretive strategies that claimed to reject them. No theory can be globally inclusive and hence conclusive of local diversities and cultural specificities. The critical discourse of Orientalism should not become a new orthodoxy that could be easily applied to all countries and all historical periods.

In fact, the very discussion of the problematic and paradoxical East-West relation involves a denial of such opposition. There are many examples of failures in a clear definition of, and distinctions between, East and West. Joseph R. Levenson, for example, was aware of this problem as early as 1953 in his classic study of Liang Qichao, a Chinese westernizer at the beginning of the century who saw the West as representing matter while China was said to stand for spiritual qualities. Levenson pointed out that Liang's "matter-spirit distinction between the Western and Chinese cultures, regardless of its justice or injustice at the moment he made it, becomes always less applicable to the actual scene."[28] And this is truer today than ever as China industrializes and modernizes in competition with the West. Another example of a rejection of sweeping distinctions of the Orient and Occident in the field of Chinese studies can be found in Benjamin I. Schwartz's celebrated study of Yan Fu, a Chinese interpreter of Western thought. Schwartz cautioned against rigid categories such as West/non-West or preindustrial/traditional societies, believing that "in dealing with the encounter between the West and any given non-Western society and culture, there can be no escape from the necessity of immersing ourselves as deeply as possible in the specificities of both worlds simultaneously. We are not dealing with a known and an unknown variable but with two vast, ever changing, highly problematic areas of human experience."[29]

In a study advanced from a somewhat different perspective, Masao Miyoshi narrates his account of the image of cultural dynamics of modern Japan, which constantly blurred the boundaries of the Self and the Other, the colonialist empire and the colonized subordinate. As "the earliest non-Western case of modern imperialist aggression," according to Miyoshi, Japan's incursion simultaneously "contained a nativist program of fighting back against the Western conquest."[30] Although contaminated with a domestic imperialist agenda that imitated the Western model of domination from the onset, Japan's defeat of the powerful Russian imperialist czarist army in 1905 paradoxically "became a model for other independent-movement leaders" such as "Sun Yat-sen of China, Ho Chi Minh of Vietnam, and Gamal Abdel Nasser of Egypt. . . ."[31] Thus, Miyoshi implies, it is difficult, if not impossible, to totally and completely separate imperialism —as reflected in Japan's military actions during World War II—and anti-imperialism—as demonstrated when Japan was subjected to Russian imperialism at the turn of this century, or to the Chinese imperial empire long before modern times. Miyoshi thus argues that any attempt to represent different realities between the First World and the Third World is "treacherous," since the very term "Third World" may imply "a racist reaffirmation of the First World with its essentialized characteristics; it can likewise celebrate placement of the First World at a more advanced stage on a supposed scale of progress and modernization. Conversely, it can signify a reactive nativist valorization of Third World communality of spirituality; it can also congratulate Third World traditionalism, proposing permanence as an absolute."[32] Arguing against an essentialist claim of a binarism in critical discourse that sees the First World and the Third World as "homogeneous" entities, Miyoshi ultimately believes that one should not just talk about "white and black, rich and poor, men and women; but rich men and poor women, or rich black women and poor white men, or even poor yellow women living in the First World and rich white men inhabiting the Third World."[33] It is only with such critical—and crucial—positioning that Miyoshi was finally able to point to the "internal colonization" within the discourse of colonialism with which the "poor and powerless of the First World are mobilized to serve as the actual agents of colonialism—often at the expense of their compatriots in poverty," while at the same time the same practice of colonization produced native elites who speak the voice of the colonizers to suppress their compatriots.[34] Critical cultural studies such as Miyoshi's have greatly enhanced our awareness and understanding of (post)colonial and (semi)colonial societies; what needs to be further explored is the internal discourse operating against imperial power within the indigenous culture, using anticolonialist discourse to dismiss the political and ideological demands of the people both in Western and non-Western societies.[35]

From yet another cultural and historical perspective, Chungmoo Choi discusses the problematics of the (post)colonialist South Korea, where the end of Japanese colonialist rule in 1945 only began for the South Korean people a new era of "colonization of consciousness" in which liberation was acknowledged in the official history of South Korea as "a gift of the allied forces, especially of the U.S.A. . . . ."[36] It was this national narrative and the subsequent American imperialists' contest with the Soviet Union that made Korean people accept "Cold War ideology as the ruling ideology of both Koreas."[37] Choi is correct in pointing out that modernization and decolonization in contemporary South Korean society meant a privileging of

Western culture, English language, world history, and finally "an admission of one's own cultural inferiority."[38] It created a "subaltern climate" in which "the 'postcolonial' Korean elite distinguish themselves
as members of the privileged class by meticulously acquiring Western,
that is, American, culture."[39] While Choi's forceful argument certainly
falls in with and furthers the discussion about the complexity and the
problematics of postcolonialist discourse that is taking place in American academia, one wonders, however, if a different or at least additional
factor is not relevant to the cultural scene that she describes: the cultural
and political arena of North Korea, where anti-American imperialist discourse applied by the official ideology is employed for a hidden agenda
of the socialist regime of Kim Il Sung. As an ally of the Soviet Union and
an old friend of China's octogenarian leaders, with whom he had fought
a common enemy in an anti-Japanese-imperialist war, Kim Il Sung more
often than not joined his socialist brothers in their anti-American and
anti-imperialist rhetoric, while playing with a delicate balance between
the two socialist-imperialist superpowers—China and the Soviet
Union—in their ideological and territorial disputes. Here, an official Occidentalism was employed in Maoist China for the sake of subjugating
its socialist brother, which paradoxically shared its master-country's attempt to promote a global discourse against Western imperialism at the
expense of the interests of the local communities both in China and
North Korea. By so doing, a neocolonialism in socialist China effectively
recovered the long-lost Chinese imperial claim on Korean subjects by
employing an anti-Western-imperialist strategy. The "imperial" China,
in turn, also had its share in making use of an anti-imperialist Korean
War in the early 1950s to carry out "mass campaigns to extend the ethos
of the [Korean] war into a passionate hunt for domestic spies and alleged or real enemy agents," especially those who had contact "with the
Guomindang or had worked in foreign firms, universities, or church organizations" before 1949.[40]

Seen in this light, one might point to a historical parallel between a
Chinese Occidentalism and a North Korean Occidentalism; in both the
image of the modern West is used as cultural and symbolic capital for
different ideological agendas. Failure to recognize this indigenous use
of Western discourses and the great variety of conditions that might
provide the focus for its utterance can lead to fundamental problems in
cross-cultural studies, as I hope this study will demonstrate. It is one
thing for cultural critics writing in the West in the area of Korean studies to condemn Occidentalist discourse. Such writings are only to be expected in the current academic tradition that unswervingly sets itself
against colonialism and neocolonialism. But it does not at all follow
that those in Korea for whom they presume to speak would necessarily
agree with their claims. And certainly it is the case, as Choi has shown,

that the discourse of classical Marxism has been employed in South Korea by dissenting intellectuals as a form of protest against a regime that has been repeatedly linked with "American imperialism."[41] But if our focus is on the use of discourse, rather than on the "truth" or "falsity" of a particular ideological position, it should be clear that underground Occidentalist sentiment in North Korea also has a potentially liberating function vis-à-vis the unrelenting orthodoxy of local Marxist indoctrination.

This is also clearly the case in the current relationship between Chinese studies in the West and lived experience in contemporary China. The leftist claims that are so frequently voiced in the West, no matter how positive a role they have or might play in the West in bringing about social changes, do not necessarily appeal to the contemporary Chinese generation oppressed by the leftist ideology. The widespread rejection of this discourse in China is as pervasive today as was its widespread acceptance when it inspired previous generations to participate in the Communist revolutionary movement. The situation could hardly be otherwise, and Orientalists in the West who fail to see this are doomed to an unending and historically irrelevant repetition of "truths" that are now widely regarded in the East as shopworn and outmoded. Shift the historical perspective just a bit, and the same holds true for many regions at the end of the twentieth century, where Occidentalist discourse can and is employed as a strategy of liberation. From this perspective, we can further problematize and enrich the debate on what Choi terms "colonial double discourse," a discourse that "has created for colonized people an illusion of living in the same social and cultural sphere as that of the metropolis, while it ruthlessly exercises a discriminatory politics of hierarchy."[42] Just as such oppression is the product of both capitalist and socialist strategies of domination, so both Orientalist and Occidentalist discourses can serve, under differing local conditions, as discourses of liberation.

It is this strategic use of discourse that the present study seeks to employ. Situated within the critical debate of postcolonial and cultural studies and locally focused on Chinese Occidentalism, it undertakes to explore the "semicolonized" Self that uses the discourse of the colonialist Other for its own political agenda within its own cultural milieu. Understood from local context, Occidentalist discourse in contemporary China is neither merely the product of an ideologically colonizing importation from the West, nor an expression of a masochistic wish on the part of the Chinese people that the more unfortunate aspects of a capitalist system be established in their country. Just as a radical feminist does not necessarily speak for her subaltern Other, who had no voice in the debate about political "correctness" among the elitist theoreticians, the often strident claims of liberal theoreticians usually operating in the West cannot automatically be taken as identical with the hopes and wishes of the non-Western Other for whom she, usually without prior consultation, purports to speak. Though such theoretical pronouncements often do address in some manner the subaltern subject, like all other utterances, they are certainly not free of the personal interests of their speakers. One must candidly admit, though such admissions are seldom found in First World academic discourse, that there is always the danger of theoretically recolonizing the Third World with Western-invented and theoretically motivated languages of "anti-colonialism." As I hope the remainder of this book will make clear, such an assertion is not made in order to deny the usefulness of Western theory, or even its potential for strategies of liberation. By reinterpreting non-Western realities mainly through the looking glass of Western theory, one might invent a new center with which a non-Western phenomenon can only be meaningfully explained by Western terminology and from a Western point of view. The natives' voices in non-Western countries should not have been "rediscovered" to promote the agendas of political "correctness" in the West. Western theoreticians—especially those "Third-World-born" critics residing in the West—who speak for the need of liberating the "Third World" from the West's economic and political power—need to be much more cautious in their claims, lest they unwittingly and unintentionally themselves become neocolonizers who exploit the cultural capital of the colonized in a process in which those voices are appropriated for reinvestment in those "banks of the West" that currently offer the highest rate of return to speculators in trendy academic markets. For one who lives in the West and speaks from the center about marginal cultures, it is extremely difficult and problematic to represent the Other. As one such critic myself, I have felt the need to constantly ask myself, "Who are we?" "Whose voice is it when we speak?" "Are we also the beneficiaries of the very system we are decrying?" One needs to persistently ask the question, "Does my study mean anything to people back home?" Clearly these are ponderous questions with no easy answers or perhaps no answers at all. But responsible criticism needs to ask them, and one cannot but lament that one does not find them more foregrounded in the exciting and stimulating studies that have been produced in the West in recent years. In any case, my study of Chinese Occidentalism attempts to address or at least to be informed by such questions as it explores phenomena such as the television series *He shang*. These programs, like some of the other subjects discussed in the pages that follow, are unquestionably politically "incorrect" by the theoretical standards of American and European academia because of their glorification of a "progressive" West. Yet they have nevertheless exerted an enormous and even liberating influence on Chinese society, an influence that directly or indirectly resulted in the 1989 Tiananmen demonstrations.

Of course, not everyone is likely to agree with the argument advanced here. But I hope that by these remarks I have shown that I am fully aware of the problematics of my own voice in this study, which in varying measure distances itself from the official voice of contemporary China, from diverse groups of Chinese intellectuals whose voices I describe as anti-official, from the Western theoreticians who dwell in the center while speaking for the marginal, and last but not least, from isolationists who think that Western theory has no value for non-Western cultures whose traditions are varyingly deemed either as superior or inferior to their Western counterparts. As a Chinese intellectual educated in the West, I cannot realistically shake off the unavoidable influence of Western culture—be it neocolonial, postcolonial, or neotraditional—since the very English language I use in writing about the voices of the Other predetermines the temporality of my own historical vantage point. By the same token, being a native Chinese does not necessarily give me an uncontested "native" voice since I cannot claim to speak absolutely for the interests of the majority of the Chinese people of both genders, all classes, all races, and different social spectrums. So long as we continue to use Chinese sources to write in the West, we should always be critically aware of what Rey Chow has insightfully termed the unequal "relationship between us as intellectuals overseas and them at home," which "will increasingly take on the coloration of a kind of master discourse/native informant relationship."[43] Such a situation has its assets and liabilities, and it certainly characterizes the arguments which follow.

In other words, although I base my research on published and unpublished materials from Chinese culture, I admit my subjectivity in selecting my data and structuring my narratives. In this regard, I agree with Silvia Tandeciarz's argument against Spivak's search for an "empirical truth" and "scientific," "verifiable," and "anthropological fact-finding" approach in examining the Third World woman. Tandeciarz believes that one should ask the better question of "whether it is to anyone's advantage to read any text as anything other than a fiction, constructed by a particular vision, which in turn is constructed by a particular experience, and whose claim to 'objectivity' thus necessarily is rendered moot" by the assumption of fictionality.[44] Tandeciarz insists that after one acknowledges the impossibility of knowing the Other, he or she could examine "how the imagining of that space construed as 'other' might serve certain ends, suggest certain alternatives that otherwise might have remained unvoiced."[45]

The issue of what alternatives, ends, and impact the writing of the Chinese Other might bring about are perhaps best illustrated in a letter from China written by Li Xiaojiang, a Chinese scholar who lived through the 1989 demonstrations, traveled to the West, and finally returned to China.

Writing in an open letter to Su Shaozhi, a Chinese scholar in exile, Li argues that overseas Chinese scholars, trained in the latest Western intellectual fashions, are extremely competent in developing profound and meticulous theoretical arguments, which unfortunately, she insists, do not often address "the real conditions prevailing in China" in the post-1989 period.[46] Upon her return from the West, Li traveled extensively to many remote regions in China, conducting investigations across the country, the conclusions of which were usually related to the current changes and transformations in China. Li pointed to the phenomenon of a perplexing discrepancy between "China will perish"—a judgment derived from gazing at China from a distance with grand theoretical analysis on the part of overseas China scholars—and "China's continued survival"—a contradiction which "leav[es] a large opening for reflection."[47] Li thus warned her colleagues in the diaspora: "We must look at what China really is, beyond 'concepts,' and beyond 'systems.'"[48]

From a slightly different angle, Zhang Longxi also emphasizes the importance and desirability of understanding China from the perspectives of those who actually live in contemporary Chinese society. Zhang argues against a trend in Western discourses involving Chinese studies which seem to have resulted from the current American leftist intellectual context rather than from "a perspective grounded in Chinese reality."[49] Sophisticated Western theory, albeit important, can be useful when understood in terms of the role it plays *within* the cultural and political environment of China. Conversely, those critics inside China without a real understanding of Western theory can and have developed their own form of articulation situated at the very center of political events: "Liu Zaifu and many other Chinese literary scholars, to put it simply, are not ivory-tower dwellers who talk about the autonomy of literature and the freedom of artistic expression only from a safe distance, somewhere outside history. They are men and women of enormous courage and moral integrity fighting for social justice and intellectual freedom in political actions."[50] The validity of this claim is self-evident, yet to acknowledge it is not to necessarily agree with the essentialist rejection of self-contained Western theory and its concomitant construction of a "true" Other. Zhang's essay, which is itself well-versed in Western theory, challenges the voice behind theory, not theory itself. It is one thing to critique theory from the perspective of indigenous Chinese society; it is quite another to advance theory merely as a means of self-empowerment conditioned by a particular moment in Western culture. Such a distinction is just what my study advocates: to reject binarist and universalist arguments grounded in an Orient constructed either by the East or by the West. Such a project thus demands both engaging with and moving away from theory, rejecting a globalizing tendency—which falls prey to Orientalism—and a localizing approach—which would once again isolate China from the rest of the world through the discourse of the official Occidentalism that this study seeks in part to explore.

In their discussions of the problematics of Western theory and Chinese experience, both Li and Zhang point to the important question of the role of intellectuals in social transformations in the indigenous cultures, an issue that is doubly complicated in China and other societies where intellectuals traveled to the West and are now living and writing in the West. Such studies in the past decades have produced many valuable perspectives exploring the indispensable and yet problematic roles Chinese intellectuals have played in inaugurating new ideas and social changes in traditional Confucian society in modern China before, during, and after the May Fourth movement. Yet it would be easy—and questionable—to overvalue the role of intellectuals. Recent works in subaltern studies, primarily initiated by Indian scholars, have explored problems within the role of intellectuals in colonized and semicolonized countries. By raising the question "Can the subaltern speak?" the Subaltern Studies Group intended to "write subalterns ('the people') back into a history dominated by two elite historiographies: one which gave pride of place to colonial authorities, the other to Indian nationalist elites."[51]

In response to such theory, Gail Hershatter pointed out that such an end aim of subaltern studies became problematic for Chinese historiography after 1949, when officially dispatched historians collected "speak bitterness" stories of worker and peasant against the feudal and imperialist past in a vocabulary supplied by the state.[52] Yet this "legacy of official subaltern-speak" should not foreclose our interrogation of the subversive voices.[53] On the contrary, by exploring the "multiple, relational degrees of subalternity," Hershatter gives a positive answer to Spivak's question "Can the subaltern speak?": some of the subaltern speak "can be understood as resistance to the dominant discourses and institutions that constrain subalterns. . . ."[54] The strength of Hershatter's essay lies in her emphasis on "local configurations" and "multiple political subjectivities" in subaltern and cultural studies, even if there remains much more to be said in order to fully and convincingly answer Spivak's question.[55]

Yet in cultural matters things are never simple or straightforward. Hershatter's conclusion, striking as it is, calls out for the problematizing that the details and localness of history can always produce. We can see this by considering an episode in the history of subaltern representation in contemporary China. During the height of the Cultural Revolution, when the Red Guards were increasingly spinning out of control in chaotic cities torn by civil war, Mao Zedong promoted the movement of "going up to the mountain areas and going down to the villages," during which millions of educated youth were coerced into settling down in remote rural areas.

The initial goal of such a movement was to provide an opportunity for the educated youth to "receive education from the poor and lower-middle peasants" so that they could eventually be accepted by the subalterns, acting like them and speaking in their voice. The following quotation from Mao Zedong, for example, was frequently used to promote a Maoist theory of subaltern representation during the Cultural Revolution, when educated youth were encouraged to reform themselves according to the role models of the subalterns in the countryside:

> How should we judge whether a youth is a revolutionary? How can we tell? There can only be one criterion, namely, whether or not he is willing to integrate himself with the broad masses of workers and peasants and does so in practice. If he is willing to do so and actually does so, he is a revolutionary; otherwise he is a non-revolutionary or a counter-revolutionary. If today he integrates himself with the masses of workers and peasants, then today he is a revolutionary; if tomorrow he ceases to do so or turns around to oppress the common people, then he becomes a non-revolutionary or a counter-revolutionary.[56]

This Maoist theory of subaltern representation is drastically different both from the local Indian subalterns in Ranajit Guha's definition and from the gendered subalterns in Spivak's definition. Most importantly, Rey Chow's explanation that "the relation between the elite and the subaltern in China needs to be formulated *primarily* in terms of the way education and gender work together" is not at all sufficient to account for the brutality and unpredictability of a dominant political power that classifies people into opposing social classes at random according to its various and ever-changing ideological agendas.[57] In the numerous political movements in the brief history of the PRC, the concept of "revolutionary subaltern" is conveniently used by the ruling ideology as a counter Other to classify a dissident as "counter-revolutionary" with the simple pretext that he "ceases to" integrate himself "with the masses of workers and peasants" or that he "turns around to oppress the common people." More often than not, even members of the subaltern group itself can be outlawed overnight as "counter-revolutionary" if they happen to step beyond the party line. Differences in gender, class, and educational level alone cannot, therefore, fully explain the complexity of the subaltern representation in the PRC.

This Maoist utopian idealism, of course, never materialized into concrete reality. For more than ten years during the Cultural Revolution, many of the educated youth were either persecuted, or in some instances, even raped, by local tyrannical party officials who claimed to represent the best interests of the subalterns, since—as opposed to the educated youth—they belonged to the class of the subalterns themselves.[58] As for the real subalterns, their illiteracy, lack of power, or even lack of a desire for power, kept them silent and invisible. The educated youth thus became a new generation of a special class of the oppressed "subalterns" whose literacy became the very reason for their being deprived of any traces of the power of discourse that they had previously possessed. Instead of realizing the initial intention of becoming one of the subalterns, they were reduced to a class less verbal and visible than the illiterate subalterns themselves. This situation predictably led to these intellectual subalterns entering into open confrontation with the ruling ideology between 1978 and 1979, a time when many of the ten million educated youths still remained in the countryside. These youths joined their effort in hunger strikes, railway blockages, and mass demonstrations for the purpose of demanding their right to go back to their home cities.[59] For the first time, the educated youths spoke up for themselves as "subalterns," but their demands had nothing to do with the interests of local subalterns whom they were supposed to embrace as role models. Their voice of protest was further recorded in post-Mao history through their writings of "wound literature" (*shanghen wenxue*) in which they expressed their grievances at being reduced to the position of subalterns.[60] One finds in these writings ambiguous feelings toward the local subalterns, some of whom suppressed them as political opponents while others sided with them against the official ideology on different occasions.[61]

This episode demonstrates the impossibility and complexity of a one-sided discourse about subalterns in contemporary China, where class categories crosscut each other and are continuously redefined by the representatives of the ruling ideology in accordance with their own interests and ever-shifting agendas. The same can be said of other political movements such as the "anti-rightist" and the Cultural Revolution, during which numerous Chinese intellectuals were sent to the country in exile to be "ideologically reformed" by the local subalterns. In the context of the cultural and political history of contemporary China, the issue of "Can the subalterns speak?" is much more complicated than those situations that have been reported, accurately or not, by Indian scholars. In fact, to many Chinese readers and critics, the question "Can the subalterns speak?" is painfully reminiscent of the familiar question "For whom do we speak?"—which was the central issue raised by Mao Zedong in his Yan'an talks of 1943. To a large extent, this document helped shape the predominant Maoist-Marxist theory of literature and art since 1949, which has persistently marked out the goal of serving the interests of workers, peasants, and soldiers. In the political and cultural history of the PRC, this supposedly subaltern theory of literature and art has conveniently justified the party's demand for "the correct attitude of the writer, the need for a popular language comprehensible to the masses, the prerequisite of 'extolling' and not 'exposing' revolutionary reality, and similar phrases which at various times have been much more than empty utterances."[62] In the "glorious" defense of subalterns—many of whom, thanks to the failure of official education programs, remain illiterate even in present-day China—the ruling ideology found a "natural" ally in the political suppression of the intellectuals whose already limited articulations of anti-official voices were rendered even more mute and powerless. Seen from this context it is ironic to note that at the very moment when the pretext for subaltern speech as an instrument of power is dying in China as part and parcel of an obsolete, radical Marxist ideology, it is being popularized in the West as an effective weapon against the mainstream claims of Western academics. While not denying its positive role in opening up theoretical issues, I nevertheless caution against the use of this once local-and-regional discourse for the sake of globalizing cultural and theoretical issues. Like other strategies of "truth" that seek to assert power both at home and abroad, this discourse may well turn out to be yet another form of the Western theoretical hegemony that it claims to displace. It is not easy for the Chinese people to erase the memory of the promulgation of an official discourse on subalterns, a discourse of power fully employed to suppress the advancement of other discourses by Chinese intellectuals. Indeed, the memories of this discourse and its tragic effects are one of the places from which I here advance my study of a Chinese Occidentalism that focuses on the role of the intellectuals in producing a counter-discourse about an imagined and imaginary West, which, as we shall see, was directed against the ruling ideology and its professed subaltern interest.

In evoking the term "Chinese intellectuals," I hardly need to point out that it is a loaded term necessarily involving diverse social groups and conflicting ideologies in different historical periods. I do not wish to claim that the post-Mao age can merely be understood in terms of a seemingly unbridgeable gap between the official and the anti-official discourses designed by progressive intellectuals. Neither do I intend to give the impression that the anti-official message alone constitutes the historical necessity of those literary and dramatic institutions under discussion. Fully aware of the danger of a binary thinking that confines intellectual inquiry, I use the terms of "official/anti-official discourses" strategically in order to identify temporary, complex, fluid, and constantly shifting historical moments in which diverse groups of Chinese intellectuals collaborated with other social forces in their confrontations with the ruling ideology. To demonstrate the complexity of those historical moments, I discuss, in chapter 2, an example of a third kind of Chinese Occidentalism in which the anti-official Occidentalism overlapped or even collaborated with the official Occidentalism of the early post-Mao regime, which manipulated the former into legitimizing the latter's political agenda. In these instances, it is precisely the "complicity" with the ruling ideology that marked the multiple historical moments of Chinese Occidentalism. This complicity marks a crucial feature of the Chinese Occidentalism and the questionable role of what Carol Lee Hamrin and Timothy Cheek termed "Chinese establishment intellectuals," who allied themselves with the authoritarian ruling elite, living and writing within the tension and conflicts between them.[63]

Yet to emphasize the politically liberating force of Occidentalism in the formation of literary and cultural history in contemporary China is not to ignore the fact that Occidentalism is multifaceted and highly problematic and can at times become ideologically limiting and confining. I therefore stress in chapter 6 the problematic nature of Occidentalism by recounting a profound irony in an earlier episode in modern Chinese dramatic history. I argue that, on the one hand, several male May Fourth playwrights considered writing about women's issues of liberation and equality important political and ideological strategies in their formation of a countertradition and a countercanon against the Confucian ruling ideology. In such a peculiar "male-dominated-feminist" discourse, they found in the image of the West a powerful weapon against the dominant ruling ideology of Confucianism. When the West is used in this way as a strong anti-official statement against Confucian traditional culture, this Occidentalist discourse can be regarded as politically liberating. On the other hand, however, in view of the particular historical conditions of women's predicament in the May Fourth period, the appeal to the Western fathers to solve the problems of Chinese women presents complex and challenging issues for feminist readings of these plays in cross-cultural contexts. Therefore, in their efforts to attack the traditional culture that oppressed women in early modern China, May Fourth new cultural fathers resorted to Western patriarchal traditions as an alternative to "liberate" Chinese women. One needs to be especially aware of the critical issues at the intersection of gender, race, nation, and class in the study of Occidentalism in cross-cultural contexts.

Chapter 7 further discusses the complex nature of Occidentalism as expressed in the 1980s and 1990s stories of the Chinese diaspora. I argue that after Chinese writers traveled to the United States and other countries, their perceptions of Others revealed more paradoxical views of the Other and Self than their counterparts in the late 1970s and early 1980s, as seen in *He shang* writers and Shakespearean producers. On the other hand, however, the increasing threat of globalization and modernization in the later period did not prevent them from constructing the Other as either a better or worse place than China, depending on their own subject positions at the moment of writing against their experience at home and abroad. Hu Ping's 1987 reportage entitled *Exchanging Revolutionary Experience in the World*, for instance, focuses on the motivations of the Chinese immigrants to escape from certain conditions in the PRC such as isolation, corruption, and bureaucracy. Cao Guilin's 1994 *A Chinese Nightingale in the Sky of New York*, in contrast, criticizes the Chinese Americans' pursuit of material wealth in his rewriting of such experiences by depicting his protagonist's literary career in the West. In these and other stories, one perceives active voices against global capitalism. Diaspora stories of the 1990s, then, expressed a more diverse expression of Occidentalism at work.

It hardly seems necessary to emphasize that this study in no way constitutes an attempt to sketch a comprehensive history of Occidentalism in modern China. Such an attempt is surely beyond the scope of any single monograph. Indeed, this work does not even claim to be a typical survey of the entire post-Mao period, whose political course is to a large extent characterized by an ambivalent and paradoxical relationship to the West. It is merely a portrait gallery of the "heroes" and "villains" in a few exciting —and, in some cases, much-neglected—moments in history when Chinese realities clashed with Western Others, confusing the traditional differences between them, and claiming the Other as access to its own cultural and symbolic capital in an indigenous battle to subvert domestic power and knowledge in both economic and political terms. By avoiding a chronological history, these fragmented "case studies" categorically question the familiar story outlined by the continuous narratives of official and national history. By drawing materials more heavily from dramatic studies than from other literary genres, I intend to redeem modern Chinese spoken drama from its marginal position both in China and in the West. While selectively celebrating the internal antihegemonic use of the image of the West in certain specific moments in contemporary Chinese history, I am equally aware of the fact that the symbolic uses of the West in Chinese texts and contexts treated here by no means offer a complete story of Chinese Occidentalism, which has rightly been characterized on both sides as problematic and contradictory ever since China's initial contact with the West.[64] The discussions of the instances of Chinese Occidentalism considered here are offered as at best partially representative and are merely meant to open up a new discourse, which mediates between theory and historical analysis of the concrete experience of the indigenous cultures. With this observation, I begin my tale, to be completed inevitably by the interrogations and interventions of others.

Chapter One

Occidentalism as a Counter-Discourse

The *He shang* Controversy

Throughout contemporary Chinese history, literary and political texts have often been composed by different and diverse groups of the intelligentsia as deliberate endeavors to promote an anti-official discourse.[1] Although impoverished in political power and material wealth, the Chinese intelligentsia has nevertheless been blessed with knowledge and literacy —qualities that have been ingeniously and repeatedly used against the "powerful" status quo. The ability to write, especially as it enables the production of anti-official agendas, points to an obvious advantage of the urban intellectuals over the peasants, many of whom have remained illiterate even in postrevolutionary China. Indeed the very act of public writing is itself a form of anti-official Occidentalism and thus a critique of Mao's antiurbanism, which, as we have seen, is itself a result of, and a reaction to, Chinese Orientalism. Yet the creation of an anti-official Occidentalism by the Chinese intelligentsia for diverse and complicated reasons is more than a coincidental product of its literacy. It was preconditioned by the parameters of Maoist political discourse, which categorized anything opposed to its political dominance as "Western" or "Westernized." To prevent China from being "Westernized" or "capitalized," for instance, was commonly advanced as the reason for starting the Cultural Revolution and for persecuting numerous intellectuals. In this situation, the adoption of an Occidentalist discourse was a strategic move by dissenting intellectuals. Accused of being "Western" both by virtue of their cultural status and their political sympathies, they had little choice but to assert that the Western Other was in fact superior to the Chinese Self. By thus accepting the inevitable official critique raised against them, whether or not it was "factually" always the case, they strengthened their anti-official status. By suggesting that the West is politically and culturally superior to China, they defended their opposition to established "truths" and institutions. In the process, these urban intellectuals created a form of anti-official Occidentalism that stands in the sharpest contrast to the official Occidentalism pervasive in government and party propaganda in contemporary China.

Nowhere is this anti-official Occidentalism more evident than in the controversial 1988 television series *He shang* (River Elegy); indeed, as we shall see, the critical debate that this series engendered can serve as an especially revealing example of the character and function of anti-official Occidentalist discourse. *He shang* was widely noted even in the West for its positive image of a scientific and modern West, indeed its almost embarrassingly positive evaluation of all things Western. Given this apparent celebration it would be easy—though facile and mistaken—to dismiss the series as an especially overt example of Western "cultural imperialism," as that term is now defined in postcolonial and Third World discourses. Seen from such a limited and mistaken perspective, *He shang* appears as but another potent example of the ideological power wielded by the West in Edward Said's account of Orientalism. Yet if considered within the cultural and historical context of post-Mao society, *He shang* can be seen more profitably as a product of anti-official Occidentalism. From this perspective it can be best understood neither as an example of Chinese naiveté nor of Western imperialism, but as a potent anti-official discourse employed by the Chinese intelligentsia to express what was otherwise politically impossible and ideologically inconceivable.

I hope to make clear by this study of *He shang* that ideas or ideological concepts, whether they stem from a politically dominant or from a subordinate culture, are never intrinsically oppressive or liberating. Certainly the appropriation of the image of the West, when put into critical use against the domestic hegemony of the ruling ideology, as was the case with *He shang*, can rightly be viewed as positive, liberating, and even desirable. Seen from this perspective, *He shang* was above all else an anti-official discourse that employed the Occidental Other, in its cultural and ideological absence, to critique the oppressive presence of official ideology. Its depiction of the West was not offered as mimesis, but as an oppositional and supplementary Other and as a counter-discourse that sought to be subversive of the dominant and official Orientalism and Occidentalism prevalent throughout Chinese culture. Thus the account of *He shang* that follows argues against the essentializing of any cultural discourse, Western or Eastern; it offers a prime example of how superficially similar sign systems can be manipulated for very different ideological ends.

Initially broadcast in June 11, 1988, the six-part television documentary series *He shang* roused perhaps the greatest national sensation in the history of the PRC television industry. *He shang* was produced by Xia Jun, a twenty-six-year-old television director and journalist. The principal scriptwriters were Su Xiaokang, a well-known reporter and a lecturer at the Journalism Department of Beijing Broadcasting College, and Wang Luxiang, a lecturer at the Chinese Department of Beijing Normal University. Others who also contributed to the writing of the narrative script were Zhang Gang, Xie Xuanjun, and Yuan Zhiming.[2] Immediately after its première, *He shang* writers received thousands of letters from audiences in all walks of life unanimously expressing their "deep gratitude" for an excellent TV program and requesting a written copy of *He shang*'s script in order to study its profound messages.[3] As a result, *He shang* was rebroadcast two months later in prime time, an unprecedented event, in spite of official efforts to ban it as a vilification of Chinese culture.[4]

One of those profound messages can be found, surprisingly, in *He shang*'s total rejection of traditional Chinese cultural fetishes. Contrary to its conventional image as the cradle of the Chinese civilization, the Yellow River is here portrayed as a source of poverty and disaster. In fact, it is depicted almost as if it were a willful human being, violent, brutal, tyrannical, periodically sweeping away millions of people and their livelihoods at free will. It seems likely that such an image of the river could not but remind many Chinese people of their traumatic experiences during the Cultural Revolution. In the television series, the river is personified as a dying old man, "alone and desolate, stubbornly waiting to die in his devastated homeland."[5] This characterization certainly defamiliarizes the common presentation of the Yellow River as a revolutionary symbol of national resistance, such as we find it, for example, in Xian Xinghai's "The Yellow River Chorus." Composed in 1939 during the Sino-Japanese War, this musical piece has been interpreted as eulogizing the "gigantic image of the Chinese nation, whose glory, diligence, and courageousness are depicted in the battlefields on both sides of the Yellow River against Japanese invaders."[6] Repeated performances of the piece after the war at crucial historical moments, such as the one after the arrest of the Gang of Four, preserved its function as an inspiration for the Chinese people's commitment to socialism, especially in times of adversity. In addition to deviating from this earlier association of the Yellow River with China's revolutionary tradition, *He shang* also rejected an earlier 1988 television depiction of the river in a series of documentary programs on Chinese landscapes; here the river was idealized for its "beauty," its "grandeur," and its personification of the "resourcefulness" of the motherland.[7]

As if such blasphemy of China's "cultural roots" were not enough, *He shang* also deconstructs other quintessential national symbols. The dragon and the yellow earth are interpreted as representing cynicism, parochialism, conservatism, confinement, and land and ancestry worship in Chinese culture. The Great Wall, China's most famous tourist attraction and historical site, is also singled out for ridicule as a defense mechanism that secluded China from the rest of the world. "If the Great Wall could speak for itself," the narrator in *He shang* assures us, "it would have honestly told Chinese offspring that it is a huge monument of tragedy constructed by the fate of history," not a symbol of the strength, glory, and enterprising spirit of the Chinese people.[8] As a kind of culmination, all of the negative aspects of Chinese culture are finally traced to Confucian ideology, whose monolithic social system resists plurality and change. *He shang* thus concludes that the yellow earth and the Yellow River cannot teach contemporary Chinese people much about the spirit of science and democracy, both of which are necessary for life at the end of the twentieth century. Similarly, those traditional cultural monuments, it is suggested, will not provide the Chinese people with "nourishment and energy"; they are no longer capable of "producing a new culture."[9]

The most critical and adversarial comment made by the television series about Chinese culture, however, is presented in its very title. The word *he* (river) refers to the Yellow River civilization and, by extension, to other primitive agricultural civilizations such as those in India and Egypt.[10] The word *shang* means "dying before one comes of age." According to Su Xiaokang, one of the main screenwriters of *He shang,* the term suggests the stagnation of the characteristic "Asiatic mode of production," which "had matured too early, thus resulting in an early stagnancy."[11] The word *shang* also suggests a survivor's mourning for the martyrs who had sacrificed their lives for their country, as evidenced in Qu Yuan's (ca. 340 BC to 278 BC) poem *"Guo shang"* (Hymn to the Fallen) in his *Chuci-jiuge* (Elegies of Chu—Nine Songs). Thus the word *shang* "crystallizes the ambiguous feelings of Chinese intellectuals in more than a century"—the more deeply they love their country, the more eagerly they long for its rebirth.[12] Using the elegy of the Yellow River as a central image, *He shang* "meditates, in all aspects, on the history, civilization, and destiny of the Chinese nation," foregrounding the imperative of "economic and political reforms."[13] To the inhabitants of the PRC, who are necessarily accustomed to reading between the lines in a strictly censored media, such statements were clear cries of protest against the current regime, which is fundamentally opposed to political reform. As Wang Jing has correctly pointed out, the message from *He shang* seemed "loud" and "clear": "Only by liberating human intelligence from the stifling sense of history will the Chinese people creatively confront the problems of the present. The past conceived as such is viewed as the antithesis rather than as the basis of what Chinese intellectuals came to revere and value in their own present."[14]

In addition to unsettling its Chinese viewers with its depictions of a dying and declining "Orient," *He shang* further shocked its audiences with a passionate account of an Occidental Other, which, it suggests, represents youthfulness, adventure, energy, power, technology, and modernity.[15] The West is characterized as a "blue ocean civilization," openly embracing the outside world and "simultaneously transporting the hope of science and democracy" across the oceans.[16] The ironies of such a depiction of the image of the West, however, were insightfully critiqued by Wang Jing as "the new fetish for the Chinese people." What "empowers the color 'azure blue' is exactly what used to empower the national symbol of the Great Wall and the dragon—namely, power in the sense of expansion, glory, and aggression."[17] Even the major successes of the West were attributed to its "right" attitude toward the sea. The rise of Athens as a marine power was viewed as having paved the way for "a democratic revolution" in ancient Greece.[18] Columbus's discovery of the New World and Magellan's journey in 1519 across the ocean, the program claims, established among other things the foundations for a bourgeois revolution. Even the history of science and technology in the West was closely related to mankind's fate on the ocean. The urgent need for building bigger and better ocean-going ships for world trade and colonialism, for example, "demanded a further development of mathematics, physics, technology, and science." This was the reason why, according to *He shang*, "Galileo published his *Dialogues Concerning Two New Sciences* in 1636, which was conducted," not incidentally, "in a ship-yard."[19]

He shang persistently lamented the historical opportunities that, it suggested, the Chinese people had lost, often by failing to heed the advice of Western men-of-letters. While Magellan was sailing across the oceans, *He shang* noted with regret, the Chinese Emperor Jiajing (Ming dynasty) declared a "closed-door" policy after a quarrel with a Japanese official over Japan's "tribute" to China.[20] The Chinese people also "did not hear in time" what Adam Smith had to say in 1776 about Chinese culture in his *The Wealth of Nations*, in which he declared that Chinese culture "suffered from stagnation as a result of neglecting overseas trade." History, the program declared, has proven correct this Westerner's view that to "close oneself up amounts to suicide."[21] As another instance of Chinese neglect of salutary components of Western culture, the program alludes to the case of Yan Fu, an important Chinese thinker and translator, who believed that Western notions such as the social contract and the will to power were useful "balance mechanisms" that could tap human potential, thus bringing about new forms of culture with vigor and vitality. Yet the conservative resistance to Western ideas was so strong in China that in his old age, Yan Fu was forced to surrender to Confucianism at the very historical moment when Ito Hirobumi, his former Japanese school-mate in a British naval college, was successfully, as the Japanese Prime Minister, leading Japan's rapid advance to a position as one of the world's powers.[22] Here, then, a Japanese imperialist, known in Chinese history books to have been responsible for both the seizure of Taiwan from China and the imposition of Japanese colonial rule in Korea, was presented paradoxically as a superior and senior Other, contrasted with an inferior and impoverished Chinese Self. It is worth noting that in *He shang* this Other is alien even though he would seem "Oriental," if not Chinese, to a non-Chinese viewer.

The details cited here are merely representative. *He shang* abounded in problematic images of China and its oppositional Others. Indeed, *He shang* amounted to no less than a rewriting of the usual Chinese versions of world history. Included were references to such events in Western history as the rise of the Roman Empire, the British Industrial Revolution, the French Revolution, and the Russian Revolution—almost all of which painted the West in favorable colors. Western thinkers were also approvingly evoked, among them Hegel, Marx, Plekhanov, Francis Bacon, Joseph Needham, and Arnold Toynbee. It seems clear that such an extremely and even one-sidedly favorable treatment of those people and events could only serve to establish a non-Chinese paradigm that could then be employed to critique things Chinese.

Naturally such a presentation drew many outraged cries of disagreement. It was reported, for instance, that "Vice-President Wang Zhen condemned *He shang* as a 'vilification' of Chinese culture and banned videotapes of the program from leaving the country," and that "in a speech to the northwest Ningxia Province on September 27, the 80-year-old conservative leader described *He shang* as having portrayed the Chinese people and their seat of civilization, the Yellow River Basin, as devoid of any merit."[23] In a literary journal, Chen Zhi'ang also observed that although *He shang* aimed at "an all-round meditation on Chinese history, civilization, and destiny," as one of its authors Su Xiaokang had claimed, it amounted in effect to a meditation on the negative aspects of the Chinese culture, which are set in sharp contrast, whenever possible, with the positive elements of the Western cultures. Quoting Lenin's remarks on the dual possibilities to be found in any cultural heritage, Chen argued that an all-round meditation on any single culture, be it Chinese or Western, must include analysis of both the negative and the positive sides. Only in this way, he claimed, could it become dialectical and, hence, convincing.[24] For Chen, the reason for the stagnation of Chinese society resides not in the negative characteristics and personalities of the Chinese people, but rather in the very fact that the Chinese feudalist society had reached its perfection too early and too securely, and hence it was difficult to surpass that stage of civilization.[25]

Other academics, of course, focused on "factual mistakes" in *He shang*. Gao Wangling noted that *He shang* expressed an "unbalanced view" of

Chinese history by "hallucinating" an idealized Western Other.[26] Using outdated research materials "from the fifties to express their disappointments in the eighties," Gao argued, *He shang* screenwriters created "acts of misunderstanding" in their proclamation of an "oceanic civilization," a myth that viewed the lack of a navigational culture as the root of China's stagnation.[27] Yet for a long time, Gao pointed out, navigation in the West was indeed limited within the "small bathtub" of the Mediterranean. Its "cultural expansion" could not possibly be compared to that of China in the same historical period, in which the latter reached out to the world on a much larger scale both by sea and by land. Neither is the "yellow earth" a particularly Chinese phenomenon. The West, too, has developed an "inland" agricultural civilization in its own history.[28]

As if to further support Gao's view, Pan Qun observed that during at least two periods in Chinese history—the early Qin dynasty and the Song and Yuan dynasties—China had developed much more advanced navigational enterprises than any other countries, including those in the West. Zheng He's seven journeys to the West across the Pacific Ocean and Indian Ocean—journeys that began in 1405 and lasted for the next twenty-eight years—were results of the open-door policies of the imperial courts. For at least one time, China, too, enjoyed a hegemony on the "blue ocean." The subsequent stagnation of Chinese society, Pan Qun concluded, was brought about by the closed-door policy of the Qing dynasty in a much later period; thus, he claimed, it had nothing to do with an absence of a "blue culture."[29] Commenting further on *He shang*'s oversimplification of Occidental-blue/Oriental-yellow civilizations, Yan Tao stated that if it were true that the ancient Greeks were a "blue-ocean culture" as *He shang* claimed, then the medieval millennium certainly had nothing to do with this "blueness." The Middle Ages were indeed much "darker" and more isolated from the rest of the world than was Chinese culture during that period.[30] As for the Great Wall as a symbol of China's defensiveness toward the outside world, Ji Ren noted to the contrary that in the Han dynasty, Emperor Wu extended the Great Wall to what is now the Xinjiang Autonomous Region for the sole purpose of protecting the "*sichou zhi lu*" (silk road), the only trade route between China and what was then known as the "*xiyu*" (western region). Thus the Great Wall significantly contributed to cultural and economic exchanges between China and the West, and therefore had nothing to do with China's "cowardice," "parochialism" and "self-isolation," as *He shang* had claimed.[31]

In all of this it seems clear that *He shang* created and propagated a misleading image of the alien West, which might well be termed Occidentalism since it provides a politically and ideologically motivated image of the cultural Other. This Occidentalist discourse in *He shang* becomes even more striking when viewed in the context of Third World discourse against a claimed Eurocentric Western domination. For example, citing Martin Bernal's argument in *Black Athena* concerning the "fabrication of Ancient Greece," Samir Amin observed, in his *Eurocentrism*, that the Western ideology of Eurocentrism was based on cultural, religious, literary, and linguistic reconstructions of a Hellenist myth with a false "annexation of Greece by Europe" from the ancient Orient.[32] Set against such a perspective, *He shang* seems to voluntarily import such Eurocentrism, rather than reject it, as many of the Third World critics seek to do. At least on first consideration, *He shang* seems to fortify the image of what Amin calls an "eternal West,"[33] with its repeated claims that a combination of the best cultural heritage of Greek civilization and Western industrialization accounts for the rapid emergence of a modern Europe. Such an image of an "annexed" Athens as the "cultural capital" of Europe[34] is most typically underscored in *He shang*'s glorifications of the rise of Hellenism, the conquests of Alexander the Great, the Discovery of the New World, and the triumph of colonialism and imperialism at various points in the text. Advocating in the East an Orientalism that Third World intellectuals like Amin would consider a distorted view of both the East and the West, *He shang* can be seen as an Oriental fabrication of the Occidental Other, an Other whose centrality is ultimately celebrated in a historical "progression from Ancient Greece to Rome to feudal Christian Europe to capitalist Europe—one of the most popular of received ideas" in the West.[35]

Moreover, *He shang*'s sympathetic portrayal of the Italian missionary Matteo Ricci—the first Westerner who "brought scientific works to the Chinese" and informed them that they "did not live in the center of the world, but live somewhere in the Northern Hemisphere"[36]—can be seen as a Chinese postcolonial affirmation of an earlier European act of cultural imperialism. This is indeed a shocking departure from what has been conventionally taught in standard Chinese history books on the imperialist nature of Western missionary activities, which are usually described as being conducted hand in glove with Western military aggression. It is thus not surprising that *He shang* mentions only in passing the humiliating Opium War, which resulted in a series of treaties and agreements including the 1842 Treaty of Nanjing that forced China to pay an indemnity of 21 million taels, to cede Hong Kong, and to open Guangzhou, Fuzhou, Xiamen, Ningpo, and Shanghai to foreign trade with most-favored-nation treatment.[37] Furthermore, the claims that the Yellow River and the Great Wall symbolize an "inward-looking," agricultural culture seem to inflict a Western "'geographic' racism," that, following the failure of "genetic racism," still attempts to explain an underdeveloped and exploited Orient by locating "acquired and transmissible traits produced by the geographic milieu" without any "scientific value whatsoever." It is amusing to note, in passing, that Amin argued that it was not possible to claim continuity in European culture in view of the fact that "the Renaissance is separated from Classical Greece by fifteen centuries of the medieval history."[38] Here, then, Amin seems to echo the opponents of *He shang*, who argued that the existence of a "blueless" Middle Ages deconstructed *He shang*'s claim of the continuity of an oceanic European culture from ancient Greece to the modern West.

A comparison of *He shang* with such a Third World critique points to a number of striking paradoxes between Amin's rather typical "anti-Eurocentrism" and *He shang*'s Occidentalism. Whereas Amin criticizes the West for regarding itself as "Prometheun *par excellence,* in contrast with other civilizations,"[39] *He shang* laments over the profound tragedy of the Chinese literati, who failed to bring into China "the spirit of Faustus and Prometheus."[40] Moreover, Amin would indeed be surprised to learn that *He shang* did not depreciate the image of China alone; it sounds an elegiac criticism for Oriental traditions as a whole. Recalling Marx's theory of an Asiatic mode of production, *He shang* claims that although in ancient Semitic languages "Asia" means "the region where the sun rises," 5,000 years later, the "Asian sun" has finally set—the ancient civilizations in the Orient have declined one after another for the simple reason that they have depended too heavily, and for too long, on an agricultural mode of production.[41]

Perhaps the greatest paradox to be found in *He shang* concerns its "misreadings" of Arnold Toynbee, whose early theory of challenge and response is cited as if it were uttered by a universally acknowledged great authority. Quoting Toynbee's view that the hostile physical surroundings along the Lower Yellow River valley engendered the development of Chinese civilization, *He shang* calls on the Chinese people to confront the hard facts of history, which, according to Toynbee's *A Study of History,* chronicle the extinction of fourteen civilizations and the decline of six, including those of the Euphrates, the Nile, and the Yellow River. The critics of *He shang* were, not surprisingly, quick to point out that this early theory of Toynbee was already considered passé in Western scholarship and that Toynbee himself had corrected these views in the 1970s: he no longer assumed that Chinese civilization was isolated and backward, but argued instead that China's "ecumenical spirit" will play a major role in shaping the future of the world.[42]

Our account of *He shang*'s uses and misuses of Toynbee is even more complicated than the bare restating of facts suggests. If *He shang* can be viewed as a profound political critique against Maoist ideology and its imperial roots, Toynbee was certainly "misreading" Chinese society when he claimed in 1976—toward the end of the Cultural Revolution—that "on the whole, the history of the Chinese Empire, which still survives in the form of the present People's Republic, has been a political success story. It contrasts dramatically with the history of the Roman Empire, which tried and failed to give lasting political unity and peace to the West."[43] Here, Toynbee completely turned around the "success story" of the West—which *He shang* screenwriters borrowed from his early works—a West that he saw in the late seventies as in the process of disintegration. Toynbee's prediction that "the future unifier of the world will not be a Western or Westernized country but will be China" is obviously unheard—or deliberately ignored—by his Chinese disciples.[44] As if to further license China as "the geographical and cultural axis for the unification of the whole world," Toynbee pointed to the "Chinese people's experience, during the last twenty-one centuries, of maintaining an empire that is a regional model for a literally worldwide world-state" and "the humanism of the Confucian *Weltanschauung*" as unique qualifications, which, ironically, are the very "cultural and historical sediment" that *He shang* screenwriters wished to eradicate from Chinese society by appealing to a "better" model in the West.[45]

Yet Toynbee and the *He shang* screenwriters perhaps have other things in common as well. Just as Toynbee sought to write a philosophy of history that sometimes plays a bit freely with historical facts, so did the *He shang* screenwriters, who sought to create a political document not intended to be accurate about the historical events it reported. Both Toynbee and the *He shang* writers were seeking a macro-historical model in order to come to terms with a teleology of their contemporary societies, be it in the East after the chaotic Cultural Revolution, or in the West after disastrous World War II. Indeed, *He shang* was never meant to be a scholarly essay. As Yuan Zhiming, one of the screenwriters, has rightly said, "*He shang* can never be qualified as an academic work; it did not even claim to address specific issues either in history or in contemporary society."[46] Thus *He shang* might more profitably be regarded as a poetic text rather than a historical one, a text that expresses a younger generation's mythic vision of the world. It is a political text reflecting Chinese intellectuals' own vision of "truth" and "knowledge." Or seen from another angle, the *He shang* screenwriters *did* attempt to be accurate, but in the construction of their program they singled out only those historical facts and data that supported their thesis. In the final analysis, whether those "facts" are accurate it not ultimately important. What is important is their critical use. Yet it is also true that Kenneth Winetrout's characterization of Toynbee's "historical" enterprise seems particularly appropriate for describing the *He shang* scriptwriters: they are "no historian[s]." For them, history "should stress pattern"[47]; "history is feeling as well as intellect"; "history is contemporary"; "history is partly myth" and "theology." Both *He shang* screenwriters and their Western counterparts believe in "historical prophecy."[48]

Indeed the debate on whether or not *He shang* is a historical or a literary text is quite beside the point. *He shang* cleverly interweaves two levels of discourses—the factual and the symbolic. By appealing to historical "facts"—which its writers selected and emphasized in order to support the polemical thrust of their documentary—*He shang* proceeds as if it were based on solid factual data and hence, empirically, rather than merely rhetorically, convincing. Yet these hard facts were, to a great extent, manipulated in order to appeal to the emotions of the contemporary Chinese audience against the ruling ideology. Thus from its very outset, the critique of *He shang* was problematic, since it was predicated on a fundamental confusion about genre. If *He shang* were considered as literature, its detractors were mistaken in their critique of its non-factuality; if it were treated as history, however, one could not account for the appeal of its rhetorical and symbolic dimension, which disqualified it as history. Indeed, *He shang* struck a cord in the national sensibility by glossing over the jump from the factual to the symbolic. It was *He shang's* rhetorical power and emotional appeal that encouraged its willing audiences to overlook the missing links and fill in the gaps between the historical and the symbolic with their own imagination, a faculty that at the moment *He shang* was aired was dominated by its predisposition against post-Mao official ideology. Indeed, there was no real engagement in the debate about the factuality in *He shang;* both its writers and supporters admitted that it would not pass muster as history. What was at stake was the ideological thrust of the series, which was both more and less than history. The rhetorical force of *He shang,* therefore, lies in its intricate interplay between history, poetry, and politics, having to do, for the most part, with the symbolic rather than with the factual. To single out any one of its three dimensions for critique is to miss the better part of the picture.

This characterization can perhaps explain the reason why, in spite of its expressed Occidentalism accompanied by self-degradation, *He shang*—a seemingly colonialist television series with otherwise dry facts, figures, and philosophical and political jargon, and without any sexual or violent content—could touch millions of Chinese from all walks of life. In fact, as Gong Suyi has observed, there emerged in the China of 1988 a *"He shang* phenomenon" in which philosophers and scholars "walked out of their studies and salons to initiate a dialogue on television screens with a national audience" concerning China's past, present, and future.[49] *He shang* was thus hailed as successfully combining both popular-cultural media and elite, scholarly discourse. It is interesting to note here that the image of the West is so predominant and paradoxical in contemporary China that even in the act of appreciating a heavily Eurocentric *He shang,* the Chinese critics did not forget to mention the difference between China and the West in "television culture" "as products of various historical conditions. . . . We should therefore not blindly accept the Western concept that sees television as part of the popular culture"; under the specific circumstances in China, "an elite cultural discourse [such as *He shang*] can be regarded as the soul of television." Popular culture thus means the "popularity" of a particular work among the ordinary people.[50] One finds in this remark an example of a deeply rooted practice of alluding to the Occident as a contrasting Other in order to define whatever one believes to be distinctively "Chinese."

The favorable reception of *He shang* can be seen from yet another angle. Immediately after its première, *He shang* became so popular that many prestigious newspapers, including *People's Daily, Guangming Daily, China Youth Daily, Economy, Wenhui Newspaper,* and *Beijing Youth Daily,* competed with one another in publishing *He shang's* narrative script. Furthermore, viewers and readers hand-copied and circulated the narrative script among themselves. These actions significantly transformed *He shang* from a media event into a literary text and an exceedingly popular text at that. Especially worth noting is its warm reception among high school students, usually a disillusioned generation that in recent years has shown little interest in the fate of its country. A high school student reported to *He shang* writers that her graduating class sacrificed its precious preparation hours for college-entrance examinations in order to study the *He shang* script together in class. "When our teacher read aloud the passage in which the Great Wall is depicted as a huge monument of national tragedy, we all applauded with excitement!"[51] A senior-high student from a poor Henan village told the *He shang* writers that since television sets are still luxury items in some remote countryside locations he had to walk a long distance, twice a week, in order to watch every single part of the series in another village.[52] High school students were by no means the only group that received *He shang* with excitement and fervor. Even the elder generation took it personally and seriously. An old "revolutionary," who fought in the war at the age of sixteen, lost sleep after watching *He shang,* pondering over the meaning of her "glorious" life stories— "How many of them were mistakes?" "How would later generations evaluate my revolutionary career?"[53] It seems clear that to a large extent the success of *He shang* can be attributed to its fundamental challenge to the Chinese conventional value system and worldview in the People's Republic.

Such an outlet of anti-official sentiments among the Chinese people inevitably drew automatic defense from those who saw the message of *He shang* as representing "anti-Marxist" and "counter-revolutionary political programs."[54] Others were disturbed by the fact that the "sacred" places along the Yellow River such as Yan'an, where Mao Zedong rallied his revolutionary forces in the 1930s, were dismissed and even profaned as poverty-stricken in *He shang*. Confronted with such criticism, Su Xiao-kang, one of the chief writers of the script, explained that while on location, his crews did go to "pay their respects" to the "revolutionary relics" in Yan'an. The whitewashed, tidy, and well-kept cave dwellings of the party leaders in the thirties did arouse in them a sense of admiration. Yet, when looking closer at the names in front of each cave dwelling, Su recalls, their hearts saddened at once when ruminating on the tragic endings of, or the tense relationships between, most of the former revolutionary leaders, such as Mao Zedong, Zhang Wentian, Liu Shaoqi, Zhou Enlai, Zhu De, and Ren Bishi. As a result, Su and his crews left with heavy hearts without shooting a single scene in Yan'an, the so-called cradle and beacon of Chinese revolution.[55]

At their next stop in Kaifeng, Henan Province, Su further tells us, his crews went straight to the small, dark room in a tightly secured bank office where Liu Shaoqi, the first president of the People's Republic, was detained for the twenty-eight days before his tragic death during the Cultural Revolution. It was Liu who supervised the implementation of the first constitution of the People's Republic in 1955. Yet, as Su Xiaokang has rightly pointed out, as an architect of the PRC legislation, Liu could not even protect his own rights as a citizen, let alone those of the president of the republic, who was, ironically, elected by the Chinese people according to the letter and spirit of their constitution. Liu Shaoqi was persecuted without any trial or legal procedure. He died in that desolate room, alone and in agony, Su emphasizes, adding the detail that his untended white hair was reported to be more than a foot long!

Su Xiaokang could not help but compare this "horror room" with Liu Shaoqi's "honorable" room in Yan'an. He perceived in them a historical connection and the inevitable tragedy of not just one individual, but of the entire generation of Chinese communists. For Su and his crews, the "sacred" place along the Yellow River region could not teach them about the "gigantic revolutionary spirit," nor could it inspire in them a sense of national pride and grandeur. It merely offered them a vivid lesson on ignorance, self-deception, and autocracy. It is high time, Su insists, that we open our eyes to the outside world and stop considering China as still "number one." It is high time that we catch up. For him, this is perhaps one of the most important messages in the entire Occidentalist discourse of the *He shang* series.

Such a remark seems to offer a perspective from which we can begin to make sense of the *He shang* phenomenon. Whatever else it might be, *He shang* is without a doubt an expression of an anti-official discourse prevalent in China at the end of the 1980s, which painted the Occident as an oppositional and supplementary Other. Clearly such a discourse served above all as a counter-discourse that aimed at subverting the predominant official ideology. Thus the majority of the audience did not care whether the historical facts were correct. They read into the contrasting Other a hope for remodeling and rescuing their own country and their own selves. Realizing this helps explain why even academics, who had earlier questioned the scholarly soundness of *He shang*, began to defend it politically after party tyrants such as Wang Zhen threatened to denounce it as "counter-revolutionary." The critical point driven home to the critics and viewers seemed to be that it is not the Chinese people who are ultimately depicted as inferior to their Western counterparts. The "inferior" China presented in the program is part of a strategy for exposing the inferiority of a monolithic, one-party system. The depiction in *He shang* of a problematic cultural past and a progressive Occidental Other were merely pretexts to debunk official ideology.

This observation is central to any understanding of *He shang*, but it also needs to be set in a broader framework. To Westerners unfamiliar with the history of twentieth-century China, *He shang*'s Occidentalism may seem striking and innovative. Perhaps to a certain degree it is. But it is important to recognize that Occidentalism has frequently been employed by the ruling classes in modern China for their own political agendas. No one can dismiss the undeniable fact, for instance, that ever since the founding of the PRC, both Mao Zedong and Deng Xiaoping have successfully used anti-imperialist discourse to stunt anti-official voices at home. During the Cultural Revolution, even Mao's former "comrades-in-arms" were persecuted as *"di, te, pan"*—enemies, spies, and traitors—who allegedly aligned themselves with Western powers and their nationalist followers; such an association with the West was even more strongly—and fictionally—created for those dissidents who openly challenged Mao's ideology. Liu Shaoqi was publicly humiliated during the Cultural Revolution for his pro-Western and pro-capitalist stance, and his wife, Wang Guangmei, was accused of adopting a Western, and hence "rotten," lifestyle. One might, of course, not idealize Liu Shaoqi, one of the top party leaders up to 1966, who was also deeply involved in the policy formation concerning China's involvement in the Korean War and other anti-Western movements. Yet the very fact that even an anti-Western president of the PRC was accused of being pro-Western, and hence, counter-Marxist and counter-revolutionary, demonstrates the powerful role that Occidentalism plays in the political drama of contemporary China.

The same is true even for Deng Xiaoping, who was himself removed more than once from the top party apparatus for the sole "crime" of introducing Western technology. It thus seemed natural for Deng to use his own brand of Occidentalism, at the beginning of the post-Mao years, to attack Mao's Cultural Revolution, his political purges, and his closed-door policies. Yet it is ironic to note that in January of 1979, when Deng was visiting the United States as the first major party leader to do so in thirty years—performing his "epoch-making" pro-Western drama—he had already started back home in China a large-scale government crackdown on the Democracy Wall movement, just as soon as his own political power was secured after Mao's death. Wei Jingsheng, the movement's leader, was sentenced to fifteen years in prison for his alleged spying activities—for providing information on the Sino-Vietnamese war to a Western journalist.

Likewise, the official reason for the 1989 Tiananmen student crackdown, announced by Deng Xiaoping himself, was that it was a "counter-revolutionary rebellion," that was caused, not incidentally, by "an international and domestic climate" in an attempt to "overthrow the Communist party and socialist system" and to "establish a bourgeois republic entirely dependent on the West."[56] The ensuing event, in which Fang Lizhi took refuge in the U.S. embassy, was manipulated to further testify to the official view that the student movement was indeed plotted by a traitor who ran into the open arms of American imperialists. Seen from these political and ideological perspectives, such events enable one to argue that it is this "Western devil" and its professed ideology—although seriously and justly critiqued by its own people in the West—that has paradoxically kept alive a myth of democracy and human rights in post-Mao China. Indeed, Deng himself is a master in annexing the Occident: he wants only Western science and technology for his economic reform, while wholly rejecting Western political and legal systems.

In view of the domestic politics in Dengist China, it is important to point out that it was almost accidental that a polemical treatise such as *He shang* could be allowed even a short life. Cui Wenhua has explained the accidental appearance of *He shang* within the limitations of a strict censorship system.[57] According to Cui, both Chen Hanyuan, the deputy director of the Central Television Station, and Wang Feng, the vice minister of broadcasting, cinema, and television, could have vetoed any film or television show at any point by simply questioning its "political healthiness." Yet, to everyone's surprise, both of them minimized their power "as the ultimate censor" and did not even suggest any changes in the script.[58] Had either one of them chosen to play his proper role as the "representative of Ideological State Apparatuses"—whose job is to purify and unify people's way of thinking—we would have probably seen an entirely different *He shang*, if we were to see one at all.[59] The appearance of *He shang*, therefore, does not testify to the soundness of the Chinese television industry, Cui argued forcefully; it illustrates, rather, how a few persons' "free will" could have instantly killed numerous movies and television programs in spite of the fact that they were the product of the talent and hard labor of many people.[60] In addition to the fact that a controversial program like *He shang* was inevitably in constant political danger in the PRC's highly centralized and tightly controlled media, it is also true, in my view, that all key persons involved in the *He shang* affair may well have had their accounts to settle with the ruling ideology. It is at least possible that they may have deliberately looked the other way because they, too, for a variety of possible motives, wanted this counter-discourse to appear. At any rate, their negligence of duty testifies to the popularity of the provocative *He shang*, which to a large extent represented the anti-official sentiments culminating in the student movement of the following year.

The accidental appearance of *He shang* can also be better comprehended when placed in the context of the power struggle within the Communist Party: without the support of Zhao Ziyang, then the Party Secretary-General, *He shang* would have been severely criticized for its pro-Western, anti-socialist, and anti-party stance, even after its seeing the light of day, as has often happened to many films and literary works after 1949. The importance of Zhao Ziyang's support was underscored in an official Chinese report after he was ousted as a scapegoat for the Tiananmen student protests of 1989. Jin Ren points out, for example, that soon after the appearance of *He shang*, Zhao encouraged his "cultural-elite activists" to write positive and even flattering reviews, although some academics questioned the soundness of its scholarship. Zhao even asked that five hundred videotape copies of the program be distributed around the country. In late September 1988, Zhao, as the Party Secretary-General, ignored Wang Zhen's request that *He shang* be criticized for its anti-socialist content during the third plenary session of the Thirteenth Congress of the Chinese Communist Party Central Committee.[61] Although Jin's account can be seen as part of another political campaign against Zhao Ziyang and hence highly questionable in its cited "facts," it at least tells us how polemical a role *He shang*—or any other work of literature and art—can play in the political dramas of the PRC. That *He shang* was part of that polemical drama is beyond doubt. Xinhua News Agency has reported that in post-Tiananmen China, a book entitled *Reappraisal of He shang* was published on November 28, 1989, by Hangzhou University Press, which had invited fourteen experts and scholars in history, philosophy, political science, journalism, and Chinese literature to a seminar in which they critiqued *He shang*'s national nihilism, historical fatalism, and systematic promotion of "complete Westernization."

To a large extent, then, the *He shang* screenwriters' initial anti-official efforts to interfere with everyday reality were subsequently used by reformist party officials like Zhao Ziyang to discredit his conservative opponents within the Chinese Community Party. This was an accidental—

but crucial—circumstance that allowed *He shang* a temporary, but highly political, life. Thus the very act of attempting to transform what Louis Althusser calls "Ideological State Apparatuses" was nevertheless appropriated by a different faction for consolidating its own power. Or seen from another angle, an anti-official discourse of Occidentalism merged with the specific agenda of a faction within the predominant official discourse, both using the image of the Other for its own purposes. Here we see an example of the many facets of Occidentalism, in which a faction among the ruling authorities supported an anti-official Occidentalism deemed unacceptable by other factions.

It was to be expected, therefore, that *He shang* became an immediate target for another political campaign against cultural imperialism in post-1989 China, which accused writers, producers, and supporters of *He shang* of being pro-Western, and hence, anti-Chinese-nationalist. A post-Tiananmen article published in *People's Daily* claimed, for example, that in the rewriting of history, *He shang* highlighted two "new epochs," the first one being "the year 1649 [*sic*], in which the British Industrial Revolution began," and the second one, the year 1987, in which Zhao Ziyang became the Party Secretary-General of the Chinese Communist Party. Thus, *He shang* is accused of suggesting to its audiences that "only Zhao Ziyang is the standard-bearer of economic reform" and that only "the capitalism which he advocated can save China." It is not surprising, then, the article asserts, that Su Xiaokang, the main screenwriter of *He shang*, "actively threw himself into the Tiananmen counter-revolutionary rebellion" of 1989, which was in itself "a result of the collaboration between the so-called 'intellectual elite' and Zhao Ziyang's political supporters."[62] The very fact that Su Xiaokang had no choice but to flee to the West further proves the highly subversive function of Occidentalism in the political arena of contemporary Chinese society. Seen in this light, the anti-official Occidentalism of the television program was in turn manipulated by the ruling clique, which, as in the case of Zhao Ziyang, collaborated with the anti-official Occidentalism in order to achieve its own practical goals in party politics. The subsequent tragedy of the Tiananmen student demonstrations is another classic example in which the masses who protested against the current regime were eventually exploited by the very ruling class that they had initially fought against.

At this point I must finally address the issue of nationalism, a confusing term that frequently surfaced in the *He shang* debates. *He shang* was on many occasions criticized for its "cultural nihilism" and its lack of the patriotism that was said to have stimulated masterpieces of literature and art in the past, inspiring many to sacrifice their lives for the dignity and integrity of the motherland. The Chinese American Nobelist T. D. Lee, for example, warned the *He shang* writers: "a nation that depends entirely on its past has no future; neither does it have any future if it totally rejects its own ancestors."[63] The defenders of *He shang* argued, on the contrary, that it expressed a deeper and more profound nationalism, the very strength of which lies in the rejection of the negative elements of a cultural tradition in order to better preserve that tradition.[64] Outside of China, Frederic Wakeman Jr. remarked that *"He shang* remains at its heart deeply nationalistic," and that despite its image, which is "hyperbolic, exaggerated, and even disproportionate if extended to the Yellow River," it nevertheless "does convey the deep patriotism that this generation ambivalently expressed" and "that has such ancient ethnic roots."[65]

It is interesting to note that both sides clung firmly to the notion of nation—nation-ness, nation-hood—as if those were politically and ideologically neutral terms. According to Benedict Anderson's celebrated study of nationalism, however, such notions are nothing but "cultural artifacts of a particular kind," that are "capable of being transplanted, with varying degrees of self-consciousness, to a great variety of social terrains, to merge and be merged with a correspondingly wide variety of political and ideological constellations."[66] Seen from this perspective, much of the political and intellectual history of modern China appears as the result of deliberate maneuverings of what Anderson terms an "official nationalism" that combines "naturalization with retention of dynastic power" in order to stretch "the short, tight, skin of nation over the gigantic body of the empire."[67] The deceptive power of such "official nationalism" was particularly telling in the civil war between the Chinese Communist Party and the Guomindang nationalists, in which both sides claimed to be patriots, thus inspiring millions of supporters from each camp to give up their lives for their diametrically opposed "glorious causes." It is the same kind of official nationalism, with only slight variations in form, that was used to justify China's territorial disputes and military clashes with India, the Soviet Union, and Vietnam, as well as the numerous political campaigns against pro-Western "counter-revolutionaries" and "foreign spies" in various ideological movements of the PRC "dynasty." Joseph R. Levenson was thus insightful when he remarked thirty years ago that in the PRC, "class-struggle provided the motor: Marxism, especially Leninist anti-imperialism, would implement Chinese nationalism. Marxist and national fervor seemed to reinforce each other."[68]

The most intriguing official nationalism of its kind—since it still has a strong appeal among the Chinese people even today—found its expression in the military and religious suppression of the national minorities such as Tibetans, Uighurs, and Mongolians, with the justification of "national territorial integrity." These are indeed examples of what I call *national-cultural-imperialism,* by which a Third World country such as

China can legitimate and exercise its own central, imperial hegemony over regional or ethnic groups in all spheres. Seen from this perspective, then, attacks on *He shang* can be viewed as yet another ideological posture in which the official claim to Chinese nationalism protects the vested interests of the conservative ruling group. Thus *He shang*'s so-called anti-nationalism can be "a means of self-definition" against the status quo in the guise of Occidentalism.[69] Its use of Occidentalism is thus a self-conscious subversion of the centrality of the official culture by moving into the very center of its own discourse a redefined and re-presented Western Other. Ironically, this is the same Other that, in the culture of its origin, has used Orientalism to enlarge its own cultural space, as Edward Said has so forcefully pointed out. Yet, as I hope this chapter has made clear, it would be a serious mistake to claim that a native self-understanding is by nature more liberating or "truer" than the view of it constructed by its Other. And it would be equally misleading to argue that Occidentalist discourse is less tied to power relationships and strategies of domination than its Orientalist counterpart. As Michel Foucault has forcefully taught us, no discursive practice is ever free from a will to power.[70]

It is from this perspective that we can finally address the issue of hegemony and its relationship to Orientalist or Occidentalist discourse. On the one hand, it is crucial to analyze the function of an imperialist discourse, such as Orientalism, that imposes on the colonial Other an economic and political hegemony. On the other hand, such a hegemony in the international arena, when situated in different cultural and historical circumstances, may also subvert a domestic hegemony within a particular culture. Thus Orientalism and Occidentalism must be seen as signifying practices having no permanent or essential content. Given their socioeconomic and political status in relationship to the West, Third World countries have rightly decried their Western Other in Occidentalist discourse. But Third World countries have an equal right to employ discourses of Occidentalism for contrary purposes, to use, "misuse," present, re-present, distort, and restore the Western Other, exploiting it as a counter-structure against the monolithic order of things at home. Thus a Third World discourse, although historically significant in the international arena in a postcolonial age, can be reduced to or appropriated as a domestic imperialist discourse for the ulterior motive of maintaining an imperial dynasty at home. It is thus one-sided to claim that "misconceptions" of the Other, such as Orientalism or Occidentalism, are necessarily imperialistic acts. It is the use to which these terms are put by those who articulate them, and by those who hear and receive them, that determines their social—and literary—effects.

The claim against imperialistic discourse can thus go both ways: if it is imperialistic for the Occident to "misrepresent" the Orient, then, the Orient can also anti-imperialistically use the Occident to achieve its own polit-ical aims at home. It is by such a political end that *He shang*'s screen-writers could justify the anti-imperialistic means with which they in-geniously fragmented and pluralized the official culture in their very invention of a West. In this case, both Orientalism and Occidentalism in whatever form never refer to a "thing-in-itself," but to a power relation-ship. Whether this projection into the Other is positive or negative de-pends, of course, on the problematic and often paradoxical social, politi-cal, and economic conditions in the indigenous culture in question—and on one's own place in structures of power. Indeed, if T. Minh-Ha Trinh is correct in observing that in the twentieth century "the West is painfully made to realize the existence of a Third World in the First World,"[71] we can also say, by the same token, that there also exists a First World whose master-slave relationship with its own people is being fundamentally challenged by a Third World discourse against the predominant ruling ideology within a Third World country itself. Seen in this light, both Third World and First World need to learn to stop feeling privileged as the Other. Only in this way can either world even hope for a corrective and critical movement in which neither a Western vision nor a non-Western vision is ultimately exempted from its own historical conditions.

Chapter Two

Occidentalist Theater

Shakespeare, Ibsen, and Brecht as Counter Others

The critical discourse on postcolonial and postmodern conditions has produced a number of exciting scholarly inquiries, among them Jyotsna Singh's insightful historical account of the cultural imperialism manifested in the productions of Shakespeare in India.[1] Singh demonstrates how the English bard "kept alive the myth of English cultural refinement and superiority—a myth that was crucial to the rulers' political interests in colonial India."[2] This study is an especially valuable contribution to the current discussion because of the way it illustrates how the construction of English literature and the exporting of the English language consolidated the political and ideological hegemony of the colonial empire in a Third World country.[3] Singh's study has ramifications beyond India. Her model can certainly be followed in producing histories of the reception of Western ideas by other non-Western cultures sharing some of the historical conditions that marked colonial India. Among these cultures is twentieth-century China, where the introduction of English and other Western literary and philosophical traditions has fundamentally shaped the theory and practice of literature since the beginning of the May Fourth movement.[4] Scholars in modern Chinese literature have contributed significantly to our understanding of postcolonial conditions in China.[5]

Arguing against cultural imperialism is, however, to explore only one side of the coin, albeit an important one. It can indeed become problematic when considered in the broader context of cultural and ideological specifics within a totalitarian society. In this chapter, I will demonstrate that on the contemporary Chinese stage, the production and reception of Shakespearean and other Western dramas—the literary and dramatic representations of an Occidental Other—can help, and perhaps even inspire, the Chinese Self to express the politically forbidden and ideologically impossible within the limitations of its indigenous cultural conditions. Thus,

43

the representation of a Western Other imposed from within—which can easily be characterized as an act of cultural imperialism—can also be understood as a powerful anti-official discourse that has been persistently employed by the Chinese intelligentsia to achieve a political liberation against the ideological oppression within a totalitarian society.

Before going into the cultural and historical specifics of the post-Mao theater, I need to clarify several points. I have so far differentiated an official Occidentalism—the Chinese government's use of the essentialization of the West as a means for supporting a nationalism that effects the internal suppression of its own people—from an anti-official Occidentalism used by certain groups of Chinese intellectuals whose knowledge and literacy are utilized in its own practice of power against the powerful status quo. These differentiations are made for the sake of argument and narration without suggesting at all a binarism that this very study seeks to critique in the first place. I do not mean to suggest that there exist two distinct discourses, known as "official" and "anti-official" Occidentalism, that are totally unrelated and completely separable. Indeed, as will be shown in this chapter, one witnesses a third kind of Chinese Occidentalism, in which the anti-official Occidentalism against the Maoist autocracy in early post-Mao China significantly overlapped with the official Occidentalism of the Deng regime, which briefly tolerated and even encouraged the intellectuals' anti-Maoist sentiments in order to manipulate them into legitimizing its political legacy.

In this instance, we see how the knowledge, qualification, and recognition associated with the image of the West became political capital both for the predominant ruling ideology of the post-Mao regime and for different groups of Chinese intellectuals who were opposed to such ideology. The "cultural capital"[6] of things Western had accumulated but remained untapped since the repression of Western ideas in the Maoist era. Indeed, its value had increased by virtue of its association with all things repressed by a tyrannical regime. Thus, the West's considerable assets were ready to be tapped for a variety of different ends in the post-Maoist era. The attractiveness of the West in early post-Mao China is best demonstrated in the popular productions of Shakespearean plays; indeed, any Western play—no matter who wrote it—could have had a following at this specific moment in time, since the very act of performing a Western play on stage was itself a form of political discourse directed against the previous regime. By liberating the previously repressed Western discourse, the post-Mao regime was able to draw upon its cultural prestige and present itself as a liberator. In this particular circumstance, the Chinese intellectuals found a temporarily overlapping space between the official ideology and the anti-official discourse. Chinese dramatists in this space could wear Western costumes and speak in the voice of the Other while spontaneously expressing their grievances against the political power, which the post-Mao regime has just inherited from its predecessor. It is thus important to bear in mind that when Chinese intellectuals were promoting the West in their theatrical productions, their seeming celebrations of the current political regime were on many occasions used to conceal criticisms of the communist system in general, which produced a Maoist regime as well as a Dengist one.

In early post-Mao China, for instance, an otherwise "alien" production of Shakespeare's *Macbeth* (*Makebaisi*) was popular precisely because the Renaissance text was appropriated by the Chinese audiences as immediately relating to their traumatic experiences during the Cultural Revolution. The Chinese intelligentsia in the early 1980s felt an urgent need to revive the Shakespearean canon after the political upheaval of the Cultural Revolution. The political atmosphere after Mao Zedong's death in 1976 and his widow Jiang Qing's later arrest endowed the play with a particular significance that Chinese who had survived the Cultural Revolution could fully appreciate. For many Chinese audiences, Macbeth's tragedy reminded them of Mao's sad history, in which a national hero, who had fought courageously for the founding of his country, was declared a traitor and finally driven to death—both spiritually and physically—by his power-hungry wife.

During a discussion of the Central Drama College production of *Macbeth* premièring in 1980 in Beijing, some critics focused on the main theme of the play and its immediate relevance to the social and political concerns of contemporary China. Xu Xiaozhong, for instance, pointed out that the play was about "how the greed for power finally ruined a great man."[7] Owing to the strict censorship by the Chinese government, which at that time was still reluctant to openly admit Mao's mistakes, there were naturally no direct connections spelled out between Mao's errors during the Cultural Revolution and the thematic concerns of the play. The similarities between the drama of Mao and Macbeth, however, were clear to those Chinese who had seen and somehow understood the play. During the two performances I attended, for example, I discussed with other audience members the play's relevance to the Cultural Revolution. Indeed, the allusions to Chinese political life were transparent to many. Zhao Xun, the deputy chairman of the National Association of Chinese Dramatists, observed that "*Macbeth* is the fifth Shakespearean play produced on the Chinese stage after the smashing of the Gang of Four. This play of conspiracy has always been performed at critical moments in the history of our nation."[8] In the same letter and spirit, the program notes of *Macbeth* viewed the play as a vivid depiction of moral decline in Macbeth and Lady Macbeth, and as a play that explored the theme of how "desire for power and ambition are the root of evil"; "those obsessed with power struggle will eventually be punished by the motherland and by the people." Thus the performance of this tragedy has its "realistic significance" especially today, it was claimed.[9] Indeed, for some members of Chinese audiences watching the Shakespearean world of intrigue and conspiracy in Macbeth, it was difficult to forget their terrifying experiences during the Cultural Revolution, a national catastrophe in which Mao and his followers persecuted numerous party officials, state leaders, and old "comrades-in-arms." Contrary to their own wishes, however, both of them—Macbeth the character and Mao the historical figure—had only brought disgrace on themselves.

In contrast to the Chinese audiences' likely reception, the producers and directors of Macbeth claimed that they sought to produce Macbeth according to the authorial intention of the playwright in order to explore the artistic style of Shakespearean drama. After the downfall of the Gang of Four, it was argued, they tried to produce as many "authentic" foreign plays as possible since they were strictly forbidden to do so during the Cultural Revolution. Even during this "purely artistic" experience, however, Xu Xiaozhong and Li Zibo, the directors of this production of Macbeth, had to admit that the play "bore a significance which reached beyond its own historicity"—"it revealed certain features of a historical period in transition from an old era to a new era."[10] Such a remark suggests their recognition that for most of their audience, Macbeth could well be a commentary on the Cultural Revolution and its lasting psychological effects. Seen from this perspective, this post–Cultural Revolutionary Chinese production of Macbeth is at least twice removed from the "original intentions" of either its early seventeenth-century English playwright or of its twentieth-century Chinese producers. Yet it would be difficult—and foolish—to fault this historical and cultural "misunderstanding" or to criticize this example of a Chinese Occidentalism. Under these circumstances, who could possibly prefer an "authentic" Macbeth in Beijing? And who could define what would constitute "authenticity" and "correctness" in these circumstances? Short of converting twentieth-century Chinese people into seventeenth-century Elizabethans, what kind of authenticity might have been possible? Indeed, it is here in the production of the English bard's Renaissance play that we see a reenactment of the twentieth-century Chinese everyday reality of intrigue and conspiracy. By acting the roles of the Occidentalist Other on stage, the Chinese people experienced a catharsis. The memory of the past was cleansed and a reconciliation with the present was at least temporarily made possible during the limited time and space of theatrical experience. Here the Occidentalist theater played an important role in the Chinese people's recovery from the tragedy of an immediate cultural past.

This enactment of the Occidental Other on the Chinese stage as a means of political liberation can also be found in other Shakespearean productions in post-Mao China. The 1982 production of *King Lear* (*Li'erwang*) by the director training class of Shanghai Drama College was applauded by the distinguished Shakespearean scholar Fang Ping because the play above all else reminded the Chinese people of the moral decline of the Cultural Revolutionary days "when human beings' souls were so polluted" that they even mistreated their aged parents—just like the two older daughters who abuse their own father King Lear.[11] Another "realistic significance" of the play, Fang continued, is that it teaches us a lesson about political struggle, in which we must learn how to differentiate friends from enemies, or how to differentiate the flattering, hypocritical Goneril and Regan from the honest and filial Cordelia. Furthermore, Fang claimed, the play bridges the historical and cultural distance between an Occidental past and a Chinese present through a vivid characterization of King Lear as "the highest ruler of a monarchy," who creates a chaotic world in which the loyal are punished and the treacherous are rewarded.[12] This could well be another allusion to Mao's irrational behavior in his old age and its tragic consequences in the life and conduct of individuals during and after the Cultural Revolution.

In contrast to these negative traits of human beings, the play was also viewed as a eulogy of the "pure love" and the "beautiful souls" of Cordelia and Edgar. It is here that we find perhaps one of the most unexpected readings of *King Lear:* "although our concept of love is different from that of the Renaissance humanist" in the Occident, Fang claimed, "we nevertheless need the same kind of beautiful soul, which is full of noble love, not just for our relatives and families, but also for our comrades, our motherland, and our glorious party. We should live as a poet, who loves everything that is beautiful."[13] This is a typical expression of early post–Cultural Revolutionary political jargon, which always demanded affirmation of a bright future for the party and its triumphant socialist course, even after a necessary exposure of the bad party renegades, such as the Gang of Four, who temporarily usurped party leadership during the Cultural Revolution. Yet Fang's interpretation clearly testifies to the multifaceted appeal of a popular Shakespeare, who was appropriated as something "Chinese" and came to play his own dramatic role in cross-cultural literary history in early post-Mao China. Indeed, a politicized Shakespeare was very popular in post-Mao China even outside the immediate stage of the theater. As Judith Shapiro pointed out, in his memoir of Mao's China entitled *A Single Tear*, Wu Ningkun—like many of his intellectual contemporaries who used literary references from Western classics—was particularly attracted to the tragedy of Hamlet, which "provided him with spiritual sustenance." Writing of his experience in the wilderness of exile, he understood Shakespeare's statement that "Denmark is a prison!"[14]

Likewise, the 1981 China Youth Art Theater production of *The Merchant of Venice* (*Weinisi shangren*) also helped establish the theme of "eulogizing *zhen, shan, mei*," or "the true, the good, and the beautiful," against "the fake, the evil, and the ugly" Cultural Revolutionary life and politics.[15] "After so many years of turning the good into the evil," Director Zhang Qihong recalled with emotion, "how urgently do we need to promote justice and friendship in our life!"[16] Such a promotion of a better life was achieved, not surprisingly, through Chinese dramatists' annexation of the Occidental play. In order to highlight such a political theme, Zhang had to abbreviate those subplots concerning religious and racial conflicts (Christian vs. Jew) in *The Merchant of Venice*—which, according to her judgment, were cultural background too unfamiliar for Chinese audiences to fully appreciate anyway—so that the major class contradictions could be foregrounded between Antonio, the rising bourgeois, and Shylock, the feudalist exploiter.[17]

To further strengthen such a politicized theme, both Portia and Jessica were beautifully portrayed for the purpose of representing "the humanist spirit of the Renaissance period," which strives for "individuality, human rights, and freedom against a feudalist autocracy."[18] Such an appropriation of Shakespearean themes for an extended political allegory was questioned by Chinese drama critics and Shakespeare scholars. Zhou Peitong argued that a culturally and racially oppressed Shylock is crucial to the integrity and complexities of the Shakespearean play, whose power lies precisely in the tragic fate of a Jewish Shylock.[19] Yet such a deviation from the original text did not bother Chinese audiences, who loved the play for its very relevance to their own Cultural-Revolutionary experiences during which they encountered too many "heartless" and "selfish" Shylocks. The "kind" and "honest" Portia thus became their new cultural model for a freer and better life.[20]

Others, however, enjoyed the play simply because it was produced as a romantic comedy that deviated from the prevailing mode of "social problem plays" in the early days of post-Mao China. Yang Tianchun, for instance, has testified that in contrast to the predominantly serious plays that merely invited one to think about social concerns, the joyful and humorous events in *The Merchant of Venice* somehow made him forget everyday reality and a painful past so that he could more fully enjoy the happy moments in this theatrical experience. This effect of the theater, Yang asserted, should be viewed as an important function of literature and art, which encourages one's new vision in and a persistent pursuit for a better future.[21] Yet it is important to note that Yang's remarks were made in 1981, when many Chinese audiences were tired of a highly political—and politicized—everyday life and an indigenous theater that was always intended as part of a political education, either to fully support the Maoist regime as had happened during the Cultural Revolution in a promotion of the "eight revolutionary model plays," or to denounce Maoist art only to valorize the new official ideology of a Dengist state. Thus a defamilarized stage representing life and love in a remote Occident offered a welcome dose of relief and recreation.

Yet however much one attempts to disassociate him or herself from the political aspects of the theater, it is still common to find, for instance, readings of *The Merchant of Venice* that link it to topical subjects such as the economic reform of post-Mao China, as demonstrated in an article entitled "A Song of an Enterprising Spirit: On the True Meaning of *The Merchant of Venice*." In this article, Hao Yin emphasized the title of the play, which, according to him, pointed to the important role of the merchant class in Venice, which was then the cradle of commercialism and capitalism in the West. Thus, he claimed, with the very title of the play, Shakespeare already affirmed the positive and heroic status of Antonio, who represents courage, virtue, and the spirit of the rising class of bourgeoisie, a class that would take the lead in the industrial revolution of England. Traditionally in Chinese Shakespearean criticism, Hao further argued, Shylock has always been inappropriately singled out as the most negative character in the play, since he, in contrast to Antonio, is a disagreeable and heartless businessman. Hao observed, however, that this Chinese degrading of Shylock had a great deal to do with traditional Chinese culture, which looked down upon merchants in favor of farmers, who were believed to be engaged in honest and productive activities. Yet, his argument continued, this anti-merchant mentality was rapidly changing in the current economic reform. Thanks to the correct party policies at present, Hao argued, peasants and farmers are now increasingly proud of becoming successful businessmen and -women and, in some cases, even millionaires. Inevitably, then, Shylock could be seen in a new and more positive light.[22]

After interpreting *The Merchant of Venice* as a play immediately relating to contemporary Chinese reality, Hao Yin went on to give a long Marxist recounting of the age of Elizabeth I, when capital was being accumulated through world trade at the highest rate. As if this sociological and cultural background were not enough to support his thesis, Hao surprisingly presented a biographical account of Shakespeare himself, who had left home at the age of sixteen, leaving behind his wife and two children. Despite the conventional explanation of "a deer incident," Hao argued, the real reason for the English bard's home-leaving was that he "was no exception from the rest of the young people of his own generation, who had chosen to travel extensively to the outside world to seek for an adventure and a career in order to find their own fortunes."[23] Seen in this light, then, Hao believed that the Shakespearean characters and themes in this play were indeed products of "a hurricane of enterprising developments in all walks of life which had swept Shakespeare away from his hometown and landed him squarely in London, the center of economic development in England at that time." This is indeed the central theme of *The Merchant of Venice*.[24] In Hao's view, then, *The Merchant of Venice* presented "a miniature world of competition in a market economy" and "promoted the idea of economic efficiency." In the last analysis, Shakespeare "provided the merchant class with a living picture of how to liberate itself from conventional modes of thinking and behavior," thus leaving a precious lesson for his readers and audiences in the many years to come.[25]

During this episode of Shakespearean reception, the evocation of economic reform seemed to support Deng Xiaoping's regime, which attempted to differentiate itself from its radical predecessors of the Cultural Revolution, who had rejected the West and its social and economic structure. In the case of Hao Yin's interpretation of the Shakespearean play, we see a complicated phenomenon in which the intellectuals' appeal to the Occident as a complementary Other to change Chinese society for the better seemed to temporarily coincide with the Dengist official ideology. Deng's regime has had a history of a love-hate relationship with the Occident, for it attempted to experiment with an Occident-like economy, without introducing Western social and ideological systems. Seen from another angle, one may also argue that the image of the West was exploited not only by the Chinese intellectuals as a powerful weapon against the ruling ideology; it has also been skillfully used, from time to time, by the Dengist reformers as a political weapon against the Maoist conservatives who resisted even economic reforms. It is thus ironic to note that when the Chinese people followed the call to duty by the Communist Party to push for political reform—reform that was also initiated by Deng Xiaoping—their historic pro-Western drama was eventually suppressed by the Dengist regime during the 1989 Tiananmen student demonstrations, when the Statue of Liberty was transformed into the Goddess of Democracy. Here the image of the West was once again rejected by Deng Xiaoping, since this image was now endowed with a political statement directed against Deng himself. We also see a typical example of how the West has become the signifier of a set of value systems, imagined and fictionalized, which are used to create a cultural and ideological message put forth in opposition to the Chinese official culture. In some instances, the West is also used as a powerful image against the official conservative Other by the official radical Self, who, ironically, as recent history has proven, allied itself eventually with the conservative group in its suppression of the Chinese people. Here we see the full implication of the problematic and paradoxical function of Occidentalism in contemporary Chinese society.

In 1988, with the benefit of the hindsight of a few years, Zhang Xiao-yang came to offer a fuller explanation of what he termed a "metamorphosis of Shakespeare on the Chinese stage." Commenting on the tremendous success and popularity of the 1986 China Shakespeare Festival, during which many Shakespearean plays were produced both in modern theaters and in diverse traditional operatic theaters such as *kunqu* (Jiangsu opera) and *huangmei xi* (Anhui opera), Zhang Xiaoyang believed that contemporary Chinese society had "the best cultural and historical conditions" to "perfectly understand" and "completely receive" the dramas of the English bard, since the unique positions of the two peoples in their own histories provided them with "the best opportunity to apprehend each other's values, experiences, and emotions."[26] To further elaborate these "shared historical conditions," Zhang Xiaoyang emphasized the fact that both post-Renaissance Elizabethan and post–Cultural Revolutionary Chinese society experienced the same transitional period from a dark, ascetic, feudalist monarchy to an open, precapitalist, and pre-modern era. Just as the Elizabethan emphasis on humanism attempted to challenge the centrality of God in the universe, the post-Mao restoration of the "self" rejected the Maoist principle of a "revolutionary," "heroic," and "collective spirit." Those cultural, sociopolitical, and ideological conditions contributed, among other things, to a formation of a "historical aesthetic consciousness" (*shidai shenmei yishi*) on the part of both the "producing subject" (*chuangzuo zhuti*) and the "receiving subject" (*jieshou zhuti*) in contemporary China.[27] Both subjects found liberation from political dominations by means of art in remote Shakespearean plays. This art "reflects reality and personal feelings, thus combining poetry, history, and philosophy most harmoniously."[28] Based on these claims, Zhang Xiaoyang reached a dramatic and perhaps even a shocking conclusion, a conclusion that paradoxically celebrates the values of the original texts despite his earlier emphasis on the historical difference separating the two cultures: "the Shakespearean workers in China of the 1980s should thus try to interpret and produce Shakespearean plays according to the dramatic principles advocated by Shakespeare himself, since this is the only way that will allow us to conform, in the same breath, to the aesthetic consciousness of both the producing and receiving subjects in our own society."[29] Strange as it may appear to connect the peculiar Chinese historical conditions with an "authentic" Shakespeare, Zhang's observation reveals at least the popularity of the English bard at the time and the Chinese critics' readiness to justify his popularity in conventional—and sometimes not so conventional—ways. It also demonstrates how the quintessential image of the West—captured by Shakespeare in his fabricated dramatic tradition—has been utilized as cultural capital with which the accumulated power and prestige associated with the West became immediately appropriated into assessments of the Chinese heritage for the purpose of changing Chinese reality.

Yet the English bard did not monopolize the post-Mao Chinese stage. Other Western plays were successfully performed and received precisely because of their ahistorical Chinese reception that had nothing to do with an "accurate" historical understanding of the original Occidental plays. Ibsen's *Peer Gynt,* for example, has been almost universally regarded by Western critics as one of the most difficult plays to produce on stage. Peter Watts, in his "Introduction" to Ibsen's *Peer Gynt,* points out that "in England, ironically enough, *Peer Gynt* is much better known from Grieg's incidental music than from Ibsen's text. Ibsen had never meant *Peer Gynt* for the stage, any more than Hardy meant *The Dynasts* or Browning *Pippa* [for theatrical production]."[30] Watts also tells us that "it was not until 1874, seven years after its publication," that Ibsen thought about asking Grieg to provide music in anticipation of a possible production. *Peer Gynt* was finally performed in Norway in February 1876, and in the English-speaking countries, "there has never been a professional production of the full text," said Watts in 1966.[31]

Whatever its difficulties on the English-speaking stage, *Peer Gynt* (*Pei'er jinte*) turned out to be a major success in Beijing, when it was performed by the Central Drama College in 1983 and 1984. For some, it was warmly received not because they understood the play in its original Norwegian terms, but rather because it evoked for them their own immediate Cultural-Revolutionary reality. One audience member who attended the play, for instance, told me that he could not help but recall in Gynt's character individuals frequently encountered during the Cultural Revolution who were afraid of being their true selves and of expressing their genuine feelings toward the people around them. During the Cultural Revolution, in order to survive politically dangerous situations, lovers, husbands, wives, parents, and children were forced to criticize and otherwise betray each other in public. People preferred to play it safe, or to "go round about"—Peer Gynt's motto throughout his life—to avoid difficulties and conflicts. To "go round about," or in Xiao Qian's Chinese translation, "*yushi raodao zou,*" was a familiar phrase for many Chinese who survived the unnerving experiences of the Cultural Revolution.[32] Chinese audiences bringing such experiences with them inevitably saw in Peer Gynt reflections of their own recent past. The play reminded them of their own problematic and fractured identities and of their own ambiguous feelings about the unsolvable conflict between personal happiness and revolutionary goals, conflicts that were highly intensified during the 10 years of the Cultural Revolution.

It was such cultural experiences that some Chinese audiences would recall when they were confronted with Peer Gynt's question at the end of the production: "Where was I? Myself—complete and whole? / Where? With God's seal upon my brow?" It was therefore no surprise that Xu

Xiaozhong, the director of *Peer Gynt,* viewed the question of "how to live one's life" as the "central psychological conflict in the divided self of Peer Gynt."[33] This question seemed to be addressed not to Peer Gynt, but to the Chinese audiences themselves who looked for an answer in their "posthumous" reflections on their previous, traumatic experiences. Gynt's question was deeply touching: "In my faith, in my hope, and in my love."[34] Solveig does not here just solve a riddle for Gynt; she answers in her own terms many of the unanswered (and even for a time unanswerable) questions of many Chinese, especially those of young people who constituted the majority of the audience for this production. Having grown up in the abnormal days of the Cultural Revolution, the young people of the early 1980s had been taught little about personal values, identity, and least of all, about love. When the play ends in Solveig's singing "in the sunshine": "I will cradle you, I will guard you;/sleep and dream, dearest son of mine," playing at once the role of mother, wife, and "purest of women," it provided an education in beauty, faith, truth, and love for the post-Mao audience.[35] Those who saw the play were enraptured not because of its Norwegianness or its romanticism, but because of what they perceived as its relevance to their situation. The production of *Peer Gynt* thus became a dramatic dialogue in which the audiences were transformed into the characters of the play, waiting for an answer from opposing characters who offered a view of life different from that of their own. Similarly to the Polish dramatist Jan Kott, who interpreted Shakespeare's *Macbeth* as the Stalinist machine of murder and blood, the Chinese audiences in 1983 recreated their own plots, characters, and dramatic scenes from their personal Cultural Revolutionary experiences while watching Gynt's "going round about" his problems and difficulties.[36] The Chinese audiences had no choice except to confront their own problems even when Gynt told them not to do so.

In addition to Shakespeare and Ibsen, Brecht was another popular Western playwright who in the late twentieth century appealed to the Chinese imagination as a counter Other. Brecht's *Life of Galileo (Jialilue zhuan),* produced in 1979 by the China Youth Art Theater in Beijing, was so popular among the post–Cultural Revolutionary Chinese audience that it ran for eighty productions, all with a full house. According to Chen Yong (Rong), the codirector of *Life of Galileo,* foreigners who saw the play often wondered how the Chinese audience would accept Brecht, who was too progressive even for the Western audience.[37] Chen believed, however, that the popularity of the play lies in the message that the production team tried to deliver. For her, Brecht's play is about the dawn of a new age, which is "necessarily accompanied by countless difficulties, setbacks, sharp contradictions and violent conflicts and even betrayals among the vanguard." Chen reassured us that such an understanding in

1979 "is particularly revealing after the crushing of the Gang of Four and as we face the reality of the Four Modernisations [*sic*] and their huge tasks, and also educates us in a general way."[38]

Yet if Chen's interpretation of *Life of Galileo* spoke only for the production crew's "good will," Lin Kehuan voiced a similar view from the spectrum of literary reception. As if to back up Chen Yong's claim, Lin explored, in a more detailed manner, how and why *Life of Galileo* would be read as if written with 1979 contemporary Chinese audiences in mind. For Lin Kehuan, Galileo represented an image of "a new man," a term that Lin quoted from Brecht as representing the authorial intention underlying the message of the play. Yet Lin Kehuan emphasized the fact that Galileo challenged the established religious "truth" in the seventeenth century with scientific evidence; with this courageous stance, Galileo indicated "the dawn of a new era"—a popular metaphor used by the Chinese people to allude to the end of the Maoist age and the beginning of a period of Renaissance. Galileo's line that "thinking for oneself is the greatest happiness of one's life" became for Lin Kehuan a motto of a new man—he was able to doubt and question the culturally dominant truth at that time.[39] This new man constantly strove to re-understand and reevaluate, not only the world around him, but also his own self and his own position in the universe.

Due to the historical circumstances of 1979 China, when Mao Zedong's mistakes during the Cultural Revolution had not yet been officially admitted by the party apparatus, Lin Kehuan had no choice but to leave his commentary implicit. Yet those familiar with 1979 Chinese society can readily apprehend the clearly implied understatement—Galileo's story of another time and place has a particular significance for the Chinese people, who were constantly told what to think during the Cultural Revolution. More critically, Brecht's play might bring back for some the painful memory of their own cowardice for not standing up for their principles against Maoist excesses. In this connection, Lin Kehuan argued that Galileo was truly "a great man" whose magnanimity resided in his open admission that he was *not* that great. Western readers may find such a view cowardly, but according to Lin Kehuan, the play emphasizes this view when Galileo tells Anthony that the real reason for the betrayal of his scientific principles was that he could not bear the painful torture imposed by the Church, not because of his clever strategy to bide his time, as Anthony wanted to make him believe. By admitting that he *was* weak, Lin Kehuan explained, Galileo proved himself a "greater man" than Anthony, who merely pretended to be great by "attempting to claim a laurel to cover up a cowardly act."[40] In 1979 China, this image of a "new man" with "true" greatness could be used in polemics against the much-too-familiar image of the "old man" Mao, who was worshipped as flawless, "forever correct," and hence, "the great helmsman of revolution both in China and in the whole world."

One of the greatest merits of Brecht's *Life of Galileo*, Lin Kehuan further argued, was that Galileo was characterized as at once "a hero and a criminal." "If we regard Galileo as a hero, he is only a weak one; if we argue that he is a criminal, he has nonetheless contributed a great deal to mankind."[41] Quoting from Marxist theory and its corresponding aesthetic principles, Lin claims that Brecht created "a dialectical character," one that radically departed from one-dimensional stereotypes who have to be either perfectly heroic or completely evil. Lin's comment on Brecht's play, of course, rejected the prevailing theory of literature and art during the Cultural Revolution, which demanded that the so-called "main heroic characters of workers, peasants, and soldiers" (*gongnongbing zhuyao yingxiong renwu*) be exclusively portrayed as "grand and tall in stature and perfect and complete in characterization" (*gao, da, quan*).[42] It is in the depiction of Galileo as a contradictory self or a split personality, Lin Kehuan tells us, that Brecht rendered a vivid, believable, and true-to-life "giant of science" during the Renaissance period. This understanding of the play may, or perhaps may not, have surprised Brecht or his more recent Occidental interpreters. Yet it is obviously a different, Chinese reading, which was possible only in the cultural and social milieu of contemporary China at the conclusion of Mao Zedong's old age.

Moreover, it is clear that Brecht's play was for some of the post–Cultural Revolutionary audiences first and foremost a familiar story of scientists and intellectuals who had frequently been purged during various political movements for openly expressing their anti-official voices. This view is supported by codirector Chen Yong's testimony that the response to the performance was "unusually strong and positive" in literary circles and among the intelligentsia, "especially the scientists."[43] Indeed, viewing the reception of Brecht's play from the perspective of more than a decade, it now seems likely that both the Chinese producers and receivers in 1979 had already perceived the defense of science and democracy as its basic theme—a theme that had been demanded by the Chinese intellectuals since the beginning of the century during the May Fourth movement and was once again invoked during the 1989 student demonstrations in Tiananmen Square.

In fact, one can well imagine that the 1979 Chinese production of *Life of Galileo* was only possible after Mao's death and before Deng Xiaoping ceased to be popular among the Chinese people. In this atmosphere it could be—and was allowed to be—understood at least partially as a limited protest against Mao's reign of terror and as an affirmation of Deng's new age of science and democracy, which the latter promised at that time. If the play were to be performed again after the crackdown of the 1989 student movement, however, the plot in which Galileo was forbidden by the Church authorities to point out a black spot in the sun—an exclusive symbol of Mao and the party's omnipotent power in contemporary China—could have been easily denounced again as blaspheming Deng Xiaoping. The Chinese audiences, indeed, would likely reinterpret the persecution of Galileo as being imposed not by the Inquisition, but by Deng's regime, which rounded up student and intellectual leaders who demanded nothing but science and democracy. Once again, it is the various social and cultural milieus of different historical moments that create an Occidental Other whom one can personally and politically relate to in everyday reality.

This trend of producing Western plays or westernized Chinese plays culminated in the China Shakespeare Festival held simultaneously in Beijing and Shanghai from April 10 to 23, 1986 on the special occasion of the celebration of the 422nd anniversary of Shakespeare's birthday. This festival was sponsored by Shanghai Drama College, Central Drama College, the Chinese Research Association of Spoken Drama, and the China Shakespeare Association. According to a review article by Zhou Peitong, twenty-six Shakespearean plays were produced during this festival in diverse dialects and dramatic subgenres such as modern spoken drama and local operas, with more than seventy different productions, including both professional and amateur theaters. In addition to scholarly exchanges between Shakespearean scholars from China, America, Italy, West Germany, and other countries, some of the plays were also performed on university campuses and in factories, where the audience from grassroots organizations received the English bard with warmth and enthusiasm.[44] Some of these plays, such as *Richard III, Titus Andronicus, The Merry Wives of Windsor, All's Well That Ends Well, Timon of Athens,* and *Antony and Cleopatra,* had never been performed before in China and are, in fact, only rarely seen even on the Western stage.

Part of the impetus for this great outpouring of Shakespearean productions was the claim that Shakespeare, above all others, is an artist who transcends cultural boundaries. For this reason, the drama critic Kong Genghong claimed, Chinese dramatists were justified in presenting at least four of the English bard's plays in the style of traditional Chinese operas: *King Lear* as Beijing opera, *Macbeth* as *kunqu* opera of Jiangsu Province, *Much Ado about Nothing* as *huangmei xi* opera of Anhui Province, and *The Winter's Tale* and *Twelfth Night* as *yueju* opera of Zhejiang Province. These productions were thus hailed by Kong Genghong as pioneering undertakings of a "Sinification" of Shakespearean drama, which he claimed enriched both the tradition of Shakespeare in the West and that of Chinese operatic theaters.[45] It was also reported that in view of the drama crisis of the late 1980s, when Chinese theater had been increasingly threatened by the television and movie industries, it was hoped that a combination of the Shakespearean heritage with that of the Chinese indigenous theaters would revive the faltering modern Chinese stage.[46]

Indeed, perhaps no other modern country has witnessed such a great number of foreign plays passing into its national dramatic repertory in such a short period. Yet through these successful productions of Western plays, the Chinese people were by no means bringing a European colonialism upon themselves. On the contrary, it is the Orient that "anti-imperialistically" used the Occident to achieve its own political aims at home through deliberate acts of "misunderstanding." It is for such a political end that the Chinese dramatists, critics, and audiences can rightly justify their "anti-imperialistic" means, with which they have successfully fragmented the official culture and the Maoist ideological superstructure in the very representation and dramatization of a Western Other. Indeed, one can perhaps even argue that modern Chinese history and China's problematic and paradoxical relationship with a Western Other can be seen as a highly theatrical event, in which the Chinese people play the roles of the Occidental Others—be they characters in Shakespearean, Ibsenesque, or Brechtian drama. The Chinese actors and actresses assume Occidental voices, wear Occidental costumes, while speaking, all the time, for the political interests of the Oriental Self. The Chinese actors and actresses carry out dramatic dialogues with the Chinese audiences, who are drawn into the Occidental plots because they see in these plots the stark reality of contemporary China. Thus such recent dramatic history, which makes prominent the presence of the Occidentalist dramatic stage in a post-Orientalist era in contemporary China, should not be slighted as a mere incident of self-colonialism by Third World people. It should rather be appreciated as an intricate event in which the East and the West are brought together under specific cultural and historical conditions in which neither the East nor the West is—or should be—fundamentally privileged over its Other.

Having thus argued for the complicated positive implications of Occidentalism in contemporary Chinese theater, I would like, however, to conclude this chapter by offering a brief consideration of the issue of voice in the Chinese representation of the Western Other. It is important to point out that when I talk about the production and reception of the Western plays in Chinese theater, I have been concerned with only a small section of Chinese urban society, in which only a limited number of Chinese intellectuals are actively engaged in theatrical activities. This limitation holds true although some of the dramatic productions discussed here were broadcast as national television programs and were thus available to a broader and more diversified national audience. The voices of the Chinese people cited in this chapter, therefore, certainly do not in all cases embrace different voices from various divisions of Chinese society; the voices of the barely literate people laboring through their lives at assembly lines and in the remote countryside seem especially in danger of being overlooked, if only because they have been largely mute in the discourses discussed here. The voice of "the Chinese people"—which intellectuals have often claimed to express in their writings—may on further inspection turn out to be merely a device by which these same intellectuals have addressed their own peculiar grievances against the status quo. Furthermore, the production and reception of Western plays can sometimes be properly viewed as the result of a collaboration of representatives of the status quo with intellectual elites who thereby become their spokesmen. As we have seen, Hao Yin's interpretation of *The Merchant of Venice* as a play promoting Chinese economic reform provides a striking example of such a collaboration.

These caveats become all the more important if we keep in mind that the majority of the Western plays produced on the Chinese stage were performed by professional theaters in urban China, which were entirely sponsored and subsidized by the Chinese government until the late 1980s.[47] Unlike theatrical professionals in the West, Chinese theaters and their personnel are, without exception, underwritten by different levels of governmental institutions. The China Youth Art Theater and the Central Drama College, for example, are directly attached to the Ministry of Art and Culture, while the Beijing People's Art Theater is supported financially by the office of the Beijing Municipal Government. One must always keep in mind this official dimension of the Chinese theater, which helps account for the frequent and much-expected calls to duty by the government and for the presence of official censors at all levels of control. But acknowledging the absence of certain voices in recent Chinese dramatic events as well as the pervasive presence of the official state apparatus in the theatrical institutions in no way denies the politically liberating function of the post-Mao theater. As I hope this chapter has made clear, the contemporary Chinese theater has, for the most part at least, successfully played within the limited space between the official ideology and a variety of anti-official discourses. With startling ingenuity, its ideological heteroglossia towers over stereotypical ideologies of both East and West and deserves far more serious attention than it has received thus far.

Chapter Three

"Misunderstanding"
Western Modernism

The *Menglong* Movement

I have in the last two chapters focused on the manifestations of Occidentalism in such popular media as television and the professional theater in post-Mao China.[1] Yet the same phenomenon can also be traced in media and traditions that are anything but popular. Consider, for example, the case of lyric poetry and its relationship to Western literary texts. Ezra Pound's Orientalism, or his discovery of the Chinese ideograph, thought to have resulted from a "misunderstanding"[2] of Chinese language and culture, is a familiar story in the West. What has not been widely known, however, is the twin story of the reception of Pound's modernist poetics in post-Mao China and the way in which it has paradoxically affected the rise of *menglong* poetry. This chapter is devoted to an examination of an Occidentalist misunderstanding of Poundian modernist poetics by Chinese poets and critics that would surprise Pound and Ernest Fenollosa. I will defend what might seem at first a surprising claim: that Chinese literary production of the 1980s—and particularly the critical debate on *menglong* poetry—is based on and conditioned by an Occidentalism and a misunderstanding of Western modernism that is as profound as its better-known Western Orientalist counterpart. From the perspective to be sketched here, we will see that it is impossible to speak of contemporary Chinese literature and its reception in the 1980s without taking into serious account the indispensable role that, as a form of ideology in the voice of a counter Other, Western modernism, in its peculiarly Occidentalist guise, has played in the Chinese debate on *menglong* poetry.

The word *menglong* in Chinese means "dim," "hazy," "shady," "misty," and "opaque." It was used by the *menglong* poets, who wrote their controversial works between 1978 and 1983, to suggest a kind of poetic quality detached from a clear-cut political message.[3] The word was also used

by the critics of *menglong* poetry to describe its "obscure" and "incomprehensible" style, which, according to them, was "unfaithful to socialist realism." In employing these definitions, both *menglong*'s advocates and its
critics built upon ideas—often vague and misleading—about modern
Western poetry. To its detractors, *menglong* poetry seemed unfamiliar,
strange, incomprehensible, and hence decadent, bourgeois, and "Western
modernist." The advocates of *menglong* poetry, however, read it as different, exciting, rebellious, and hence avant-garde, revolutionary, and innovative. As we shall see, what was most striking about the role of Western
modernism was that both *menglong*'s advocates and its detractors misunderstood Western modernism in fundamental ways. Here, then, is a particularly telling example of an ambivalent misunderstanding across cultures, one that, taking our cue from Harold Bloom in his *The Anxiety of
Influence,* we might call "poetic misprision."[4]

At the beginning of the century the Chinese ideograph was imported
into the West by Pound on the claim that it would, because it was Chinese
and thus foreign, fill a lack in Western poetics. Sixty years later that very
same poetics, composed at least partly of Chinese materials, was advocated in China by the defenders of *menglong* poetry precisely because it
was Western and not Chinese, and therefore would lead to a kind of
"purer" poetry that would make up for what was lacking in Chinese literature! It is no surprise then, that *menglong*'s critics viewed it as Western
and thus decadent. But the ironies run even deeper: just as Pound's importation of what was "Chinese" into Western culture had profound ramifications for Western literature, so the importation of Western modernist
poetics into post-Mao China transformed Chinese literary practice.

Initially the advocates of *menglong* poetry were widely understood to
be calling for a replacement of the prevailing Chinese poetics—which was
dominated by ideological and political content—with the poetics of Western modernism. But this claim seemed premised on at least two kinds of
misunderstanding in the Chinese reception of *menglong* poetry: first, of
menglong poems themselves and, second, of Western modernism. Although frequently accused of following Western modernist poetics, the
menglong movement in its early stage[5] was a direct outgrowth of the political, ideological, and social conditions of post-Mao China. Reacting
against the earlier dominant mode of hymnal poetry that seemed to exist
only to praise Mao and the party, *menglong* poets gave expressions to disappointment with the party's lost idealism, corruption, and bureaucracy.
In fact, some of the early *menglong* poems were so realistically oriented
that they still sang hymns to Premier Zhou Enlai, who was more popular
than other top party leaders and hence represented an ideal proletariat
and revolutionary leader. Some of the early *menglong* poems, for example,
first appeared in *Today* (*Jintian*), an underground literary journal, as part

of the Democracy Wall movement in Beijing, which was banned by the government in 1980 as "anti-socialist" and "anti-party."[6]

In a 1992 interview in London, Bei Dao, a key player in *Today*'s publications from 1978 to 1980, described how the first issue of *Today* was posted on the Democracy Wall in Xidan, right after they printed it on December 23, 1978, for lack of a better channel to distribute it. It was the second unofficial journal (*minkan*) ever to appear on the wall.[7] Bei Dao believed that *Today* was so closely connected with the political events that the participants were perplexed from the onset by the choice between literature and politics.[8] In her 1997 essay entitled "Today and I" (*Jintian yu wo*), Xu Xiao also explained the unavoidable issue of politics at that time. Although the *Today* group intended to pursue a free spirit of humanism (*ziyou de renwen jingshen*) against party doctrine, they could not really pursue their purely artistic endeavor even if they wanted to. "In a highly politicized society, we were born politicized and hence had no choice but to be polemical." She told stories of several young people involved in the publication of *Today*, who did not write literary works themselves but were attracted to the *Today* group for its anti-official agendas.[9]

Dissatisfied with the PRC literary tradition, *menglong* poets called for a "truth-telling" literature that moved beyond the Maoist ideology and education they had grown up with since 1949. Xiao Xiao, in a study of underground literature during the Cultural Revolution, summarized the multifaceted reading traditions in the PRC, which might help us understand where the *menglong* generation had come from. According to Xiao, during the seventeen years prior to the Cultural Revolution, book publishing limited itself to (1) works by Marx, Engels, and Mao; (2) Chinese and Soviet revolutionary literatures; and (3) Chinese and Western classical works. During the Cultural Revolution, when schools and libraries were closed down, however, some young people circulated among themselves "gray-cover books" (*huipi shu*) and "yellow-cover books" (*huangpi shu*) published from the 1960s to the 1970s as "inside reference books" (*neibu duwu*) for high-ranking party officials. In the early 1960s in the wake of the Sino-Soviet split, Xiao pointed out, World Knowledge Press (Shijie zhishi chubanshe), People's Literature Press (Renmin wenxue chubanshe), and Sanlian Publishing House printed works by Soviet writers to help CCP officials understand the nature of "Soviet revisionism." Likewise, in the early 1970s, other works against Stalinism and on American politics and Western literature were published to help party officials better understand the changing dynamics in the Sino-Soviet and Sino-American relationships. Quoting from the *Catalogue of the Inside Reference Book Publications from 1949 to 1979*, Xiao Xiao reported that close to 1,000 books on Western theories and literatures were published during the Cultural Revolution in comparison with 1,041 titles that had appeared from

1949 to 1966. In the complete isolation from the outside world during the Cultural Revolution, therefore, these books were aggressively circulated among urban youth and those sent down to the countryside, including those associated with the *Today* group, thus creating one of the few channels of communication between the young generation and the rest of the world. Ironically, those books originally intended to educate Chinese officials to eliminate revisionist and bourgeois ideologies instead confirmed the doubts of the lost generation and contributed to their enlightenment. According to Xiao's surveys, the forty most influential works for this generation included critical reflections on Communist revolutions, such as Leon Trotsky's *The Revolution Betrayed* and *Stalin, An Appraisal of the Man and His Influence*, and Anna Louise Strong's *The Stalin Era*. Some young people were shocked by the similarities between Maoism and Stalinism in the personality cult and the persecutions of their political enemies. Whereas Edgar Snow's *Red Star over China* revealed for the first time Mao's problematic personal life with women, the Cuban revolutionary Che Guevara's *The Diary of Che Guevara* and William Shirer's *The Rise and Fall of the Third Reich* awoke them to the problems of idealism and the corruption of power. Other so-called bourgeois Western works included Arnold Toynbee's *A Study of History*, Harry Truman's *Memoirs*, and Henry Kissinger's *The Necessity for Choice*. Western literary titles consisted of Albert Camus's *The Stranger*, Samuel Beckett's *Waiting for Godot*, John Osborne's *Look Back in Anger*, Jack Kerouac's *On the Road*, and Jean Paul Sartre's *Nausea*, only a few of which can be considered as "Western modernist." This is not to deny that some *menglong* poets were indeed influenced by Western modernism.[10] Yet their Western modernist education was accompanied by other Chinese and Western traditions as well. Jiang He's early poems, for instance, reflected his attachment to Pablo Neruda and Elizabeth Barrett Browning.[11] In her early career, Shu Ting meticulously copied the poems of Pushkin, Tagore, Byron, Keats, and works by Chinese writers such as He Qifang and Zhu Ziqing.[12]

Despite this multifaceted reading background, critics still singled out Western modernism as the main negative influence that made the *menglong* poets depart from their own Chinese tradition. Yet from its very beginning, *menglong* poets invoked the Chinese tradition and reality as a source of artistic innovation. Indeed, the social content of some of the early *menglong* poems, such as Jiang He's "Monument" (*Jinianbei*), "Funeral" (*Zangli*), and "Unfinished Poem" (*Meiyou xiewan de shi*), still belonged to the realist tradition that dominated Chinese literary production since the May Fourth movement of 1915–1925. Jiang He's "Funeral," for instance, depicted political events such as the April Fifth Tiananmen incident of 1976, in which Chinese people publicly mourned Zhou Enlai's death to protest against Cultural Revolutionary leaders. This movement distinctly paralleled that associated with the 1989 Tiananmen student demonstrations, in which Chinese people mourned Hu Yaobang's death to voice their outrage at Deng Xiaoping's regime. At its best, early *menglong* poets carried out the pre-Mao literary legacy of "the May Fourth men of letters," whose "sense of mission," according to Leo Ou-fan Lee, "impelled them to see themselves as social reformers and spokesmen for the national conscience."[13]

From its very beginnings, *menglong* poets also invoked the classical Chinese tradition as a source of artistic innovation. In their manifesto, *menglong* poets declared their "New Poetry" as neither symbolist, surrealist, misty, nor impressionist; rather, they asserted, it embodies "a national spirit, the voice and pulse of the thinking generation, a reaction to the poetic disease of the past two decades." In order to drive home the point that *menglong* poetry was not influenced by "Western monsters," the manifesto spelled out ways of "reviv[ing] the rich visual-imagist tradition of Chinese poetry," which, it was admitted almost as an aside, "may coincide with contemporary Western poetics. But it is certainly not worshipping and fawning upon things foreign." Where the influence of Western modernism could be found, it was said to aim at a deeper understanding of "the true value of our own artistic tradition."[14] The movement's manifesto defended itself against imputation of Western influence, which was simply a way of stigmatizing it as an oppositional movement.

Despite all these complexities, however, critics chose to deliberately misunderstand *menglong* poets as following a decadent Western modernism that was dominated by nothing but "sex" and "money."[15] What inevitably resulted was a series of critical and even ideological debates on whether *menglong* poetry was acceptable to the canonical tradition of Marxist aesthetics and its demand for socialist realism. For some time, then, *menglong* poets were fiercely criticized for imitating Western modernism, for having alienated themselves from the popular and revolutionary taste of the Chinese audience, and finally, for writing elitist poems that few could comprehend. Whereas some chose to misunderstand *menglong* poems in this manner, others refused even to make an effort. "The best way to deal with these incomprehensible poems," Miao Deyu once said, "is not to read them at all. We would rather save our precious time to read those works that we can understand."[16] Here we see a particularly important aspect of the official use of Occidentalism in contemporary China expressed in the voice of conventional critics: the West is invoked and criticized for its cultural identity as the counter Other, which is thought to deviate from the predominant Communist ideology. The state and official ideology conveniently explored and employed the image of the Occident as a powerful weapon against the anti-official discourse as evidently expressed in *menglong* poetry.

But the ironies of misunderstanding *menglong* poetry go even deeper. Both the *menglong* poets themselves and their critics misunderstood Western modernist aesthetics even while invoking it. Both sides claimed that Western modernism was a "self-expressive" movement, a term that many Western scholars would tend to more easily associate with the poetic conventions of Romanticism that Pound and his Western contemporaries had sought to displace by importing, among other things, the Chinese ideogram. In fact, the entire debate on *menglong* poetry pivoted upon this central issue: Should the New Poetry—a term used both by critics and defenders of *menglong* to suggest an ideal future trend in the development of contemporary Chinese poetry—be mostly an expression of the self, as the *menglong* poems allegedly were? Or should it be an expression of the revolutionary, socialist idealism with the interests of the people and party at heart? Related to this issue was the recurrent concern of whether the New Poetry should imitate Western modernism or whether it should follow three indigenous Chinese poetic traditions—the classical, the folkloric, and that of the May Fourth movement.

Behind these literary issues lie, of course, the ever-present political and ideological concerns that have dominated Chinese poetics for the last several decades. Chief among them are questions about literature's function in promoting China's "four modernizations"—industry, agriculture, technology and science, and national defense—which take the West for their models. The question of how far the Chinese should go in adopting Western models in all spheres of life was therefore naturally raised. If it is necessary to import Western technology for a modernization in economic terms, should China also adopt Western philosophical and aesthetic models seen as outgrowths of a "decadent" capitalist society? Since in the Maoist interpretation of orthodox Marxism, literature and art were considered a crucial part of a socialist superstructure that in the last instance determined the nature of an economic base, many wondered if the "bourgeois ideology of modernism" would not become detrimental to modernization in socialist China. Such questions, needless to say, were based on various acts of misunderstanding Western modernism and its ideology. One of its striking features was the Chinese readers' neglect of the historical fact that the modernism advocated by T. S. Eliot and Ezra Pound, which had dominated the West in the first decades of the twentieth century, was by the 1970s becoming passé. Yet in the 1980s, when the Chinese writers and readers looked toward the West for an aesthetic model for cultural, political, and economic reform, ironically they picked up on a modernism that had long been superseded in the West. As Leo Ou-fan Lee has rightly pointed out, "For a present-day Marxist critic in the West, it must be equally incredible to find [in post-Mao literature] the linkage not only between humanism and Marxism, but between humanism and modernism as well."[17] Here we have a typical case in which ideological and social differences produced literary misunderstandings.

It is no wonder, then, that the Chinese misunderstood Western modernism in nearly every way possible. As I have already suggested, Western modernism was labeled as self-expressive, which somehow became connected with *menglong* poetry, viewed also as self-expressive, hence modernist and bourgeois. The characterization of Western modernism as self-expressive seems hardly surprising when viewed in the context of its early reception. Yuan Kejia's *Collected Works of Foreign Modernism,* for instance, was conditioned by the ideological and political considerations still prevailing in early post–Cultural Revolutionary China. Yuan simply used the orthodox Marxist theory of the West's historical development to explain its modernist phenomena as end-products of "a decadent bourgeois society which declined into a monopolistic capitalism in the 1920s." Western modernism was thus characterized by Yuan as a literature of alienation within capitalist societies—alienation of man from other men, from society, from nature, and from his own self.[18] One of the prominent features of Western modernist works, according to Yuan, is its focus on "a disillusioned self," "the pathos of a lost self and the frustration of an unsuccessful search for such self."[19]

Surprisingly, however, it was the defenders of the *menglong* movement who first used the term "self-expression" and "Western modernism," though they did so on separate occasions. Xie Mian argued, in "After the Peace Was Gone," that the young poets of the *menglong* school attempted to restore to their rightful place "individuality," "dignity," and "self-respect," which had been dismissed in revolutionary poetry. Wang Xiaoni's poem "Holiday, Lakeside, Random-thoughts" (*Jiari, hupan, suixiang*), for example, focused on expressing personal feelings without apparent concern for a social reality; it thus reaffirmed the legitimacy of individuality as a basic theme in *menglong* poetry.[20] In another essay, Xie Mian noted that the *menglong* movement represented "the emergence of a group of new poets who wrote some 'eccentric' or 'odd' poems after courageously adapting certain techniques from Western modernist poetics."[21] These separate statements on self-expression and Western modernism set up a framework for the forthcoming debate on *menglong:* both critics and supporters combined these two terms as chief characteristics of the *menglong* movement.

As if to follow up on Xie's endeavors, Sun Shaozhen's 1981 seminal article "A New Aesthetic Principle Is Emerging" further complicated the issue of self-expression. Celebrating *menglong* poems as successful expressions of "a set of new aesthetic principles," which rejected both the "popular songs of the 1950s to sing hymns to the party" and the "revolutionary marching songs" of the 1960s to depict the "selfless spirit" and "heroic struggle" of the masses, Sun argued for an end of political monism in order to exert an artistic freedom that would explore human feelings as a basic concern in literature.[22] Although Sun centered his argument on "self-expression" (*biaoxian ziwo*), he never related it to Western modernism. Only in his concluding paragraph did he touch upon the necessity of borrowing literary legacies "from other nations," which "will enrich our own heritages to create artistic works of a higher level."[23] By "other nations," of course, Sun could very well refer to diverse literary traditions of many different countries and periods. The term "Western modernism" was never invoked in the entire essay. Its publication, however, immediately triggered off a critical debate. Thus it was Sun's opponents, such as Cheng Daixi, who first directly connected self-expression with Western modernism: "almost all artists of Western modernism," Cheng claimed, "regard 'self' or 'ego' as the only object for representation. They attempted to express this 'self' with obscurity (*menglong*), absurdity, fantasies, and incomprehensibility," which represented for Cheng "the common features of Western modernism." To support his unfavorable view of modernism, Cheng Daixi cited T. S. Eliot's *The Waste Land* as "expressing an individual's totally disillusioned self." Similarly, Eliot's involvement with the magazine *The Egotist* aimed at nothing but a vigorous promotion of self-expression.[24] Here it is important to note that the idea of self-expression attributed to the modernism of Pound and Eliot was in fact what the critics of *menglong* considered themselves to be reading *against*.

Surprisingly, however, *menglong* defenders willingly followed up on this attempt to further relate Western modernism to *menglong* poetry. In his essay "The Emergence of New Groups of Poetry—On the Modernist Tendencies in Contemporary Poetry in Our Country," Xu Jingya boldly rejected the entire poetic tradition of the Mao era and argued for an importation of Western modernist features as exemplified in *menglong* poetry.[25] Citing Hegel's "dialectic," which postulated "symbolic art, classical art, and romantic art" as three stages of artistic development in human history, Xu argued that modernism was the next logical step and hence the highest stage of development of literature and art for all mankind. Sooner or later, Xu said, this irresistible trend will become predominant in China. In Xu's essay, self-expression had become an important Western modernist feature that could somehow revive the dying poetic tradition in contemporary China. Yet, as if to assert his own critical difference from an Occidental Other, Xu remarked that *menglong*'s self-expression was existentially related to "the happiness of one's country and people" and thus "much wider in scope than its Occidental counterpart," which "expressed a pure 'self' isolated from society."[26]

Xu's opponents, of course, did not lose the opportunity to reaffirm how self-expression was indeed a central characteristic in bourgeois ideology and hence should be completely repudiated. Xu's supporters, however, defended him by arguing that Western modernist techniques were nothing new or foreign. Xia Zhongyi noted, for example, that Pound and Kafka used similar techniques in "Metro" and *Metamorphosis* as those employed in Li He's poems and Feng Menglong's *Lasting Words to Awaken the World* (*Xingshi hengyan*). Nobody has labeled these traditional Chinese writers as being "Western modernist." Xia thus claimed that Western modernism perhaps had its origins in the classical Chinese tradition. It was only new in its "provocative world view which is not useful for our socialist literature."[27] The ensuing critical campaign against Xu's "daring manifesto on Chinese modernism" involved major literary journals such as *Literary Gazette, Poetry Monthly,* and *Contemporary Trends in Literature and Art,* and finally culminated in Xu's 1984 "Self-Criticism" in which he had to admit that it was "ideologically wrong" to "blindly follow" the concept of self-expression advocated by Western modernists. By virtue of his literary misunderstanding of Western modernism, Xu was made a scapegoat in the ongoing "anti-spiritual pollution" campaign, in which Deng Xiaoping's party apparatus railed against an overflow of "decadent influences from the West." Here we see a typical example of how a literary practice is preconditioned by the cultural and ideological specifics of a society at a given historical moment.

This peculiar Chinese appropriation of Western modernism—marked either by claiming it as Chinese in origin in order to defend it, or by rejecting it precisely because it was not Chinese—became a common feature in the ensuing debate on *menglong* poetry. The single most striking fact about this debate is that both the defenders of the Western tradition and the critics of its use in China shared the same limited view of the way that modernism was understood in the West. Both sides were arguing about modernism, but neither was looking seriously into what Pound, Soviet critics, or Western Marxists had said about China or modernist conventions. Thus all theoretical and most practical literary production in China was based on a misunderstanding of Western modernism as dominated by self-expression. As I have already suggested, such a view is a radical departure from the Western interpretation, which has emphasized a "historical sense" as a striking feature of Pound's modernist poetics. "So far as 'personal utterance' meant self-expression," David Perkins testifies, for example, "Pound usually rejected it. But that poetry should reflect life, not art, he affirmed often and with fervor, for he was struggling against himself."[28] Pound's ideogrammic method was understood in the West as a rebellious act against the romantic tradition of self-expression and hence an "objective" presentation and "impersonal" method.[29] Pound's ideological concerns in his whole career, including the extreme case of his enthusiasm for Fascism, demonstrate how preoccupied he once was with the economic and social orders of his times. "How to write concerned him far less than how to govern," Perkins writes of Pound's life before the war. "Where formerly he had advised and aided Eliot and Joyce he now tried to advise senators and congressmen, Roosevelt and Stalin."[30]

In the West, therefore, Pound is hardly regarded as an artist who believed in the "art for art's sake" ideology of which the Western modernist movement in China was accused. It is thus not accidental that in the numerous Chinese articles on Pound and his modernist movement, very few of them mentioned Pound's imprisonment after World War II for his collaborationist activities. The fact that a heavily ideologically oriented Chinese criticism should choose to neglect Pound's pro-Fascist political record tells us how far the Chinese critics went to misunderstand Pound and his modernist ideology—perhaps deliberately so. But just as strikingly, Pound's defenders seemed equally unaware of his concern for social issues. In fact, the whole political dimension of Pound's modernism, if known, would have been a source of embarrassment to both sides.

Equally embarrassing to Chinese critics was that Eliot also saw Pound's "method as a modernist gesture of doing away with romantic notions of 'originality' in poetry," a gesture that was anything but a promotion of self-expression.[31] Eliot himself emphasized the necessity of a "historical sense" for an artist who is always forced by tradition to escape from his personality and emotions in order to surrender himself continually to tradition. Thus self-expression even in the "most individual" part of a work asserts only the "immortality" of the dead poet "most vigorously."[32] As if to "protect" Eliot and Pound from a posthumous Chinese contamination, Western literary theorists have likewise persistently argued for the anti-institutional dimension to the modernist movement, which would not celebrate self-expression. Peter Bürger observed that "we should come to see that avant-garde artists were actively attacking the institution of art. Their effort was not to isolate themselves, but to reintegrate themselves and their art into life."[33] For Bürger, then, modernist movements "negate those determinations that are essential in autonomous art: the disjunction of art and the praxis of life, individual production, and individual reception as distinct from the former."[34] For Matei Calinescu, however, it would even be "so difficult" to conceive of Eliot and Pound as "representatives of the avant-garde," since they "have indeed very little, if anything, in common with such typically avant-garde movements as futurism, dadaism, or surrealism."[35] The rejection of the past tradition in the modernist movement is highly paradoxical since "the anti-traditionalism of modernism is often subtly traditional."[36] It is thus not the emphasis on the self, but the subtle sense of tradition that is characteristic of modernism, at least according to the views of the major explorers of this movement in the West.

In the process of misunderstanding Western modernism, Chinese critics also misinterpreted *menglong* poetry, which is neither self-expressive nor egoistic. Indeed, *menglong* poets frequently used "I" to speak for a collective "you" and "we," who are disillusioned with their former revolutionary idealism. Jiang He's "Unfinished Poem" published in *Today* in 1979, for example, depicts Zhang Zhixin, a revolutionary martyr who was imprisoned, tortured, and finally executed during the Cultural Revolution for openly challenging Mao's ideology. At the beginning of the poem, the "I" speaker projects himself into a female "you," the heroine. The entire objective world in the poem—the prison wall, time, and history—is in conflict with "I," the poetic persona, who also speaks for an implied "you"—the prisoner who is nailed on the wall:

> I was nailed upon the prison wall.
> Black Time gathered, like a crowd of crows
> From every corner of the world, from every night of History,
> To peck all the heroes to death, one after the other, upon this wall.
> The agony of heroes thus became a rock
> Lonelier than mountains.
> For chiseling and sculpting
> The character of the nation,
> Heroes were nailed to death
> Wind-eroding, rain-beating
> An uncertain image revealed upon the wall—
> Dismembered arms, hands and faces—
> Whips slashing, darkness pecking.
> Ancestors and brothers with heavy hands
> Labored silently as they were piled into the wall.
> Once again I come here
> To revolt against fettered fate
> And with violent death to shake down the earth from the wall
> To let those who died silently stand up and cry out.[37]

In this poem, the "I" is at once a historical "I," or a Whitmanesque collective "I"—those Chinese persons who can readily identify with Zhang's fate. The "I" speaker perceives in Zhang the pathos of her nation, lonely, suffering, and in need of salvation. History, time, and the entire world are all at odds with the lonely heroes who are "sculpting" "the character of the nation" while their ignorant "brothers" are toiling away time to build up the prison wall, willingly and silently. The heroic "I" thus regards himself as an unhappy child of an unfortunate nation, alienated from his own people, neglected and unappreciated. "I" is determined to wake up this unfortunate land: "Once again I come here / To revolt against fettered fate / And with violent death to shake down the earth from the wall." The "I" in this poem stands for a new generation that urges "those who died silently" to "stand up and cry out" for truth, justice, and happiness.

In the second episode of the "Unfinished Poem," "I" changes into the voice of a mother whose daughter is sentenced to death as a political prisoner:

II. Suffering

I am the mother. My daughter is about to be executed.
Gun-point walks toward me, a black sun
Upon the cracked earth walks toward me.
I am an old tree. I am a bunch of dried fingers.
I am those convulsed wrinkles upon the face.
The land and I both bear together this catastrophe,
Heart thrown upon the ground.
My daughter's blood is splashed into the mud,
Hot and flowing, my child's tears run upon my face;
They too are salty.
As in winter, small rivers, one after the other freeze,
One after the other stop singing.
I am sister, I am daughter and wife.
Lapels and hems are torn, hair falling,
Not leaves.
Spindrift flies from rocks.
My hair is an ocean.
I am father, I am husband, I am son.
My big hand bumps and jolts upon the hair-ocean.
Bone-joints dully cracked.
I am boats and vessels.
I am cut jungles
While still growing robustly.

The "black sun" stands out here as a strikingly defamiliarized image for the Chinese readers in the late 1970s who were still habituated to the "red," "rising," and "never-setting sun"—persistent symbols of Mao, the party, and the "socialist motherland" in revolutionary poetry. A typical example is "Our Great Motherland" (*Women weida de zuguo*) by He Jingzhi, a much celebrated poet in the sixties:

The red sun rises in the east,
Its splendor shines upon the Four Seas,
Our great motherland
  Stands, towering and proud.
With the hands of a giant,
The spirit of a hero,
It rearranges the vast countryside.
Just look how spring fills South China,
  Flowers bloom beyond the borders;
A thousand wonders,
  Ten thousand spectacles.

> The Three Red Flags meet the east wind,
> Gales and thunders of revolution come rolling forth.
> O! Our great motherland
> Advances toward the new age of socialism!
> The great Mao Tse-tung,
> The great Party,
> Guide us
>   Toward the bright and glorious future![38]

Here we see a once popular revolutionary poem in post-1949 China in which the "red sun" glorifies the "wise leadership of Chairman Mao" and the "bright" future of socialist motherland. In the *menglong* poem just cited, however, the sun and its encoded ideology are subverted to express the sorrows of a mother—"an old tree" with "dried fingers" who mourns for the loss of her daughter. This "I" naturally refers to all mothers, daughters, fathers, and sons—an impersonal "we" who long for a new life that would not be smothered by the "black sun." This episode witnesses fourteen uses of "I" or "my." Yet as Jiang He himself once explained, these "I"s indeed remain "selfless"; the first-person pronoun does not express one's private feelings and emotions. On the contrary, it embodies "an epic dimension" in order to encompass the "national spirit" of the Chinese people, which is at once heroic, as expressed in Zhang Zhixin's deed, and tragic, as reflected in the indifferent "brothers and ancestors" who facilitated the imprisonment of the heroine.

The epic qualities of Jiang He's poetic oeuvre culminated in his monumental work "Oh, Motherland" (*Zuguo a, zuguo*), also published in *Today* in 1979:

> At the places where the heroes have fallen
> I rose up to sing a song for the motherland
> I placed the Great Wall on the northern mountains
> As if lifting up the heavy fetters of a thousand years
> As if holding towards heaven a dying son
> Whose body is still convulsing in my arms
> At my back, my mother
> Nation's pride, suffering, and protest
> A sign of uneasiness flickers
> In the eyes of heartless history
> Then, deeply inscribed on my forehead
> A glorious scar
> Smoke arose from behind my head
> Numerous white bones crying out, dispersing with the wind
> Like white clouds, like a cluster of pure pigeons[39]

Despite the lack of punctuation, the poem has a clear political message. The ancient battlefield at the Great Wall no longer testifies to the past glory of an invincible motherland as it once did in revolutionary poetry. It is now compared to a dying son in the arms of "my mother"—the Great Wall—who is suffering, protesting, uneasy with a "glorious scar inscribed" on her forehead. In the next few stanzas, the "I" speaker "follow[s] the white pigeons/With indignation and passion/Traveling through many ages and places/Even through battles, ruins, and corpses/Slashing the ocean waves as winding mountains/Bleeding, lifting up and sending off the bloody sun." Throughout the poem, "I" identifies himself with "mother" and "motherland," pondering her children's fate and sorrow. "I" also questions the "bloody sun" in a bleak landscape left with tears, corpses, and ruins. "I" is at best an "allegorical self-expression," which speaks for a new national consciousness. Whatever self-expression one might find is meaningful only when it is merged with the present and future of the nation in the flow of history. Jiang's poems are indeed direct products of the ideological conditions of early post-Mao China. Accusing them of being "Western," "modernist," and "egoistical" literature in this case is irrelevant to the actual practice of *menglong* poetry, but was made up out of the necessities of the political concerns of early post-Mao China.

If Jiang He's early *menglong* poems belong to the May Fourth realist tradition, the woman writer Shu Ting's poems reflect yet another May Fourth theme, the search for romantic love and freedom, which has been fully explored in Leo Ou-fan Lee's *The Romantic Generation of Modern Chinese Literature*. If anything, Western readers would never have expected Chinese modernist writers to write love poems, or at least the conventional kind. Yet this is precisely the main subject matter of Shu Ting's early poems. With a distinctively feminine voice, simple, supple, and perhaps even delicately timid, Shu Ting's love poems touched the readers—especially young readers of her own generation—who were emotionally "thirsty" in the dark ages of the Cultural Revolution, during which love was suppressed as bourgeois ideology. In the first stanza of the poem "To An Oak Tree" (*Zhi xiangshu*), published in *Today* in 1978, for instance, we perceive a romantic yearning to reshape an unsatisfying present with an idealistic search for a selfless love:

> If I were to love you—
> I won't be like those upward-climbing trumpet creepers, who show
>   themselves off by borrowing your higher branches;
> If I were to love you—
> I would never mimic those sentimental birds
>   forever chirping their monotonous songs for some green shade;
>   nor would I be just a mountain spring
> making a gift of refreshing coolness all year long;
>   nor just the loftiest mountain peak,

adding on to your height or augmenting your majestic mien;
   not even the sunlight,
   nor even the spring rain.
No, not any of those can come close to my love for you!

I want to nestle to your side and turn into a kapok tree,
assume the shape of a tree, to stand alongside of you:
the roots—tightly held beneath the ground;
the leaves—touching themselves in the clouds.
And with the passing of every breeze,
we would salute each other, reverently.

   But—no one is there
to hear and understand our words.
You have your branches of brass and trunks of steel—
   sharp as blades, sharp as swords,
   and sharper than lances;
I, too, have my sturdy red flowers,
as heavy as heaved sighs,
as brave as a hero's torch.
We share freezing cold, thunderstorms, wind and lightning;
together we enjoy evening mists, auroral clouds, and rainbow;
seemingly forever parting and clinging to each other for life.

   So great is our love for each other,
     never-yielding and always loyal:
   I love—
not just your tall, robust body,
but also your stubborn stance, the ground beneath your feet.[40]

In this poem we see at least three literary traditions at work: (1) May Fourth realism, (2) European romanticism, and (3) a uniquely Chinese combination of these two seemingly disparate movements. Whatever Western traits they contain, they are not modernistic. Love in this poem, for example, is reminiscent of the Kantian definition of love: "good will, affection, promoting the happiness of others and finding joy in their happiness."[41] While it is of course possible to understand these lines in a sexual manner, the lovers here seem to enjoy first of all a spiritual union in which their leaves are "touching themselves in the clouds." Once viewed as a forbidden subject in revolutionary poetry, the romantic love of this poem protests against the conventional love for Mao and the party. Yet at the same time, this poem participates in the realist movement, since the Self is indeed employed as a political strategy against the Other of the ruling ideology. In this regard, then, Shu Ting's love poems can be regarded as only superficially romantic, or romantic with a different emphasis: they recall the Byronic revolutionary battle for Greek national freedom. Seen in this light, Jiang He's realist poems can in turn be regarded as romantic; he expresses, above all else, patriotic feelings for a national salvation, as demonstrated in his "Oh, Motherland." This romantic and realist temper in *menglong* poems is thus identical to the Byronic mind: "When a man hath no freedom to fight for at home/Let him combat for that of his neighbors;/Let him think of the glories of Greece and of Rome, /And get knocked on his head for his labors."[42]

However Western these poems may seem, the romantic and realist traits of *menglong* poetry can be viewed as a continuation of the contemporary Chinese literary tradition, which was from time to time open to foreign influence from 1949 to 1966, before the Cultural Revolution. The majority of PRC readers were certainly more familiar with romanticism and realism than modernism in the early post-Mao period. The much-honored Soviet concept of critical realism, for example, canonized Balzac, Tolstoy, Gorky, Chekhov, Mark Twain, and Charles Dickens as progressive writers. Romantic texts by Byron, Wordsworth, and Goethe were taught as Western classics in universities before the Cultural Revolution. Shelley's "The Revolt of Islam" and "England in 1819" were interpreted as ideological protests against injustice and oppression. His famous line "If Winter comes, can Spring be far behind?" from "Ode to the West Wind" was even employed as a well-known revolutionary motto by Lu Jiachuan, a Marxist character who sacrificed his life for the future of a new China in *The Song of Youth* (*Qingchun zhi ge*), one of the most popular novels in the late 1950s and early 1960s.[43]

Seen in these cultural specifics of the contemporary Chinese literary scene, what Chinese critics considered as "egoistical" (a concern with the self) in *menglong* poetry may indeed be "egotistical" (a sense of personal superiority over one's physical and social surroundings). The *menglong* movement represents not a private, unrepresentative, onanistic self-reference, but what might be called "allegorical self-expressions" in the Whitmanesque tradition, which is at once egoistical and egotistical. Whitman spoke of the "I" as emblematic and allegorical ("I am large; I encompass all things"), as well as of the "I" as individual and private. Here a private "I" and a public "I" are merged and integrated, forming an image that is superior to the poet's social and cultural parameters. Seen from these perspectives, then, one may be able to contrast *menglong* poetry more appropriately with, on the one hand, the Western modernists—who were impersonal, even if they were egoistical—and, on the other, with the May Fourth writers—who were both personal and egotistical.[44]

We have so far mapped out at least two areas of misunderstanding of *menglong* poetry: Chinese critics misunderstood it as self-expressive, and this misunderstanding was, in turn, based on a misreading of Western modernism. In the remainder of this chapter, I would like to further address the question of how and why these related acts of misunderstanding came about: they had less to do with Western modernist influence *per se* than the expected results of the conflicting horizons of literary expectations by various groups of readers at the specific moment when *menglong* poetry first appeared. Generally speaking, despite the claim of its critics, *menglong* poetry was largely "incomprehensible" or "obscure" only to certain groups of readers, who were mostly members of an older generation. In this reading community, the readers' ideological and aesthetic principles were preconditioned by their own education and experience before the Cultural Revolution, which, up to that moment, remained basically unchanged. Such readers, like others in China, suffered through many political upheavals. Unlike other readers from a very disillusioned younger generation, many of them could still somehow maintain their revolutionary idealism in spite of their personal sufferings and momentary doubts. Some even had vested interests in holding onto the revolutionary ideology: they had spent all their lives fighting for the revolution and were now occupying positions of power in the literary establishment. The passionate exposure of the dark side of everyday reality presented by the "doubting Thomas" generation, therefore, offended not only their literary sensibilities, but political, cultural, and ideological ones as well. Changed images such as the "black sun" thus became puzzling, obscure, unacceptable, and hence, inevitably, Western modernist.

The generation gap between these two groups of readers was most clearly brought into the open by Gu Gong, father of the *menglong* poet Gu Cheng. His son's poetic lines such as "Who is moving in the distance?/It is the clock's pendulum, /Hired by the god of death/To measure life" were, he claimed, too "depressing" and too "terrifying" for him. He thus confessed in an article on *menglong* poetry: "I have never read this kind of poetry. When I marched and fought in the war, the lines of poetry we chanted were bright and exalted, like bomb shells bursting, like flaming bullets. Not like this! Not like this at all!" Like many other readers of an older generation, Gu Gong simply could not understand "why in the depths of their souls are there such 'glacial scars,' such 'doubt'—or, even worse, such thoughts as 'Who is coming—the god of death.'"[45]

In addition to ideological differences, the formal features of *menglong* poetry further frustrated some traditional readers. The image in Maoist poetry of the "never-setting" and "indispensable" sun on which both the

natural and human world depend for vitality is now described in Bei
Dao's "The Snowline" (*Xuexian*) as something that can be easily forgotten:

> Forget what I've said
> forget the bird shot down from the sky
> forget the reefs
> let them sink once more into the deep
> forget even the sun
> only a lamp covered in dust and ashes
> is shining
> in the eternal position[46]

In Bei Dao's "Cruel Hope" (*Canku de xiwang*), the sun is associated with a
funeral procession and the death of science and reason: "striking up a
heavy dirge/dark clouds have lined up the funeral procession/the sun
sinks towards an abyss/Newton is dead." In the same poem, the sun can
even become unpredictable:

> What's that making an uproar
> it seems to come from the sky
>
> Hey, sun—kaleidoscope
> start revolving
> and tell us innumerable unknown dreams[47]

The older generation would have reiterated their unshakable belief in the
"omniscient" sun even when the socialist course to which they were devoted turned out to be not-so-smooth sailing. Under no circumstances
could they have written such provocative lines as these: "Thus perhaps /
we have lost / the sun and the earth / and ourselves" and "Hope / the
earth's bequest / seems so heavy / silent / cold / Frost flowers drift away
with the mist."[48] Not being able to understand these lines, some readers
chose to dismiss them as "bourgeois," "decadent," and "Western modernist." This generation gap explains the reason why some of the well-
established poets and critics of the older generation such as Li Ying, Tian
Jian, Ai Qing, and Zan Kejia took the lead in campaigning against what
they called the "unhealthy" trend in *menglong* poetry.

From its very beginning, however, *menglong* poetry was accepted by
many readers of the younger generation—the same generation that produced it—and even by some not-so-young critics such as Xie Mian, who
was attacked for favoring *menglong* poetry at the expense of his successful career of promoting revolutionary poetry. As time went by, however,
the defamiliarizing aspects of *menglong* poetry gradually gave way to a
process of familiarization. More and more readers began to realize that
menglong poems were not so obscure after all, but quite clear and direct in

their images. Much of the credit for popularizing *menglong* poetry, however, should be given to the critical debate itself. Both supporters and critics were given many forums to clarify their own views on *menglong* poems and on the assumptions evoked by such terms as Western and Chinese traditions. Miao Yushi noted that in the very debates on *menglong* poetry in which most theoretical and poetic issues were addressed, both sides found more and more common ground in their seemingly irreconcilable stances. Those who regarded *menglong* as obscure and suffocating now began to accept it as one of the many possible poetic trends. Indeed, the *menglong* debate even educated Chinese readers in a new artistic taste. Poems such as "Autumn" (*Qiu*) and "Night" (*Ye*), which earlier had seemed difficult to understand, now began to make sense. This transformation demonstrated that "the public's reading habits and our critics' way of artistic evaluation have been undergoing a spontaneous change in the last few years."[49]

Underlying these changes, of course, was a much more relaxed ideological and political atmosphere for artistic creation than was present in the immediate aftermath of the Cultural Revolution. Critics and readers became more tolerant of opinions different from their own and from the current policies of the ruling ideology. When these non-literary changes occurred, past acts of misunderstanding were gradually turned into acts of understanding. The *menglong* poet Gu Cheng was thus correct in saying that "after the poet had smashed the old reading habits with the creation of his new poems, both the author and his readers will experience a rebirth together."[50] Yet it must be emphasized that this rebirth was made possible only with readers' changed horizons of literary expectations and their new interpretations, which were conditioned by the political and ideological circumstances at a specific historical moment. As theorists like Hans Robert Jauss have argued, the transformation of a literary system and its various meanings are due to events both in the aesthetic and in the socioeconomic systems of a culture.[51] If, as seems to be the case, the only meaning that a text can have is the transitory one residing in the minds of its readers, then perceived meaning is, in a sense, predetermined by the preceding literary and cultural experiences of the reader. The historicity of *menglong* poetry, as we have seen, resides not within the text, but outside the text, in readers' interpretive processes of understanding and misunderstanding. Or said otherwise, its historicity can be situated entirely within the texts that were themselves the products of a social-economic-political moment.

Yet the story of the acceptance of *menglong* poetry, both by diverse groups of readers and by the ruling ideology, is even more paradoxical than just described, for the process of familiarization with *menglong* poetry also resulted in a parallel process of familiarization with Western modernism. What used to be foreign and negative gradually became domestic and positive. These new horizons of expectations concerning Western modernism, not surprisingly, altered, among other things, the literary and political perception of Ezra Pound, who was suddenly received not only as a native Chinese, but also as a classical Chinese. It became fashionable to argue, for example, that Western modernism was not harmful after all, since it was originally inspired by the classical Chinese tradition. Ironically, therefore, the same Pound who was held responsible for initiating Western modernism by misunderstanding classical Chinese poetry in the West was now glorified in the East as a talented China-hand who revived Western literature through his understanding of a Chinese tradition. By extension, then, things Western, or Chinese with Western influence, became less terrifying than before, because they seemed to ultimately reaffirm the superiority of a Chinese heritage. Zhou Qiwan argued, for example, that the *menglong* tendency was by no means Western. It was in fact so uniquely Chinese that even Pound had to borrow it from Li Bai's poems in order to establish his own imagist movement in the West. The same was true for other genres, Zhou argued. Zhang Xun's symbolist painting in the Tang dynasty, for instance, influenced impressionist art in the West while Chinese operatic theater inspired Brecht's expressionist theater.[52] Seen in this light, then, Zhou believed, one should no longer condemn modernism as reflecting decadent and capitalist ideology. To do so naturally implies a rejection of our own national legacies such as Tang poetry, Sung lyrics, and Yuan drama, traditions emanating from a feudalist society that Marx considered as a much more backward historical period than capitalism.[53] Here we see a surprisingly paradoxical twist: Pound's modernist poetics not only rescued the *menglong* movement, it also sanctioned for the Chinese their own classical traditions, which were recognized as positive and historically progressive only after they were valorized by "Western monsters."

In such a dialectical process of literary reception, the changing fate of Pound and his modernist movement in turn altered once again the interpretations of *menglong* poetry. Shi Tianhe suggested that *menglong* be renamed "imagist poetry" after its ancient predecessors such as "When a Crane Cries" (*He ming*), in *Elegantiae* (*Xiaoya*) from *The Book of Songs* (*Shijing*). The ironic fact here, according to Shi, was that Western imagist poems seemed to be very popular among *menglong* poets who claimed to have borrowed them from the West, whereas Chinese classical imagist poems were greatly admired by modernists such as Pound. It seemed that Chinese poets "were anxious to break away from their own tradition by importing the imagist methodology from the West," whereas Western imagist writers "sold their Chinese goods back to the home market after processing them in the West."[54] In Shi's opinion, then, Pound became a Western salesman who was desperately in love with Chinese goods, and eventually proved to the Chinese themselves that his poetic goods were of indigenous provenance. Pound, who by Western accounts misunderstood classical Chinese poetry, was now portrayed in China as a disciple of the Chinese cultural past, which *menglong* poets had tried so hard to escape, only to find themselves embracing it in the same manner as their Western "poetic-parents."

In fact, in these Chinese accounts, not only did Pound help Chinese writers and readers discover their own literary tradition, but he also offered a solution to the dilemma of *menglong* poets. Huang Ziping noted two polarities in the writings of the young poets after the Cultural Revolution. On the one hand, they were more philosophical and abstract, focusing on a contemplation and even negation of the past cultural tradition. On the other hand, they demanded the fullest expression for deep, emotional, and personal feelings. It was Pound's concept of image—one that "presents an intellectual and emotional complex with a quick rendering of particulars without commentary"—that offered the young poets a delicate balance between a philosophical "cool-headedness" and an "enthusiastic expression," thus helping them achieve "a sudden emancipation from spacial and temporal confinements."[55] It is worth noting here that Huang was especially cautious in delineating Pound's relationship to *menglong* poetry—the young poets merely "seemed" to be inspired by Pound's theory. It was, of course, extremely hard for Huang to prove that these young poets actually had any direct contact with Pound's imagist theory, since most of Pound's poems had not yet been translated into Chinese at that time. The important point for the present argument is Huang's implicit recognition that a rereading of Pound's poetics as something fundamentally Chinese, classical, and therefore beneficial brought about a new way of understanding *menglong* texts, which only a few years earlier were conceived of as having been influenced by "Western monsters."

Equally striking in the history of the *menglong* debate is that so much was written on Pound's modernist poetics that it soon became part of the critical vocabulary of literary discourse. For a while, it seemed that a critic in contemporary China could not talk about *menglong* without somehow bringing in Pound's modernist poetics. Pound's name was even frequently invoked in fields not directly relevant to modern poetry such as in discussions of the classical tradition. Xiao Chi argued that Western tradition, which is based on the classical genres of drama and epic, emphasized imitation of human actions, whereas the Chinese tradition, with its emphasis on poetry as a high genre, focused on expressions of human feelings through depictions of natural images. In his conclusion, Xiao says quite unexpectedly: "Chinese classical poetry has been greatly admired by Ezra Pound, one of the architects of Western modernist poetics. As has been pointed out by Michael Alexander, 'This use of nature as a language is a permanent contribution of China to Pound. . . . (*The Peetic Achiekement of Egra Pounda* [sic] by Micheal Alexander).'"[56] Spelling mistakes in the English book title here were frequent occurrences in the Chinese journals at a time when the press could not catch up with the fashionable trend of constantly citing Western sources. Later on, Xiao obviously realized the irrelevance of Pound to his discussion: when he included this essay in his book *The Aesthetics of Chinese Poetics*, published in 1986, he left out the concluding paragraph on Pound.

The acts of literary reception that formed part of the *menglong* debate were brought about by acts of misunderstanding or misuse. According to the conventions of comparative literary studies as they are usually practiced, such acts of misunderstanding are to be deplored as a product of a regrettable ignorance, or a negative example of a Chinese Occidentalism. But it would be a mistake to dismiss the various misunderstandings of Western modernism so strikingly apparent in the *menglong* debate merely as the products of ignorance. Such acts of misunderstanding were one of the few possible ways that Western modernism could become meaningful to different reading communities in the early days of post-Mao China, when cultural exchange with the Western world was neither common nor deemed desirable. Whatever "Western modernism" might have meant to Chinese readers at that time, it played a major role in initiating artistic movements, which were not limited to lyric poetry, but included other genres such as the novel, the film, and the play. However understood, Western modernism has played such a pioneering role in the making of contemporary Chinese literature that no one in the post-Mao era could seriously talk about contemporary Chinese literature and its critical scene without coping with Western modernism and its influence. To a great extent, then, it was an act of misunderstanding that made possible cross-cultural literary relations between China and the West in the past decades.

The critical debate over the *menglong* movement, taken in its narrower sense, was short-lived, since this type of poetry was finally accepted by the official culture; it became canonized and anthologized as one of the leading poetic trends in modern China. Yet the place of the Western tradition in contemporary Chinese literary production was by no means settled. To some extent, it was precisely because of different layers of misunderstanding among the Chinese readers and writers that Western modernism became, for better or for worse, a reference point that defined and conditioned specific forms of literary production and reception. The emphasis on self-expression, for instance, was still regarded as an important feature of Western modernism. This so-called "Western" sense of the self was further explored by some *menglong* poets in their efforts to develop new kinds of poetry—*national epic poetry* (*minzu shishi*), *searching-for-roots poetry* (*xungen shi*) in 1984, and subsequently, *abstract poetry* (*chouxiang shi*), and *philosophical poetry* (*zheli shi*) in 1988.

In their national epic poetry, *menglong* poets such as Jiang He and Yang Lian began to dig into past cultural traditions in order to express a new national consciousness—or to use a then-fashionable Jungian term—to describe the "collective unconscious" of the Chinese people.[57] It is interesting to note in passing that here we see another typical example of misunderstanding in the Chinese reception of Western literary theory. C. G. Jung was very popular in China around 1985, when Chinese intellectuals were looking for what they called the "historical, social, and collective conscious of the Chinese people" (*lishi de, shehui de, jituan de yishi*) which was expressed in Chinese myth, religion, dreams, and literature.[58] In the West, however, Jung's notion of the archetypal and primordial images is understood as precisely not culturally specific, but universally inherited in the collective unconscious of the human race in spite of the diverse social conditions of each culture.

Perhaps anxious to transcend the tradition of which they had by now become a part, the young poets sought to move beyond their once provocative *menglong* poetry by pursuing instead philosophical themes that were now reflected in their descriptions of historic sites and their cultural heritage. Ancient myths became popular subject matter, in which legendary heroes moved high mountains, shot down nine superfluous suns, and patched up the broken sky to restore the natural order in the universe. The once "bleeding" and "bloody" sun now appeared soft and loving again, caressing the river and land that raised generations of Chinese people. In his poem "Chasing the Sun" (*Zhuiri*), Jiang He wrote with passion and tenderness: "When he [*Kuafu*] started his journey to chase the sun / he was already old / otherwise he would never go after the sun / youth itself is the sun."[59] The Chinese national spirit is best expressed in a harmony between man and the universe:

> Legend goes that he drank up all the waters in the Wei and Yellow River
> In fact he made himself a cup of wine and passed it to the sun
> Indeed he and the sun were intoxicated a long time ago
> He washed himself and got dry in the sun

Similarly, in the next stanza:

> When the sun settles in his heart
> He feels that the sun is so soft that it hurts
> He can now touch it
> He is old
> His fingers shaking like rays of sunlight.[60]

This urge to recover "authentic" classical Chinese traditions was, of course, part of an emerging movement known as *searching-for-roots literature*, a movement that was itself a reaction to a love for Western literature. It found its best expression in A Cheng's novellas *The King of Chess (Qi wang)*, *The King of Forest (Shu wang)*, and *The King of Kids (Haizhi wang)* and in a number of regional literatures such as "literature of western Hunan Province" (*Xiangxi wenxue*), as represented in the works of He Liwei, "literature of Jiangsu and Zhejiang Provinces" (*Wuyue wenxue*), as represented in the works of Li Hangyu, and "literature of western regions" (*xibu wenxue*), as represented in a variety of works in fiction, reportage, drama, and film. Starkly stated, the goal of "searching for roots" was a native Chinese literature wholly free from Western influence. Yet paradoxically this new indigenous trend engendered heated controversies about the "Chineseness" of specific elements of the new literature, which were grounded in fundamental issues involving correct understanding as well as misunderstanding of Western literary traditions.

At the same time searching-for-roots literature was becoming a rising genre, it was challenged by a more vigorous generation of Chinese modernism as represented by the experimental works of Liu Suola and Xu Xing. Their experiments with unpunctuated sentences, psychological explorations, and fragmented and reversed time schemes were viewed as strong reactions against realism and parochialism and as inescapable results of misunderstanding Western modernism. Commenting on Liu Suola's novella *You Have No Other Choice (Ni bie wu xuanze)*—a modernist-like story describing the everyday routine of a group of cynical college students—Liu Xiaobo pointed out that Liu Suola borrowed only superficial features from Western modernism such as black humor. Her characters do not express a modernist sense of the absurdity of life. The loneliness, indifference, and cynicism in Liu Suola's work belong, on the contrary, to the May Fourth realist tradition in which the dissatisfied Chinese people were partially awakened to the necessity for social change. The escapism reflected in Liu Suola's work, Liu Xiaobo further claims, goes back to the Daoist philosophy that regards "non-action" (*wuwei*) as the perfect state of human beings in harmony with the universe.[61] What Liu Xiaobo implies is that to read Liu Suola's work as Western modernist is to misread literary traditions in both the East and the West, both modern and traditional.[62]

Yet such misconceived modernist works played an important role in the ongoing battles between "indigenous Chinese" and "Western"-oriented writers. A voice of *différence* was consistently expressed by several established writers who remained popular precisely because they still somehow belonged to the predominantly realist tradition of an earlier period. The realist writers at that time such as Zhang Xianliang, Jiang Zilong, Liu Xinwu, and Zhang Chengzhi still appealed to a large group of readers with their social concerns and their quotidian, yet elegant and natural prose styles. This realist approach defamiliarized the reader's "horizon of expectations" based on Western models and renewed from time to time the lost capacity of readers for older Chinese literary conventions. As if to compete with modernist and provincial trends, realist writers updated their approach in order to make an old tradition look new. A good example is Zhang Xianliang's novella *Half of Man Is Woman* (*Nanren de yiban shi nüren*), which probed deeply into the repressed social and sexual life of a group of political prisoners in the Mao era.[63] His daring and detailed depictions of sexual desire and its consequences—a forbidden subject barely touched on in the past—won him a large following in the realist tradition. By doing so, Zhang Xianliang paradoxically embraced the Western tradition, which was then understood in China as emphasizing sexual and private experience, as we have seen in the *menglong* debate. The desire to make things "new" was, of course, self-deceiving, since what the Chinese writers believed to be new turned out only to be old, returning either to the Chinese or to the Western traditions, or a combination of both. Literary history, then, has to be constantly misread in order for latecomers to claim that they have made things new.

This somewhat sketchy account of certain episodes in contemporary Chinese literature provides us with enough data for understanding contemporary Chinese literary production and its reception, and its relation to Western traditions. One can perhaps argue that Chinese writers in the last decade have been motivated by opposing desires, to forsake what is indigenous to Chinese culture in order to incorporate into it apparently alien elements, and, on the other hand, to repudiate alien, Western elements in order to create things more original than one's immediate predecessors. It is the dynamics of Occidentalism that have played an important role in the formation of contemporary Chinese literary and cultural history. Underlying these opposing desires are fundamental acts of misreading and misunderstanding, not only of the Western literary tradition *per se* but also of the indigenous Chinese tradition as well. The history of the most recent Chinese literature can thus be analyzed as a dynamic process mediated between earlier literary traditions and the individual talents who tried to surpass these traditions in the cross-cultural arena.

In terms of T. S. Eliot's theory, the development of contemporary Chinese literature can be outlined, at first glance, as a fierce and seemingly irreconcilable battle between tradition and individual talent. The three literary movements in contemporary China—urban modernism, searching-for-roots or regional literatures, and traditional realism—were all motivated by the desire to make things new. Urban modernism, for instance, declared its originality by appealing to Western modernism, as shown earlier in the brief discussion of Liu Suola's novella *You Have No Other Choice*. In a similar manner, regional literatures claimed their "personality" by reacting against such Western trends, as demonstrated in urban modernism, and developed their own regional style with local dialects and characters, as in the case of Gao Xingjian's play *Wildman*. Traditional realism, likewise, further explored its own imagination in updating the realist approach in order to make an old tradition look "new," as shown in Zhang Xianliang's novella *Half of Man Is Woman*. Yet, despite its claims of individuality and originality, socialist realism could at best merely conform to earlier literary traditions, such as the May Fourth movement and classical literature, which it had tried so hard to misunderstand in order to exert "revisionist ratios." Thus the *menglong* poets had to resort from time to time to the Chinese classical poetic tradition while embracing Western traditions; the novelists and short story writers who advanced urban modernism had to constantly tell their Chinese stories in Western style. Regional literatures could not survive without using mythical, folkloric, and cosmological images—elements of Chinese traditional culture. Yet these Chinese stories had to be narrated with a modernist sense of time and space initially explored by Western modernism. Similarly, the writers of the socialist realist school had to modernize their stories with Western concepts while still pledging its allegiance to the May Fourth movement and to the classical tradition. Literary history, then, has to be constantly misread and misunderstood in order for the latecomers to claim that they have made things new.

By way of concluding this chapter, I would like to emphasize that the story of *menglong* poetry as recounted here illustrates the way Chinese literary production of the early post-Mao period—and the critical and poetic discourses associated with it—is conditioned by a misunderstanding of twentieth-century Western modernism. I hope I have shown that such acts of misunderstanding are to be appreciated, not regretted as an expression of Occidentalism or of a self-imposed act of Western colonialism, since they offer one way to understanding the larger arena of Chinese-Western literary relations. Such a perspective, in contrast to the traditional quest for correct reading and the commonplace privileging of understanding, views misunderstanding as a legitimate and necessary factor in the making of literary history and of cross-cultural literary relationships. In speaking this way, I mean to evoke a conception of misunderstanding that is *sociological rather than epistemological*. By talking about acts of misunderstanding, I do not mean to suggest the preexistence of an epistemologically grounded proper or correct understanding of the text or a literary movement to which a misunderstanding can be opposed. I hope that it has become apparent that my argument strongly rejects such a claim. By "misunderstanding" I mean a view of a text or a cultural event by a receiver community that differs in important ways from the view of that same phenomenon in the community of its origins.[64] Misunderstanding in this paradigm is the natural result of a cultural dialogue between readers both within and between cultures who attempt to analyze, in the words of Barbara Johnson, "the specificity of a text's critical difference from itself" in light of their own specific place and time in history.[65] Indeed, in this model for studying the role of misunderstanding in cross-cultural literary relations, there is no such thing as understanding without embodying in the same term a self-understanding or reunderstanding, which is also to say a misunderstanding if conceived from the traditional point of view. Or to reverse the same argument, there is no such thing as misunderstanding without an admission that this misunderstanding is the only way to understanding.

By "misreading" in this study, I mean *reading, rereading, writing,* and *dialoguing*. It is a *reading* of the text that is radically different from a mere discovery of the "verbal meaning" according to the author's logic, attitudes, and world, as postulated in the Hirschian model. In cross-cultural literary study in particular, misunderstanding refers to a *reading* or *rereading* of a foreign text that departs radically from a so-called "proper" and "correct" understanding in its culture of "origins." If we expand Roland Barthes' view of a "writerly text," we could say that misunderstanding is also an act of *writing* or *rewriting,* in which a foreign reader "writes" a text of his own—producing a reading of the text according to his own cultural and literary experience without merely accepting the meaning already given, thus dismantling the foreign text into an endless plurality and openness to a free play of *différence*.

By "misunderstanding," I also mean an act of dialogue between text and interpretation, between past and present, and perhaps most importantly in the study of cross-cultural literary relations, between individual readers and their various social and historical formations. In this dialogue, the foreign reader imagines a question, looks for an answer in the text from another culture, and comes up with a misreading as a solution to his question. Acts of misreading and misunderstanding are mechanisms with which literary production and literary reception can be dialectically and dialogically mediated between different cultural and literary traditions.

To further stress the central role of misunderstanding in the formation of literary history and its process of canonization, I would like to argue that acts of misunderstanding were in the first place categorized as such by a ruling ideology as improper and erroneous. It is the will to power on the part of the ruling ideology that decides for us what a "truthful" discourse is and what a "proper" way is for understanding such a truthful discourse. The function of an official discourse, therefore, is not so much

to assert as it is to exclude, to keep what is contrary to the culturally sanctioned forms from being said, or to prevent the end results of misreading
and misunderstanding from being produced. Acts of misunderstanding
carry out an anti-official task that points to those very oppositional values
of truth that have been ideologically excluded from the past tradition as
illegitimate claims. These acts can thus be regarded as a central act of a
Foucauldian archaeological search for the formation of a new literary history—one that delineates the "surface disorder of things."[66] They can also
be explored as concrete ways in which readers as individuals assert their
own values, or their own ways of understanding and reunderstanding. A
study of the dichotomy between understanding and misunderstanding of
literary texts will therefore reveal for us how a system of constraints was
established in which certain norms, values, and literary practices were
sanctioned in order to dismiss others as erroneous.

In cross-cultural literary studies, furthermore, the study of the political
and ideological functions of the misconception of the Other in a particular culture—be it the Orient or the Occident—can help us explore fundamental ways in which the official history, official culture, and above all,
official discourse that constitutes and validates them, are being challenged in the disguise of a counter Other. Occidentalism and Orientalism
of whatever kind can thus be explored as inseparable parts of a political
exercise of power that celebrates the individual's desire to dominate his
own discourse against the constraints of a monolithic official culture. The
uses of the West as a counter Other in post-Mao cultural and literary debates play a seminal role in the political and ideological defamiliarization
of the institutional truth valorized as such by the dominant cultural tradition within contemporary Chinese society. In either case, it is the particular Chinese cultural and ideological conditions that make the uses of
Occidentalism possible and meaningful. To misread a foreign Other is for
many a way of exposing a kind of ideological impress on truth in one's
own literary and cultural traditions, or a kind of political impress on a
proper or correct understanding of such truth. Occidentalism in these
contexts disrupts the traditional habits of thinking in the Orient and
forges a new way of understanding traditional values.

Chapter Four

A *Wildman* between the Orient and the Occident

Retro-Influence in Comparative Literary Studies

Our discussions of *He shang,* the Chinese reception of Occidental theater, and the Chinese debate on *menglong* poetry in post-Mao society have demonstrated that in twentieth-century literary study it is impossible to separate Oriental and Occidental traditions.[1] Certainly one can no longer talk about Ezra Pound and his modernist poetics without mentioning his Chinese "parental tradition." Neither can one discuss the *menglong* debate without exploring the theory and practice of Pound and other Western predecessors. Indeed, to a marked extent, one can claim that Chinese literary and cultural studies are tied unavoidably to their Western counterparts. For sinology, then, world literature and culture can no longer be ignored or assigned a secondary status as mere source or influence. Neither should they be simply labeled as expressions of Occidentalism and hence dismissed as acts of cultural imperialism.[2] Especially in view of the increasing exchanges between cultures, sinology cannot exist without Western contacts and apart from the contexts of Western texts. Neither is it possible to speak of a Western tradition that is uncontaminated by things Chinese. This situation points to yet another important aspect of the way that Occidentalism can be viewed, in certain cases, as a positive and liberating force in recent Chinese literature and culture.

Let me cite a single example from literary history. Maxine Hong Kingston's *The Woman Warrior* may seem to be one of the first Chinese American novels to make a major impact on twentieth-century American literature. Yet *The Woman Warrior* is popular among Western readers not because it offers descriptions of a minority, or peculiarly Chinese experience, or because it expresses a kind of Orientalism from the particular point of view of Chinese American people, but rather because the Chinese experiences are depicted, in the words of King-kok Cheung, "in a mode that reflects their own multicultural legacies." Kingston's seemingly Chinese accounts are typically Western, since she has "instated [herself] in the American tradition by hitting upon a syncretic idiom at once inherited and self-made."[3] The latest addition of Asian American writings to American university curriculums further proves the necessity and inevitability of cultural diversities that bridge East and West.[4]

Yet Kingston's self-articulation of both Western and Chinese experiences is by no means a new invention. Long before Kingston, Ezra Pound's reading of Chinese poetics, or his "expressed Orientalism," was already inseparably tied to the Occidental tradition itself. It is in this sense that we say the poetics of Pound and of *menglong* are both Chinese and Western, both Oriental and Occidental; they are inclusively both and hence exclusively neither. In order to fully understand a so-called "Chinese" tradition, therefore, one must look at how the very Chineseness of this tradition has already been "contaminated" by Western readers in the course of cross-cultural literary reception. To understand what Chinese culture has meant in the West for generations of sinologists, then, one must encounter the reception or mis-reception of Chinese culture by Marco Polo, Matteo Ricci, Arthur Waley, and Gary Snyder, to name only a few. In a similar manner, a thorough study of any contemporary Chinese literary phenomenon has a great deal to do with Occidental influence, as we have demonstrated in the discussion of *menglong* poetry. To simply dismiss the works of Pound, Kingston, Polo, Ricci, Waley, and Snyder as expressions of Orientalism is to erase a better part of cross-cultural literary history and communication.

To further illustrate the unavoidable and inevitable mutual contaminations in the literary traditions and political histories between the Orient and the Occident, I will recount, in this chapter, an interesting episode in the reception of a contemporary Chinese play—Gao Xingjian's *Wildman* *(Yeren)*. This play has been reviewed by diverse reading communities as, paradoxically, at once Chinese and Western, classical and modern, and traditional and avant-garde. I hope to demonstrate through the discussion of this reception history that it is often difficult for us to determine the cultural identities and national origins of a particular play, text, or event. Above all else, I want to point out that it is impossible to fully appreciate Gao's play without coming to terms with its roots in both Occidentalism and Orientalism.

In May 1985, when Gao Xingjian premièred his third play, *Wildman*, in Beijing, China, its critical reception was quite different from that of his first two plays, *The Alarm Signal (Juedui xinhao)* staged in 1982 and *The Bus Stop (Chezhan)* in 1983.[5] Both of his earlier plays have been immediately recognized by audiences and critics alike as being strongly influenced by the Occidental modern theater—by such people as "the formidable French dramatist" Antonin Artaud, and "a host of writers and theorists of the Theater of the Absurd."[6] The Occidental critics themselves were unanimous in reviewing *The Bus Stop* as "the first play to introduce elements of the Theater of the Absurd to a Chinese audience."[7] Their Oriental counterparts, likewise, expressed a similar view. One of the striking features of *The Bus Stop*, as Wang Xining argues in a review in *China Daily*, is that it successfully "dissected modern Chinese urban society in a manner reminiscent of Beckett's *Waiting for Godot*."[8]

However, *Wildman*, the third of Gao Xingjian's plays to be performed, elicited a quite different critical response. On the one hand, some Chinese and Western critics were still enthusiastic about its Western style and technique. Others, however, pointed to a new turn in Gao's interest, one that drew on the rich resources of Chinese theatrical traditions. Those who celebrated the return of Chinese tradition in Gao's latest play insisted that it owed its success mainly to its endeavor to enrich "the range of expression open to artists in all performing arts in China."[9] What is perhaps most interesting in this critical disagreement is the way that it heightens our awareness of the complexity of cultural relations underlying the play and leads to what has already become a central question on the part of the audiences—is the play primarily founded on a Chinese or a Western model? This disagreement about *Wildman* has been further complicated by Gao's own declaration of intention, which stresses his allegiance to the classical Chinese traditions in theater. In the postscript to the published form of the play, Gao explains that *Wildman* is an attempt to realize his ideal of establishing a modern theater by drawing on traditional Chinese opera, characterized by its artistic techniques of singing (*chang*), speech (*nian*), acting (*zuo*), and acrobatics (*da*).[10] Interestingly enough, in characterizing this native Chinese tradition Gao uses the term "total theater" (*wanquan de xiju*)—a term that cannot fail to suggest to the Occidental consciousness the work of Antonin Artaud, and indeed the whole *Gesamtkunstwerk* tradition since Wagner—to designate his ideal theater in which artists would easily "recover many Chinese artistic techniques already lost in the last century."[11]

Gao explicitly claims in his postscript that *Wildman* does not attempt to win over its audiences by the art of dialogue, a feature that he associates with the Occidental drama; instead, he claims, it seeks a full employment of the traditional Chinese operatic, and above all, nonverbal technique of dance, music, images, costumes, and make-up to compose a "dramatic symphony" consisting of several different themes, themes that overlap harmonies and disharmonies in order to fashion a "polyphony" (*fudiao*). In *Wildman*, therefore, both language and music are used in such a way that they create a "structure of multi-voicedness" (*duoshengbu jiegou*).[12] Just as a symphony seeks to create "a total musical image," Gao asserts,

Wildman "tends to realize a total effect of action through multi-voicedness, counterpoints, contrasts and repetitions."[13] For the visual aspect of the play, Gao symphonizes a "multi-layer-visual-image" through the use of dance, flashback scenes, shadows, and movements. Actors in *Wildman*, therefore, must possess the skills required by the traditional Chinese theater: they must perform at once as a dancer, a singer, an acrobat as well as a speaking character. Costuming, our playwright demands, should not only be strikingly bright in color, as is required by the traditional theater to enhance the visual and physical effect on the senses of the audience, but it should also "truthfully reflect the local color of the mountain area along the Yellow River," which provides the play with its geographical background. A faithful portrayal of the primitive and natural lifestyle of the mountain folks, Gao Xingjian insists, is crucial for a successful production of the play. Fortunately, Lin Zhaohua, the Beijing director of *Wildman*, fundamentally preserved the Chineseness that Gao Xingjian so painstakingly spelled out. *Wildman* was for the most part performed in the local dialect of the Sichuan Province, with episodic scenes that remind one of the traditional "opera-drama sketches" (*zhezi xi*), interspersed with local folk songs, national minority dances, and Han epic singing.

In addition to the traditional Chinese theatrical conventions consciously explored both by the playwright and the director, *Wildman*'s dramatic structure and theme can also be seen by many as indigenously Chinese. Unlike Occidental drama, which usually has an Aristotelian plot with a beginning, a middle, and an end, *Wildman* carries no obvious storyline. Instead, the play consists of a series of diverse episodes peopled by nameless characters who move in a more or less definite and identifiable place. The play is set in contemporary China in the rapidly vanishing virgin forest of Sichuan Province, where some scientists and local people believe in the existence of wildmen, a sort of manlike monkey believed to offer the much-sought missing link of traditional evolutionary theory. A nameless scientist, designated in the script only by the character name "ecologist," goes into the forest to undertake research on wildmen, hoping to learn not only something about these strange "living fossils," but also about the preservation of a natural environment that he believes is ultimately linked to the continuation of the human species.

In his travels, the ecologist encounters lumberjacks and local officials who make their fame and living by destroying the forests. By virtue of their occupations, these people threaten the living environment of wildmen and thus come into conflict with the ecologist. In the course of the play the ecologist also sets himself in opposition to other city-dwellers, who, like him, have ventured into the forests for the sake of tracing the whereabouts of the wildmen, though motivated by purposes quite different from his own. A newspaper man—again the character has no name

and is designated only by his profession—for instance, is merely interested in hunting for exotic news to please his readers in the city. Similarly,
scientists representing opposing sides in a scholarly debate are at work
collecting data only to prove or disprove the existence of the wildmen.
Unlike the ecologist, they have no interest in investigating living creatures
and their environmental conditions in order to protect them. They bribe
innocent local people, especially children who cannot even understand
the issues at stake, in order to prove the existence or nonexistence of wildmen, thus bringing about quarrels, disputes, and disharmony in the
mountain village in which peace, unity, and harmony once prevailed.

Another episodic strain of the play concerns a school teacher who de-
votes all his time and energy to attempting to rescue an epic of the Han
nationality—the only one of its kind—by writing down the performance
of an old and dying epic rhapsodist. This epic, *The Song of Darkness* (*Hei'an
zhuan*), recounts the history and development of the Han nationality from
the time of its childhood—when it first began to separate itself from the
wildman—up to the present time. Because of its nature and scope, the
ecologist and teacher believe that the epic should be regarded as a national treasure, "as precious as panda and wildman" for the Chinese
nation. Integrated into this episode are other overlapping themes and
subplots that deal with problematic and still-unanswered questions in
contemporary China about love, marriage, ethics, custom, tradition, corruption, and even ideological issues left unresolved from the Cultural
Revolution.

Wildman is infinitely more complex than I have just indicated here, but
enough has been said, I think, to indicate the ways in which the play offers a view of an exceedingly problematic world full of contradictions and
disharmonies. Yet unexpectedly at the end of the play we are offered an
episode that is connected with many of the play's diverse concerns. Here
a wildman appears to a little boy in a dream. The wildman imitates the
boy's language and gestures, dancing with him happily and running with
him into the depths of the forest. While these actions are taking place, the
audience becomes increasingly aware of the epic singing and folk music,
which grows louder and more prominent in order to furnish an accom-
paniment to the scene. Central to this moment in the play's economy is a
silent but nonetheless real dialogue between this child of modern man
and his predecessor, between "mankind and Nature."[14] The image created
by this last scene—one so strongly suggestive of harmony and cosmic totality—is clearly related to the spectacular ending of the traditional Chinese theater, which overwhelms its audience with a *Gesamtkunstwerk*-like
effect of singing, dancing, and acting. Such an ending thematically em-
braces the Daoist vision of a harmony between nature and culture. It provides its audience with a catharsis that supposedly enables them to come

to grips with the cosmic and mythological forces in the universe. As Lin Zhaohua, the director of the play, points out, ultimately *Wildman* is about harmony, "a harmony between people and their nation, a harmony among people themselves. It urges the audience to think about its relationship to nature and to culture, especially ancient culture."[15] It seems clear, then, that both in form and content *Wildman* can be viewed as a contemporary restoration of the theatrical, cultural, and philosophical traditions of China.

Yet it would be a serious mistake to see in Gao Xingjian's play only a recuperation of indigenous Chinese traditions. As the terminology in which Gao describes his play suggests, anyone acquainted at all with the modern Occidental theater will not fail to be immediately impressed by the way it seems to exploit conceptions of the theater strikingly similar to those advocated by Antonin Artaud's notion of total theater and Brecht's theory of epic theater. Artaud spent much of his life longing for a theater of "a pure action," of a latent force beyond rational speech or language, beyond "a written text" and a "a literary tradition." He therefore sought to create a theater wholly unlike the Occidental theater of his time, which would present an "archetypal and dangerous reality, a reality of which the Principles . . . hurry to dive back into the obscurity of the deep."[16] Artaud believed that fixed text, language, reason, order, even civilization itself with its attendant traditions were barriers to the human spirit. He therefore called for a theater of physicality that was to create "a metaphysics of speech, gesture, and expression" that would be capable of throwing its spectators back to real life, not by imitation or illusion, but by a mystical, ritual, primitive, or archetypal spectacle of signs and gestures that would speak for the antirational elements in human experience. Artaud therefore proposed to resort to mass spectacle, providing his audience with a "pure experience" that would create a sensation of totality, awakening in them an intuitive force, expressed in a theater of the body that is not subversive of the mind. If language is used at all, Artaud observed, it must be a language beyond words and senses capable of evoking that which cannot be spoken. He therefore called his ideal theater "a sacred theater" because it was to have "the solemnity of a sacred rite. . . ."[17] Thus the Artaudian theater aims at a more universal, primordial force deeper than any psychological or social reality, a force that touches on "an idea of Chaos, an idea of the Marvelous, an idea of Equilibrium."[18]

All of these Artaudian elements of the theater can easily be identified in *Wildman*. By means of nonverbal elements, *Wildman* provides for its audiences the kind of total and physical experience that Artaud so painstakingly emphasized. The time span of 8,000 years in *Wildman's* action, and the invocation to Pan Gu, the Chinese god of creation in primordial times, suggest to spectators a cosmic view of the universe. The sharp contrast between the nonverbal, primitive wildman and the verbal but confused, problematic modern man shocks the spectators and thus attempts to throw them into a mystical and ritual experience deeper than any psychological or social realities. The world of *Wildman* extends far beyond the boundaries of anything uniquely Chinese and modern; indeed, the play seems finally concerned with issues that belong to a world much larger than the one codified in the details of its dialogue, language, and setting. Much of the effect of the play is achieved by its spectacular physicality, which seeks to create the sensation that Artaud claimed would simultaneously "touch on Creation, Becoming, and Chaos."[19]

To a large extent, then, *Wildman* can be seen as having participated in the traditions of the Artaudian theater, with its "passionate equation between Man, Society, Nature and Objects."[20] All of these concerns are crystallized in the last scene, where, as we have already seen, amidst a mixture of pantomime, mimicry, and musical harmonies and rhythms, a wildman, the image of the primitive and the natural, dances with a little boy, a symbol of the childhood of civilization. At the end of the play, we are provided with the following stage directions:

> (They [the WILD MAN and XI MAO, the little boy] run onto an elevation at the back of the stage. XI MAO does a forward roll. He turns expectantly to the WILD MAN, who clumsily does the same. XI MAO runs, calling to the WILD MAN, who runs after him. They play hide and seek. XI MAO looks out from behind a stone. The WILD MAN sees him and runs toward him. XI MAO runs toward the elevation, and the WILD MAN follows. Gently, music starts and their movements slow down until they look as though they are in a slow-motion film. Then they perform a dance. XI MAO is nimble, the WILD MAN clumsy. When XI MAO and the WILD MAN play together, the WILD MAN tends to copy XI MAO's movements, even when in slow motion. The WILD MAN should always have his back to the audience. XI MAO draws back into an area of light at the rear of the stage, in front of a backdrop depicting the forest. All performers enter wearing masks, each mask expressing a different shade of emotion. The "happier" masks should be in the center of the stage. All move slowly toward the WILD MAN, to the rhythm of the LUMBERJACKS' dance and the melody from the song of the TEAM OF SISTERS. The sad cries of the OLD SINGER are heard, gradually fading out. XI MAO is seen and faintly heard saying, "Xia, xia, a shame, xia, xia, xia, xia. A shame, a . . . shame." Curtain.)[21]

All these and other theatrical conventions seek to put the audience into a state prior to language and therefore to help them to break away from the intellectual subjugation of language, thus conveying to them a sense of "a new and deeper intellectuality which hides itself beneath the gestures and signs, raised to the dignity of particular exorcisms."[22] With this world of "the Absolutes" and "the invisible" cosmic forces, *Wildman* also meets the demands of the Artaudian theater for a "religious ritual," and therefore moves toward what Leonard Pronko has characterized as "that meeting point where human and nonhuman, meaning and chaos, finite and infinite, come together."[23]

Yet as soon as one has identified the similarities between *Wildman* and its Western counterparts, he/she may also be tempted to "decenter" this claim by arguing for the opposite "truth." Artaud emphasizes the dynamics of action, the higher forces of violent physical images that "crush and hypnotize the sensibility of the spectator," even to the extreme exclusion of any copy of life or any concern with any aspect of social and psychological realities of human society.[24] Within his limited concern of trying to restore theater "to its original direction, to reinstate it in its religious and metaphysical aspect," Artaud makes explicit that his theater must "break with actuality," and that its object must not be to "resolve social or psychological conflicts" or "to serve as battlefield for moral passions."[25] The function of theater, he insists, is to express objectively certain secret truths that "have been buried under forms in their encounters with Becoming."[26] For him, language, tradition, and the theatrical masterpieces of the past are responsible for the decline of Western theater. If a contemporary public does not understand *Oedipus Rex*, he argues, it is the fault of this ancient Greek play, not of the public, since the latter has learned too well what the theater has been—it dealt with the themes of incest, morality, destiny, falsehood, and illusion. A concentration on social realities and their attendant problems is regarded in the Artaudian model as being outside of the legitimate concern or the proper domain of theater.

While recognizing Artaud's claim of "total theater," one can also be immediately brought face-to-face with the ways that *Wildman* rejects some of Artaud's conceptions. There can be no denying that *Wildman* is firmly foregrounded in contemporary Chinese society; its concerns, as we have noted earlier, are occasional in the best sense of that term. Though its episodic structure forecloses the possibility of its offering a solution at the end of the play, *Wildman* nonetheless raises in a striking and even direct way unanswered and perhaps unanswerable questions about love, marriage, tradition, bureaucracy, science, morality, and even the current national preoccupation with ecology and environmental protection. It is true that *Wildman* can be categorized as a traditional dance and music drama, and that in this sense it seems to meet Artaud's demand for a form of theater that is closely related to ritual and religious ceremony. But it is also true that its basic thematic matter is concerned with a conflict between nature and culture that is specific to this moment in late twentieth-century Chinese history. In fact, precisely because these thematic concerns are historically so far removed from the primitive and the ritual experience in which they are theatrically mediated to us, the play is able to go beyond

Artaud by combining that sense of primitive "magic culture," which Artaud's theater seeks, with much that is not Artaudian—an entirely modern world with its own social and psychological dimensions.

The same dichotomy between that which belongs to the total theater and that which does not becomes apparent when we attempt to locate the kinds of theatrical gestures and movements that *Wildman* employs. From one perspective the play's actions seem to harken back to that moment when religious ceremony emerged from its purely ritualistic origins and was transformed into the beginnings of what we know as theater.[27] On the other hand, the play's action goes beyond the first becoming of the theater, beyond anarchy, chaos, and disorder. It includes elements that we associate with a "mature" theater by a combination of the verbal with the nonverbal, the actual with the imaginative, the social with the psychological, and above all, the sensational with the individual. *Wildman* is at once descriptive and narrative, spectacular and physical. The opposing claims for the traditional and the modern, the intellectual and the physical, seen by Artaud as irreconcilable or as hurled against each other, are here coupled together. It is perhaps in this sense that *Wildman* realizes the ideal of a theater of totality that goes well beyond Artaud's demands and in which the basic disparity between Self and Other, subject and object, reason and sensation, language and signs are finally engulfed and united.

But Artaud is not the only Occidental theoretician of the drama whose work is relevant to *Wildman*. Gao Xingjian observes in his postscript that *Wildman*'s emphasis on the *mise en scène* and spectacle does not aim at creating verisimilitude. It is intended, on the contrary, for reminding its audience that it is acting, not real life. Gao therefore expressly requires that masks be used in the production of *Wildman* in order to emphasize the dichotomies, contradictions, or multi-voicedness within the characters. At the outset of the play, the actor who plays the part of the ecologist steps out of his character and exhorts his audience to enjoy the play fully without worrying about the whereabouts of the actors, who may sometimes be sitting in the audience. There need not be, he implies, any barriers between the world of the audience and the world of the play. In the middle of the play, for instance, the ecologist takes off his mask more than once in order to assume his identify as an actor. In this guise he recites poems and provides background information. Earlier, at the outset of the play, he even narrates what would normally be regarded as stage directions and theatrical comments. In this way, the actor openly disowns his character. He calls attention to his many different roles—the ecologist, the actor who plays the ecologist, and the stage director. He is, he reminds us, at different times all of these figures, and yet he is really none of them. Such a discourse seems intended to prevent us from establishing an emotional identification with the ecologist or any other character. All of these devices, of course, are suggestive of the Brechtian theater. In his article "*Wildman* and I," Gao Xingjian openly admits such a Brechtian influence, especially as concerns the now classic theory of the "alienation effects."[28] For him, Brechtian distancing devices help break down the conventional notion of the theater as representation of real life.[29]

But just as our observation of the Artaudian elements in *Wildman* led us also to see the presence of the opposite, so here too the Brechtian nature of the drama is undercut in our very act of recognizing its presence. Brecht's alienation effects aim basically and fundamentally at keeping the spectators from being emotionally involved so that they can intellectually contemplate the possible meanings of the play. In the postscript to *Wildman*, however, Gao Xingjian paradoxically specifies that the director should create in the play a kind of "cordial and warm atmosphere" in which the actors directly communicate with the audience (a Brechtian technique as well as one that recalls the works of Thornton Wilder) so that the audience can feel free and happy to participate in the total experience of the theater as if they were enjoying an entertainment during a festival (a notion that is un-Brechtian). The production, our playwright specifies, should also leave enough time between each act so that the audience is able to think intellectually, reflect, and ponder over what they have just experienced sensationally. *Wildman*, therefore, offers its audiences a multiple, polyvalent, and even contradictory experience in which the body and mind, the primitive and the contemporary, the universal and the local, the sensational and the intellectual, the subjective and the objective, the illusionary and the actual are all joyfully united and combined. It is at once Brechtian and anti-Brechtian, Artaudian and anti-Artaudian. It is at once both and yet neither.

Gao Xingjian's *Wildman*, therefore, presents to us a strange and yet stimulating dramatic phenomenon that raises in a radical way a number of theoretical issues that are not restricted to "the dramatic" in the narrower sense of that term, but that reach into the history of literature in general, and, as the rest of this study will suggest, into the theory and practice of comparative literature in particular. Gao's play raises questions of the first order about the canonical practice of influence study, which "posits the presence of two distinct and therefore comparable entities: the work from which the influence proceeds and that [to] which it is directed." That is to say, cross-cultural literary studies, as a comparative discipline, have depended largely on what Ulrich Weisstein called "the key concept in Comparative Literature studies," which are characterized as one-to-one relationships between "emitter" and "receiver" texts.[30] At first sight, the general concerns of this chapter—the relationship between one national theater and another—seem to be the proper subject for this kind of influence study.[31] On further consideration, however, these concerns challenge the validity and legitimacy of such a traditionally conceived influence study. It will be the burden of the rest of this chapter to set the discussion on *Wildman,* and the Western dramatic theories on which it seems to draw, within a broader context of some critical discourse of canon formation in the West and the East alike.[32] A clarification of this notion will eventually help us better approach the problems of Occidentalism and Orientalism in cross-cultural literary studies. It will become clear that the various expressions of Occidentalism in contemporary Chinese theater and of Orientalism in Western receptions of traditional Chinese theater are invariably inseparable parts of formations of literary histories both in the East and in the West.

I would like to comment first on the notion of influence on which this study has sought to shed light. I propose a study of *retro-influence* across different historical periods in which a rereading of an *emitter* text in light of its modern parody can generate a misreading or rereading of its emitter text. My account of *menglong* poetry offers such a typical case of retro-influence, in which the Chinese readers' reinterpretation of Pound's modernist emitter texts as something Chinese in turn generated a new way of understanding *menglong receiver* texts as truly classical. In this way, both the emitter text and the receiver text changed and exchanged meanings in the reader's acts of reading, misreading, writing, and dialoguing within different cultures and across various historical periods. This study of misconception of the Other—be it a literary text or an image of a counter Other in the form of the Orient or the Occident—in light of reception theory further testifies that literary misunderstandings of both home and foreign cultures, on the part of both the author and the reader, are as much the production of literary reception as they are of literary production, and that readers' horizon of expectations are at least as decisive in literary systems as authors' intentions.

In the dialectical process of naturalizing text—be it "original" or "parodic"—there can be no origin, no beginning, no end, no privileged text. Both the original and parodic text can be considered as precursors to be appropriated in relation to each other. Both can be read either ironically or earnestly, either parodically or originally. There is no hierarchy in any scheme of reading, but only an exchange of shared properties of *différences.* In this way, the historicity of literary studies, the interactions between reading experiences in past and present, will all be constantly set in a dialectical process within a new historical context. An old text, therefore, will always appear to be new for the reader who responds to the past work in order to outdo or refute it. From this perspective, it is possible and perhaps even fruitful to pursue influence study in a backward way— not from text A to B to C in a linear or chronological manner, but from C to B to A in a retrogressive or achronological order. Consequently, the

emphasis of influence study will no longer be placed on a "proper understanding" of either the source text, or the parody text, but rather on the
reader's creative act of misreading and misunderstanding with regard to
his changed and changing perspectives in a new historical context.

In a similar and yet slightly different way, our discussion of *Wildman*
has also suggested that it is exceedingly difficult, if not impossible, to determine which cultural tradition evoked in *Wildman* is the emitter and
which is the receiver. Did the Chinese traditional theater influence the
West by means of Brecht's theories, which, as Brecht himself admitted,
were derived in some sense from Chinese sources? In that case, Chinese
theories of drama made a detour through Western cultural traditions only
to come back to China to exert an influence on the modern Chinese theater. Or did Artaud and Brecht influence Gao Xingjian, who, in turn,
found in the West that which had been lost in the contemporary Chinese
theater? Or is it, more simply, the case that Gao reached back into his own
national traditions to create his play?[33] To raise this question is to see that
it is impossible simply to posit the "presence of two distinct and therefore
comparable entities."

The question of whether *Wildman* is indigenously Chinese or character-
istically Western can here be seen as deeply puzzling. *Wildman* appears to
be both, and yet it can never be proven to be one or the other. As we have
seen earlier, *Wildman* has been received as the most Chinese play Gao had
ever written, and this very Chineseness in the play has even been declared as part of his own attempt to rescue modern Chinese theater from
being too influenced by its Western counterparts. However, as soon as we
have discovered everything that can be identified as Chinese, these characteristics can immediately be decentered in order to prove just the opposite claim. We might, then, be tempted to say that the play is the product
of Western influence. But clearly the matter cannot be solved so facilely.
Furthermore, talking about the play's Westernness invites yet another
confusion: one perceives at the same moment the Artaudian as well as the
anti-Artaudian elements, the Brechtian as well as the anti-Brechtian characteristics. It seems pertinent, therefore, to first of all attempt to decide, if
ever possible, the nature of Chineseness and of Westernness in the context
of our discussion before we can even begin to discuss, and therefore to
challenge, the concept of the relationship between an emitter and a receiver in the traditional mode of influence study.

But our difficulties are not due solely to the complications and contradictions embedded in the term *Western dramatic tradition*. The words *Chineseness* and *the Chinese theater* have a similarly long and seemingly confusing history, and this history is further complicated, in the West at least,
by generations of Western critical acts of misreading and misunderstanding. As Leonard C. Pronko has pointed out in his *Theater East and West*, the

traditional Chinese theater "has had a history of singular miscomprehension and misinterpretation in the West."[34] When one considers the sheer difficulty of communicating across cultural boundaries, it is easy to agree with Pronko's claim. But Pronko's implied evaluation of misunderstanding and misreading, common as they are, constitutes at best only a partially valid view of these activities. Pronko assumes that miscomprehension and misinterpretation are undesirable activities, and that it is the task of cross-cultural studies to remove them. But as a good deal of literary theory has insisted, misreading and misunderstanding are not wholly negative actions. On the contrary, for critics like T. S. Eliot and Harold Bloom, these once-thought negative activities are the means by which literary history is made and—I would add—cross-cultural communication takes place.

For Eliot, Bloom, and a number of other theorists, Western literary production is motivated by an intense quest for the novel, or the apparently new. "Strong" writers and critics seek ways of escaping—or apparently escaping—the parental tradition in which they have been formed, and the processes of misunderstanding and misreading provide a convenient means for their accomplishing this goal.[35] In an attempt to say what apparently had not been said before, some Western writers turned, and continue to turn, to the novelty of exotic literature. But the exotic literature was not studied or appropriated for its own sake. Rather it was appropriated and reworked for the apparent strangeness that it offered to audiences. Yet paradoxically, the otherness could not be allowed to remain as otherness, for in order for Western audiences to appropriate it in some way, the strange had to be made familiar; the exotic had to be domesticated, even if in the process it ceased to be exotic. To take the specific example of classical Chinese drama, eighteenth-century European writers, motivated by an "anxiety of influence," turned to it as a source of novelty. Yet in order to make these strange texts comprehensible, they misread them by making them conform to traditions of Western drama. Let us first of all consider briefly the process by which this paradoxical transformation took place.

Fan Xiheng, in his essay "From *The Orphan of Zhao* to *Orphelin de la Chine*," describes a brief history of the transformation of a Chinese Yuan drama into Western dramatic repertory. This Yuan drama, known as *The Great Revenge of the Orphan of Zhao* (*Zhaoshi gu'er da baochou*) is attributed to Ji Junxiang and was first performed in China around the late thirteenth century. The same play was later rewritten by another anonymous author under the title of *The Story of the Orphan of Zhao* (*Zhaoshi gu'er ji*). According to Fan Xiheng, Ji Junxiang's Yuan drama was first translated into French in the 1730s, which brought about other translations into English, German, Italian, and Russian. This Chinese Yuan play has thus over the centuries inspired several generations of Western dramatists such as the English writer William Hatchett, who adapted Ji's Chinese story into his *The Chinese Orphan,* and the Italian playwright Pietro Metastasio, who wrote his own version of *Eroe chinese,* to name only a few. A better-known case, of course, is Voltaire's *Orphelin de la Chine,* which was so successful in its Paris première that it was immediately translated into Italian and English.[36] Yet, this process of transformation was by no means one-sided. Not only did the original Chinese text inspire Western readers, the Chinese readers, upon reading their Western peers' recreation of the Chinese text, did not hesitate to translate Western texts back into the Chinese language again. During World War II, for instance, a Chinese writer by the name of Zhang Ruogu translated Voltaire's French play, which was originally based on Ji's Chinese orphan story, into an abridged prose version "in order to raise the morale of the Chinese people in their struggle against Japanese invaders." Incidentally, Zhang Ruogu's translation of Voltaire's French play was initially inspired by Zhang Yuanji's *The Integrity of the Chinese Nation* (*Zhonghua minzu de renge*), a narrative published during the period of the Sino-Japanese War in the 1930s, in which Ji Junxiang's orphan story was retold as an earlier example of the Chinese people's "great revenge" on invaders.[37]

Among several Western transformations mentioned above, one of the earliest creative misreadings was William Hatchett's well-known adaptation of the Chinese Yuan drama, published in England in 1741. He attracted an audience and gained a certain amount of notoriety for himself with his new work using a borrowed exotic story and a foreign "parentage." Having to cope with the burden of his own Western tradition in order to find for himself a place in his own cultural tradition, Hatchett creatively changed the Chinese Yuan play and actually presented it as "an English neo-classic play, observing the unity of time," although in fact his Chinese parental story takes place over some twenty-five years.[38] It is clear that the so-called Chinese influence at this early stage of cultural exchange amounts to nothing more than an expression of the European taste for the exotic, the different, the dissimilar, which must be garbed in Western clothing to make it attractive. The image of the Chinese theater that Hatchett's work suggests is only a Westerner's own arbitrary interpretation, or better, misinterpretation and misunderstanding of it. It is a product of a Western search for things anew—foreign manners, interesting events, plots, or characters of curiosity. Yet in Hatchett's play these elements end up conforming to the older taste and tradition for which they were intended as an antidote, in this case, the neoclassical theater.

But this account is not complete in itself. It does not represent a naïve moment in Chinese-Western cultural relationships. Attempts like Hatchett's to offer to the West such distorted and creative introductions of the

Chinese theater decisively shape the literary and theatrical expectations of the Chinese theater. The word *Chineseness*, therefore, inescapably meant for the eighteenth-century English audiences something drastically different from what it meant in its original Chinese setting. Such audiences found in the Oriental theater what on first consideration seemed unavailable in their own. And these exotic elements found there and introduced to the West were always strikingly different from their Chinese sources in terms of style, symbol, movement, make-up, and music. Even in the twentieth century, despite increasing knowledge of and contacts with China and Chinese scholars, the reception of the Chinese theatrical tradition by figures like Bertolt Brecht was still to some extent inspired by a creative misunderstanding of the ingenious works of his own tradition and appropriated in such a way as to enrich his own limited space of imagination. Since Brecht appeared on the historical scene much later than predecessors like Hatchett and Voltaire, he explored with much more vigor than his predecessors what had been left unsaid in the Western reception of the Chinese theater. In order to outwit his Western predecessors, Brecht's creative misreading of the Chinese dramatic tradition was, to employ again the mechanism described in T. S. Eliot's "Tradition and the Individual Talent," a conformation and submission to the two cultural traditions. At the same time, it was an oedipal rebellion against both.

Brecht's surrendering to the Chinese parental tradition has been documented extensively both in Chinese and Western scholarship. Ding Yangzhong, a Chinese scholar who popularized Brecht through his many articles and lectures in post-Mao China, describes Brecht's interest in the philosophical thoughts of Mo Zi, Confucius, and Mao Zedong; he "chose the parabolic form to treat philosophical matters" in *The Good Woman of Setzuan* and performed in the Berkiner Ensemble *Hirse for die Achte (Millet for the Eighth Army)*, which was an adaptation from the Sino-Japanese War play *Food (Liangshi)*.[39]

It is also a well-known fact that Brecht's concept of *"Verfremdungseffekt"* first occurred in his essay entitled "Alienation Effects in Chinese Acting," written in 1936, occasioned by Brecht's seeing Mei Lanfang's performance in Moscow. Brecht was deeply impressed by the Chinese actor, "who constantly keeps a distance between himself, his character, and the spectator. . . . Consequently he never loses control of himself; his performance is constantly on a conscious, artistic level with all emotion transposed."[40] As Pronko rightly points out, however, the alienation effects that Brecht believed to have been inspired by Chinese acting arose in fact from his unfamiliarity with the Chinese stage conventions. Chinese spectators were expected to react emotionally to the sad or happy scenes in Chinese opera. Pronko has also observed that Chinese music, originally used to appeal to deep emotions, was interpreted by Brecht as a means to break illusion and to establish distance.[41] In terms of the present argument, Brecht rebelled against his Western predecessors, who first introduced the Chinese theater to the West, by pointing out those elements of Chineseness in the Chinese theater that they failed to perceive. He was therefore no longer interested in the exotic foreign manners and curious plots, as were his predecessors. Above all, he was not interested in seeing the Chinese tradition as neoclassical and hence Aristotelian. His notion of alienation effects which he believed to be Chinese, however, as Pronko has rightly pointed out, inspired only his own version of reading the Chinese performing arts. His unfamiliarity with the Chinese theater, however, paradoxically made him conform to the earlier tradition of his own Western predecessors, who revised Chinese theater in order to make it palatable to the West.

Seen from this perspective, Brecht is no "genius," nor is he a "strong" poet. For all of his attempts to do otherwise, he only repeats what his Western predecessors had done in the past. His misreading and misunderstanding of the Chinese theater, and as the result of it, his creative notion of alienation effects are no more ingenious than his parental interpretation of a Chinese neoclassical drama. At the same time his deliberate misuse of the Chinese theater also betrays him as an unfaithful critical offspring to his Chinese ancestors. By an act of creative treason, however, he paradoxically fits himself into the foreign tradition as well as his own. He is therefore making a place for himself only by standing on the shoulders of ancient "giants" in two traditions.

Like Brecht, Gao Xingjian proved himself no exception in following this law of the formation of the literary history. Coming quite late on the scene of the Chinese dramatic imagination, Gao Xingjian tried to create things new for his Chinese audience by introducing exotic and foreign theatrical traditions in his first two plays—*The Bus Stop* and *The Alarm Signal*. As we have already mentioned, his first two plays were heavily influenced by such Western dramatists as Artaud and Beckett. Later on, however, when Chinese audiences were overwhelmed by a flood of Western-style theater on the Chinese stage after the open-door policy was instituted, Gao Xingjian abandoned his Western critical parents and returned to his own Chinese traditional theater. In this way he was able to meet the changing literary expectations of his Chinese audiences. Yet for reasons already suggested, his return to his own cultural tradition was in fact a return to the Chineseness of a theater that had earlier appealed to his Occidental peers and was appropriated by them through acts of creative misreading. Once again, then, we have an example of belatedness in which a poet of a later generation, in this case Gao Xingjian, felt compelled to find things new in a foreign culture, a culture that in fact is originally his own.

In this case Gao was fortunate enough to live in a time and place that enabled him to embrace simultaneously his own literary tradition—"to recover many Chinese artistic techniques already lost in the last century"—at the same time he could use something newly created by his Western predecessors out of *his* (Gao's) own tradition. As a critical playwright owing debts to numerous predecessors from more than one culture, Gao benefits from both cultures, the Orient and the Occident, and from both historical heritages, the ancient and the modern, but he does so in a way that depends on misreading and misunderstanding in every case and in every direction. Because of this he ends up belonging exclusively to neither the Orient nor the Occident, but inclusively to both.

These remarks help us to understand the strange reception history of *Wildman* in which the play has been claimed by more than two national parentages in the critical reviews. On the one hand, *Wildman* can be perceived as a Chinese play only by those whose dramatic expectations are confined to a knowledge of the traditional Chinese theater. On the other hand, however, it can be regarded as being influenced by the Occidental theater only by those who take the concepts of Artaud (who was influenced by Balinese drama) and Brecht as purely Occidental, thus disregarding their debts to their Oriental traditions. In both cases, however, readers from different cultural backgrounds, with different dramatic and cultural expectations, inevitably receive *Wildman* differently. It could not be otherwise, even for those Chinese readers knowledgeable in Occidental theater or for Orientalists who are acquainted with Chinese dramatic traditions. Just as producers of texts can only write from within their own historical and cultural space—and in Gao's case, that space was both Oriental and Occidental in paradoxical ways—so readers can only read on the basis of their own place in history.

Chapter Five

Wilder, Mei Lanfang, and Huang Zuolin

A "Suggestive Theater" Revisited

There is yet another way in which Gao Xingjian's *Wildman*, his most "Chinese" play, can be viewed as essentially "Western," for it seems to stand under the undeniable "influence"—as that term is used in the most conventional sense—of one of the most important plays of the twentieth-century theater in the West, Thornton Wilder's *Our Town*, an "Oriental" play itself according to its own Occidental reception. Here we see an important fact about the formalistic features in contemporary Chinese theater—it is inevitably conditioned by various Chinese receptions of Occidental dramatic traditions and practices. Both the formal and thematic parallels between *Wildman* and *Our Town* are indeed striking. Just as *Our Town* opens with a stage manager placing a table and several chairs here and there on an empty stage to remind the audience that they are about to watch a play, not an illusionary real-life story, at the beginning of *Wildman*, the ecologist likewise explains to the audience that the play's action is not limited to the stage itself; it occurs everywhere in the theater, including the audience's seats. Furthermore, the play is divided into three chapters, not three acts, since there will be no curtain in his show.

Each chapter may overlap with another, the audience is told, and may itself be further divided into many different episodes. In the second chapter of *Wildman*, for instance, the mountain villagers are summoned for a meeting, in which a reporter urges the villagers to provide him with detailed information as to where and when they had indeed seen a wildman and, if possible, what its appearance and speech are like. This is then followed by a series of seemingly unrelated episodes without any change of scenery: a school teacher attentively transcribing a rhapsodist's performance of *The Song of Darkness* for the preservation of this oral history of the Han nationality; a little boy telling his mother about seeing a wildman not long ago; a village girl expressing her sympathy and concern for

the ecologist, who had just been through a painful divorce; the rhapsodist telling the ecologist the tragic story of an old scientist who had
been persecuted to death during the Cultural Revolution for trying to
rescue wild birds in the forest; the scientist tricking the little boy into admitting that, contrary to his early statement, he did not see a wildman after all, thus proving the scientist's theory of the impossible existence of
wildmen. The final two episodes shift from an arranged marriage for the
village girl by her poor parents to her desperate confession of love to the
ecologist, who declines her devotion in order to bury himself in his writings, which call for a national campaign to protect nature from the im-
pending destruction of culture and civilization.

These individual events in *Wildman* aim at presenting a panoramic
view of history and reality. With a rearrangement of different time
schemes of past, present, and future, *Wildman* possesses an epic dimension that moves freely in time and space in order to remind its audience
that it is a play about everyone's story, not just about one person's particular problem in a specific historical time. The ecologist's current concern
with environmental protection, for example, is integrated with the rhapsodist's narration about the scientist who had sacrificed his life for the
protection of nature. In a similar way, the ecologist's unsuccessful marriage to a city-dweller, who resented his working all-year-round in the
desolate wilderness, is blended with an innocent village girl's love for
him and her tragic show of being forced into an arranged marriage by a
patriarchal society. All of these nonlinear episodes provide telling contrasts between a problematic modern civilization and a primitive setting;
the contrast is further intensified by depicting the deteriorating fate of the
forest, unprotected from advancing industrialization. By juxtaposing
what he calls "contrapuntal oppositions" (*duiwei*), Gao Xingjian fore-
grounds diverse historical perspectives, rather than a specific aspect of
contemporary reality. In between the pauses among the episodes
(*jingchang*), Gao Xingjian observes, "the audiences are left with some time
for themselves to experience the sensations and to think and reflect upon
them."[1]

Such a theatrical theory and practice is markedly parallel to Thornton
Wilder's *Our Town*. Like Gao Xingjian's *Wildman*, *Our Town* also achieves
an epic dimension by showing, in the first act, a flashback scene in the
past—"a day in our town," May 7, 1901—an ordinary day that every one
of us lives.[2] In this connection, Donald Haberman has drawn attention to
Wilder's "constant and deliberate rearrangement of time,"[3] which "reminds the audience that what they are witnessing happened a long time
ago."[4] When the Stage Manager first introduces Mrs. Gibbs, he adds that
"Mrs. Gibbs died first—long time ago in fact."[5] Thus Wilder provides the

audience with what Haberman has called "glimpses of future time—that is, time after the action of the play but before the time of the audience" in order to remind the audience that what happens on the stage has little to do with the chronological progression of historical time, thus preventing ordinary events "from being overlooked."[6]

Although the culturally significant events described in *Wildman* drastically differ from those seemingly ordinary incidents located in turn-of-the-century New England in *Our Town*, both plays share the same timeless, episodic structure that presents a macrocosmic view of life. Both plays constantly employ the present time of the play to symbolize a larger temporal view of past, present, and future. Both plays are about much more than simply Emily and George, or an ecologist and a wildman. Both are in some sense stories of mankind, of its historical past and contemporary reality, its struggle against time and its efforts to preserve natural life and cultural heritage. Both plays are narrated by insightful observers—the Stage Manager and the Ecologist—who convey to the audience their apprehensions over the meaning of life and their nostalgic feelings for an irreversible past.

Once we recognize the connections between Gao Xingjian's and Wilder's play, we encounter the same problem that we dealt with in the previous chapter on the problematic and paradoxical relationship between Gao Xingjian and Brecht—who had been influenced, first and foremost, by the traditional Chinese theater but was somehow taken by the Chinese audience as being foreign and hence exotic. We are confronted with the same issue: was Wilder's *Our Town* a precursor text that influenced Gao Xingjian, or did both Gao Xingjian and his American counterpart simultaneously resort to their parental traditions—that of the Chinese traditional theatrical conventions that had taken a detour to the West in the last century? In fact, if we examine the history of the reception of *Our Town* in the West, we realize that there is another similarity between the two plays in question: like *Wildman*, *Our Town* has been claimed by two theatrical traditions—that of the Orient and that of the Occident.

In the first place, Wilder's *Our Town* has been celebrated as the most genuinely American (as distinct from Americanized European) play. Richard H. Goldstone, for example, has emphasized that Wilder's play broke with the nineteenth-century European "realistic-naturalistic theater" as represented by Ibsen and Chekhov's models.[7] *Our Town* has thus been considered as the first national play that has its "roots in the cultural soil of America,"[8] since the story appeals to millions of Americans "as a reassurance" of the "American dream."[9] Despite the attempts to trace Wilder's roots from his European precursors in Shakespeare, Ibsen, and the Greek and French dramatists, it was Theodore Dreiser, and Gertrude

Stein, his own contemporary Americans, who are cited most frequently as immediate influences on Wilder. Claus Clüver argues, for example, that although there are striking parallels in scenic techniques between Wilder's *Our Town* and André Obey's adaptation of Shakespeare's *The Rape of Lucrece* for the Compagnie des Quinze, staged in 1931, Obey's play did not serve as an important source of influence on Wilder's *Our Town*, but "merely confirmed what he had already found, possibly inspiring its extension in some small ways."[10] Indeed, Wilder is considered so native American that he could even provide the effect of American folk art—"the play comes before the audience like a late nineteenth-century painting depicting the customs, colors, and destinies of ordinary lives."[11]

Yet as soon as we have accepted the claim that *Our Town* is a typical American play, we can immediately argue for just the opposite view—that it also seems to have strong ties, especially formal ones, to the theatrical conventions of classical Chinese opera. Describing Wilder's plays as a "world of pretense," Rex J. Burbank has argued for Wilder's Orientalism as a protest against his own Occidental dramatic traditions—that he attempted to consider the "slice-of-life" realism of his times by depreciating the value of conventional scenery and sets. Thus, Burbank says, Wilder was supported "by the Chinese, whose classic drama has only placards to identify the scenery."[12] Donald Haberman has studied in some detail the relationship between Wilder's play and the Oriental theater, especially that of the Chinese theater: Wilder grew up in China when his father served as Consul General both in Hong Kong and Shanghai. There might indeed be a direct connection between Wilder's theatrical conventions and that of Mei Lanfang, "the great Chinese actor, and certainly one of the great actors of any style," who visited the United States in 1930. "Fortunately, Wilder," Haberman tells us, "as someone's guest, saw one of Mei Lanfang's extraordinary performances," when the tickets for his performance were virtually unobtainable because of the Chinese actor's great popularity among American audiences.[13] Haberman even claims that Wilder demanded from the actors of *Our Town* that "they attempt something like Mei Lanfang's expression of a reality above the casual and a permanence beyond the brevity of each performance."[14]

Commenting on the possible effect of what is known as the "symbolic" aspect of Mei Lanfang's art on Wilder's use of pantomime, Haberman argues that "in *Our Town* it was used mainly to express the chores about the home: preparing meals, stringing beans, mowing the grass, delivering the paper and milk—activities that are repeated either daily or seasonally."[15] In this connection, Haberman cites Wilder as saying in 1938: "The theater longs to represent the symbols of things, not the things themselves."[16] This statement coincides with a frequently argued claim that the essence of traditional Chinese operatic theater is "symbolic." The traditional Chinese theater is, of course, characterized by a lack of realism in perform-ance and a scarcity of scenery. The location of different scenes can simply be announced by dramatic characters, described by pantomimes, or un-derstood by different arrangements of simple properties—a table may symbolize, at different times, a family sitting room, a scholar's study, a judge's court, or even indicate a city wall overlooking a battlefield. Walk-ing in a circle around the stage may symbolize a long journey, or, shout-ing "I demand you come down" suggests two characters at two levels of a house, although both of them are acting on the same floor of the stage.

Obviously, the text of *Our Town* employs, in many different ways, a sim-ilar symbolic mode of dramatic action. The play begins with an "empty stage"—"No curtain. No scenery," as the text puts it. Four chairs are used throughout the play in the most economical way, serving as kitchen and Main Street in Act One, which symbolizes, in the words of Wilder's text, "Daily Life"; as benches in Mrs. Gibbs's garden, dinner table and an iron-ing board in Mrs. Webb's home, and church pews in Act Two, which sym-bolizes "Love and Marriage."[17] In Act Three, "Death and Rebirth," ten or twelve chairs are placed in three openly spaced rows to represent graves in a cemetery. All other props are represented by the pantomime of the ac-tors. Within this bare setting, Emily moves freely from her new grave back to her "twelfth birthday," an event which leads to the painful realization of how unaware she had been of the meaning and wonder of daily life when she had a chance to fully enjoy it. Throughout the play, Wilder gives careful, deliberate stage directions to make sure that the required pan-tomimes are performed in a specific manner:

> Dr. Gibbs has been coming along Main Street from the left. At the point where he would turn to approach his house, he stops, sets down his—imag-inary—black bag, takes off his hat, and rubs his face with fatigue, using an enormous handkerchief.[18]

The word "imaginary" is repeatedly used throughout the play—both Joe Crowell, Jr., and Si Crowell hurl "imaginary" newspapers into door-ways[19] whereas Emily carries an armful of "imaginary" schoolbooks.[20] On this bare stage without many props and stage setting, Wilder successfully explores the "myth" and "truth" in art and life.[21]

The use of narrator–stage manager is another feature in *Our Town* that bears a pronounced similarity to Chinese operatic theater. This cross-cultural parallel escaped even the notice of Peter Szondi in his well-known study "The Epic as *I* as Stage Manager: Wilder."[22] In the tradi-tional Chinese theater, actors often present a straightforward exposition of character and event. When a character enters he usually announces his identity, narrates his background, and sometimes even

indicates what he intends to do at that particular moment of the ongoing play. Let us take for example the chief landmark of classical Chinese
drama entitled *Autumn in Han Palace* (*Hangong qiu*) by Ma Zhiyuan. This
play describes the sorrow of Zhaojun, the legendary beautiful woman in
a Han palace, who asks her lover-emperor to send her into exile to the
remote kingdom of the Tartars in order to keep peace on the Chinese
border. After a sorrowful farewell with her lover and her homeland, at
the end of the long journey to the frontier, Zhaojun drowns herself in a
river in front of the Tartar Khan. In the prologue, the Tartar Khan initi-
ates the play by an elaborate self-introduction: "I am the Emperor
Huhanya [Tartar Khan]. My ancestors have long lived in the desert ruling unchallenged all the land in the north. Hunting is our livelihood,
fighting our occupation."[23] At the onset of the play, he briefs the audience on his own position and his tribe's historical association with
China, thus foreshadowing Zhaojun's tragic fate at the end.

As if to imitate its Chinese counterpart, *Our Town*, likewise, opens with
an explanatory monologue by its principal character—the Stage Manager.
Slightly different from the first-person narration of his Chinese counterpart, however, Wilder's Stage Manager describes the title, the time, and
the place of the play in a third-person voice:

> This play is called *"Our Town."* It was written by Thornton Wilder;
> produced and directed by A. . . .
> The name of the town is Grover's Corner, New Hampshire,—just across
> the Massachusetts line: longitude 42 degrees 40 minutes; latitude 70
> degrees 37 minutes.
> The First Act shows a day in our town. The day is May 7, 1901. The time
> is just before dawn.[24]

The Stage Manager then gives a descriptive account on the daily routine
of the town and introduces characters with information on their past and
present. Before Doctor Gibbs appears on the stage, for instance, the Stage
Manager says: "There's Doc Gibbs comin' down Main Street now, comin'
back from that baby case. And here's his wife comin' downstairs to get
breakfast." Then, the Stage Manager moves immediately to narrating the
doctor's future—"Doc Gibbs died in 1930. The new hospital's named after him."[25] What fundamentally renders the Stage Manager's monologue
different from its Chinese counterpart is that, in addition to introducing
the background and characters, the Stage Manager also helps provide the
play with a kind of abstraction and historicity: he moves in and out of
stage actions, between various characters, historical eras, and geographical locales.

In Act One, for example, after his character's acting-out of day's events
in the morning, the Stage Manager interrupts the play by inviting a pro-

fessor to give a "scientific account" of "the meteorological conditions" and "anthropological data" of Grover's Corners.[26] This is then followed by a "political and social report" from Editor Webb, who even directly answers the audience's questions on the little town's past. A second interruption is brought about after the acting-out of the town's life in the afternoon. At this point, the Stage Manager looks back at the town from the future time after the play's enactment: many years later, he tells us, Howie Newsome still delivers milk as an old man; Mr. Morgan's drugstore is now "citified"; and the Cartwrights become richer and richer, etc. Then the scene shifts back to the evening life of the town. In Act Two, the Stage Manager intrudes upon George and Emily's wedding day by tracing back in time, first, "how big things like that began" and, second, "how the parents took it" as a way of representing "what Grover's Corner thought about marriage" as a whole.[27] In a more intriguing way, in Act Three, the Stage Manager stops the funeral scene by asking Emily to relive her twelfth birthday so that she will "see the thing that they—down there—never know,"[28] thus making Emily appreciate a seemingly unimportant day in her life.

As if to smooth out the historical abstraction in the play, the Stage Manager constantly breaks the illusion of the theater by playing different characters—as Mrs. Forest, who forbids George to practice his baseball on Main Street in Act One; as Mr. Morgan, who sells ice cream soda to George and Emily in Act Two; and as the church minister, who marries the young couple in Act Three. He also assumes, on a more symbolic level, the role of a journalist, a historian, a commentator, and above all, a philosopher, who talks about the "universal truth" that also relates to one's personal microcosm. He is, indeed, as Goldstone has noted, "a composite of what Wilder himself, by 1937, was becoming—or at least what he was role playing."[29] Seen in this light, therefore, we might conclude that on the one hand, Wilder's play is close to Chinese theatrical conventions, which emphasize a "fluidity" and a "plasticity"—a complete freedom in time and space. On the other hand, however, Wilder went beyond the Chinese tradition by adding an objective dimension to a subjective mode of narrative, thus rendering his play a blend of philosophical discourse.

To a great extent, then, the reception of Wilder's *Our Town* simply repeats *Wildman*'s story in a slightly different manner: similar to Gao Xingjian's play, which was confusedly viewed as under the impact of Brecht and of Chinese operatic theater, *Our Town*, likewise, replicates a story of mixed and diverse traditions frequently found in the history of cross-cultural literary studies. With both Oriental and Occidental characteristics, *Our Town* became a universal "little town," which, in the words of the dramatic character Rebecca in the play, is not just located in the

"Western Hemisphere," but also "on the Earth," within the "the Solar System," and in "the Universe."[30]

Yet Wilder's connection with Brecht is by no means limited to the sheer resemblance of his (Wilder's) play to that of Gao Xingjian. We mentioned earlier the interesting fact that Wilder saw the art of Mei Lanfang, who toured and performed in Seattle, New York, Chicago, Washington, D.C., San Francisco, Los Angeles, San Diego, and Honolulu for six months in 1930.[31] That was five years before Brecht saw Mei Lanfang's play in Moscow. Thus, though they came from different continents, both Wilder and Brecht were inspired by the same Chinese artist to create their own versions of Occidental epic theater. Or put otherwise, by embracing the same Chinese artist in different historical moments, they both returned to their own ancient roots in the Occident—that of the non-Aristotelian theater of Shakespearean drama, which allies itself with the open form of Corneille, Pirandello, Chinese opera, and more recently, of Gao Xingjian, to which Wilder's *Our Town* bears striking similarities both in form and theme. Moreover, this Occidental adaptation of traditional Chinese theater in the 1930s was somehow paradoxically rediscovered by the post-Maoist Chinese writers in the 1980s, and was "mistakenly" regarded as Western, foreign, exotic, and hence desirable.

Yet Wilder was not the only American who was deeply touched and profoundly educated by Mei Lanfang's performance. Stark Young, a well-known American drama critic, also watched Mei Lanfang's performance in 1930. In his subsequent articles, Young noted specifically the Greek and Elizabethan parallels to Chinese operas: the theater mechanics of the Elizabethans, the similarities to Greek type scenes—"the Parting Scenes, Recognition Scenes, Ironic Scenes"—and the ancient Greek method of "rising into music where the pitch of the dramatic idea and emotion seems to require it."[32] Indeed, according to Mei Shaowu, Mei Lanfang's son, Young was so impressed by Mei Lanfang's acting that he called on Mei in person in New York and told him that in seeing the performance style of Chinese opera, it "suddenly dawned on him that he had found the key to the solution of some problems in his theatrical studies." It is through the classical Chinese art that "he was able to understand the ancient Greek theater even better."[33] Once again, we see an intriguing case in which things Chinese in literary studies could be interpreted as things Western. More importantly, a tradition as remote as the Chinese opera can serve to help Westerners reunderstand and reappreciate their own traditions. In a similar manner, Gao Xingjian "misread" Brecht's theater as at least partially "non-Chinese," and only because of its unfamiliarity judged it helpful in bringing theatrical innovations to his own modern Chinese theater.

In this regard, Tao-Ching Hsü seems to have missed the point when he comments that Mei Lanfang's 1930 American performance was a financial success, but without "any noticeable influence" "so far as the dramatic art is concerned."[34] This is certainly not true if we look at its warm reception by Stark Young and others. Perhaps it takes time for different generations of readers, such as Brecht, Young, and Wilder, to assimilate Mei Lanfang's art into that of their own traditions, as this study has attempted to demonstrate. More recently, for instance, in an insightful essay, Georges Banu has these words to describe the lasting influence of Mei Lanfang's 1935 Moscow performance on European theater artists such as Stanislavsky and Meyerhold, Craig and Brecht, Eisenstein and Piscator, Tairov and Tretiakov:

> Attending a performance is not necessarily synonymous with *seeing* one, but the great majority of the artists present at Mei Lanfang's Moscow performance did see, for they came with expectations—expectations born of artistic crisis. Each in his own way had already made a case against the Western actor and envisioned his regeneration, if not, as Gordon Craig was demanding, his extinction. "Let him be annihilated if he is condemned, but let him be revived if he is viable," proclaimed Meyerhold without hesitation. . . . Their search, not always clearly formulated, found a model in the theater of China. Mei Lanfang was living proof that the actor they envisioned could exist. What is the theater if not the incarnation of the invisible in a corporeal body? The Chinese actor was the crystallization of their visionary spirit.[35]

The traditional Chinese theater is, of course, not the only source of inspiration from the Orient for Western modern dramaticists. Earl Miner, in his *The Japanese Tradition in British and American Literature,* has chronicled Stark Young's early attempt in the 1920s to synthesize the theories and practices of Arthur Waley, Ezra Pound, and W. B. Yeats concerning the Japanese nō drama in order to "advocate a new style of acting and production" on the American stage.[36] Among those who had joined efforts with Young in this connection were, according to Miner, Brecht, who adapted "the stylized forms and philosophical content of nō to the Expressionistic stage," most noticeably in his *Der Jasager* and *Der Neinsager,* and Wilder, "whose *Our Town* is in part indebted to nō for its bare stage technique and whose one-act plays often have a stage-manager who speaks the thoughts of the characters like the chorus in the nō."[37] Miner considers Wilder "the most successful American playwright to use nō techniques."[38] One should not be surprised, though, to learn from Miner that here, too, Wilder's "deep interest" in nō is once again coupled with the "major influence" of the "bare stage" technique in the "theater of Elizabeth and Philip II and III," as Wilder himself had confessed.[39] Miner provides an excellent orientation

to the way that Wilder used diverse theatrical traditions—both the Oriental and the Occidental—to forge his own dramatic style; one could not
overestimate the dynamics of the process of cultural exchange through
which Wilder rediscovered in the nō theater the dramatic conventions of
his own ancestors of the Elizabethan age, the values only reaffirmed by,
paradoxically, a remote Oriental tradition.

On a broader level, the similarities between the Chinese, Greek, and
Elizabethan theaters have been explored to some extent by both Western
and Chinese scholars. One of the most extreme viewpoints on the subject
has been expressed by J. Dyer Ball, who quotes from an unidentified
source the claim that the "whole idea of the Chinese play is Greek. The
mask, the chorus, the music, the colloquy, the scene and the act, are
Greek." According to this source quoted by Ball, the Chinese took the
Greek idea and "worked up the play from their own history and their
own social life." In fact, it is suggested that the whole conception of the
drama is essentially alien to Chinese culture, with only Chinese details
and language transplanted into a foreign form.[40] Although this view lacks
solid historical evidence, it nevertheless represents an interesting attempt
on the part of a turn-of-the-century Western China-watcher who tried to
introduce China to the West from an overtly Eurocentric perspective.

A more substantial work of comparison between Chinese theater and
its Western counterparts can be found in Tao-Ching Hsü's *The Chinese
Conception of the Theater*—a major study in English of the Chinese operatic
theater—with insights into Western dramatic models. More than 100
pages in this study, for example, are devoted to such topics as "the Chinese and the European theater," in which the Chinese theater is compared
with Greek acting space, formal elements, emphasis on skill and training,
dance and music, and festival atmosphere. Similarly, the Chinese theatrical tradition is also contrasted with the *commedia dell' arte* in popular taste,
conventions, improvisation, types of characters with the Elizabethan theater in open stage, lack of realism and scenery, sensuous elements, audiences; and finally, with other European theaters such as the medieval
drama, the Roman and Restoration theater, the Italian and German opera,
the Spanish and French drama in their use of fool and jester, the machinery of court pageant, and the convention of men playing women. Tao-
Ching Hsü's erudite study is another classic example of how Chinese
studies, even in the classic field, have to be considered with things Western, even ancient Western.

The process of cultural exchange under discussion here is a two-way
street. Just as a foreign literature seemed to clarify Wilder's relationship
to his own tradition, so the foreign reception of an art can inform its indigenous readers who previously overlooked it. Again, Stark Young's
view of the Beijing opera provides a striking example. In contrast to the

conventional view of Beijing Opera as essentially symbolic, Young suggested, to the contrary, that Mei Lanfang's art is essentially realist. Young was astonished at "the precision of its realistic notations and renderings." It was, for him, a kind of realism that amounts to "an essential quality in some emotion, the presentation of that truth which confirms and enlarges our sense of reality."[41]

Interestingly, Young employs a significant phrase—"essential quality"—a word that seems to coincide with the prevailing theory of the "suggestive theater" (*xieyi xiju*) advocated by Huang Zuolin, one of the most celebrated drama directors and critics in contemporary China.[42] Throughout thirty years of teaching and directing both Occidental and Chinese plays, Huang Zuolin gradually developed a dramatic theory of his own, a theory that he first articulated in 1962 and gradually popularized in the 1980s.[43] He argues that the future orientation of an ideal Chinese theater should be envisioned as a combination of three divergent views on theater, those of Mei Lanfang, Stanislavsky, and Brecht, or a combination of the best of the dramatic traditions inherited both from the Orient and Occident. For him, the basic difference between the three traditions lies in the fact that "Stanislavsky believed in the 'fourth wall,' Brecht wanted to demolish it, while for Mei Lanfang such a wall did not exist and so there was never any need to pull it down, since the Chinese theater has always been so highly conventionalized that it has never set out to create an illusion of real life for the audience."[44] Huang Zuolin thus concludes that "realism is the keynote of Western art" and suggestiveness, of Chinese art.[45]

Huang Zuolin explains that in the 2,500 years of the development of world drama, the illusionary theater that preaches the "fourth wall" has a short history of only ninety-three years. Yet "even during this brief period not all playwrights have used it."[46] Brecht, among others, "proposed to pull down the fourth wall and dispel the illusion of real life."[47] Brecht thus criticized Stanislavsky's method of "transmutation (of the actor into the character played)" as "a very tricky business," since no actor, Huang Zuolin quotes Brecht as saying, can "enter his part for long" without exhausting himself and then starting "to imitate some superficial characteristics of his role."[48] Yet these difficulties, Huang Zuolin reports Brecht as saying, "would not beset an actor of the traditional Chinese drama who simply 'quotes' from his character" artistically from beginning to end.[49] Huang Zuolin thus sees the ideal Chinese theater of the future as a combination of the "four inner characteristics"—that of the suggestiveness of life (not "as it is," but as it is "extracted, concentrated, and typified"), of movements ("human movements eurythmicized to a higher plane"), of language ("not plain vernacularism" but "lyrical"), of *décor* ("not the real environment but one designed to achieve a high artistic

level")[50]—with the four outer features of Chinese theater, namely, fluidity, plasticity, sculpturality, and conventionality.[51] It is in this regard that
Huang Zuolin exemplifies Mei Lanfang's art as the "ideal method" to
"combine the 'inner technique' of introspection with the outgoing techniques of representation" by way of analyzing what Brecht had reflected
already on the Chinese theater and its counterparts.[52]

This discourse, with its free movement from the Occidental dramatic
tradition to that of the Oriental, proves that the study of a Chinese theater
seems to require Western elements to reach its full articulation. In order to
analyze Mei Lanfang's ideal method, for instance, Huang has to deal with
Stanislavsky, the Russian artist whose theory has influenced the modern
Chinese stage, and ultimately, with the German "parentage" in Brecht,
whose impact on Chinese theater in the twentieth century has already
"contaminated" at least two generations of Chinese dramatists such as
Huang Zuolin and Gao Xingjian.[53] Yet, in the process of formulating his
own dramatic theory and practice, Huang Zuolin, like many strong readers, has to scrutinize Brecht's "misreading" and "misunderstanding" of
the Chinese theater. Huang Zuolin once described how during his studies
in England in 1936, he experienced "great national pride" upon reading
the English translation of Brecht's 1935 essay on Mei Lanfang's performance. It is worth noting a historical coincidence here: Huang Zuolin first
encountered a Western appropriation of the Chinese opera six years after
Wilder saw Mei Lanfang's performance in America, and two years before
Our Town's première.

Despite his admiration for "Brecht's power of observation," however,
Huang Zuolin realized that Brecht "had only a fleeting 'glimpse' of the
Peking opera, and therefore inevitably made some inaccurate observations."[54] Huang points out, for instance, that Brecht believed that a general in Chinese opera would "wear as many ribbons on his epaulettes as
the regiments he commands." In fact, he actually wears "four little flags
regardless of the size of his army."[55] Huang Zuolin further observes that
"mistakes like this are of no importance"—Brecht is still a "great artist"
whose "comments on Mei's exquisite performance are an indication of his
deep insight into the Chinese theater."[56] For Huang Zuolin, then, Brecht's
misreading of some details of Chinese art does not prevent him from understanding the main feature of Chinese theater—the famous *Verfrem-
dungseffekte*—an ideal theater for which both Brecht and Huang Zuolin
were searching at approximately the same historical time. Huang, therefore, "cannot but admire these apt and precise comments made by Brecht,
who was a foreigner and who had had very limited contact with China's
performing arts."[57] It is precisely because of this foreigner's acts of misunderstanding, however, that the history of modern Chinese theater and
its theoretical premises in the past thirty years have taken on a different

tone—a fact that can be verified by the coming into being of Huang Zuolin's paradigmatic theory of the theater and its being put into practice by his numerous students, including Gao Xingjian. It is thus no exaggeration to claim, as did Adrian Hsia, that Brecht's seeing Mei Lanfang in 1935 "also marked the beginning of Brecht's reception in China," without which much of the history of modern Chinese drama and its theory would have been written quite differently.[58]

Indeed, when examining closely the reception of Huang Zuolin's 1979 production of Brecht's *Life of Galileo* in China, one may not be surprised at Huang and his codirector's own readings of the play, which could probably account for the success of the production. Indeed, as I have already described in chapter 2, *Life of Galileo* was so popular among the post–Cultural Revolutionary Chinese audience that it ran for eighty productions, all with a full house. According to Chen Yong, the codirector of *Life of Galileo*, the popularity of the play lies in the meaning and message that its production team tried to deliver. For the Chinese audience in 1979, Brecht's play was about the coming into being of a new age—a peculiar Chinese interpretation, which "is particularly revealing after the crushing of the Gang of Four."[59]

This popular reception of Brecht may also help explain why, in contrast to the popularity of *Life of Galileo* in 1979 China, the Chinese production of Wilder's *Our Town* (*Xiaozhen fengqing*) in 1987 by the Beijing Experimental Theater did not arouse the same enthusiasm. To the best of my knowledge, there were only two brief accounts of *Our Town*, one of which focused, however, on its role as a Sino-American cultural exchange event, since it was directed by Lois Wheeler Snow, the widow of Edgar Snow, known as "a great friend of the Chinese people" during the revolutionary war period.[60] Only a stage photo of Emily and George's wedding was printed in *Drama Journal* in 1987 with a brief description of the play: "This play describes the ordinary daily events—through which one experiences the boundless universe—in a small town in America at the turn of the century."[61] One would perhaps assume that Wilder's "universal" story of a little town in New England in the twentieth century would have gained easier access to the Chinese people than a more remote story of Galileo. The audience's indifference to *Our Town*, of course, could also be attributed to the decline in theater attendance, or a "drama crisis" as some critics had then termed it, by the time of its production in 1987.[62]

This episode of cross-cultural literary history reveals to us once again how the meaning and the relevance of a text is reinterpreted by the particular receiving culture at different historical moments. Wilder's *Our Town* came relatively late in the Chinese theatrical scene, when audiences had already been flooded with an overdose of Western plays, including Shakespeare's *Romeo and Juliet* (1981, Beijing and Shanghai, in the Tibetan language), Arthur Miller's *Death of a Salesman* (1983, Beijing, directed by Miller himself), and Eugene O'Neill's *Anna Christie* (1984, Beijing), to mention only a few titles. Although Shakespearean plays were especially favored during this period, as I have recounted in chapter 2, there was by no means a lack of other foreign dramas appearing on the stage. Japanese, Indian, Soviet, Greek, French, and East European dramas were also performed in this period. This belatedness no doubt contributed to the inability of Wilder's at least partially "Chinese" play to attract a significant Chinese audience. Or perhaps, for some audience, its very "Chineseness" made it too familiar to appeal. Yet paradoxically, its partial "Westernness" can perhaps also bear at least part of the blame; whatever its merits, *Our Town* arrived at the wrong time in the wrong place, when things Chinese had been overtaken by numerous things Western. One found, for instance, Chinese theater full of foreign characters and costumes; Chinese bookstores crammed with bestsellers by William Faulkner or James Bond thrillers. Indeed, wherever one looked, the horizons of Chinese literary and dramatic expectations seemed drastically affected by things non-Chinese. Yet Wilder and Brecht's efforts to search for an ideal modern theater should not be regarded as merely a partial success. Apart from bringing on the horizon new theatrical conventions in the West, more significantly, they joined their efforts in contributing to the formulation of Huang Zuolin's concept of the suggestive theater, which has already established itself as an important school in Chinese theater.

Such remarks suggest that it is time to pause and consider the territory thus far traversed in this study of cross-cultural influences within a culture and across different cultures. From Shakespeare to his Chinese producers, from Pound to *menglong* poets, from Brecht and Artaud to Gao Xingjian, from Wilder and Stark Young to Huang Zuolin, for many Chinese writers, the tradition, in Eliot's sense of the term, is both the Chinese tradition and the Western tradition, both the Oriental and the Occidental. To claim that the Chinese is more traditional than the Western for a contemporary Chinese writer is to misconstrue in a very fundamental way the current Chinese literary scene. Eliot's philosophy concerning tradition and the individual talent, although it was developed solely with Western literature in mind, can provide fundamental insights into contemporary Chinese production and reception. From this perspective we can more "traditionally" separate the components of the current Chinese literary scene into Chinese and Western, but only in order to make clear how individual writers find themselves in profound conflict with both, as they seek for "originality" in order to make a place for themselves and their writings.

In our account of the *menglong* debate and of Gao Xingjian's controversial plays, for example, both the writers and their critics appealed to the Western parental poets as sources of imagination, only to realize finally that their resort to modernist tendencies was in fact a return to the "Chineseness" of a tradition that had earlier appealed to their foreign predecessors, and was thus appropriated by them through acts of creative misreading. Here again, then, we have an example of a belatedness in which later poets—in this case, post-Mao writers—felt compelled to find things new in a foreign culture, a culture in fact "originally" their own. Yet the post-Mao writers were fortunate enough to live in a time and place that enabled them to embrace simultaneously their own literary tradition and something newly "created" by their Western parental critics out of *their* own tradition. As latecoming critical offspring owing their debts to numerous traditions from more than one culture, the post-Mao writers benefited from both cultures, the Orient and the Occident, and from both historical heritages, the ancient and the modern. Yet they did so in a way that depended on misreading and misunderstanding on every hand and in every direction. Because of this, it seems fair to say, they end up belonging exclusively to neither East nor West, but conveniently to both.

The implications of this observation seem clear: what is important for us to pursue in our critical inquiry is the unending dynamics of interactions and interrelationships between traditions and individual talents, between literary production and literary reception. Needless to say, we cannot decline or even separate one "comparative entity" from the other. Neither can we fruitfully determine such things as *emitter, receiver, origin, beginning, causality, continuity,* and *canonicity.* Each term is inextricably tied to its opposite. There is no final reference, only shared properties of *différence.* Within that *différence* what is Chinese may appear as Western; what is Western may appear as Chinese. There is no ontologically grounded truth by which we can distinguish Chineseness from "Westernness." It is thus important to reiterate my argument that for sinology, references to Western literature and culture can no longer be simply dismissed as expressed acts of colonialist Occidentalism. Rather, all that is Other and alien to it—which is to say, all that is Occidental—must now be recognized and inscribed within its proper context.

If such claims seem surprising, they are also obvious. In twentieth-century cross-cultural literary study it is almost impossible to separate different national traditions. As our study has shown, Wilder's *Our Town* is regarded, on the one hand, as the most American play to mark the beginning of a national theater. On the other hand, we have also demonstrated how this very American play is indeed influenced by things Chinese, or at least could be read as basically an Oriental play.

Thus, it perhaps may not be an exaggeration to claim that a knowledge of the classical Chinese theater is required for an understanding of certain crucial features of a typical Western drama. In an equally paradoxical way, on the other hand, the traditionally isolated field of sinology, as we now look at it, has already undergone such a prolonged and complicated history of cultural exchange through a detour of various nations that it has already turned into one that is entwined with everything Western as well as non-Western. Just as the *menglong* movement cannot be meaningfully discussed without exploring its Western roots, twentieth-century Chinese experimental theater such as that explored by Gao Xingjian, and the theory and practice of Huang Zuolin's suggestive theater, would not make sense to us unless the critical content and vocabularies of Western theater of the absurd, epic theater, and total theater are brought into full play.

Chapter Six

Fathers and Daughters in Early Modern Chinese Drama

On the Problematics of Occidentalism in Cross–Cultural/Gender Perspectives

Throughout this study, we have emphasized the politically liberating force of Occidentalism when used as a counter-discourse in the formation of literary history in contemporary Chinese television culture, drama, and poetry. In the account of the television documentary *He shang* in chapter 1, for example, I stressed the anti-official function of Occidentalism, which was employed by Chinese intellectuals as a powerful strategy against the predominant official ideology. Yet, this is not to argue that Occidentalism is not highly problematic and cannot at times become ideologically limiting and confining. As a way of pursuing this study of Chinese Occidentalism in an inclusive manner, with a deliberate open-endedness that matches the very subject under scrutiny, I stress in this chapter the problematic nature of Occidentalism by recounting an earlier episode in modern Chinese dramatic history. I argue that, on the one hand, a group of male May Fourth playwrights considered writing about women's issues of liberation and equality important political and ideological strategies in their formation of a countertradition and countercanon against the Confucian ruling ideology. In such a peculiar "male-dominated-feminist" discourse, they found in the image of the West a powerful weapon against the predominant ruling ideology of Confucianism. When the West is so used as a strong anti-official statement against Confucian traditional culture, this Occidentalist discourse can be regarded as politically liberating. On the other hand, however, in view of the particular historical conditions of the May Fourth period, which was characterized by its embracing an anti-imperialistic agenda as its top priority, the appeal to the Western fathers to solve the problems for Chinese women can present complex issues for feminist readings of these plays in cross-cultural contexts.

Indeed, from our privileged position of hindsight, we might even argue that the construction of a utopian model of the West in *He shang* has its historical roots at the beginning of the century in the May Fourth Occidentalist discourse. This discourse was fundamentally torn between a tendency to look toward the West as a liberating model and a countertendency to resent it for its very otherness. This countertendency was based on a repugnance for things Western because it seemed that the West, however "free," was fundamentally opposed to all that is Chinese. Such a divided and paradoxical mentality toward the West can be best illustrated in the two plays that I discuss here. In Chen Dabei's *Miss Youlan* (*Youlan nüshi*), the Chinese woman who longs for a Western education as an escape from her confined traditional family life is killed. This tragic ending at least suggests the playwright's sympathy with the Western-oriented "new" woman of China, whose dream can never be fulfilled in a Confucian society. As if written as a response to Chen's Occidentalist play, however, Ouyang Yuqian's *Homecoming* (*Huijia yihou*) describes a Western-educated Chinese man who has to choose between his traditional Chinese wife and his Western mistress. The play closes without a solution, leaving the audience to its own conclusions. If drama, which is about a resolution of dramatic conflicts, cannot provide one with an answer as to which to choose—the East or the West—what about fiction? What about poetry? What about theory? What about history? What about life?

It is here that Chinese drama in the 1920s provides an interesting point of comparison with the Western discourse on genre and gender. In the Western discussion about the ideological positioning of literary texts, questions about the relationship between gender and genre have frequently been brought to the foreground. The novel, for example, is often said to occupy a central position in women's literary production and its reception. According to this view, with the rise of industrialization, women gained relatively early access to the domestic form of the novel since it is "the prime example of the way women start to create themselves as social subjects under bourgeois capitalism—create themselves as a category: women."[1] In a similar and yet different manner, fantasy, utopian, and science fiction writings by women have been construed as political texts of subversion in which women envision a violent attack upon the symbolic order of the patriarchal society with their nonrealist forms.[2] In contrast to these individual feminine appropriations, the theater is usually viewed as collective, and hence as a medium predominantly controlled by the voice of men.[3] In "Writing like a Woman," Terry Lovell argues that women's preoccupation with the novel stems from their deep insecurity. Women can only function in a domestic space that has been made possible by the social arrangement appropriate for their culturally determined roles.[4] The relative invisibility of women's participation in theater reveals the limitation of their role in literary production in the more public and collective arenas.

These observations, especially when they are placed in a cross-cultural literary and sociopolitical scene, prove at best inadequate. I will, in the following pages, explore the gender/genre issue by situating the development of modern Chinese spoken drama in the historical and cultural context of the May Fourth movement, which looked toward Western political, cultural, and literary models in its formation of a "new-culture" discourse directed against traditional Confucian ideology. I argue that some dramatic works of the May Fourth period are gender-ambiguous: these works were initiated and dominated by male playwrights who nonetheless perceived in women's problems a source of inspiration for their anti-official discourse against the established Confucian traditional culture and its implied truth. In the very beginning of the formation of modern Chinese drama, therefore, several male playwrights considered writing about women's issues an important political and ideological strategy in their formation of a countertradition and a countercanon. Parenthetically, moreover, this phenomenon seems to have coincided with that of some of the fiction writers of the same period, who, as noted by Ching-kiu Stephen Chan, tended to position their "own dilemma of identity" in relation to "the alien, repressed, but emerging 'other' of the woman in question."[5] The dominant intellectual (male-centered) self thus "wanted desperately to re-present *himself* via a mutation in the crisis of the 'other.'"[6]

In contrast to the Western feminist accounts of drama as a public form hardly open to women's participation, the story of the rise of a modern Chinese drama is closely tied to the development of a specific kind of women's theater, in which male playwrights spoke for women and in the name of women in order to free Others—including themselves—from a burden of an ancient and oppressive tradition. This political content of early modern Chinese drama helps account for its rapid formal development based on the models of Ibsen's plays into a full-fledged genre in a relatively short period of time. Thus, the harmony of form and content in modern drama—which Peter Szondi has viewed as impossible in the Western dramatic tradition since the disintegration of conventional meaning at the hands of playwrights such as Ibsen and Chekhov—is to some extent paradoxically achieved on the modern Chinese stage, a stage directly inherited from the traditions of the Occident.[7]

From the onset of the May Fourth literary movement, the issue of women's liberation was closely associated with the emancipation of individuals of both genders and all classes. Leading intellectuals such as Chen Duxiu and Hu Shi attacked the Confucian ideal image of women and its patriarchal practices such as foot binding, arranged marriage, the concubinage system, chastity, child marriage, and a lack of educational opportunities. The May Fourth men of letters shared the belief that Chinese women were collectively placed at the bottom of the patriarchal hierarchy and thus needed a drastic reversal in their social position. Women's liberation was incorporated as an integral part of these men's defense of individualism and their appeal for a new Chinese culture, an appeal paradoxically based on the models of the Other culture. Chen Duxiu, for instance, was inspired by the Russian October Revolution's call for "the emancipation of all mankind," while Hu Shi's American experience taught him the value of science, democracy, and equality for men and women alike. Thus Elisabeth Eide is right in noting that in the May Fourth literary movement, women's "emancipation was used as a radical ideology or as an eruptive force in relation to tradition." "A liberation of the individual will from the collective will of either family or society," she says, "concerned both sexes" in their joined efforts to destroy the existing society.[8] This call for liberation was echoed in the fiction writers at the time: both male and female writers explored the issue of women's oppression and confinement in the traditional society in works such as Lu Xun's "The New Year Sacrifice" (*Zhufu*), "Regret for the Past" (*Shangshi*), and "Divorce" (*Lihun*), Bing Xin's "Two Families" (*Liange jiating*), and "The Final Consolation" (*Zuihou de anxi*). As Yue Ming-Bao has correctly pointed out, however, "the failure on the part of Lu Xun and other May Fourth intellectuals to recognize the connection between women and language led to the perpetuation of the silencing of female voices."[9] "Even though the writers are sincere in their intentions to defend women," Yue further argued, "their writing betrays the discursive habits of patriarchal tradition which excludes women's experiences from its articulation."[10] And yet there is a paradox here, one that some Western feminist theater critics might find surprising: the rapid development of modern Chinese fiction, with its call for liberation of both men and women from an enslaving past, was to a great extent brought about by Hu Shi's introduction of Western drama. Ibsen's play *A Doll's House*, for example, inspired the creation of numerous Nora-type characters in the fiction of this period.[11] Thus in contrast to the Western scene, in which women were believed to have identified more readily with the "private" form of the novel, in the modern Chinese scenario it was the public and political form of the theater transplanted from an alien soil that inspired and promoted the domestic form of fiction.

While the May Fourth fiction writers were attracted to the ideological concerns in Ibsen's plays, the dramatists of the same period took over both the form and content of Western models as weapons against the traditional Chinese operatic theater and the ideology that it expressed. As Hong Shen has documented, in 1919 Qian Xuantong called for the closing down of the obsolete operatic theater dominated by the gentry class in order to promote a "real drama" (*zhenxi*) for the ordinary people. What he had in mind seems clearly to have been inspired by Western realist plays. In a similar way, Zhou Zuoren repudiated the operatic theater as "a de-humanized literature" (*feiren de wenxue*) and argued instead for a new drama, which he termed "a humanistic literature" (*ren de wenxue*). Even those who advocated a reform, rather than an abolition, of the operatic theater equally stressed the old drama's offensive political and public implications. Song Chunfang, for example, spoke for the preservation of a national theater on the ground that the new drama, the product of European and American ideologies, could undermine the traditional cultural values and consequently lead to social corruption. As if to present an antithetical view against Song's argument, however, Hu Shi went so far as to list Western subgenres such as problem play, symbolist play, psychological play, and satirical play as diverse possibilities for creating a new drama on the Chinese stage.[12] Hu Shi even wrote a one-act play himself, entitled *The Greatest Event in Life* (*Zhongshen dashi*).[13] Significantly, this play was subsequently canonized in modern Chinese literary history as the first successful attempt at modern spoken drama based on Western theatrical forms.

Strikingly, this first modern dramatic piece by a leading male writer can be read as an early "feminist" text that depicts a heroine who elopes with her Japan-educated lover against the will of her parents who have arranged her marriage to a total stranger.[14] Hu Shi's "women's play" exposed already in 1919 the traditional marriage institution as a central source of women's oppression under patriarchy.[15] Yet, unlike the major voices of Western feminists, the anti-Confucian content of this play situated the issue of women's liberation in the broader context of May Fourth discourse, which called for the liberation of individuals of both genders and all classes. Within the play, Confucian ideology threatens to ruin the happiness of both men and women, both the heroine and her lover. In fact, Hu Shi's play was regarded as so subversive of the patriarchal tradition that its script was finally returned to him from the dramatists who had planned to stage it, since no woman at that time dared to play the heroine who eloped with a Western-minded man.[16] The prominent drama critic Hong Shen once noted that the very fact that no woman in that historical period was courageous enough to play the part of a "Chinese Nora" illustrates the play's social significance in a "feudalist society."[17] Once again, though in contrast to the usual Western feminism in which women's voices were said to have been silenced by men, we have here a paradoxical situation in which women's concerns were expressed by a male playwright. Yet in the last instance they failed to be enacted by women participants in the gaze of predominantly male spectators in traditional Chinese society.[18] This situation points to a marked difference between the two cultures. In the West, according to theater feminists cited above, the production of dramatic texts was carried out almost exclusively by males who served as spokesmen for patriarchal ideology, but the performance of these texts was open to female enactment. In certain cases in early modern China, male participants represented women's interests far more significantly than did their Western counterparts, but the prevailing patriarchal culture prevented women from giving them an authentic feminine expression or interpretation on the stage. In this regard, Randy Kaplan has noted male playwright Tian Han's "sympathetic depictions of contemporary Chinese women grappling with contemporary concerns that were not only peculiarly Chinese but peculiarly female."[19] "In Tian Han's early dramaturgy," Kaplan argues, "when women fail, it is not because they are women and therefore must inevitably fail, but because they are women born to a male-controlled tradition that devours human potential for compassion."[20]

This particular gender-ambiguous feature of early modern Chinese drama is even more fully expressed in the works of Guo Moruo, another important May Fourth male writer. In his *A Trilogy of Three Revolutionary Women (Sange panni de nüxing)*, Guo Moruo reversed the fate of three legendary ancient women and reinterpreted their stories as indictments of the traditional threefold obligations of women to their fathers, husbands, and sons. In the first play, *Zhuo Wenjun*, the title heroine elopes with her lover, Sima Xiangru, thereby challenging both the strong will of her father and the Confucian ideology as a whole, which expects a widow—such as she is—never to remarry in order to be chaste to her late husband. With good reason, this anti-patriarchal play was enthusiastically staged in 1923 by the students of Women's Normal College in Shaoxing, Zhejiang Province (Zhejiang Shaoxing Nüzi Shifan Xuexiao). It was soon banned by the local "fathers," who condemned the play as corrupting young people's minds.[21] In a somewhat similar manner, the trilogy's second play, *Wang Zhaojun*, depicts the title heroine as a dignified courtesan who rejects the love of the Han emperor—the most powerful "father" of all in prevailing patriarchal hierarchy—by willingly marrying an outsider from a "barbarous" tribe.[22] Guo Moruo's characterization of Zhaojun as a female rebel against the Han imperial court deviated radically from past historical accounts, which portrayed her as a submissive courtesan waiting patiently all her life for the occasional favor of the Han Emperor. In a way more politically relevant to the contemporary Chinese reality of the 1920s, Guo Moruo's third play, *Nie Ying*, presents the title heroine as a martyr who stands by her patriotic brother against outside invaders. It is important to note that the writing of *Nie Ying* was occasioned by the historical event of the May Thirtieth movement of 1925, in which the Chinese people protested against the British policemen who had killed Chinese students and workers in Shanghai. Guo Moruo confessed that *Nie Ying* was "a bloodstained memento" of this national event: it premièred in Shanghai Grand Theater on July 1, 1925—one month after the May Thirtieth movement—and was enthusiastically applauded as a powerful anti-official and anti-imperialist play.[23] Here we see once again the inseparable connection between the emergence of women's theater and the formation of May Fourth discourse, which positioned itself against all cultural fathers—the domestic father in *Zhuo Wenjun*, the imperial father in *Wang Zhaojun*, and the imperialist father in *Nie Ying*.

In his subversive plays against what he termed "male-dominated society," Guo Moruo exposes the twofold oppression of Chinese women by both the other sex and the other class.[24] As is characteristic of May Fourth writers well versed in Western tradition, he introduces Correa Moylan Walsh's *Feminism* as an alternative approach to Chinese women's predicament. He applauds Walsh's attempt to combine socialism, which "awakens one's class consciousness," with feminism, which "appeals to one's gender awareness," thus emphasizing "a liberation of all women, which can only be achieved with the liberation of mankind as a whole."[25] Imbued with such strong ideological convictions, Guo Moruo's women's trilogy has naturally been criticized as "didactic," as "propaganda," and as "mere mouthpieces" through which the writer expressed "his own ideas and opinions."[26] This criticism may be true, but his polemical dramatizations of ancient Chinese women, however, are political subversions precisely because they are didactic. They above all else depict "the contradictory position of women in history"—the difference between women as active, productive, historical beings and women "as a sign, a construct created in culture."[27] The historically active women, who affected the lives of kings and emperors, but who were construed by male ideologies as subordinate and lesser human beings, are in these texts returned to their true status, much to the aggravation of the predominant male-culture, which had already conveniently produced misogynistic and distorted theories of women's situations. In his women's trilogy, Guo Moruo re-historicized patriarchal myths into tales of women with courage, integrity, wisdom, and power, thus remythologizing Chinese reality into national allegories in his attempt to create a political space for women as part of his strategy against the ruling ideology in traditional China.

Less known than Hu Shi and Guo Moruo's May Fourth women's theater both in the West and in China is Chen Dabei's *Miss Youlan*.[28] Published in 1928, *Miss Youlan* is indeed a surprisingly advanced *pièce bien faite* in the tradition of Occidental playwrights such as Eugène Scribe and Alexandre Dumas fils, with its dramatic devices such as accelerating suspense, mistaken identity, and the disclosure of a withheld secret.[29] The play is set in the 1920s in Beijing. As the play unfolds, Miss Ding Youlan is grief-stricken by her father's decision to marry her to a rich warlord's son who has contracted some sort of venereal disease from his amorous adventures.[30] In the process of trying to commit suicide, however, Ding Youlan realizes that her life could become meaningful again if she joined other young people in their efforts to build a better life in a "new China"—a typical call to the young and the oppressed people in the May Fourth literature. Before she has a chance to do so, however, Ding Youlan accidentally discovers that her half-brother, Ding Baolin, is in fact an illegitimate child of Liu Ma and Zhang Sheng, the servants in the house. Sixteen years ago, both Mrs. Ding—Youlan's stepmother—and Liu Ma were pregnant at the same time. It was agreed that if Mrs. Ding's baby turned out to be a girl, she would be traded with Liu's baby, if the latter were a boy, since a girl could never inherit a family fortune. Although a boy was finally born to Mrs. Ding, he was so sick that the exchange was still considered necessary. Thus Mrs. Ding's real son, now named Liu Fenggang, was taken to Liu Ma's house, where he somehow survived. Liu Ma never openly acknowledged that she was supposedly the "mother" of Fenggang, since Confucian male-dominated society expects a widow never to remarry, let alone to have an illegitimate child. In the *scène à faire*, Miss Ding Youlan brings her real brother, Fenggang, beaten up as an apprentice in a tailor's shop, to her father, thus arousing the hatred of Mrs. Ding, who instantly shoots her to death. The spoiled "young master" Baolin, upon learning the truth that he is illegitimate, loses the will to live, scared by the miserable life of Fenggang whom he has up to this point constantly insulted and abused.

Chen Dabei's *Miss Youlan* was readily viewed by its critics as "full of suicides, threats, blackmail, shooting, unexpected revelations and confessions, through which it was hoped to stimulate the interest of the audience."[31] Situated in the critical debate surrounding Western feminist issues, this play can be recognized as an important cultural text on women's predicament in early twentieth-century China. The play expresses, among other things, the concern of a May Fourth male playwright with the economic, cultural, and political oppression of women. Through the interweaving of plots and subplots, Chen Dabei draws our attention to the specifics of the cultural and economic dimensions of women's subordination, exploring the common practice of marital law, sex preference, and reproductive history in a patriarchal society, and its political institutions that render woman invisible and powerless. Miss Ding Youlan's tragedy exposes the nature of the family as a father-dominated unit mediating between individuals and the patriarchal society. Her father, like most of the fathers in traditional Chinese society, exerts power on women both in and around the household. He forces his daughter to marry a stranger in order to adhere to his culture's ideal image of "a model family," which is "blessed with a husband, a wife, a son, and a daughter, who will become the richest man's wife in the city and will produce many grandchildren."[32] In the process of achieving such a goal, the father victimizes other women as well. It is indicated in the play that Ding Youlan's birth mother was her father's concubine, who died in sorrow after she gave birth to Ding Youlan, a member of the inferior sex. Thus Chen Dabei's play explores above all else the historical and cultural conditions that deprive women of their reproductive choice. Women's fertility is not merely biological and private, but also political and cultural, being primarily shaped by Confucian men's needs and desires in their power relationship to women.

Outside the immediate family circle, moreover, other women such as housemaids Liu Ma, Zhen'er, and Xi'er bear perhaps the heaviest weight of the Confucian patriarchal tradition, which discriminates against both women and men of the lower classes. As a practice common in traditional Chinese society, Zhen'er and Xi'er are sold to this rich household as servant girls, since their parents could not afford to raise them at home. These women are constantly insulted and abused by Baolin, the so-called young master. Ding Youlan relates to these poor women and demands that Baolin show respect for the female servants as human beings. She asks Baolin how he would feel if he were poor and his sisters were insulted by a rich master. Without knowing it, Ding Youlan is actually suggesting what would have been a real situation: if Mrs. Ding had not switched her baby with Liu Ma, Baolin's poor sisters could have easily been sold into slavery. This mistaken identity is not merely used to enhance the theatrical effect whereby the audience enjoys the dramatic reversal of the fate of the characters who are themselves blind to the real situation; it is also employed to foreground the themes of gender and class as important ideological issues for the May Fourth playwrights.

To some extent, then, Chen Dabei's sympathetic portrayal of women seems to confirm the Western cultural feminist view of women's superior quality of mind and spirit in their efforts to disrupt the established gender hierarchy.[33] Ding Youlan is depicted, to use Alison Jaggar's phrase, as having "the spiritual power of experiencing a mystical sense of connection or identification with other people."[34] She regards her maid Zhen'er as a "close friend," confides in Zhen'er her dream of getting an American education and her nightmare in which she was dragged into a dark world together with other "fellow sisters."[35] Ding Youlan also senses, through a superior faculty of intuition, that the poor apprentice Fenggang might be her real brother and goes out of her way to help him. Indeed, almost all the women in the play—with the exception of Mrs. Ding, to whom I shall

return later—are depicted as wiser, more sensitive, and more sophisticated than most of their male counterparts. The father and the son are
characterized, in contrast, as aggressive, ignorant, and vain.

In other dramatic moments, however, the play seems to acknowledge
the theoretical thrust of the Western materialist feminist view of the 1980s
which treats woman as a "historical subject whose relation to prevailing
social structures is also influenced by race, class, and sexual identification."[36] The play can be read as if to point out that in addition to gender
difference, class distinctions and the cultural biases that derive from them
further separate or destroy even the patriarchal family itself. Fenggang is
frequently abused because he is believed to be the son of two poor servants. Zhang Sheng, his biological father, is equally victimized by a cultural father of a higher class. Indeed, it may be argued that by creating two
complicated and interwoven families—that of a rich gentleman who raises
a servant's son, and that of a poor man who brings up a young master—
Chen Dabei's play can be read as having symbolically dismantled the Confucian social hierarchy in order to expose the cultural and material basis
for the subjugation of individuals. The somewhat romantic characterization of Miss Youlan—the Other woman who moves beyond gender and
class difference by helping poor maids and an apprentice—is therefore idealized as a catalyst to disintegrate a father-centered society that victimizes
both men and women.

Despite his sensitive portrayal of oppressed people, however, Chen Dabei
reveals nevertheless his male-dominated point of view in his treatment of
Mrs. Ding. Perhaps less obvious than Youlan's portrayal as the victimized
daughter is the patriarchal misogyny in the depiction of Mrs. Ding as the
stereotypical stepmother who maltreats and even kills Youlan, the stepdaughter. Mrs. Ding is in fact made into a scapegoat by the patriarchal society that forces her to trade her child in order to protect her limited right as a
wife—a vulnerable position that could easily be lost to another concubine if
she fails to bear a male heir. Indeed, this misfortune has already happened
to Mrs. Ding's predecessor—Ding Youlan's birth mother, who died in sorrow after giving birth to her, instead of a son. It is thus crucial for Mrs. Ding
to secure her own position with the birth of a son at all costs. To a large
extent, then, the unhappy stepmother/daughter relationship in this play is
a cultural construct of the patriarchal society that deprives women of their
economic and political means to be independent and render them into mere
machinery for reproduction. Both stepmother and stepdaughter are
victimized at different levels by the same phallocentric tradition, which ac-
culturalizes women's relationship into tension, competition, and alienation.
Chen Dabei's almost farcical depiction of the stepmother reveals a male-
centered point of view so deeply rooted in Chinese culture that even a self-
proclaimed rebel against this cultural tradition can paradoxically support or

even further create the misogyny and the mistreatment of women. One may even argue that in the process of representing a women's problems and concerns, Chen Dabei unwisely divides women into the stereotypically "good" and "bad," thus affirming the subjectivity of male spectators and leaving some of the women unarticulated within his dramatic discourse.

Striking as it is, the patriarchal misogyny in the depiction of Mrs. Ding is not the only dramatic moment that unveils Chen Dabei's limitations as a May Fourth playwright from feminist perspectives. In the valuable process of carrying to the full the anti-official task against the gentry and warlord at home, however, Chen Dabei paradoxically resorts to the imperialistic "father" of an equally patriarchal West that suppressed its own women. We are told, for instance, that Ding Youlan's father forbids her to go to school on the ground that it might turn her into a social rebel—a consistent theme in May Fourth literature, which, among other things, identifies the family as institutional imprisonment of the individual and education as a means by which to escape it. In her desperate attempt to run away from an arranged marriage, however, Ding Youlan naively appeals to Western "fathers" and the educational institutions that empower them. She begs her stepmother to give her the dowry her birth mother had left her so that she can use it for the expense of going to an American school. She is, of course, heartbroken when this dream to be free and independent is finally shattered by her "domestic" stepmother's refusal to help. Such an idealistic view of the West as a sympathetic father is also revealed in the brief appearance of the good-natured Wang Huiqing, who helps Fenggang escape from his persecutors. It is important to note that Wang is designated in the play as "a university teacher of the English language," hence by implication, a nicer and fairer person.[37] Before Ding Youlan's death, moreover, she begs her father to save Baolin, her "fake" brother, by sending him to a public school to receive an education so that he can become a useful person on his own. By "education," Ding Youlan means the new-style school that teaches English and science, school based on Western models, which are ideologically opposed to the private tutorial system in which students are forced to learn by rote Confucian classics.

All these utopian images of the West disclose the complicated, perhaps even contradictory Self of the May Fourth playwrights who journeyed to the West—either physically or spiritually (or both)—in search of a new model for literature and society. It should be briefly mentioned that for the May Fourth playwrights, the notion of the "West" is broadly understood as including everywhere "foreign" (*yang*). What is often regarded as the first performed modern Chinese drama—an adaptation of George L. Aiken's dramatic version of Harriet Beecher Stowe's novel *Uncle Tom's Cabin*—was staged in 1907 in Japan, the "Eastern foreign country" (*dongyang*) where Chinese dramatists first learned about European theatrical conventions through Japanese drama reformers. (It is interesting to note a striking paradox in Chinese-Western literary and intellectual relations: while holding up American founding fathers' ideals whereby everyone was "created equal" as a weapon against Confucian tradition, the Chinese dramatists were nevertheless attracted to *Uncle Tom's Cabin,* the most popular play on the American stage before and after the Civil War, for its powerful attack on black slavery and for the subsequent liberal critique exposing the hypocrisy of the founding principles of the United States.) Other prominent dramatists such as Hong Shen and Xiong Foxi studied drama in America, one of the "Western foreign countries" (*xiyang*). Such broadly defined Western experience naturally helped promote a pro-Western mentality among the May Fourth playwrights. We see, therefore, a profound irony in modern Chinese history: initially inspired by the anti-imperialist event of the May Fourth movement of 1919, May Fourth playwrights nevertheless found in the image of the West a powerful strategy in speaking the politically inconceivable and the ideologically impossible against the dominant ruling ideology, which was viewed as in every way opposed to the "progressive" and "democratic" West. Rightly or wrongly, therefore, the West was employed, in the same way as women's liberation, by the May Fourth playwrights as a strong anti-official statement against the Confucian tradition. Thus, speaking in the name of women may not necessarily mean that women's interests are spoken for: women's theater can at the same time consolidate the interests of Western patriarchal fathers who were promoted, willy-nilly, by a group of "new-culture" men at home. Here we see a family romance, which, since it extended across cultures, is even more complex than that imagined by Harold Bloom. In it, May Fourth domestic sons rebelled against their Confucian fathers by attempting to liberate their sisters from their domestic fathers. Yet in order to do so, the sons appealed to a new surrogate father—Western imported tradition—which included its own form of patriarchal domination of women. The end result was that domestic sons' apparent liberation of their sisters turned out to be a selling of them into new bondage in order to achieve their own new cultural freedom, which even in its Western form, existed more for men than for women. In this sense, Chen Dabei belonged to the problematic generation of what Tani E. Barlow terms "a modern, post-Confucian, professionalized intellectual, who oversaw the appropriation of foreign signs into the new, domestic, urban, mass market, print economy, an 'intellectual' who signaled a shift from widely diffused textuality of the old society to the scriptural economy of realist representation in a modern peripheralized world economy."[38]

Such a paradoxical view of the West is not merely unique for the dramatists of this period, nor was it peculiar to male writing only. Bing Xin, among the first May Fourth women writers, also shared a pro-Western-patriarchal vision. Strongly influenced by her patriotic father, who fought in the Sino-Japanese War of 1894–1985 (in which Chinese resisted a Japanese attempt to annex Korea and invade China), Bing Xin participated in the May Fourth student movement in Beijing against the northern warlords and foreign imperialism. Yet as if to contradict her anti-imperialist stance, her first short story, "Two Families" (*Liangge jiating*), seems to hold up the Western educational system as a remedy to contemporary Chinese women's problems.[39] In the story, Bing Xin compares two families. In an "ideal" family, a British-educated husband collaborates with his wife in translating English books into Chinese language, bringing up a well-behaved child in peace and harmony. In an "unhappy" family, an uneducated wife spends all her time playing mahjong, neglects her children, and drives her husband to despair. At the end of the story, the I-narrator's mother, upon learning about the death of the unhappy husband, singles out a lack of education as the cause for his wife's failure in making a happy family. It is indeed shocking to see how patriarchal this story truly is: the sole purpose for a woman's education is to better fulfill her domestic duty as a "virtuous wife and good mother"—the very Confucian ideology that the May Fourth writers were trying to eliminate. An education in English language and literature is represented as a romantic exile from social and cultural suppression at home. It is thus important to note how a much-celebrated woman writer in modern China does not necessarily speak for women and in the name of woman. As Shoshana Felman has rightly pointed out: "To 'speak in the name of,' to 'speak *for*,' could thus mean, once again, to appropriate and to silence."[40] Seen in this light, Bing Xin presents herself as a privileged and superior woman who sees her sisters' problems in male terms, especially in Western male terms. Certainly Bing Xin would have been surprised by Betty Friedan's remarks on "feminine dis-fulfillment" in 1960s America, where the well-educated, "suburban," and "perfect wives and mothers" suddenly realized that it was the same old issue of education that made them unhappy and frustrated again in their role as housewives who felt shut in and "left out."[41] Thus the American dream of being "respected as a full and equal partner to man in his world," cherished and perpetuated by Chen Dabei and Bing Xin's women characters, was shattered even within American society itself.[42] It would seem that in the West women's early demands for education and equality were manipulated by a patriarchy that turned women's expectations into a new social order of the "ideal family." Such a situation stands in stark contrast to the fantasies and hopes expressed by female characters in early modern Chinese drama.

In order to further explore the Chinese use of the image of liberated Western women, I now wish to dialogically juxtapose *Miss Youlan* with another May Fourth play—Ouyang Yuqian's *Homecoming*.[43] Ouyang Yuqian's play describes how Lu Zhiping, a Chinese student at "New York University," marries a Chinese American woman, Liu Mali (Mary Liu), and returns to his hometown in Hunan Province to divorce his wife, Wu Zifang, whom he had married without love as tradition dictated. After his homecoming, however, Lu is deeply touched by the love and devotion of Wu, who has taken good care of his father and grandmother during his many years of absence. He also begins to appreciate the primitive, yet serene and peaceful, life in the countryside uncorrupted by modern industrialization. While he is about to ask for his wife's forgiveness, however, Liu Mali arrives, claiming to be Lu's real wife and threatening to wreak revenge on him if he rejects her at this point after many years of deception. Wu Zifang, by contrast, is understanding and forgiving. She trusts her husband with his own decision. Being the legal wife does not necessarily give her the right to claim her husband, she says. She wants to stay married only on condition that he truly loves her. After all, she has never been dependent on her husband, who has been away for so many years, and she never will be. She has her own little world that enchants her and people around her whom she loves. The play ends at this point without closure: Lu leaves home to talk to Liu Mali in another city, promising his folks that he will make the right decision.

At first sight, *Homecoming* seems to be at every turn and in every direction opposed to Chen Dabei's *Miss Youlan*. Ouyang Yuqian's sympathetic depiction of the sensible Chinese woman above all else celebrates the Confucian expectation of a woman as virtuous wife, good mother, and submissive daughter-in-law. Wu spends most of her time taking care of her grandmother-in-law—her role model who remained a widow most of her life in order to bring up her son and grandson. As if this were not enough, Wu goes so far as to offer to play the role of her granddaughter-in-law even if and after Lu divorces her so that the old woman could be spared the news of her grandson's infidelity. Here, at least two generations of women sacrifice their womanhood for the preservation of a patriarchal family as if it were "natural," while unknowingly protecting it as a social and cultural construct. Seen in this light, *Homecoming* can readily be seen as an anti–May Fourth play written at the beginning of the twentieth century, in which woman's social status is unjustifiably incorporated into an ideologically questionable "pastoral" view of the very Confucian society that "new-culture" writers have tried hard to subvert. It is perhaps from this perspective that Hong Shen, a prominent modern Chinese drama critic, noted that if acted improperly on the stage, this play "could easily become a shallow play defending a traditional ideology by attacking the overseas Chinese" who journeyed to the West in search of a better society.[44]

On the other hand, however, Ouyang's seemingly pro-patriarchal concept of woman can be read as the product of a "dialogical imagination" working against the imperialistic vision as represented by Chen Dabei, who sees Western education as a source of inspiration for Chinese women's liberation.[45] In my view, Ouyang's *Homecoming* can be interpreted as a sequel, as it were, to Chen's play: it above all else addresses the question of what would happen to Miss Ding Youlan if and after she leaves home. Would she be able to cope with the dire consequences of obtaining an American education? Could she become as estranged from her Western experience as she was from her imprisonment at home? Would Miss Ding in America become so educated and independent that she would freely marry a man who was "her equal" only to find out later, as does Liu Mali, that he already has a virtuous wife at home—the very traditional role Miss Ding refused to play in the first place? Does Western education necessarily provide woman with a better choice, or does it further entrap her in a more subtle yet a more brutal way? By rejecting her tyrannical Chinese father, isn't Miss Ding mesmerized by yet another "father"—the Western-educated but dishonest Lu Zhiping? Is it possible for a woman to transgress the masculinity of powerful male institutions, both marital and educational, both at home and abroad? It is perhaps ironic to note that to some extent Wu Zifang, the Chinese wife in Ouyang's play, is better off precisely because the marriage was prearranged by her parents—the kind of marriage that forced Miss Ding to leave home in the first place. Wu is after all competing with an outsider who has no home to return to and no culture to identify with. Thus the future Miss Ding in America—or the present Liu Mali in China—can be regarded as a female transgressor who is confined both abroad and at home. The portrayals of a Western/comical Liu Mali and a Chinese/dignified Wu can thus be viewed as the exhaustion of the utopian model of the West in China and as a negation of the educational system that formulates knowledge and power even in a cross-cultural arena.

By juxtaposing two fully opposed types of women—the Chinese domestic woman and the Western professional woman—Ouyang's play seems to depict the issue of women's liberation in the broader context of national liberation from yet another angle. Solutions to particular Chinese problems may subject Chinese women to a double jeopardy imposed by both domestic and international fathers. The hope for a better and freer life for women lies perhaps in a combination of the consciousness-raising of the women as individual subjects against the male-dominated tradition with the formation of a new cultural identity as a social group, without necessarily projecting one's future onto a romanticized Other. Seen in this line of argument, Wu Zifang can be considered as superior to and more independent than her Western counterpart: she lets her husband choose of his own free will without insisting on her legal status as his wife. Although seemingly bound to the patriarchal tradition, she is in fact more liberal than the seemingly liberated woman from the Occident precisely because she has given up her rights as the "legitimate" wife of tradition. Here, then, an act against the patriarchal society does not necessarily mean the abandonment of things Chinese and familial. Wu Zifang is stronger not because she is Chinese and protected by domestic and marital institutions, but because she is superior to her environment, to other men and women around her. At least, Wu can be interpreted as a supplement, or a counter Other to Miss Ding Youlan, whose anti-patriarchal act cannot be complete until it is dialogically combined with the anti-Western-logocentric thrust as expressed in *Homecoming*. It is important to note that Ouyang leaves his play open-ended so that the dialogical voices of two oppositional women provide its audience with food for thought and freedom of choice. As these plays clearly show, the two seemingly contradictory thrusts of anti-Confucianism and anti-imperialism in the May Fourth discourse were, to a large extent, constantly renegotiated in the ongoing dialogue between what is represented by Chen Dabei's *Miss Youlan* and Ouyang Yuqian's *Homecoming*, crying out its own version of truths without a single moment of reconciliation and compromise.

By way of conclusion, I would like to point out that in studying the changing traditions of women's theater in a cross-cultural context, it is imperative that we explore certain major issues encountered in Western feminist discourse. The exploration of feminist concerns demonstrated in Chen Dabei and Ouyang Yuqian's May Fourth plays, for example, can offer other readings that have not yet been explored in the canon of modern Chinese drama. The work of a less-studied playwright such as Chen Dabei could yield a new array of meanings under postmodern conditions. On the other hand, by examining modern Chinese drama through the perspectives of Western theories, as I have tried to do here, we can further the Western critical discourses that have often claimed to reach conclusions without, for the most part, taking into account non-Western literary and dramatic phenomena or the cultures in which they are embedded. As I have argued, some of these conclusions seem inadequate when judged against the practices of modern Chinese drama.

At the same time, however, we have seen that male playwrights' being aware of, or addressing, women's problems does not *necessarily* create a "women's theater" *per se*. At the very moment when women's predicament is sympathetically depicted on the modern stage, the dramatic voices of the Other can advocate patriarchal traditions either in a domestic form or in cross-cultural contexts. Indeed, we must be aware of the fact that the very process of raising women's consciousness—the May Fourth writers certainly did that—can at the same time be maneuvered into a reformulation of a "new-culture" discourse as patriarchal as its predecessor. With the hindsight made possible by the 1989 Democracy movement, which witnessed the suppression of powerless individuals from both genders and all classes, moreover, one might argue that not only is the May Fourth goal of individualism and democracy far from being accomplished in present-day China, but most importantly, just as the May Fourth discourse was later used by Mao Zedong to justify his so-called "new-democratic revolution" and Cultural Revolution, women's issues could be seen in the same light as having been utilized by the May Fourth men-of-letters to speak for men, or the "new-culture" men, in their political struggle against the old men, the Confucian men. The May Fourth plays discussed in this chapter can thus be read both as liberating drama and as documents that appropriate women's issues in order to legitimize and promote the pro-Western and anti-traditional canon. In the everlasting battle between the old men (Confucius, Mao Zedong, and Deng Xiaoping) and the new men (the May Fourth, Maoist, and post-Maoist intellectuals), women's issues—indeed all issues concerning individual rights and freedom from all kinds of culturalization and politicization—can be raised, but in the last instance buried after a new ideology has secured its position in power. The lesson to be learned, therefore, is that criticism is best served not by separating dichotomies such as Orient/Occident, Self/Other, traditionalism/modernism, and male/female, but by questioning these binary oppositions and engaging in a constant dialogue without ever claiming one version of "truth" at the expense of celebrating the diversities of all "truths."

Chapter Seven

China Writes Back
Reading Stories of the Chinese Diaspora

This chapter focuses on stories from the Chinese diaspora written in the Chinese language and their portrayal of multiple and overlapping national identities. Unlike the best-selling women's autobiographies such as *Wild Swans,* which begin by stressing the suffering in China and end usually in celebration of a "free" West for an English-speaking audience,[1] these stories were written in the Chinese language—some by overseas students themselves—for an audience at home who shared their vision of a troubled and yet hopeful China. Situated in the native circumstances, these narratives provide a dialogic space that transforms geographic regions into diverse cultural conceptions of the Self and Other. As these authors search for their own identities in a cross-cultural context, they inevitably express their own subjectivities—either in terms of "Chinese" or "non-Chinese" or everything else in between—against multifaceted nationalist and imperialist backgrounds.

I put "Chinese" in quotation marks to indicate the complexity of the very concept of Chineseness, which has undergone scrutiny in critical investigations of the Chinese diaspora. In *Ungrounded Empires,* an informative study of the cultural politics of modern Chinese transnationalism, Aihwa Ong and Donald Nonini argue against an essentialist approach of equating "Chineseness" with having Chinese values and norms. They propose to understand it as inscribed and multiple "relation[s] of persons and groups to forces and processes associated with global capitalism and its modernities."[2] Terms such as "Chinese culture" and the like are thus studied as discursive tropes "constantly cast and recast in cultural terms"; they "do not merely explain Chinese identity" but "in large part *constitute* Chinese identities and transnational practices, and are therefore in need of deconstruction and study."[3] I agree with Ong and Nonini's project of exploring "the multifaceted and shifting experiences of diaspora Chinese

Student identities will be formed in UK but this is not to say they are coming over for 'to speak out against global capitalism'. They are consumers of it and want to gain ~~peace~~ from it.

140   *Chapter Seven*

living under, yet reworking, the conditions of flexibility" without grant-
ing China "a privileged ontological or epistemological position."[4]

My discussion of these stories of Chinese diaspora, however, furthers
this project by focusing on an unstudied aspect of Chinese transnationalism. Before these writers' sojourn abroad, what were the native circumstances and conditions that motivated their emigrant experience? During
their sojourn abroad, how did they define themselves as "Chinese" in order to construct their own identities in opposition to everything else they
construed as "un-Chinese" in cross-cultural and global contexts? In addition to, or in the midst of, their Asian Pacific economic and cultural activities, what were the discursive powers at work that negated or compen-
sated for their status in their immigrant countries? When we talk about
Chinese transnationalism in the geopolitics of the twentieth century, to
what extent can we recover the subject positions of Chinese writers who
narrated their own diaspora experience in the Chinese language for a domestic readership within China? In addition to a "business speak,"[5] as
discussed in Ong and Nonini's work, can one detect a "China speak" that
explores the use of cultural capital, such as storytelling and image making, to advocate a special kind of Chinese identity, as a critical strategy of
speaking out against global capitalism in reaction to local conditions? Can
Chinese stories—however problematic they are in epistemological and
critical terms—be seen as narrative forms against late capitalism and
modernization when examined within their local contexts?

Furthermore, to connect with the central concern of this study, I would
like to address the issue of what happens to the construction of foreign
countries after Chinese writers travel abroad and see the life of Others
with their own eyes. Stories of the Chinese diaspora, therefore, can to
some extent be seen as a series of sequels to *He shang* and Chinese Shakespearean theater, as discussed in chapters 1 and 2. Unlike the previous
works in this study, however, stories of the Chinese diaspora, precisely
because their writers have traveled to other shores, reveal more complex
and paradoxical views of the West and other countries. Although some of
the writers still idealize the West in order to address issues at home, others continue their China-oriented critique but also express their disillusionment with the West and other places. In nationalist terms, some of the
protagonists' experiences abroad as being viewed as inferior Others indeed create new impetus for them to embrace China as the motherland
that they had once reluctantly left behind but whose spiritual rejuvena-
tion they have continuously longed for. In ideological terms, after rejecting socialism in China as a totalitarian regime, they wonder, once abroad,
if capitalism can become the solution to the prevailing social problems
both in China and in the rest of the world. Negotiating this in-between
space, they examine the diversity between what they perceive as "Chi-

Chen sees a benefit of people negotiating different cultural spaces and over time as their subjectivities about the 'other' and themselves will change. International sojourns empower one to speak in an active voice against global Capitalism' (pg 142)

China Writes Back 141

nese" and "non-Chinese" values, while sorting out the lessons to be learned from these cultures. It is from this in-between space that they write back, with multiple subjectivities constantly in flux and in negotiation with each other.

This is not to claim, however, that the 1980s and 1990s representations of the Other are essentially different from each other. Neither do I imply that *He shang* and Chinese Shakespearean theater were the only kinds of Occidentalism available in this same period of early post-Mao China, or that the stories of the Chinese diaspora discussed below are exclusive or monolithic in their views of China and other cultures. For anyone familiar with the landscape of cultural China, it is clear that the constructions of the West and China are almost always dialogical, multifaceted, and paradoxical in every period, and different from writer to writer, or even from piece to piece authored by the same writer. For this reason, I will discuss two very different works written by Hu Ping—one written in 1987 and the other in 1997—to demonstrate how his construction of America varies according to the changing perspectives of the author and his different understandings of America and China at given historical moments.

This chapter continues to consider the complex and paradoxical role of Occidentalism in the construction of Chinese identities both at home and abroad. The chapter also continues the discussion of the question "can China speak" as its own agent and in its own voice against a persistent anxiety expressed by some scholars in Chinese literary and cultural studies, whose works—while valuable in many other aspects—have a tendency to reduce twentieth-century Chinese writings to mostly subjugations to Western colonialism and imperialism. While taking into consideration the importance of the colonial experience imposed on the Chinese people in the twentieth century, this chapter reminds its readers, once again, that twentieth-century Chinese literary and cultural histories cannot always be seen as *reactive* to and preconditioned by a so-called predominant Western colonialization, but as formative sites where Chinese writers can and have been *actively* constructing their own stories, from their native perspectives, and with a voice of their own. As I have shown in the introduction, overemphasizing Chinese experience in the twentieth century as predominantly colonial and semicolonial not only plays into the Maoist game of official Occidentalism, which utilized its anti-Western and anti-imperialist agendas to oppress its own people; more significantly, it virtually grants the West more power than it deserves, indeed discursively constructing a more powerful West than it actually was militarily in the first half of the twentieth century. Even in the 1990s, when globalization and modernization presented more challenges than ever before, Chinese writers spoke up against such domination in their own Chinese diaspora writings. These stories, I hope, will demonstrate that Chinese intellectuals in the twentieth century have not simply occupied a passive position vis-à-vis Western domination. As my discussion below of Cao Guilin's *A Chinese Nightingale in the Sky of New York* (*Niuyue shangkong de Zhongguo yeying*, 1994) will show, writing about diasporic life in the Chinese language can produce a particular kind of discursive power that rewrites one's sojourning experience in America, thus empowering one to speak in an active voice against global capitalism.

In talking about an active diasporic voice in cross-cultural contexts, I am fully aware of the pitfalls of Chinese nationalism, or what Michelle Yeh rightly characterizes as assumptions that "stem from a nationalistic, sinocentric framework that reifies China and the West."[6] What I want to challenge in the following discussions is precisely the dualistic divide between China and the West and the thorny issues of Sinocentrism on the one hand and Eurocentrism on the other. As I have already pointed out in earlier chapters, the critical debates that have appeared in the form of "China versus the West" are indeed cultural, ideological, and linguistic constructs to validate a particular agenda, on the part of the official ideology, in the form of a counter-discourse conducted by Chinese intellectuals to oppose such an ideology, or as a collaborative effort by both parties to construct the West for their sometimes commonly shared goals. In other words, this picture of the dualistic China/West, or official/anti-official, is the very one I intend to disrupt as a discursive strategy of political and cultural identities. The tendencies of Sinocentrism and Eurocentrism can indeed be found in the stories of the Chinese diaspora. I intend to investigate the native circumstances—and most significantly, the cultural, political, and economic factors at work—that provided fertile ground for such contradictory sentiments at different moments of historical narratives.[7]

While pursuing similar critical issues treated in the previous chapters on television documentaries, poetic texts, and theater productions, this chapter considers narrative genres in the forms of short story, novel, reportage, and autobiographical writing. Although the limited space of one chapter does not allow me to delineate the historical scope of these genres in their earlier prototypes, a brief analysis of some of the precursor texts seems necessary to provide readers with some of the persistent themes and critical issues at stake. I therefore choose, in the first part of this chapter, a few representative stories of Chinese abroad from the 1920s, a particularly significant moment in Chinese literary and cultural history, when some May Fourth writers traveled to different foreign countries in search of an elixir that would rescue China from decline. By comparing stories of the 1920s with the 1980s and 1990s, I do not mean to present them as coherent narratives in a linear line of historical development, nor to suggest that stories of Occidentalist writings about the diaspora can be explained within a single theoretical framework. In fact, I intend to explore how the motivations of the students in post-Mao China resemble or differ from those in the 1920s, and how post-Mao writers inherited even more complex cultural and ideological traditions, Confucian and Maoist, capitalist and post-socialist.

Yu Dafu's "Sinking" (*Chenlun*, 1921), one of the most popular pieces in the May Fourth literary canon, reflects the complexity of the Chinese diaspora stories. The story portrays a Chinese student studying in Japan, then a popular destination because of the relatively low tuition fees and shorter distance from the homeland, and because more schools were open to Chinese students there than in its American and European counterparts. Considered the "Eastern foreign land" (*dongyang*) in contrast to the "Western foreign land" (*xiyang*) of America and Europe, Japan also appealed to Chinese students as a place where Western knowledge and technology had already been incorporated into its own culture. Kirk A. Denton has succinctly depicted this paradoxical position of Japan for Chinese students: this "symbolic ambiguous" island nation stood, in the minds of Chinese intellectuals, as "both the cause of Chinese national humiliation (i.e., defeat in the 1894–95 war, the Twenty-one Demands, and the Treaty of Versailles) and the shining paragon of an Asian nation which had successfully modernized along the Western model."[8] Apart from "a sense of national shame" and "haunting questions about why Japan had succeeded in national modernization when China was failing so miserably," Denton points out, Yu Dafu's work also reminds its readers of the dramatic "contrast with the days when China was learned master and Japan humble pupil."[9]

Like many Chinese students in Japan at that time, the protagonist in "Sinking" is studying medicine, as so willed by his elder brother, but he finds himself drawn to English and German romantic poetry as an escape from his depressing experience as an inferior Chinese looked down upon as a "Shina," a derogatory word used by the Japanese to discriminate against the Chinese. His situation becomes worse as he struggles without success against what Denton calls a "profound sense of lack, both sexual and national." After sleeping with a Japanese woman, he feels worthless as a weak Chinese (nation) who could not find the inner strength to resist outside power.[10] In the in-between space of Japan, Denton points out, the protagonist's dilemma cannot be explained simply as being torn between traditional China and the modern West. Furthermore, the protagonist is, like many other writers of this time, "at once attached and repelled" by both iconoclasm and nationalism in response to the impact of Western imperialism, since "the Western model of self needed for the iconoclastic stance is ultimately terrifying to the Chinese intellectual because it cuts him off from the possibility of linkage as a means toward social and national renewal."[11] As we shall see in the following discussion, May Fourth writers related to various discourses (such as Chinese traditionalism, Western enlightenment, Japanese modernism, Korean nationalism, Soviet socialism, and American liberalism) in ambivalent ways at different historical moments. Protagonists in such stories as "Sinking," therefore, cannot be reduced merely to "victims of Japanese imperialism's subjugation of China."[12] From a different perspective, one could even argue that "Sinking" pioneered a form of Chinese diasporic writing that locates the land of the Other as an inevitable space of awakening, both in personal and political terms. By situating his protagonist in Japan, the author brings out even more acutely the protagonist's sense of being an inferior Chinese. The author speaks out, in a distinctively "Chinese" voice, against deteriorating circumstances back home (in an iconoclast spirit) and against racial discrimination (in a Chinese nationalist spirit) through the narrative space of his protagonist. Viewing Yu's works as mere reflections of colonial experience dramatically reduces the complexity of the May Fourth writings, especially those written away from China, which sometimes take a different perspective on things Chinese and foreign. Furthermore, such monolithic readings also disregard the complexity of the narrative structure, which inevitably consists of dialogues, distances, and ironic tensions among author, implied author, narrator, reader, implied reader, and protagonists, as Denton has cogently described.[13]

Equally important in modern Chinese literary history, but less studied in the English language scholarship, is Lu Xun's short story "Professor Fujino" (*Tengye xiansheng*, 1926). A more upbeat story than "Sinking," "Professor Fujino" expresses another paradoxical view of the Japanese. In this autobiographical piece, Lu Xun (the I-narrator) describes Professor Fujino, his anatomy teacher at the Sendai Medical School, who treats him with respect as a new student from China. Unlike some of his contemporaries, Professor Fujino does not look down on the Chinese; on the contrary, he studied Chinese in high school and admires Chinese culture.[14] Concerned that the narrator's Japanese might not be fluent enough to follow his lectures, Professor Fujino decides to look over his student's class notes, and he carefully corrects them. After the narrator is ranked sixty-sixth among the 142 students for his examination scores,[15] however, prejudiced Japanese classmates accuse him of cheating, citing as evidence the many marks Professor Fujino had made in his notebook, which apparently indicated what the exam questions would be. Since China is a weak country, the narrator reflects, it is assumed that an average grade is too good to be true for an inferior Chinese man with "low intelligence." Such a racial sentiment was popular in Japan especially after the Russo-Japanese War, which, although fought in Chinese territory, resulted in Japan's control of China's Lüshun port and the South Manchurian Railway as well as other privileges after Russia's defeat. Worse than this national humiliation, the narrator has to bear the insult of the Japanese student who writes the anonymous letter accusing him of cheating, which begins with a quote from the New Testament: "Repent ye, for the kingdom of heaven is at hand." This was a popular phrase in Japan at the time, because Tolstoy used it to advise the Russian czar and the Japanese emperor against their war policies. Nevertheless, it was absurd to use this phrase to hurt an innocent Chinese student.[16] Pondering over the foreign aggressions against China in the past sixty to seventy years, including Japan's condescending view of the Chinese as poor citizens of a declining Qing dynasty, the narrator wonders if medicine is the best means to help bring about a healthy China. His sense of mission becomes clearer after the famous slide incident, in which he sees Japanese soldiers executing a Chinese man accused of spying for Russia, while other Chinese look on indifferently. This becomes a turning point for him in his decision to give up medicine in order to pursue a literary career, whereby he can educate the Chinese people.

In her *Primitive Passions,* Rey Chow describes the same incident, but from an earlier and much-cited text: Lu Xun's preface to his *Call to Arms* (*Nahan*). Exploring this occasion as "the beginning of a new kind of discourse in the postcolonial 'third world,'" Rey Chow goes beyond the usual autobiographical reading by defining it as the beginning of a "discourse of technologized visuality" that explains "an experience of the power of a spectacle transmitted by the film medium"—hence, an emerging modernity.[17] Lydia Liu, on the other hand, discusses the same incident from both texts but focuses on "the violence of representation," which raises important issues in the formation of Lu Xun's discourse of Chinese national characters, a theory he borrowed from the American missionary Arthur Smith, though not without reservation, given "his situated subjectivity as a Chinese."[18]

Whereas both postcolonial readings enhance our understanding of the problems confronting a major Chinese writer under imperialist conditions, I want to emphasize the other side of the story: Lu Xun's portrayal of a Japanese man as an inspiring model for his literary career, which subsequently enabled him to write against Japanese imperialism. Paying particular attention to the context of "Professor Fujino," one might argue that his contact with Professor Fujino as a Chinese abroad played an equally important role in his "turning point"; it facilitated the slide incident and situated it in the narrative space of his depiction of a sympathetic Japanese teacher/mentor. He saw in the professor an embodiment of their shared hope for a new China. He treasured him as a "great man," even though his name remained unknown in Japan.[19] He regretted that he never fulfilled his promise to send him a photograph of himself, nor did he ever write to him. Yet he hung the professor's photograph in his study to remember him by, especially to inspire him when he felt lazy or tired in the middle of the night. It was therefore in Japan, where racism against the Chinese ran rampant, that Lu Xun/the I-narrator spoke against such experiences in his creation of a positive Other in Professor Fujino. Lu Xun's depiction of Professor Fujino as a Japanese mentor can be seen as disrupting the stability of an ontological "Chinese" or "Japanese" identity, or as either "the oppressed" or "the oppressor." It provides a narrative space in which binary categories such as these are interrogated in their local and personal contexts.

In the following discussion of other stories of Chinese abroad, we witness a similar pattern in which foreign role models, mother figures, and women friends (especially lovers) in remote countries play a significant role in the construction of what the protagonists believe to be their "Chinese" identities, although the protagonists usually live among racist foreigners. It is sometimes in a seemingly strange foreign land that Chinese protagonists find a catalyst by which they transform themselves into stronger persons, whose stories abroad, in turn, become significant ingredients for their creative writings as literary figures of the May Fourth period. Even in an unequal relationship between China and its "superior" Others, there are particular moments when some of the foreigners provide the Chinese abroad opportunities to liberate themselves from their trapped past and from a sense of subjugation to colonialism.

An interesting case in point is Guo Moruo's "Late Spring" (*Canchun*, 1922). Also set in Japan in the 1920s, the story reads almost as if it were a critical response to the dark world of "Sinking." Whereas the protagonist in "Sinking" thinks about drowning himself after a sexual liaison with a Japanese prostitute, in "Late Spring" the I-narrator takes care of a Mr. He, who had attempted to drown himself in the sea upon hearing of his father's death in China. After visiting his friend in the hospital, however, the narrator, while away from home for the first time, dreams about the Japanese nurse he met during the day who takes care of Mr. He. At the very moment when he is about to examine her shapely body for possible tuberculosis (since he is a medical student), his friend interrupts him with the shocking news that his wife has just killed his two sons in revenge for his infidelity. Awakened from his nightmare, the narrator rushes home, only to find his sons and wife safe and sound, his wife smiling at his confession of his fleeting thought of betrayal. In a way similar to "Sinking," "Late Spring" expresses the loneliness and alienation of Chinese students abroad. The narrator laments that Mr. He would choose to die in a foreign land, away from home. While helping his friend to overcome his grief, however, the narrator, in an almost comic manner, comes to appreciate the love and understanding of his wife only after his encounter with a Japanese woman. Rather than a sexual lure to decadency and despair, as seen in "Sinking," here the dream world of an imagined sexual endeavor allows the narrator to fantasize about an *affaire d'amour* that never materializes in the "real" world of the narrative space. The encounter with the Japanese woman thus functions as a catalyst for him to appreciate his own family and culture. This instructive event thus frees him from the otherwise subjugated position as a Chinese in the diaspora. Against such local and personal backgrounds, the meaning of "Japanese" becomes fluid, changeable, and subjective according to the narrator's specific experience in the land of the Other. The stories of the Chinese turn out to be those not of a downtrodden racial group but of individuals, such as a friend trapped in his own tradition and an overseas student confused by his sexual desires while seeking his personal and cultural identities.

In contrast to Guo's story, which focuses on the libido and the unconscious world, Li Jieren's "Sympathy" (*Tongqing*, 1923) records a more down-to-earth experience: the sixty-two days the I-narrator spends in a French hospital, where he overcomes the fear of dying in a foreign land. Indeed, one way to read "Sympathy" is to interpret it as expressing the narrator's ambiguities about both modern French society and his own Chinese traditions. In a clearly iconoclastic spirit, for instance, the narrator begins his diary by stating that after having searched for sympathy for many years without success in China, he unexpectedly finds it in Paris after only ten months. "Whatever you fail to find, your best luck is to search outside of your own country," he declares.[20] He feels fortunate to have received high-quality care in a hospital established for poor people who cannot afford medical treatment and is especially grateful to an amiable doctor and a blue-eyed, beautiful nurse. He discovers that the city of Paris is in fact divided into twenty *arrondissements,* many of which have established hospitals that are free of charge for poor people. He also depicts a loving relationship between himself and Mrs. Ximen, who, having lost her own son in World War I, offers a motherly love for a "sick child" from China.[21] When she visits him in the hospital, he cannot help but embrace her as if she were his own mother. The war-torn history of both countries has resulted in bonding between otherwise strangers. He does not suffer any discriminatory treatment as an inferior Chinese, even though the Chinese had been depicted as the "sick men of East Asia" (*dongya bingfu*); instead, he is taken care of as a "sick man" in a foreign country without money, family ties, and relatives.

It is, however, from the position of a Chinese intellectual who is proud of his own ancient civilization and culture—which he feels all the more keenly once he is away from home—that the narrator also expresses his misgivings about what he understands to be the "French

culture." Mrs. Ximen finds it hard to comprehend the fact that because
of his determination to study abroad, it will probably be eight years before he sees his wife again. In the past thirty-eight years, Mrs. Ximen
declares, she has followed her husband everywhere he has gone; unless
one is not in love or has no choice but to be drafted for the war, French
couples can never be parted, even for a week. The narrator wonders
how he can possibly help a French woman understand his situation: his
wife still lives in his hometown in China with his mother, and he bid his
farewell only a few days after their wedding. Above all else, how can a
French woman understand that both he and his wife are indeed very
much in love? Nor can she understand that for a Chinese couple, geographical distance can only make their hearts grow fonder, and that
they can indeed resist any temptations while apart. In his belief that the
Europeans have stronger sexual desires than the "Far Eastern peoples,"
the narrator further essentializes the French as being physiologically
different from the Chinese. In his view, European women seem to believe they are born for love whereas European men are born for the
sake of providing such love. By contrast, Far Eastern peoples, the narrator claims, are gentler and more implicit in their expression of love
and hence prone to being misconstrued as lacking unconditional or
passionate love.

Yet as soon as the narrator essentializes the Chinese as spiritually more
sophisticated than the French and hence advances a Chinese nationalistic
position, he is perhaps at the same time led by his own iconoclastic stance
to advocate a "strong subject, perceived as autonomous from political
power and conventional social values."[22] Echoing the May Fourth sentiment of "saving the children" from a cannibalistic Confucian society, he
expresses his concerns for the future generations in China if Western individualism, enlightenment, and humanism are not properly introduced.
It is perhaps why he goes so far as to claim that the French are indeed an
innately superior race to the Chinese: French women enjoy robust and
physically impressive men, and French men adore healthy, mature
women; shouldn't we Chinese worry about a weaker quality of offspring,
since we Chinese men prefer weak, delicate, precious, and useless
women, like Lin Daiyu in the *Dream of the Red Chamber,* while our Chinese
women desire effeminate men?[23]

The story is ultimately more complicated than what I can account for
in the limited space here. Suffice it to say that the author/narrator's
search for a better model for social progress in the West leads, in part, to
a self-imposed racial view that favors the French over the Chinese. Such
a stance becomes even more problematic when the narrator depicts the
so-called equality between black men and white women in France. He
encounters in the hospital, for instance, a middle-aged black man who is

visited by a gorgeous white woman; apparently, she is deeply in love with him. He claims that it is not uncommon for the French to see black men walking arm in arm with white women in the streets, but for people from the Far East such as himself, it nevertheless takes a while to get used to. Does the author/narrator depict the French as less prejudiced toward the black than the Chinese, or does he construct a Chinese national identity that is at once inferior to the French and superior to the black? Or does he construct a series of contradictory images that reflects his ambivalent attitude toward his own culture and Others?

In my view, one way to explain the ironic tensions between iconoclasm and nationalism in this story is to examine the narrator's personal circumstances at the moment of writing. The narrator states that although being sick far away from home is not desirable, his misfortune nevertheless turns out to be a good thing, for he has a chance to see the "real picture" of France from the unique perspective of commoners in a hospital established for them, which is a perspective unavailable in China.[24] Being poor, sick, and foreign, he is particularly impressed by the social equality between the rich and the poor, which the French at least attempted to address. The issue of class equality, therefore, might have affected his view of racial equality and explain his particular attention to the seemingly acceptable practice of interracial relationships. A plunge in class status, from a cultural elite at home to a poor student in a foreign land, therefore, may have played a role in his perceptions of the race/nation issues in France. This overemphasis on equality could also partially explain his comment that even poor French workers appear to have the same kind of mannerisms and sophistication as the senior advisors to the prime minister, unlike in China, where one can hardly miss the differences between the elite (*shangdeng ren*) and the commoners (*xiadeng ren*). The essentialist racial characterization in this text, however problematic, stems from the author's overall concern with social equality both in China and abroad and accounts for his construction of what he calls "the true spirit of the French commoners" (*Faguo pinmin de zhen jingshen*) after his own near-death experience.[25]

These intersecting views of class and race can also be understood from the intellectual contexts of the period. One can trace, for instance, this image of France as a mythical place where one can pursue social equality to the time prior to the May Fourth period. As Peng Ming points out, Chen Duxiu, in his pre-Communist days, looked to the "French civilization" as an inspirational model for the future of a better China. In an essay entitled "The French and Modern Civilizations" (*Falanxi ren yu jinshi wenming*), published in the first issue of *New Youth* (*Xin qingnian*, then called *Qingnian*), Chen declared that although people from other Western countries contributed to European civilization as a whole, the French were indeed the pioneers who had made the earliest and most significant contributions. Like many of his contemporaries, Chen was attracted to the French Revolution, to its "Declaration of the Rights of Man," and to its motto, "Every man is equal before the law."[26] This intellectual tradition partially led to the work-study program for Chinese students in France that began in 1912, a program that from 1919 to 1920 alone brought as many as 1,600 Chinese students to France. In his 1920 farewell speech to students departing for France, Wu Yuzhang explained their purposes abroad: France was "the center of European civilization with new academic achievements and technological innovations"; it was also an important site for investigating the unfolding Bolshevik revolution.[27] From a different, yet related, perspective, delving to the bottom of this advanced capitalist society to work alongside the proletarian class was seen as one of the most valuable training experiences for the first generation of Chinese communists.[28] Against such diverse intellectual backgrounds, the narrator's positive, yet questionable, depictions of France[29] can be seen as reflecting his own search for a spiritual China yet to emerge as an equal player to the West, however imagined that West turns out to be.

In contrast to Li's "Sympathy," which constructs France as a place of paradoxes, Jiang Guangci's "On the Yalu River" (*Yalujiang shang*, 1926), set in the early years of the Soviet Union, depicts a socialist country as an inspirational space to collect heroic stories.[30] In an interesting structure of a story-within-a-story, the narrator, a Chinese student studying in the Soviet Union, recounts the story of Yungu, a Korean woman who sacrificed her life in the nationalist struggle against Japanese occupation. While staying in Moscow at a nunnery that serves as a makeshift dormitory for foreign students, the narrator and his Persian roommate take to heart the tragic love story of Li Menghan, their Korean roommate. The fates of Li and Yungu, who grew up together as sweethearts in Korea, were sealed by their common family and national history. After Japan's occupation of Korea in 1910, the Japanese murdered Li's father after he assassinated a Japanese police officer; Li's grief-stricken mother threw herself into the sea to protest her husband's murder. Yungu's parents took Li in, and Yungu comforted and took care of him as a mother. To flee from Japanese persecution, Yungu sent Li across the Yalu River to escape to China and later on went across the Chinese border to join the Soviet Red Army to fight for the independence of Korea and other oppressed countries. Six years later, however, Li was grief-stricken by the tragic news that Yungu had been tortured to death in a Japanese prison in Korea as a leader of national independence. Li still mourns for the beauty, purity, and nobility of his fiancée, a saintly woman who is irreplaceable in his heart. This story of a Korean heroine—a story that traveled across various countries—helps a Chinese national in the Soviet Union confirm his shared destiny with other oppressed peoples in the world. This story of multiple perspectives and geopolitical locales thus constitutes for him a new Chinese identity, which is not confined by his own national and racial boundaries.

At the intersection of race and nation, moreover, gender politics also plays a role: a maternal figure becomes inspirational to male audiences both in the dormitory and beyond the immediate narrative space, thereby validating the Bolshevik revolution, a model for the Chinese and Korean revolutions. Indeed, the image of Yungu adds an interesting dimension to the group of new women Hu Ying insightfully studies in her *Tales of Translation*, which "traces the production, circulation, and appropriation" of imported images of Western women in the late Qing period, such as the Lady of the Camellias, Sophia Perovskaia, and Madame Roland. Similar to Madame Roland, Yungu has also been "cast in a range of roles, from a helpful mate to her husband to a powerful political activist in her own right." She thus helps "narrate the complex relationship between imagining a foreign other and reimagining the self amid the interplay of local and global forces."[31] She is depicted at the same time, however, as a virtuous woman who showed filial piety to her parents and her fiancé, according to the decrees of traditional society. The image of Yungu might suggest a possible solution to the dilemma of the May Fourth generation with regard to its ironic tension between iconoclasm and nationalism. One might argue, for instance, that a happy medium is achieved in the characterization of Yungu as a self-conscious nationalist against Japanese colonialism and her filial piety to her parents, who, although aristocratic in family background, nevertheless became patriots against foreign occupation, thus preempting the necessity for the iconoclastic stance sometimes required of modern heroes and heroines.

The reimagining of the Self and the Other at the intersection of the local and the global becomes more intricate in Zhang Wentian's novel *Journey* (*Lütu*, 1924), set in 1920s America, where he lived from August 20, 1922, to the end of 1923.[32] Historians have neglected this chapter of Zhang's life and stress instead his later and longer experience in the Soviet Union, where the CCP sent him in 1925 to receive formal communist education. An emerging young leader by the age of twenty-five, who was thoroughly trained in Marxist and Leninist theories of socialist revolution, he was dispatched back to China in 1931 by the Comintern to assume a leading position in the CCP.[33] In our context of stories of the Chinese diaspora, then, what does Zhang's early piece on America, written before his Soviet experience, tell us about his perception of a capitalist country? How did he construct an America in relationship to his knowledge of other foreign cultures and literatures? What in his view of America reflected his experience as an overseas Chinese in the 1920s? Similar to many of his contemporaries, Zhang was influenced by progressive journals such as *New Youth* and *Shenbao,* and had already published numerous essays, prose, and new poetry while participating in the political debates on labor issues, rural society, cultural movements, and marriage and family relationships.[34] He also brought out scholarly essays on the literary theories of Tolstoy and Oscar Wilde, and was among the first few Chinese scholars to examine Goethe's *Faust* and its spirit of fully participating in life's journey, in spite of all obstacles.[35]

Recognized as a young literary talent and translator, Zhang Wentian was invited by fellow members of the Young China Study Association (Shaonian Zhongguo Xuehui) to study in San Francisco while working as an editor for a Chinese newspaper. Three months later, however, after his arrival in the United States, Zhang expressed his resentment at the racial discrimination and materialist pursuits in America in a letter to Yu Dafu on November 22, 1922. As a lonely foreigner living in the "Sahara desert" in the West, Zhang also missed China, his homeland.[36] In the library at the University of California at Berkeley, Zhang continued his study of world affairs, which only confirmed his belief in socialism, especially after he had lived in America and witnessed its social evils with his own eyes. To his Chinese readers, he wrote about his excitement over the successful new economic policies in the Soviet Union. He also analyzed the political situations in postwar England, Germany, France, and America. He predicted (rightly, as it turned out) that in spite of the ongoing negotiations of treaties and war reparations between these countries, the irreconcilable differences among them as both new and old imperialist rivals would no doubt bring about another world war some twenty years hence. He urged the Chinese people to overthrow the capitalist system and to build China into a "shining and gigantic country" that could become a model for all oppressed people from the so-called "weak nations."[37]

On one level, *Journey* can be seen as a blueprint of how these idealistic visions can be achieved through one individual's quest for love and for the meaning of life. Writing in America at this particular moment in his life, Zhang combined his Marxist tendencies with his romantic spirit— acquired through Western literature—in his depictions of the numinous journey of Junkai and his entanglement with three women: a Chinese woman and two American women. Instead of assigning to each woman the distinction of being either a Chinese or American woman, however, the author creates in each a substitute for what is missing in the protagonist's life at a particular moment. The first part of the novel, for instance, begins with Junkai, an engineer in an American company in California who is dispirited by racial discrimination and boredom. He has just received a heartbreaking letter from Yunqing, his lover in China who is about to marry a stranger, according to her mother's wish. Yunqing's letter plunges him into a deep depression, which results in his lying in bed for eight days. It is during this period that Anna enters his life. This blue-eyed, blonde, American woman seems to understand his pain without any explanation. Although an American in appearance, Anna acts and speaks in a way very similar to Yunqing; indeed, she replaces Yunqing as his loving companion in America, in a foreign land where the protagonist misses his female companion even more than before.

The story then shifts back to China, explaining in a flashback Junkai's reason for coming to America in the first place. Two years earlier, in the suffocating, humid city of Tianjin, he was working at an engineering company in a job he resented and was living a tedious life without purpose. Drowning in alcohol and loneliness, he accepted an invitation to work in San Francisco. He knew that living in America would not necessarily mean a better life; he might feel even more lonely than before and perhaps might even die as "a dog" overseas.[38] In this moment of despair, with no prospect of happiness in either country, he encountered Yunqing on his way from Tianjin to Shanghai. An innocent, lively, and beautiful woman who breathed new life into his existence, Yunqing revived his spirit and inspired him to search for a better life. Although she had agreed to fulfill her mother's wish and go ahead with her arranged marriage, Yunqing promised Junkai to remain his true love forever and to cheer him on as he journeyed to America. In this depiction of Yunqing, the author provides the protagonist with a timely object of romantic love to substitute for his unrequited love for his motherland. Whereas her suffering allegorizes the misery of China under Confucian bondage, Yunqing's devotion energizes him while at the same time releasing him from his ties to China.

It is important to note that in the character of Yunqing, Zhang Wentian also was speaking from his own experience as a victim of the system of arranged marriage. Similar to Yunqing, he had married a stranger for fear of breaking his mother's heart. When he writes of Junkai's forgiving the "cruelty" of Yunqing's mother, after Junkai's realization that an arranged marriage is what a loving mother is expected to do in a Confucian society,[39] Zhang is in effect forgiving his own mother. Zhang further depicts Junkai as having been trapped in the same dilemma, but in this case the timely death of his parents relieved Junkai of the need to go through with his arranged marriage. One detects here a strategy of double substitutions: by offering Junkai a way out of his arranged marriage, Zhang rewrites his own life experience in a scenario that best resolves the tension between his filial piety and his rebellion against such tradition. By projecting onto Yunqing his own past experience, Zhang accentuates the tragic effects of Confucianism on a female victim while at the same time preserving for the male protagonist the role of her supporter against tradition.

Whereas the first part of the story begins in America and traces the protagonist's life back to China, the second part focuses on his experience in the United States. Projecting his own view of China into his American characters, Zhang depicts Anna's mother as extremely progressive; she does not take for granted China's inferior position in the world. In their first conversation, Anna's mother voices her dissatisfaction with a hostile world in which human beings are divided by national and racial boundaries, such as the Chinese, Japanese, Americans, and British, whose prejudice and hatred have resulted in world wars. She also expresses her resentment upon hearing Chinese being addressed as "Chinamen" and "Chinks," or Japanese as "Japs." To her, such racism merely proves the ignorance of those Americans who fail to appreciate China's ancient civilization.[40] Such views have apparently deeply affected Anna, who admires the Chinese so much that she falls in love with Junkai. She writes him weekly letters to discuss world affairs, especially with regard to China, and comforts him during their walks together along the moonlit river in Yosemite. He cannot, however, allow himself to return her love for fear of forgetting Yunqing, who depends on his love letters to help her endure her meaningless existence in China.

While distancing himself emotionally from Anna, however, Junkai is drawn to Margaret, a Berkeley student of French literature who is equally devoted to China. Margaret becomes even more irresistible after she finally confides her own tragic love story to Junkai. She vowed never to get married after her conservative mother from New England drove away her true love, a struggling novelist with few financial prospects. Upon hearing Margaret's story, Junkai feels happy for the first time since his arrival in America, for he has finally found a soul mate who resents the materialist aspects of America as much as he resents China's centuries-old traditions. He discovers in Margaret an equal, who, similar in fate to Yunqing, proves nevertheless stronger in her will to fight against her mother's prejudice. Embodying the same kind of femininity as Yunqing and Anna, Margaret demonstrates a braver spirit than his own. As a leftist from Berkeley, Margaret indeed revives his early desire to participate in the Chinese revolution. Inspired by the recent establishment of a revolutionary party in China, Margaret encourages him to go back to his home country, where he can make a difference. The second part of the story ends with Margaret's death in a hospital in Chicago, on her way to join Junkai on the West Coast before their journey together to China. No longer able to fight alongside him in China, she urges him to overcome his sentimental mentality: her last words are "charge on, my Junkai." The third part of the story shifts back to China, where Junkai has been appointed deputy commander of the revolutionary army. After Yunqing nurses his wounds, he returns to the battlefield, where he dies. He is remembered by his comrades as a worthy member of the revolutionary party of "Grand China" (*Da Zhongguo*).

Before all this happened, there had been one more important moment in the story back in America: after having discovered that Junkai was indeed attracted to Margaret, a heartbroken Anna threw herself into the river. Eventually, he lost two American women, whose memory urged him on in the struggle for a better and stronger China. This episode reminds me of an intriguing scene in David Hwang's play *M. Butterfly*, which premiered in 1988. The play, based on a true story, is a reversal of the Western masterpiece *Madame Butterfly*, in which a Japanese woman kills herself for an American GI. Hwang's play tells the story of Rene Gallimard, a French diplomat whose fantasy of being loved by a butterfly lures him to fall in love with Song Liling, a Chinese woman who turns out to be a man. Hwang's play thus pokes fun at the cultural stereotype of "yet another lotus blossom pining away for a cruel Caucasian man, and dying for her love."[41] In one scene, Song challenges Gallimard's favorite fantasies about submissive Oriental women killing themselves for cruel white men. Whereas the French man considers such stories "beautiful," he would probably consider a blonde homecoming queen a "deranged idiot" if she fell in love with a short Japanese man who treated her cruelly while turning down "marriage from a young Kennedy."[42]

Such an unlikely story of a Western woman falling in love with an Oriental man, however, indeed occurs in Zhang Wentian's *Journey*, in which not just one but two beautiful American women—one blonde, one brunette—die for a Chinese man. Not only did a beautiful blonde kill herself for the love of a "sickly" Chinese with no financial prospects, but an intelligent American brunette even began her own journey to follow him to China to fight for his country. Zhang did see his story of racial, gender, and class equality as "beautiful," one for which he had fought all his life, as his later revolutionary career proved. Almost seventy years before Hwang, then, Zhang concurred with Hwang's critique of a racist America where "race and sex intersect the issue of imperialism."[43] In Zhang's story, however, the Westerners who die for an Easterner are women and not men, therefore further dissecting the stereotypical and binary view of the imperialist (masculine) West and colonized (feminine) East that Hwang so brilliantly satirizes. On different levels of narrative strategy, the signifiers attached to the West and the East are constantly in flux, having to do less with geographical divides than with diverse cultural conceptions. At certain moments in the story, both China and the United States are seen as inspirational: the romantic landscape in California, with its waterfalls, moonlit rivers, camping grounds, and national parks, seems to coexist in Junkai's mind with the peaceful rural area of his home in China,[44] inspiring his wish to serve it better upon his return from America. At other moments, however, America is seen as equally corrupt and demoralizing and, like China, in need of political reorientation. Taken as a whole, the story depicts America neither as an ideological ideal against which China should measure its progress nor as a monolithic space of capitalist evils without spiritual pursuits. In the combined voices of one Chinese man and two American women in their quest for a better world, the story cuts across boundaries of sex, race, and nation to critique the negative aspects of both countries while embracing their constructive elements. Whereas the criticism of America's racial discrimination and unequal power relationships, voiced by Anna's mother and Margaret, demonstrates that the West is not monolithic, Junkai's protest against China's stagnating history and his people's lack of spirit questions the simple equation of "West = imperialism, China = victims of such imperialism." To some extent, the story reads almost like an international romance between an enlightened Chinese man and two Renaissance American women, who bridge two cultures in their imaginary ideal. In this romantic entanglement, a "perfect" Chinese woman in Yunqing provides another soul mate to Junkai, who understands his journey between East and West.

Considering the Chinese diaspora stories of the 1980s in the intellectual contexts of the 1920s stories discussed above, how did the motivations of the students in the 1980s resemble or differ from those in the 1920s? How did the writings of the Chinese diaspora help us understand the Chinese conceptions of the Selves and Others in a post-socialist state grappling with the aftermath of Maoist China, which also demanded a reintroduction of Western science and democracy? Despite their obvious differences, the 1980s shared a surprisingly similar cultural atmosphere with that of the 1920s. Like the 1920s, which witnessed intellectual ferment and a sense of immense possibilities, the 1980s marked a new era, welcomed as a chance to overcome the cultural and ideological legacy of Maoist China. Both periods expressed a sense of backwardness when China opened up to the outside, with a steady flow of Chinese students going abroad. In their very popular reportage entitled *Exchanging Revolutionary Experience in the World* (*Shijie da chuanlian,* 1987), Hu Ping and Zhang Shengyou recorded the historical contexts of this new wave of students going abroad.

In borrowing the phrase "exchanging revolutionary experience," Hu and Zhang were drawing from their immediate past history. The phrase originally referred to the mass movement in 1966 of more than fifty million Red Guards who traveled to different parts of China to spread Mao Zedong's message about the necessity of the Cultural Revolution. Hu and Zhang saw this movement as one of the origins of the overseas student movement of the 1980s; some of these students were indeed ex–Red

Guards themselves. Similar to the Red Guards, whose destinations were revolutionary sites such as Beijing, Yan'an, Shaoshan, and the Jinggang Mountains, Chinese students also had their clear goals: North America, Japan, France, and Italy, with the United States as the most popular destination. Unlike the Red Guards, however, who returned to their hometowns a few months later, Chinese students seldom went back to China, many of them settling down instead as overseas Chinese. In contrast to the passionate yet quickly waning Red Guard movement, the trend of Chinese students going abroad was still gathering momentum and would consequently exert a lasting impact on China.[45] How did the country respond to this tremendous change? Was this trend beneficial to China? What were the reasons behind this trend? What did this phenomenon tell us about the mentality and hopes of the people going abroad and the people they left behind? These were some of the issues that drove the writing of Hu and Zhang, which was supposedly based on real people and real events.

To explore these questions, Hu and Zhang began their study by examining the devastating impact of the "brain drain" on China. At the China Opera House, for instance, four out of five actresses who had played the title role of *Carmen* in five years during the early 1980s had left the country to become foreign stars.[46] Its symphony lost one-third of its players, who after having received training worth tens of thousands of government dollars, were easily lured away to music schools abroad by small financial aid packages. One professor lamented that throughout his teaching career in half a century, he had never seen so many students so eager to leave him for foreign universities. To answer the charge that these students worshiped things foreign and had deserted China, which needed their talents the most, Hu and Zhang explored the roots of the problem: China's neglect of its own talents. In a 1986 article, for instance, the *Wenhui Newspaper* reported that at least two-thirds of the technicians and scientists in Shanghai had not been able to put their expertise to use, with another third never appointed to the positions appropriate for their training. Consequently, many intellectuals sought employment unconnected with their training because it paid a better salary and benefits. In an opening bid for managing positions in a Hilton Hotel, three hundred people applied, most of whom were university lecturers and advanced graduate students in other fields. In tough competition, one out of eight were hired, almost the current ratio for the competitive selection of graduate students in Chinese universities.

To further explain why some young people were anxious to leave China, Hu and Zhang narrated the story of Ouyang Caiwei, whose parents and grandparents were returned students from foreign countries. Because her mother had studied English at UCLA in 1947, Ouyang was denied entry to college during the Cultural Revolution, in spite of her mother's explanation that her study abroad was sponsored by a women's association that supported Asian and African students, which had nothing to do with the imperialist U.S. government. At the age of thirty-seven, Ouyang decided to follow in her mother's footsteps. She wanted to make more money abroad while training herself to be a better scientist in a more advanced country. Ouyang made it clear that her journey abroad would be for only a few years and that she would definitely return to China. "I am from the Third World. I will come back after I have improved myself. Who would rather live in the First World only as a Third-World citizen?"[47]

Through this story and others, Hu and Zhang demonstrated that "worshipping things foreign" could not fully explain why so many Chinese people chose to leave. By going abroad to improve their livelihood, these people had succeeded where their government had failed. The movement to study abroad could thus be seen as "tidal waves gushing through the two valleys of hope and disappointment." Until we have established a new system of respecting individual talents, Hu and Zhang argued, the movement to "exchange revolutionary experience in the world" would continue to gain momentum. "We pin our hopes on the economic and political reform of China," Hu and Zhang concluded. When China eventually becomes a strong nation in its own right, they predicted, another global movement to "exchange revolutionary experience in the world" would begin; the final destination, however, would be China, with a constant flow of talents from the West to the East. Such a prediction was not a self-congratulating and farfetched daydream, Hu and Zhang claimed, since many experts already believed that the twenty-first century would indeed be the century of Asia, with the economic and political success of the Pacific Rim.[48] In Hu and Zhang's reportage, one detects an approach that assumes China will become a superpower, a vision of a "grand China" such as Zhang Wentian projected into his nationalist heroes in the 1920s. It also echoed the optimistic post-Mao discourse of openness and reform expressed by *He shang* and Shakespearean theater in the 1980s, which addressed mostly the domestic situation in China.

Hu and Zhang's reportage provided a look at the sociopolitical circumstances within China that influenced Chinese students' going abroad in the 1980s, giving the point of view of one outside the movement. Zhou Li's *A Chinese Woman in Manhattan* (*Manhadun de Zhongguo nüren*, 1992), in contrast, offered an insider's account of her personal journey, with a focus on her life in America and its impact on her reflections of China's past.[49] It has been reported that within five months of its initial release, Zhou's book was reprinted four times with at least 500,000 copies sold throughout the country. One private book dealer profited from such a sudden demand of the book by reportedly wholesaling 60,000 pirated copies. Eventually, this book made it to the top of the list of best-selling literary works in the Fifth National Book Exhibition, a fact that, according to one critic, testified to "readers' enthusiasm unprecedented in the past few years."[50]

First published in Beijing, in July 1992, as "autobiographical fiction," supposedly based on the exotic experiences of a native-born Chinese woman living in the West, *A Chinese Woman in Manhattan* was said to have touched many hearts[51] with its exceptional tale of how a poor Chinese woman, presented in the text as an I-narrator, became rich and famous in Manhattan in less than four years after her arrival in the United States in 1985. Added to this "American-dream" story were passionate accounts of the narrator's unrequited love for various Chinese men during the Cultural Revolution when love affairs were sometimes made or broken on the basis of political considerations. For many Chinese readers, this cross-cultural success story surely seemed to continue the literary traditions of "wound literature" and "reflective literature" (*fansi wenxue*), which depict the suffering and sacrifice of young people and of their parents during the Cultural Revolution and which were popular in the days after the death of Mao. Yet at the same time, this book was noted for its having moved beyond post–Cultural Revolutionary traditions in its creation of a new world of literature, where an ordinary Chinese woman had risen to the top of the American world through her extraordinary talents and by the sheer force of her will.[52]

The book was very popular in 1992 with its wide spectrum of readers, many of whom read, cried, and admired the "spiritual strength" of the author.[53] What is the charisma, one critic asks, of this Chinese woman in Manhattan that appeals simultaneously to old and young, to intellectuals and to entrepreneurs as well?[54] The solution to the mystery of the book's attraction to contemporary Chinese readers can probably be discerned in a discussion of the book in a Chinese publication, which enthusiastically describes its "enlightening revelation of a success story of a single Chinese woman across the oceans," its "intimate remembrance of the arduous journey from Shanghai to the Northeast wilderness during the Cultural Revolution," and finally, its "inspiring emotions of Chinese national pride" and a longing for the motherland that permeated the book, as one critic claimed.[55]

Yet *A Chinese Woman in Manhattan* became an even bigger sensation when several overseas readers in the New York Chinese community furiously challenged it. Several recent immigrants who personally knew Zhou Li accused her of falsely using their names in her fiction in order to emphasize her success while fabricating her accounts of the way that other Chinese failed in American business while she succeeded spectacularly. Contrary to the claim made in the book that the author lived in a luxurious apartment near Central Park and traveled all over the world for business and pleasure, they pointed out that she actually continues to live with her family in a shared apartment in one of the poorest neighborhoods in New York.[56] In contrast to the claims of being a millionaire, they said she could not even afford her own office space to carry out her business activities.[57] "Not being rich is, of course, no crime," they argue, yet it is a crime to poison the minds of young Chinese who are naively deceived by Zhou's fantasy of an easy access to the "American dream."[58] By the standards of her overseas critics, Zhou's book is especially "harmful" since she claims that ninety-five percent of her "autobiographical fiction" was based on factual and personal experience. Yet this is not the case and that very fact challenges the thematic and ideological claims of the book in a very fundamental way. "How many tragedies would this book help bring about for young people" who read it with sincerity and goodwill?[59] The "myth of the West" has to be quickly exposed to gain a balanced and realistic view of the West.[60]

Elated by the successful sale of her book in China, however, Zhou Li declared that her next "biggest dream" was to produce an English translation so that it would become a best seller in the West as well as in China. If this really was a wish on her part, and not part of the elaborate fiction about herself that she has already constructed, it seems surprising. It is difficult to believe that even a newcomer to American culture could be so totally unaware of the fact that, if available in English, her book could be easily singled out as extraordinarily imperialist, racist, and sexist in the claims that it advances. At the beginning of the book, the I-narrator brags of her success in America while describing in great detail the failure of the American people in their own country. She remarks on the racial differences between herself, a poor Chinese woman who became a millionaire in a foreign land where she had to overcome numerous linguistic, cultural, and social obstacles, and those "gorgeous" American waitresses and secretaries working under her. These unfortunate Americans, who, "although blessed with all the advantages granted by God"—"white skin," "blue eyes," and "native language"—could only "live a poor life" with minimum wages and "extreme pressure from work."[61] She asserts the superiority of white Western men over their non-Western, non-White counterparts in telling how she snatched such a man away from her American girlfriend, who had helped her since she first came to America. Having experienced many sorrows in her relationships with different men in China, Zhou says, it was this Western man, with "white, smooth skin," and "beautiful European features," who had finally given her true love, genuine sexual pleasure, and a beautiful son who had European features. In contrast to her admiration of white males, however, Zhou deeply resents African Americans. She reports how she felt insulted as a Chinese national when an African American policeman attempted to stop an illegal

Chinese artist painting in the streets of New York: "Aren't you blacks usually drug-dealers, robbers, murderers, and rapists yourself?" She asks indignantly, "Why don't you punish them?"[62]

Most ironically, while complacent about Chinese supremacy over other ethnic groups in the West, the I-narrator consciously acts both as a subordinate in Western hierarchical society and as its active agent in pursuing its interests in her native land. She depicts herself as a broker constantly shuttling between China, where Third World cheap labor and raw material were willingly provided, and metropolitan New York, the center of world trade. She celebrates the image of New York City as the center of Western imperialism and colonialism: "Park Avenue represents the splendor, luxury, generosity, and might of a golden empire"; "Manhattan is a miracle," and New York is the "most charming city in the world."[63] Some Western readers are likely to read such claims as hilarious and unintended affirmations of their author's ignorance of the United States. But as the earlier ideologically questionable remarks about race and gender make clear, such an overt affirmation of Western imperialist power has serious ramifications. One of these has to do with the image of China as a nation that emerges from this discourse. The image of China as one's motherland is mixed together with the I-narrator's self-esteem; being successful in America somehow testifies to the power of her motherland, which produces glorious offspring. The image of the Chinese nation as a soft, feminine, forgiving motherland, embracing its children from overseas in spite of their condemnation of her past abuses, may evoke what Homi K. Bhabha calls the revelation of an "ambivalent margin of the nation-space," which can "contest claims to cultural supremacy, whether these are made from the 'old' post-imperialist metropolitan nations, or on behalf of the 'new' independent nations of the periphery."[64]

Yet it is precisely this questionable nationalist discourse that has touched the hearts of so many Chinese readers. He Zhenbang argues, for instance, that the I-narrator's so-called arrogance is indeed "an expression of patriotism": "every single business deal she helps to bring into China from America is itself a concrete act of such patriotism."[65] From a slightly different angle, Zeng Zhennan also believes that many readers were attracted to *A Chinese Woman in Manhattan* not because it "aroused one's curiosity about making a fortune overseas," or because it somehow "offered the knack of successful business" from a "young Chinese woman." Rather, many readers were won over by the I-narrator's depiction of commercial practice, which "has already been elevated to a spiritual world of self-definition and self-perfection," thus "entering the temple of literature with aesthetic values."[66]

At least at the time of this writing, Zhou has not seen the fulfillment of her wish that her "autobiography" be translated into English. Were it available in a Western language, however, it is easy to imagine what the response would be. Some Western reviewers and readers would find it an easy object of angry criticism for its self-imposed Orientalism, imperialism, and nationalism. Its glowing celebration of the West could readily be utilized by "Third-World-born" critics writing in the West to advance their own agenda of trashing Western culture even while enjoying its benefits. Other critics, foreigners and native-born alike, might find in this book a vivid demonstration of how China is in dire need of a grand Western theoretical framework in order to be aware of its subject-slave position. It would be difficult to fault any of these perspectives as valid responses, but only partially and incompletely so, to Zhou's extraordinary work.

Yet anyone who attempts to chronicle the course of the Chinese debates on this book will be struck by how the Chinese critics and readers heatedly discussed this book in their own terms, which are at best only partially connected with issues that motivate current Western academic discourse. Even those Chinese respondents who condemned the book, and did so from a variety of different perspectives, did not seem to be affected by the large volumes of recent translations of Western literary and cultural theory, including theories of postmodernism and postcolonialism. The Chinese debate on the Chinese book carried on within Chinese contexts—I will briefly recount that debate in the next paragraph—renders the political intervention of Western dicourse irrelevant and powerless within its confines. Indeed, a colonialist critique on this book, which, as I have suggested, is easy to produce in the current Western intellectual atmosphere, would almost certainly sound to many Chinese readers and critics as nothing more than a repetition of the official ideological discourse, which has always deemed the West as a dangerous Other attempting to colonize and subvert Communist China. It would not be easy for many Chinese participants in the debate over the book to forget their traumatic experiences during the Cultural revolution, which was supposed to have supported the "Third World Revolution" through its own "struggle for a continued Chinese socialist revolution." Such anti-colonialist and anti-imperialist discourse and its subsequent ideology officially imposed in China also led to the losses of innocent life in the Korean War as well as of valuable resources in Vietnam at a time when millions of Chinese people were impoverished. For many Chinese people who had lived through the tyranny of a Communist system, anti-colonialism and anti-imperialism cannot be taken as mere intellectual discourse; it partially symbolizes for them a strategy of political suppression and economic deprivation. And it is precisely this perspective that rightly renders so much of Western theory more than suspect and ultimately irrelevant to their own experience, as they— in contrast to critics in the West—have experienced it and understood it.

Let us briefly examine, then, the main issues of the debate in the reception of this work in the China of 1992. Some critiques were concerned with the "literary value" of the book. Bewildered by the almost unanimous positive reactions, which claimed it was a "masterpiece," Wu Liang argued that *A Chinese Woman in Manhattan* lacked literary creativity. It is, in this critic's account, at best nothing more than a journalistic account of overseas experiences, the factuality of which could never be verified. Although sharing certain features with "wound literature," *A Chinese Woman in Manhattan* is for him nevertheless a step backward from such tradition both in linguistic and ideological terms. It expresses, he says, nothing more than a familiar "bourgeois world view" that "defines flowers, banquets, holiday vacation, sex, and affluence as the index of one's happiness"; the author was thus only "intoxicated by her own success."[67]

In contrast to such a view, Yang Ping believed that the author of *A Chinese Woman in Manhattan* functioned as a Chinese huckster selling to her home market an "American dream" of individualism, which Arthur Miller already criticized in his play *Death of a Salesman*. Added to this American dream, Yang correctly pointed out, was a "Chinese 'ugly duckling's'" dream of a "white knight," which was drawn from the author's own values and a broader "rich-and-famous dream" that "permeates our own historical times."[68] Yet at the very moment when we "join the parade celebrating the American dream, we have at the same time lost our own dream." But, the critic says, such an American dream, nevertheless, will "eventually be destroyed because the Chinese people will never accept an American way of life based on plundering resources in the world."[69]

Many others, however, argued that there was nothing wrong in indulging an American dream if it simply means striving for individual happiness, a dream that everyone in the world shares. Why shouldn't we, they ask, import an American dream in order to realize our own dream? Why are so many people having problems accepting other people's success, especially a woman's success?[70] Following the same line of argument, one critic further states: "it is extremely irritating for a male reader if a 'small woman' can demonstrate her success through economic power."[71] What hides behind the image of a "bragging businesswoman," Li Shidong claimed, was a real Chinese experience that demonstrates the strength of spiritual qualities.[72] For the Chinese reader, the questions that this book raises are, and rightly so, about the Chinese experience, its past and present, and its hopes for the future.

There are, of course, many reasons for the popularity of *A Chinese Woman in Manhattan* and the intensity of discussion it provided. It is important to note that the American success story is situated at the very beginning of the first chapter, and this account serves as a point of departure for the narrator's journey into a tragic past. Chapter 2 revisits her happy and innocent childhood and her traumatic initiation into adolescence during the Cultural Revolution. Chapters 3 and 4 detail her passionate and frustrated love experiences in the wilderness and are followed by the last chapter, which depicts the protagonist's fulfilling career and happy family life in America. Throughout the book, a depiction of the West, which is readily seen as largely imaginary by those who have lived there, is rendered credible to those who have not by the precise, realistic, and vivid representations of a Chinese past that was personally witnessed by many of the book's Chinese readers. The positive depictions of her white American man and her new country as a land of milk and honey are then not so much expressions of a craving for everything that is Western but rather a longing for a China free of tyranny and abuse. There is also a longing for the happy adolescence she could have had if the social and political conditions in China had been different. Indeed, at the end of the book, there is even a temporary moment of reconciliation with her past sufferings. The protagonist is depicted as sitting by a campfire at the Grand Canyon, a quintessentially American location. Yet here she nostalgically finds in her Western man's face the familiar features of the Chinese man she fell in love with fourteen years earlier in the Chinese wilderness. Both Western and Chinese man are for a moment equally "charming, smart, and brave." For a long time before this moment of peace and happiness, it was China's rejection of her both as an acceptable citizen and as a passionate lover that made a Western man's affection and the Western order of individualism so enchanting to her.[73]

Close examination will show how this coming together of American and Chinese experience recurs throughout this book, even as it sets about at every turn to separate East and West in an almost Manichean manner. Even in Zhou's account of life in America, one finds constant allusions to Chinese experience. Oliver Stone's 1991 motion picture *JFK*, for example, reminds her of an episode in her childhood when she and twelve other girls quietly mourned the "heroic" act of Lee Harvey Oswald, who sacrificed his own precious life to assassinate John Kennedy, thus heralding what they were told was the inevitable end of capitalism and imperialism. They did not realize, however, that Kennedy was deeply loved by the American people as "the youngest president in American history" who, among other things, "successfully handled the Cuban Missile Crisis and saved America from destruction." She thus gains insight into and questions the making of history as ideological impositions separating peoples from different cultures.[74] Here, as elsewhere in the book, one finds an implicit critique of the official Chinese Occidentalism imposed by the ruling ideology in Maoist China, which imagined a West as an Other subversive of revolutionary and proletarian China. And it is this critique that makes, what for the Western reader is regarded as little more than a wholesaling of the Western imperialist and patriarchal system, something quite different for his Chinese counterpart. For many Chinese the book can be read as a discourse of power against the official culture of the state-party apparatus. The fictional depiction of an imagined West, rendered as all the more believable by the author's claim that it is an autobiographical fiction, is particularly appealing to many Chinese readers as an alternative to the social reality of contemporary China, where success is usually attributed to family background and privilege. It is only from the perspective of the cultural specificities of contemporary Chinese society that an overt celebration of American imperialism and colonialism can "be liberated from the symbolism of the fetish and serve as the real source of inspiration for those who now turn toward it in search of an answer," to borrow Wang Jing's powerful critique of *He shang*.[75] The sense of history, albeit of the contemporary period and from a cross-cultural perspective, is similar to that conveyed in *He shang*, whose "project of the liberation of the present from the burden of history" is both "contradictory" and "paradoxical."[76]

To understand *A Chinese Woman in Manhattan* in this way is not, however, to claim that it cannot be appropriately understood in other, and markedly different, ways, including those advocated by critics speaking from a post-colonialist perspective. It would be difficult for a Westerner, or even someone who has lived in the West as a foreigner, not to be troubled by the book's racism and sexism. Its constant tone of self-promotion is bound to disturb many readers. Yet the conclusion to be drawn from these differences is not that its author is ideologically naïve or the hapless and helpless victim of an irresistible Western ideology, but that writing and reading are always initiated as local activity, always at least partially determined by the exigencies of time and place. Critics who miss this point, who constantly lament an Occidentalism or Orientalism, which, their protests notwithstanding, consists of essentialist perspectives often condescending both to West and East, may advance what they think of as Western theory, but will utterly misconstrue the experiences of those whom they claim to describe and whose interests they claim to advance. The success of *A Chinese Woman in Manhattan* is hardly surprising and is certainly not to be lamented, at least from a native Chinese perspective. By narrating a personal story that highlights her seduction of a Western man and her conquering Western culture, the Chinese female protagonist of this autobiography has captured a Chinese readership, which, against the constraints of both its own national government and theorists in the West, aspires to "Western" experiences, surely not as they "really are" but as they are imagined by the Other who understands and uses "the West" for its own theoretical and pragmatic interests.

In the process of the Occidentalizing manifest in Zhou's book, the paradoxical relationships between Self and Other, between various kinds of East and West, are made clear. On one level the protagonist's experiences in the West place her in a hegemonic relationship to her own people. Here the universalizing Western master narrative finds a problematic voice in the China-woman subject, whose own national tale of an oppressive Chinese society, especially during the Cultural Revolution, is ultimately lost in her exotic tale of her adventure in the West. The tale of the Other thus renders silent the tale of the Self, paving the way for a globalizing discourse that glorifies the image of the Others who are still imagined, even by one who has physically been there herself. In this regard, the critique of the post-colonialist theorist is apt.

Yet even such overt colonialist and Orientalist discourse in *A Chinese Woman in Manhattan* is not monolithic, despite initial impressions. It cannot in the last instance be reduced to binary oppositions, which speak either for or against the Self or the Other, or for or against diverse views of the East or the West. In this book, as always in a discourse that is cross-cultural in its concerns, the reflection of the Self is embedded within the representation of the Other. A good example is the manner in which the book's narrative voice employs a racist discourse to describe African Americans who ruthlessly murdered a Chinese artist in New York. The message that this voice bears is, on the one hand, all too recognizable as an expression of the prejudiced and unjustified beliefs of white Americans. But on the other hand, it is also clearly homebound, since it immediately raises questions about who should shoulder the responsibility for those talented Chinese artists plying their trade in American streets: "Oh, my motherland, why do you force your splendid offsprings to drift in a foreign land?"[77] Similarly, the nostalgic feelings toward one's childhood, lost love, and longing for the homeland form the central messages of *A Chinese Woman in Manhattan*, in spite of the fact that such Occidentalist discourse is and will remain problematic when expressed through the image of the Other.

How had these paradoxical views of America and China evolved five years later in 1997 in Hu Ping's second popular piece of reportage,[78] entitled *Immigrating to America (Yimin Meiguo)*? As if echoing Zhou Li's autobiography, which narrated her own reasons for living in America, Hu Ping provided a more personal picture than that of his 1987 reportage with regard to the irreversible trend of immigrating to America in the late 1990s. After his own trip to America and interviewing many new Chinese Americans, Hu admitted that he was wrong in 1987 to believe and report as a fact an expert's prediction that only one-tenth of Chinese students would choose to stay in America. Neither was he right when he forecast that the destination of the "brain drain" would redirect itself from the West to the East. Indeed, the statistics now seemed even more astonishing: each year, more than 40,000 students were still flooding into America from China, surpassing Japan (30,000) and South Korea (10,000). Among the nine million Asian Americans, two million are now Chinese Americans. Confronted with a shared choice made by numerous Chinese people, one cannot simply dismiss Chinese immigrants as isolated cases. Nor can one easily reject America by producing a series of "Say No" books to boost a self-deceptive Chinese nationalism, Hu declared. Looking back at the twentieth-century history of China and the West, Hu argued that, whereas on the one hand China had no doubt suffered from a hundred years of imperialist aggression and humiliation, it was important to remember that China's isolation and rejection of modernization and individualism had also contributed to its national disasters. During his trip to America, Hu felt obligated to listen to, understand, and narrate the stories of new Chinese immigrants in order to decipher the history of the nation and the souls of the Chinese people.[79]

To achieve this goal, Hu divided *Immigrating to America* into two parts. The first, entitled "The Trials and Tribulations of the Insignificant" (*Jiemo cangsang*), narrated a story that "belongs to the era of isolation and complacence" in the early 1960s, when China rejected everything foreign as either imperialist or social imperialist. Not only America and Europe were denounced as imperialist enemies; even students from a few socialist countries were closely watched to make sure they were living by the strict rules of this purely revolutionary country in the East. An Yi was one of the unfortunate ones, a girl from Beijing who in 1963 fell in love with Qiaodi, a blond-haired, blue-eyed Albanian student. For this innocent love, An Yi paid the price of two years in prison without a trial and many more years of labor on a prison farm. An Yi could not understand why it was criminal to date an Albanian from our "brother" country, "the only socialist lamp in Europe," as the official media had so claimed. After all, she did not love just any Caucasian from a capitalist country. She was told that it was a criminal offense nevertheless because, with so many Chinese men available, she had chosen instead to love a foreigner. She was accused of being a "foreigner's prostitute" (*yangji*) and, as such, was criticized in prison study sessions by a real prostitute, who claimed that at least she had provided sex for workers, officials, and college students. Hence, she served the Chinese people and did it only for money. An Yi, on the other hand, shamelessly loved a foreigner for free.

An Yi could never fathom why anyone would forbid love relationships among people of different skin color and nationality. Neither could she understand that her affair had indeed crossed boundaries of sex, class, race, and nation. In the early 1960s, people involved in love affairs outside of wedlock could be accused of being "a bad element" (*huai fenzi*) and even end up sentenced to prison, as she was. One also needed to worry about the party doctrines against marriages across class lines. A member of a worker's family, for instance, was discouraged from involvement with someone born into the family of an ex-capitalist or a KMT official. In addition to these taboos of sex and class politics, dating an Albanian raised the complex issue of race and nation. Even at the time when China promoted friendship with a few socialist states, it still could not approve of Caucasians, who suggested colonialist history and Western imperialism. The category of "foreign," therefore, could become suspect, especially for those who ventured into the dangerous territory of love and sex. In Qiaodi's case, though he was from a socialist country and born into a revolutionary family, being white was a mark against him.

It is interesting to recall here our earlier discussion of Zhang Wentian's *Journey*, in which idealist relationships indeed transcend the boundaries of class, race, and nation. In the real world of 1960s socialist China, however, where Zhang's dream of equality for all people had supposedly been realized, An Yi had to endure punishment for a crime she never understood. After working on a prison farm and experiencing public humiliation during the Cultural Revolution, she finally married a man seventeen years her senior and was sent back to his hometown in a poverty-stricken village in Hebei Province, where she could not even feed her son. She finally managed to leave in 1982 after her divorce. In her subsequent years, while raising her two children from two marriages, An Yi sometimes thought about Qiaodi: as a son of a guerrilla fighter during World War II, how did he manage an increasingly harsh life in post-socialist Albania, where "the red flag had already fallen to the ground"?[80] She had also heard from Meng Baige, her former inmate friend who was also accused of being a "foreigner's prostitute" for having married a Russian from the Soviet Union. Calling from Japan, Meng advised An Yi to come there to marry a rich man for a better life. An Yi also heard from Jiang Ying, another former inmate friend. In 1975, when the PRC granted special amnesty to ex-KMT officials, Jiang quickly married one of them, whose hometown was Beijing, thus becoming eligible to return to Beijing with him. She mocked her own fate years later: "The KMT has finally brought me back to Beijing after the CCP had kicked me out."[81]

Indeed, An Yi's fate turned out to be worse than that of those ex-KMT and others wrongly accused as foreign spies and counterrevolutionaries, whose verdicts were usually reversed in the post-Mao era. Her case could not be cleared, since there was no official party document with regard to merely a few convictions of "foreigner's prostitutes" before the Cultural Revolution. Worse still, she heard that nowadays there were so many real foreigner's prostitutes that a high-ranking official had recently ordered they be severely punished with jail sentences or time at labor farms. One African man even published an article in his home country claiming that Shanghai girls were indeed the best prostitutes, who always took the initiative, had good hygiene, and charged a low fee. An Yi's brother lamented her misfortune of being a falsely accused "foreigner's prostitute" whose chance for being vindicated had recently been ruined again, this time by real foreigner's prostitutes. Just when China's door had been opened a crack, he complained, how could Chinese women use that opportunity to perform such shameless acts?[82]

These stories of the insignificant explored the cultural and historical circumstances that motivated Chinese people to leave China. Hu Ping warned his readers that nowadays many young people took for granted their undeniable rights to marry foreigners and live abroad without being aware what a high price An Yi had paid for her rights to love across national boundaries. Remembering this past history would not only ensure that China did not slide back into the Maoist era; it would also help people fully understand why so many Chinese are still leaving China in search of a better life. In the second part of *Immigrating to America,* which "belongs to a new era of openness and reform," Hu Ping was particularly interested in discovering "the psychological space" (*xinli kongjian*) of Chinese Americans who had immigrated to America in the past ten years. Why did they decide to stay on? What were their dreams and aspirations? Some of them, according to Hu, wanted to "experience a different way of living" (*huan yizhong huofar*), one not controlled by the changing policies of the party nor confined by the Chinese mentality of jealousy and pettiness.[83] Tired of iron rice bowls offered by a collective society, they wanted to see for themselves to what extent they could achieve their potential as individuals. One couple, for instance, gave up the husband's comfortable party position in China to start a restaurant in Mineral Well, Texas. Using Mao's strategy of "surrounding the cities from the countryside," they avoided major cities where restaurants faced tough competition and finally won the business of this small town. They also integrated themselves with the Western cowboys and Texas culture, following the spirit of one of Mao's sayings made popular during the Cultural Revolution: "We Communists are like seeds and the people are like the soil. Wherever we go, we must unite with the people, take root and blossom among them."[84] Contrary to their Maoist heritage, however, they were not there to liberate people from poverty in Texas but to realize their own modest dream of owning a small farm and traveling all over the world just like their American neighbors. To make this dream come true, they worked from nine in the morning to midnight every day, knowing full well that "accumulated working hours were printed on the other side of each green dollar note they make."[85] Ironically, these former urban youths who were sent down to rural areas during the Cultural Revolution had given up their once passionate dream of building collective farms in the socialist countryside. As it turned out, it was finally in America that they could look forward to their own private farm in a foreign land. They therefore could not accept the dark depiction of Chinese American life in recent

Chinese television dramas, which characterized Chinese Americans as suffering "coolies" in a racial and capitalist America. If that were the case, many illegal Chinese would have left the country on their own, without any help from the U.S. Immigration and Naturalization Service.

Hu Ping did not, however, present a rosy picture of America without a racist past and present. Tracing the civil rights movement, Hu analyzed the two hundred years of continued struggle on the part of African Americans to achieve equality in racial, social, and political terms. He believed, however, that a subjugated racial group also needed to look within itself for a catalyst for change. The Irish immigrants, for instance, who came in large numbers to build the transcontinental railway, were looked down upon by many of the British immigrants who had settled in Boston and other East Coast areas. The way some of the British Protestant settlers treated the Irish Catholics was similar to the way Shanghai urbanites treated rural people from the northern part of Jiangsu Province (*Subei ren*), Hu claimed. After generations of united effort, however, Irish Americans surpassed other ethnic groups in political power, in effect taking over Boston's city hall: since the 1920s, almost all the mayors there had been Irish, except for two Italian Americans. Moreover, in 1960 John F. Kennedy became the first Irish American U.S. president. Likewise, Japanese Americans, despite having been rounded up in interment camps during World War II, had also improved their social and economic status through their own achievements, as especially evident in the Japanese American influence in Hawaii. Chinese Americans, Hu Ping believed, were increasingly becoming aware of their collective history in order to improve their lives in America. Many have said that even though they felt, as first-generation immigrants, "marginal" to the mainstream (*bianyuan ren*), they believed their children would become more integrated into American society. Perhaps one of them would even become the first Chinese American U.S. president.

At the conclusion of *Immigrating to America*, Hu Ping noted that thirty years had passed between the story of the insignificant "foreigner's prostitute" and that of Chinese Americans, with the theme of revolution giving way to the theme of construction. The only thesis of his book, Hu claimed, is that "it is not necessary to invite historians to repeat the familiar story of the closed-door policies and missed opportunities for China since the late Qing dynasty. The post-1949 history itself has already taught us that China must be open. The most recent events in the last 18 years have demonstrated that China must open up even more to the world."[86] Declaring that China and America were two of the most creative countries in the world, Hu pinned his hope for a better China and for the world on the mutual understanding and acceptance among people of diverse cultures and histories. In Hu's work, one witnesses an interesting case of Occidentalism, in which America is constructed as an equally "great" Other to China through two sets of double images. American history is characterized both by racial discrimination against minority groups and by the collective efforts of the minority groups who have overcome such discrimination to achieve economic, cultural, and political success. On the other hand, contemporary China is depicted both as backward and hopeless in the closed-door period of Maoist China and as vibrant, dynamic, and hopeful, as seen in the success stories of the overseas Chinese, once freed from its past. By claiming that Chinese Americans would eventually become equal to and as influential as any other ethnic groups in America, Hu Ping expressed his hope that mainland China would benefit from the enterprising spirit of both Chinese Americans and other ethnic Americans.

Hu Ping's upbeat reportage, however, did not represent exclusive pictures of America and China in the 1990s. Whereas Hu's work continued to promote economic reforms in response to a Maoist past that had rejected materialist pursuits, other writers in the 1990s depicted the consequences of such reform: the search for wealth at the expense of spiritual fulfillment and moral values. Such a double-edged critique against Maoist and post-Maoist ideologies found its best expression in Yan Li's short story "The Behavior of Blood" (*Xueye de xingwei*, 1993), written in Manhattan, New York. The main character of the story is Li Xiong, who has inherited the practice of "blood transfusions" from his grandfather. Having been publicly humiliated as a former landowner before 1949, his grandfather insisted before his death that he undertake a series of blood transfusions. In this fashion, his landowner's blood, which the Red Guards had once said would flow through his arteries forever because his grandfather, Li Xiong's great-great-grandfather, was a landlord, could be replaced with the blood of poor peasants, so that his offspring would be free from political persecution. This anti-Maoist plot satirizing the Maoist "blood theory," which divided the Chinese into opposing social classes according mostly to their family background, is juxtaposed with the anti-capitalist plot of the protagonist's story in America. After unsuccessful attempts at studying in universities, investing in the stock market, and running his own company in America, Li Xiong adopts his grandfather's solution to replace his own blood with Coca-Cola, the most potent fluid from the most successful business in the world, which he believes will remake him into a promising entrepreneur. Naturally, Li Xiong's chain restaurant business turns out to be such a success that he is well on his way to becoming a billionaire. Li then discovers a talented poet, who happens to have written these words before their meeting: "New York washed the blood of the world's heart, /transferring it into Coca-Cola that flows into the world."[87] Elated that "great minds think alike," Li invites the poet to write a biography of his own life in America, so that the poet's vision could be proven to have already been realized in Li's commercial success story.

Li's biography, however, turns out to be a best seller, with the unfortunate result that many aspiring young people begin imitating Li's blood transfusions in hopes that they too can become rich and famous. They end up instead in hospital emergency rooms, where they are treated for serious illnesses resulting from the transfusions. To stop such a crisis, Li Xiong has no choice but to sign a contract with the U.S. government specifying that Li declare his biography a science fiction written by a crazy poet, while keeping his real story a secret for five years to allow the government time to conduct research on his blood transfusions. The story ends with Li Xiong's commercial success remaining relatively intact, rescued by his poet friend's reluctant agreement to declare himself, and his poetic imaginations, illusionary and hence unacceptable to the mainstream culture. With these fanciful plots told in the manner of science fiction, Yan Li indeed satirized a capitalist society that neglects poetic talents while taking any kind of incredible financial success at face value. By situating his story in the cross-cultural space between China and America, Yan Li discarded the extremes of both Maoist China and post-Mao ideology, which promoted an American economic success story under the pretext of improving the livelihoods of Chinese people, while on the other hand denouncing the former when a different nationalist agenda warranted such an attack. The story raises crucial questions: Is post-Maoist China a better alternative to the Maoist era? What price does a post-socialist society have to pay to avoid the pitfalls of its socialist past?

At this point, one can note the possible autobiographical aspects of the story. Yan Li's grandfather committed suicide in 1968 during the Cultural Revolution; Yan Li was a *menglong* poet who hand-copied Alexander Pushkin's poems at the age of sixteen in 1970[88] and had participated twice in the controversial Star Exhibitions (*Xingxing huazhan*) of 1979 and 1980.[89] After coming to America in 1985 as a self-sponsored college student, Yan Li probably experienced a dilemma similar to that faced by Li Xiong and his artist friend between business and artistic pursuits. What marks him as different from the characters in the story, however, is that Yan Li has successfully established his own Yixing Poetry Club (Yixing Shishe) in New York as a known poet, painter, and photographer.[90] One can thus imagine that Li Xiong's struggle to reconcile his successful business career with a struggling artist's attempt to achieve poetic recognition expresses at least in part the author's desire to live in an ideal society, which is available neither in the Maoist nor in the post-Maoist models. In this regard, Xu Xiao was correct in pointing out that some of the *menglong* poets, who were once "spiritually homeless" in socialist China, remained so even after they had joined the "movement to exchange revolutionary experience in the world." After having lived in the United States, their disillusionment with the American dream prompted them to embrace Marxism again and reject capitalism. For instance, Mou Zhijing, the former editor of the *Middle School Red Guard Newspaper* (*Zhongxue Hongweibing bao*) who had courageously published Yu Luoke's controversial essay "On Blood Theory" (*Chushen lun*) during the Cultural Revolution, made attempts to join the American Communist Party but ultimately failed to do so, for fear of losing his job. He now had no choice but to remain homeless forever—the destiny, Xu Xiao believes, of this entire lost generation that went from being Red Guards, to *menglong* poets, and finally to Chinese Americans.[91]

If part of Yan Li's story is about poetry, Cao Guilin's fiction *A Chinese Nightingale in the Sky of New York* (*Niuyue shangkong de Zhongguo yeying*, 1994) is about performance and writing. *A Chinese Nightingale* picks up where his earlier novel, entitled *Beijing Sojourners in New York* (*Beijing ren zai Niuyue*, 1991), left off. *Beijing Sojourners* tells the story of an ex-musician, Wang Qiming, and his relentless search for financial success in America.[92] In *A Chinese Nightingale*, the plot is reversed: here, Wang Qiming rejects his business career to pursue his literary efforts. After his wife and daughter steal his property and business, Wang buries himself in writing. He writes in his basement, in the park, sometimes even without eating and sleeping.

In fact, in writing his autobiographical fiction, *A Chun*, in which he relives his first few years in America, Wang is honoring his devoted lover, A Chun, the female protagonist in *Beijing Sojourners*. In rewriting A Chun's story within the narrative framework of *A Chinese Nightingale*, however, he focuses on the loving relationship between the two, not on their efforts to achieve financial success. In another story, entitled *Green Card*, Wang Qiming depicts the sorrows and sacrifices of Beijing girls who are reduced to prostitution in order to eke out a living in America.[93] Writing of Chinese diasporic life, therefore, is another way of reliving immigrant life, providing him a second chance to "do it right." A Chinese American writes back in his own voice, against his own enchantment with the American dream and the post-socialist fantasy of economic success that justifies corruption and the increasing gap between the rich and the poor.

Yeying in *A Chinese Nightingale* reverses the image of the Chinese musician whose artistic talents cannot be recognized in a foreign country. Yeying (which means "nightingale") is an opera star who has conquered the stage in America and other countries with her brilliant performances. Most significantly, as the first reader of Wang's works, she convinces him that he is pursuing a worthy career in writing the real-life experiences of first-generation immigrants, the broken dreams and struggles that they seldom shared with friends and relatives at home. Yeying also writes at the same time. As an adjunct professor of music, she writes scholarly essays on Chinese folk opera, its history, development, and significant contributions to world music. As if to accentuate this theme, all characters in the story are divided into two camps according to their attitudes toward writing: the bad characters (such as Wang's wife, his daughter, and her greedy American boyfriend) destroy Wang's writings; the good characters (a priest, his American friends, and other struggling artists) support and protect Wang's writings.

One such ally is Yeying's former teacher in China, who is now pursuing a Ph.D. in America. He composes Western opera with Chinese stories as a way of introducing Chinese civilization to the world. He therefore appreciates Wang's efforts to "give up a business career to pursue literary writing" (*qishang congwen*). The teacher perceives the journey to the West undertaken by "cultural immigrants" (*wenhua yimen*) as worthwhile only if they can succeed in the challenging project of "transplanting Chinese culture to the West."[94] Here we see an interesting repetition of the earlier concept of "*tiyong*," or "using Western means while preserving Chinese essence." Caught between the tensions of their socialist past and post-socialist realities, while equally disillusioned by communist and capitalist systems, Chinese American writers such as Cao Guilin in the 1990s felt even more at a loss about their identities, ambitions, and values, and they had no choice but to resort to a kind of Chinese nativism. Successful artistic performance was now seen as the superior means of using Chinese cultural and symbolic capital to override the values of business success. Performing artists such as Yeying and her teacher thus believe in using Western operatic form to preserve and promote Chinese culture. They fail to realize, however, that in the very process of transplanting their culture, they have already changed it to fit into a Western environment. Their belief in Chinese folk opera as representing Chinese cultural essence becomes a cultural form of filial piety. Unlike their predecessors in the stories of the 1920s who were torn between iconoclasm and nationalism, Chinese intellectuals in the 1990s were confronted with even more complex burdens of various traditions: Confucian, socialist, liberal, capitalist, modernist, popularist, and what can be grouped under the umbrella of "Western." On the other hand, they also had to deal with various kinds of nationalisms, such as colonialist nationalism, anticolonialist nationalism, socialist nationalism, cultural nationalism, military nationalism, state nationalism, and popularist nationalism, which is a task much more complex and multifaceted than that confronted by their predecessors in the 1920s.[95] Such are also the new challenges of understanding Occidentalist writings in the 1990s, where the constructions of Selves and Others involve explorations of diverse traditions and varied reactions in cross-cultural and cross-historical circumstances.

Cao's fictional works, of course, cannot resolve all of these issues, but suffice it to say that in *Beijing Sojourners* and *A Chinese Nightingale,* Cao created a new Chinese identity, one of multicultural perspectives that do not take for granted any ideological legacies without seriously challenging their pitfalls. In the combination of two Chinese lovers, A Chun as a business partner and Yeying as artistic mentor, one also witnesses a return to the idealistic pursuit expressed in Zhang Wentian's *Journey,* in which two American women sacrificed their lives for Junkai's love and his revolutionary career. Despite a seemingly similar plot structure of two women loving one man (albeit from different nationalities) to provide him the perfect romance, the irony remains that Junkai does not survive, while Wang Qiming does. Wang, however, does not choose to live in Junkai's cherished homeland of China, where he dies, but in America, a paradoxical place as described in his favorite lyric of A Chun: "If you love him, send him to New York/because it is heaven, /if you hate him, /send him to New York, /because it is hell."[96] While rejecting his earlier pursuit of materialism, as Junkai had, Wang nevertheless has also abandoned Junkai's belief in socialist China, thus inviting readers to reflect upon the intricate relationship between post-socialism and post-colonialism, a new experience beyond Zhang Wentian's story of the 1920s. As Lydia Liu rightly points out in her insightful study of Cao's first novel, socialist histories in China and other countries from the former Eastern European bloc, though important parts of Marxist movements in the world, have not received enough critical attention in transnational studies, raising the possibility that transnationalism and post-socialism will cancel each other out in "their theoretical possibilities."[97] Though the story reverses the plot structure and character portrayals of *Beijing Sojourners, A Chinese Nightingale* expresses similar concerns about the relationship between post-socialism and transnationalism. It provides us with another opportunity to examine the overlapping and coexisting phenomenon of Occidentalism at the intersection of post-socialism and post-colonialism, without taking lightly what has happened in the native land that produced such discourses in the first place.

I hope I have made it clear through this brief discussion of Chinese diasporic stories that the constructions of Selves and Others in this genre are always multivoiced and locally oriented, even when, as in expressions of Orientalism and Occidentalism, it may seem otherwise. What makes the stories of the Chinese diaspora in the 1990s more complicated than their predecessors in the early 1980s, however, is that they express more disparate expressions of Occidentalism that can take aim at Maoist China as well as post-Maoist China, against ideological isolation from the West and against pursuing the American dream without political critiques. They are mixed with even more multifarious images from the popular and in-formational cultures in the form of television dramas and best sellers. One also needs to consider seriously the impact of popular media such as tel-evision series, talk shows, movies, popular music, best sellers, VCDs, and DVDs on the Chinese imagination and the exploration of what Geremie R. Barmé has called the "nonofficial" or "counterculture."[98] In our sensi-tivity to forms of discourse, we need to be attentive to their local posi-tioning, and above all, to the ways that in their discursive use and con-sumption they may well be strategies of bondage in one world, yet strategies of liberation in another. It is intellectually limiting to judge all Orientalist discourse in the West without taking this localness into ac-count, or to treat it as if it had only negative and sinister effects. If Chinese producers of culture choose Occidentalist discourse for their own utopian ends, it ill behooves those who watch from afar to tell them condescend-ingly they do not know what they are doing. I can only hope that the ac-count given here of Occidentalism in contemporary China might aid Ori-entalists and Occidentalists alike in understanding this fundamental axiom of any form of cultural studies that is faithful to its own founding notion of culture.

Notes

INTRODUCTION

1. For an informative survey of Chinese views of America in the form of travel accounts, official diaries of visiting diplomats, and short essays by leading intellectuals, see *Land without Ghosts: Chinese Impressions of America from the Mid-Nineteenth Century to the Present,* trans. and ed. R. David Arkush and Leo O[u-fan] Lee (Berkeley: Univ. of California Press, 1989). For an early review symposium on Edward Said's *Orientalism* by Asian studies scholars published in *The Journal of Asian Studies* 39:3 (1980), see Robert A. Kapp, "Edward Said's Orientalism: Introduction," 481–84; Michael Dalby, "Nocturnal Labors in the Light of Day," 485–93; David Kopf, "Hermeneutics versus History," 495–506; and Richard H. Minear, "Orientalism and the Study of Japan," 507–18. Simon Leys, in his *The Burning Forest* (New York: Holt, Rinehart and Winston, 1986), rejects Said's Orientalism as a contention that "certainly does not apply to sinologists" since "the intellectual and physical boundaries of the Chinese world are sharply defined; they encompass a reality that is so autonomous and singular that no sinologist in his right mind would ever dream of extending any sinological statement to the non-Chinese world" (96). For a study on Orientalism and nationalism in the context of contemporary Chinese literary and cultural studies, see Xiaobing Tang, "Orientalism and the Question of Universality: The Language of Contemporary Chinese Literary Theory," *Positions* 1:2 (1993):389–413.

2. Arif Dirlik, "Marxism and Chinese History: The Globalization of Marxist Historical Discourse and the Problem of Hegemony in Marxism," *Journal of Third World Studies* 4:1 (1987):158. In his definitive study *The Origins of Chinese Communism* (New York: Oxford Univ. Press, 1989), Dirlik also traces the problematic relationship between socialism worldwide and the Chinese transplantation of Marxism and socialism from 1917 to 1921. Dirlik comments on China's reaction to the outside world:

> Global problems were China's national problems, and China's national problems were global problems, all of them rooted in the capitalist world system. Awareness of worldwide social conflict resulted in a new reading of China's problems, in other

177

words, while the evidence of social conflict within China endowed worldwide developments, including the Russian Revolution, with an immediacy of meaning. Social revolutionary ideology, which *as* ideology had a history of nearly two decades in Chinese radical thinking, had found its substance. In this context, socialism, with its promise to end the conflicts created by capitalism, found a ready audience. (9)

3. For an English translation of Lin's essay, later published as a booklet, see Lin Piao (Lin Biao), *Long Live the Victory of People's War! In Commemoration of the 20th Anniversary of Victory in the Chinese People's War of Resistance against Japan* [*Renmin zhanzheng shengli wansui*] (Beijing: Foreign Languages Press, 1965). Citations are quoted from this translation.

4. Lin Piao, 48–49. For a discussion of the related issues of race in Chinese history, see Frank Dikötter, *The Discourse of Race in Modern China* (Stanford, Calif.: Stanford Univ. Press, 1992). Dikötter rightfully points out:

Although there is nothing in Mao's writings which deals directly with the idea of race, it is clear that his sense of nationalism was based on a strong racial consciousness and a sense of biological continuity. Like most politicians who grew to maturity in Republican China, he perceived the Chinese 'nation' (*minzu*) as a biologically distinct group: being Chinese was a matter of 'culture' as well as 'race.' As a student of Li Dazhao, it is also likely that he coalesced the notions of 'class' and 'race' into a vision of the struggle of the 'coloured people' against 'white imperialism'. . . . The race problem had become a class problem. (192)

For examples of China's relationship to Third World countries, see Alan Hutchinson, *China's African Revolution* (London: Hutchinson, 1975), and Philip Snow, *The Star Raft* (London: Weidenfeld and Nicolson, 1988).

5. Maurice Meisner, *Marxism, Maoism, and Utopianism: Eight Essays* (Madison: Univ. of Wisconsin Press, 1982), 98.

6. Meisner, 100.

7. Jonathan D. Spence has pointed out the hegemonic nature of such a discourse. He believes that Lin Biao's 1965 statement "became a basic formula for Chinese foreign policy during the Cultural Revolution, and was interpreted by many Western observers to mean that China sought to play a dominant role in creating global upheavals that might lead to a weakening of the capitalist nations." See his *The Search for Modern China* (New York: Norton, 1990), 627.

8. Douwe Fokkema made a similar point. See his "Orientalism, Occidentalism and the Notion of Discourse: Arguments for a New Cosmopolitanism," *Comparative Criticism* 18 (1996):237.

9. Edward Said, *Orientalism* (New York: Vintage, 1979), 1.

10. Said, *Orientalism*, 3.

11. Uta Leibmann Schaub, "Foucault's Oriental Subtext," *Publications of the Modern Language Association of America* (hereafter cited as *PMLA*) 104:3 (1989):308.

12. Gautam Dasgupta, "*The Mahabharata*: Peter Brook's 'Orientalism,'" *Performing Arts Journal* 30:3 (1987):10.

13. Dasgupta, 14.

14. Ernest Gellner, "The Mightier Pen? Edward Said and the Double Standards of Inside-out Colonialism," review of *Culture and Imperialism*, by Edward Said, *Times Literary Supplement* 19 Feb. 1993:4.

15. Gellner, "The Mightier Pen?" 3. Gellner's point is not without problems: it views "Confucian-collective spirit" as a better option to non-Western societies without taking into account the controversies over Confucianism in Chinese scholarship.

16. Gellner, "The Mightier Pen?" 4.

17. Eqbal Ahmad, review of *Culture and Imperialism*, by Edward Said, *Times Literary Supplement* 2 Apr. 1993:17.

18. David Davies, letter, *Times Literary Supplement* 19 Mar. 1993:15.

19. Gellner, reply to letter of Edward Said, *Times Literary Supplement* 9 Apr. 1993:15.

20. Fred Inglis, "A Peregrine Spirit with an Eye for Eagles," review of *Culture and Imperialism*, by Edward Said, *The Times Higher Education Supplement* 5 Mar. 1993:27.

21. Inglis, 27.

22. Edward Said, letter, *Times Literary Supplement* 19 Mar. 1993:15.

23. Kwame Anthony Appiah, "Europe Upside Down: Fallacies of the New Afrocentrism," *Times Literary Supplement* 12 Feb. 1993:24.

24. Appiah, 24.

25. Appiah, 24.

26. Appiah, 24.

27. Diana Fuss, *Essentially Speaking: Feminism, Nature, and Difference* (New York: Routledge, 1989), 2.

28. Joseph R. Levenson, *Liang Ch'i-ch'ao and the Mind of Modern China* (Cambridge: Harvard Univ. Press, 1953), 8.

29. Benjamin I. Schwartz, *In Search of Wealth and Power: Yen Fu and the West* (Cambridge: Harvard Univ. Press, 1964), 2; citation and comments by Paul A. Cohen and Merle Goldman in their "Introduction" to *Ideas across Cultures: Essays on Chinese Thought in Honor of Benjamin I. Schwartz*, eds., Paul A. Cohen and Merle Goldman (Cambridge: Council on East Asian Studies, Harvard Univ., 1990), 4.

30. Masao Miyoshi, *Off Center: Power and Culture Relations between Japan and the United States* (Cambridge: Harvard Univ. Press, 1991), 40.

31. Miyoshi, 41.

32. Miyoshi, 41.

33. Miyoshi, 42.

34. Miyoshi, 42.

35. Miriam Silverberg has also discussed the impossibility of separating gender and ethnic relations "into neat binaries of male/female" and binaries of colonial Japan/colonialized Korea and China during the World War II period in her "Remembering Pearl Harbor, Forgetting Charlie Chaplin, and the Case of the Disappearing Western Woman: A Picture Story," *Positions* 1:1 (1993):32. Silverberg narrates the story of Ri Ko-ran, daughter of a Japanese colonial official working in Manchuria, who was idolized as a Chinese movie star by Japanese audiences, although she was in fact a Japanese growing up in Manchuria and Beijing. In this episode in which "the colonizer is passing as colonized" (35), thus acquiring power and knowledge of both the Other and the Self, one sees the danger of idealizing Oriental cultures as monolithically the "oppressed" and the "subaltern" on the part of the Western cultural critics as well as of the indigenous

cultures in question. Silverberg's insight that "national-ethnic fluidity" prevails "because historical exigencies countered political ideologies of racial identity/ purity" (63) once again warns us against any essentialization of a culture as either the "Other" or the "Self," the colonizer and the colonized. Others have also studied the impact of Japanese colonialism and imperialism on the making of literary and cultural histories both in colonial Japan and in the East Asian countries colonized by Japan. See, for example, James A. Fujii, "Writing Out Asia: Modernity, Canon, and Natsume Soseki's *Kokoro*," *Positions* 1:1 (1993):194–223. Commenting on the "ongoing reproduction of amnesia that underwrites" the reception of the canonical work by Soseki, which forgets the colonial history of modern Japan (194), Fujii demonstrates how *Kokoro* "continues to be read in ways that ignore the specific conditions of Japanese modernity and nationness that give rise to this text. What must be endeavored is to bring into focus the oft-neglected relationship between Japan and its Asian neighbors as a way of thinking about Japanese modernity and 'modern Japanese literature' (which is always marked by the West)" (197). Working in different cultural contexts, Ann L. Stoler challenges binary categories of "colonizer" and "colonized" by showing them as having been "secured through notions of racial difference constructed in gender terms," as demonstrated in the experience of European women during the colonial rule of French Indochina and the Dutch East Indies (651). See Ann L. Stoler, "Making Empire Respectable: The Politics of Race and Sexual Morality in 20th-Century Colonial Cultures," *American Ethnologist* 16:4 (1989):634–59. From a different angle, John L. Comaroff problematizes the notion of colonialism as "a coherent, monolithic process" by narrating how, in 19th-century South Africa, three equally important colonizing groups such as "settlers, administrators and evangelists contested the terms of European domination" (661). Comaroff confirms the points of view expressed in some recent anthropological scholarships against an essentialist view on colonialism: "that colonialism simply does not have a single, transhistorical 'essence,' neither political nor material, social nor cultural. Rather, its form and substance are decided in the context of its making" (681). See John L. Comaroff, "Images of Empire, Contests of Conscience: Models of Colonial Domination in South Africa," *American Ethnologist* 16:4 (1989):661–85.

36. Chungmoo Choi, "The Discourse of Decolonization and Popular Memory: South Korea," *Positions* 1:1 (1993):80.

37. Choi, 80.

38. Choi, 82.

39. Choi, 82.

40. Spence, 531–32.

41. Choi, 88–96.

42. Choi, 82.

43. Rey Chow, "Against the Lures of Diaspora: Minority Discourse, Chinese Women, and Intellectual Hegemony," in Tonglin Lu, ed., *Gender and Sexuality in Twentieth-Century Chinese Literature* (Albany: State Univ. of New York Press, 1993), 33.

44. Silvia Tandeciarz, "Reading Gayatri Spivak's 'French Feminism in an International Frame': A Problem for Theory," *Genders* 10 (Spring 1991):79.

45. Tandeciarz, 79.

46. Li Xiaojiang, "Open Letter to Su Shaozhi," trans. Feng-ying Ming and Eric Karchmer, *Positions* 1:1 (1993): 270.

47. Li Xiaojiang, 276.

48. Li Xiaojiang, 278.

49. Zhang Longxi, "Western Theory and Chinese Reality," *Critical Inquiry* 19 (1992):127.

50. Zhang Longxi, 112.

51. Gail Hershatter, "The Subaltern Talks Back: Reflections on Subaltern Theory and Chinese History," *Positions* 1:1 (1993):105. For studies on and by the Subaltern Studies Group, see *Subaltern Studies* (Delhi: Oxford Univ. Press), 7 Vols.; Gayatri Chakravorty Spivak, "Can the Subaltern Speak?" in Cary Nelson and Lawrence Crossberg, eds., *Marxism and the Interpretation of Culture* (Urbana and Chicago: Univ. of Illinois Press, 1988), 271–311; Spivak, "A Literary Representation of the Subaltern: A Woman's Text from the Third World," in her *In Other Worlds: Essays in Cultural Politics* (New York: Routledge, 1988), 241–68; and Rosalind O'Hanlon, "Recovering the Subject: *Subaltern Studies* and Histories of Resistance in Colonial South Asia," *Modern Asian Studies* 22:1 (1988):189–224. O'Hanlon's essay was cited by Hershatter.

52. Hershatter, 108.

53. Hershatter, 108.

54. Hershatter, 111, 119.

55. These two terms are Tani E. Barlow's in her "Editor's Introduction" to the issue of *Positions* in which Hershatter's essay appears, vi.

56. Mao Zedong, "Qingnian yundong de fangxiang" [The orientation of the youth movement], *Mao Zedong xuanji* [Selected works of Mao Zedong] (Beijing: Renmin chubanshe, 1964), 530. English translations are from *Selected Works of Mao Tse-tung*, Vol. 2 (Beijing: Foreign Languages Press, 1975), 46.

57. For Rey Chow's comment on Ranajit Guha and Spivak, see Rey Chow, "Against the Lures of Diaspora," in Lu, ed., *Gender and Sexuality*, 44.

58. Examples of such abuse can be found in Deng Xian's astonishing narrative history of those educated youth who lived in Yunan Province for ten years. See his *Zhongguo zhiqing meng* [The dream of Chinese educated youth] (Beijing: Renmin wenxue chubanshe, 1973), 124–27. For an early account of this movement in English, see Thomas Bernstein, *Up to the Mountain and Down to the Villages: The Transfer of Youth from Urban to Rural China* (New Haven, Conn.: Yale Univ. Press, 1977).

59. Deng Xian, 170–377.

60. "Wound literature" was first attributed to Lu Xinhua's short story "The Wounded" [*Shanghen*] published in *Wenhui bao* on 11 Aug. 1978. For English translation of representative works, see *The Wounded: New Stories of the Cultural Revolution*, 77–78, trans. Geremie Barmé and Bennett Lee (Hong Kong: Joint Publishing, 1979). For examples of post-Mao literature in English translation depicting the lives of educated youth in the countryside during the Cultural Revolution, especially with regard to their use of knowledge and their interaction with local subalterns, see Ah Cheng, "King of Children" and "King of Chess" in his *Three Kings: Three Stories from Today's China*, trans. and intro. Bonnie S. McDougall (London: Collins-Harvill, 1990), 155–215, 27–94. See also Laifong Leung, *Morning Sun: Interviews with Chinese Writers of the Lost Generation* (Armonk, N.Y.: M. E. Sharpe,

1994). Using an ironic title borrowed from Mao Zedong's once famous quotation that "young people, full of vigor and vitality, are in the bloom of life, like the sun at eight or nine in the morning," Leung recorded interviews with twenty-six contemporary Chinese writers who were themselves members of the "educated youth," spending their most precious years laboring away in the countryside, disillusioned and deceived by an idealist Maoist ideology.

61. The problematic and intricate relationship between modern Chinese writers and the subalterns they claim to represent in their literary and political imaginations dates back long before the founding of the People's Republic of China. For an anthology in English on the images of the peasants represented in modern Chinese literature from the 1930s to the 1980s, see Helen F. Siu, comp., trans. and intro., *Furrows: Peasants, Intellectuals, and the State* (Stanford, Calif.: Stanford Univ. Press, 1990). Siu rightly notes that "urban Chinese intellectuals have concentrated on portraying a social world they seldom grasp. Whether objects of abuse in traditional society or objects of transformation in the decades of socialism, the peasants have been, in the eyes of these writers, as much a political and moral metaphor as living, suffering, and functioning human beings. However unreal these literary images of peasants may be, they reveal the evolution of the writers' fitful, ambivalent, but compelling relationships with the peasantry on the one hand and with state-building efforts on the other hand" (Siu, vii). Once again, the "subaltern-speak" was presented completely by elitist intellectuals with the very absence of the subalterns' own voice. The representations of the subalterns are merely used to illustrate "the odyssey of modern Chinese intellectuals" (Siu, vii), not the odyssey of the subalterns themselves. For source materials available in English on rural and urban women in 1980s China as subalterns, see Emily Honig and Gail Hershatter, *Personal Voices: Chinese Women in the 1980's* (Stanford, Calif.: Stanford Univ. Press, 1988).

62. Leo Ou-fan Lee, "The Politics of Technique: Perspectives of Literary Dissidence in Contemporary Chinese Fiction," in Jeffrey C. Kinkley, ed., *After Mao: Chinese Literature and Society 1978–1981* (Cambridge: Council on East Asian Studies, Harvard Univ., 1985), 162. For an English translation of Mao's "Talks," see *Mao Zedong, "Talks at the Yan'an Conference on Literature and Art": A Translation of the 1943 Text with Commentary*, trans. Bonnie S. McDougall (Ann Arbor: Center for Chinese Studies, Univ. of Michigan, 1980).

63. For a comprehensive study of the Chinese establishment intellectuals, see Carol Lee Hamrin and Timothy Cheek, eds., *China's Establishment Intellectuals* (Armonk, N.Y.: M. E. Sharpe, 1986), especially the "Foreword" by John Israel and "Introduction: Collaboration and Conflict in the Search for a New Order" by Timothy Cheek and Carol Lee Hamrin, ix–20. For important works on Chinese intellectuals in early modern China, see Chang Hao, *Chinese Intellectuals in Crisis: Search for Order and Meaning (1890–1911)* (Berkeley: Univ. of California Press, 1987); Vera Schwarcz, *The Chinese Enlightenment: Intellectuals and the Legacy of the May Fourth Movement of 1919* (Berkeley: Univ. of California Press, 1986); and Jerome B. Grieder, *Intellectuals and the State in Modern China: A Narrative History* (New York: Free Press, 1981). For the roles of intellectuals in the PRC, see Merle Goldman with Timothy Cheek and Carol Lee Hamrin, eds., *China's Intellectuals and the State: In Search of a New Relationship* (Cambridge: Council on East Asian

Studies, Harvard Univ., 1987). See also Li Zehou and Vera Schwarcz, "Six Generations of Modern Chinese Intellectuals," *Chinese Studies in History* 8:2 (1983–84):42–56. In this essay, modern Chinese intellectuals are divided into distinct and yet problematically overlapping groups of the 1911 generation, the May Fourth generation, the 1920s generation, the Anti-Japanese War generation, the 1940s and 1950s generation, and the Red Guards generation. For important works on Chinese intellectuals and power, see Tani E. Barlow, "*Zhishifenzi* [Chinese intellectuals] and Power," *Dialectical Anthropology* 16 (1991):209–32. Barlow argues that the Chinese intellectual "has positioned itself between internal and external others" (209) and that they appropriate signs such as Woman, Sexuality, and the master narrative of privileged modernist discourse "out of the 'stronger' European language into the 'weaker' language and local context" of China (212). I agree, in particular, with her argument regarding the younger generation of intellectuals in the post-Mao era, whose rhetoric in the Western signs of "democracy," "liberty," and "modern" "refers to a 'West' that never was and is a weapon against the autocratic China they know too well" (224). See also Rey Chow, "Pedagogy, Trust, Chinese Intellectuals in the 1990s—Fragments of a Post-Catastrophic Discourse," *Dialectical Anthropology* 16 (1991):191–207, for an examination of Chinese intellectuals' agency in Chinese politics.

64. Although there are no substantial studies exclusively on Chinese Occidentalism, China's interaction with the West has been a persistent concern in Chinese studies. For a selected few related to literary and cultural studies, see, for example, Leo Ou-fan Lee, *The Romantic Generation of Modern Chinese Writers* (Cambridge: Harvard Univ. Press, 1973); Paul A. Cohen, *Discovering History in China: American Historical Writing on the Recent Chinese Past* (New York: Columbia Univ. Press, 1984); Bonnie S. McDougall, *The Introduction of Western Literary Theories into Modern China, 1919–1925* (Tokyo: Center for East Asian Cultural Studies, 1971). For recent critiques on the problematics of Chinese studies and their related issues from new and different perspectives, see Rey Chow, *Woman and Chinese Modernity: The Politics of Reading between West and East* (Minnesota: Univ. of Minnesota Press, 1991); Tani E. Barlow, "Career in Post-war China Studies," and Lydia H. Liu, "Translingual Practice: The Discourse of Individualism between China and the West," both in *Positions* 1:1 (1993):224–67 and 160–93 respectively.

CHAPTER 1

1. Portions of the introduction and this chapter appeared in *Critical Inquiry*, 18:4 (1992):686–712. I wish to thank Lyman P. Van Slyke, David A. Schabes, manuscript editor, and an anonymous reader for *Critical Inquiry* for their valuable comments, and the Second Walter H. Shorenstein Conference in East Asian Studies at Stanford University for providing a forum for it.

2. An English translation of *He shang* can be found in Su Xiaokang and Wang Luxiang et al., *Deathsong of the River: A Reader's Guide to the Chinese TV Series Heshang*, intro., trans. and annot. Richard W. Badman and Pin P. Wan (Ithaca: Cornell Univ. East Asian Program, 1991), 93–222.

3. Wang Dan, "Biyao de bianhu" [A necessary defense], in Cui Wenhua, ed., *He shang lun* [About *He shang*] (Beijing: Wenhua yishu chubanshe, 1988), 205.

4. For an insightful cultural critique of *He shang*, see Wang Jing, "*He shang* and the Paradoxes of Chinese Enlightenment," *Bulletin of Concerned Asian Scholars* 23:3 (1991): 23–32. The same issue of the *Bulletin* features a symposium on *He shang* which includes essays by Mark Selden, "Introduction," 3; Stephen Field, "*He shang* and the Plateau of Ultrastability," 4–13; and Edward Gunn, "The Rhetoric of *He shang*: From Cultural Criticism to Social Act," 14–22. For a summary, analysis, and review in English of *He shang*, see Frederic Wakeman, Jr., "All the Rage in China," *New York Review of Books* 2 Mar. 1989:19–21. For earlier accounts of *He shang* in English, see "Television in China: Rolling River," *The Economist*, 19 Nov. 1988:105; and Geremie Barmé, "TV Requiem for the Myths of the Middle Kingdom," *Far Eastern Economic Review* 1 Sept. 1988:40–43. For a summary of the content of and initial debate on *He shang* in English, see "Controversial TV Series 'River Elegy,'" *China Reconstructs* 38 (Jan. 1989):47–49.

5. Su Xiaokang, "Longnian de beicang—guanyu *He shang* de zhaji" [The sorrow of the year of the dragon—sketches from *He shang* on location], in his *Ziyou beiwang lu: Su Xiaokang baogao wenxue jingxuan* [Memoir on freedom: selected works of Su Xiaokang's reportage] (Hong Kong: Sanlian shudian, 1989), 270.

6. "Huanghe dahechang" [The Yellow River chorus], in *Cihai* [Chinese encyclopedia] (Shanghai: Shanghai cishu chubanshe, 1979).

7. Examples of these television programs included *Tangfan gudao* [The ancient route to the West in Tang dynasty], *Huashuo Changjiang* [On the Yangtze River], *Huashuo Yunhe* [On the Grand Canal], and *Huanghe* [The Yellow River].

8. Su Xiaokang and Wang Luxiang, et al., *He shang* [River elegy], in Cui, *He shang lun*, 24. All the quotations from *He shang* are from the same script. English translations are mine.

9. Su and Wang, *He shang*, in Cui, *He shang lun*, 74.

10. Huo Xiangwen, "Guanyu *He shang* timing dawen" [Reply to a reader's letter on the title of *He shang*], *Renmin ribao* [People's daily] 26 Sept. 1988:8.

11. Su Xiaokang, "Longnian," 273.

12. Huo, 8.

13. Su Xiaokang, "Huhuan quan minzu fanxing yishi" [Calling on the self-reflective consciousness of the Chinese nation], in Cui, *He shang lun*, 87.

14. Wang Jing, 24.

15. Such a view of America can be traced back historically to the turn of the century when, according to R. David Arkush and Leo O[u-fan] Lee, "many Chinese were—and continue to be—impressed by the dynamism and youthful vigor of individual Americans, the same youthful energy decried by earlier European visitors as uncouthness and lack of sophistication" despite Liang Qichao's warning that "American capitalism" "was likely to eventually replace England's imperialistic might and could overwhelm international geopolitics." See Arkush and Lee, 9.

16. Su and Wang, *He shang*, in Cui, *He shang lun*, 70.

17. Wang Jing, 30.

18. Su and Wang, *He shang*, in Cui, *He shang lun*, 70.

19. Su and Wang, *He shang*, in Cui, *He shang lun*, 71. I am aware that the actual date for Galileo's *Dialogues Concerning Two New Sciences* is 1638. This kind of factual error is typical in *He shang*.

20. Su and Wang, *He shang*, in Cui, *He shang lun*, 71.

21. Su and Wang, *He shang*, in Cui, *He shang lun*, 71.

22. Su and Wang, *He shang*, in Cui, *He shang lun*, 73. A post-Tiananmen movement article, which accused *He shang* writers of taking "a reactionary political attitude," pointed out that when Ito Hirobumi went to England to study naval military technology for half a year, Yan Fu was only nine years old; they could not possibly have been schoolmates. Such corrections of factual errors dominate the official critique of *He shang*. Starting on 9 Aug. 1989, *Beijing wanbao* [Beijing evening post] ran a special column entitled "The Many Errors in *He shang*"; a total of 101 articles had appeared in this corrective series. The *Renmin ribao* editor claimed, in his editor's note published in *Renmin ribao* 19 Dec. 1989:6, that he selected some of these articles from *Beijing wanbao* to benefit his own readers. English translations of selected articles can be found in "Report Views Errors in 'River Elegy,'" *National Affairs* 26 Jan. 1990:25–31.

23. Pui-yee Lai, "Intellectuals Alarmed by Film Series Clampdown," *Morning Post* 17 Oct. 1988:9.

24. Chen Zhi'ang, "*He shang* zi shang" [The elegy of *He shang*], *Wenyi lilun yu piping* [Theory and criticism of literature and art] 1 (1989):54.

25. Chen Zhi'ang, 57.

26. Gao Wangling and Wu Xin, "*He shang* fanying le yizhong shiheng xintai" [*He shang* reflects an unbalanced mentality], in Cui, *He shang lun*, 186.

27. Gao and Wu, 181.

28. Gao and Wu, 181–82.

29. "Nanjing Daxue Zhongguo Sixiangjia Yanjiu Zhongxin juxing *He shang* zuotanhui" [Nanjing University Research Center for Chinese Thinkers held seminar on *He shang*], *Guangming ribao* [Guangming daily] 20 Nov. 1988:3.

30. "Nanjing."

31. Ji Ren, "Wanli Changcheng shi fengbi de xiangzheng ma?" [Is the Great Wall a symbol of a closed-door policy?], *Renmin ribao* 15 Aug. 1989:6.

32. Samir Amin, *Eurocentrism*, trans. Russell Moore (New York: Monthly Review Press, 1989), 93. See also Martin Bernal, *Black Athena: The Afroasiatic Roots of Classical Civilization*, vol. 1 of *The Fabrication of Ancient Greece, 1785–1985* (New Brunswick, N.J.: Rutgers Univ. Press), 1987.

33. Amin, 89.

34. Amin, 93.

35. Amin, 89–90.

36. Su and Wang, *He shang*, in Cui, *He shang lun*, 36.

37. For a classic account of imperialism and a standard textbook used in Chinese universities, translated into English, see Hu Sheng, *Imperialism and Chinese Politics*, trans. Foreign Languages Press (Beijing: Foreign Languages Press, 1955). The original Chinese text was first published in 1948. The publisher of the English translation notes: "This book is not only a history of imperialist aggression against the Chinese people and the abnormal political relations that arose from it, but also an analysis of the Chinese people's struggle against imperialist aggression and for national independence, democracy and freedom. Taking the point of view of historical materialism, it deals with the great revolutionary tasks which the masses of the Chinese people accomplished in various historical stages, and criticizes the erroneous views of certain bourgeois historians."

38. Amin, 96, 94.

39. Amin, 99.

40. Su and Wang, *He shang*, in Cui, *He shang lun*, 72.

41. Su and Wang, *He shang*, in Cui, *He shang lun*, 10.

42. See Dong Yue and Liu Jun, eds., *"He shang* weixin zhuyi lishiguan pouxi—shoudu bufen shixue gongzuozhe pipan *He shang* jiyao" [On a metaphysical view of history in *He shang*: Minutes on a critique of *He shang* by historians in Beijing], *Renmin ribao* 23 Oct. 1989:6. The article mentioned that five scholarly journals in Beijing, including *Lishi yanjiu* [History research], *Shixue yanjiu* [Research on historical studies], *Jindaishi yanjiu* [Modern history research], and *Shijie lishi* [World history], jointly sponsored a meeting in which a number of historians were invited to criticize *He shang* as a piece of "pseudo-science" and "pseudo-scholarship" in order to clear away its "negative influence on the society as a whole." An English translation of a slightly different version of this article can be found in "Historians in the Capital Criticize *He shang*: A Summary," in Su and Wang, *Deathsong of the River*, 311–27.

43. Arnold J. Toynbee and Daisaku Ikeda, *The Toynbee-Ikeda Dialogue: Man Himself Must Choose* (Tokyo: Kodansha International, 1976), 232.

44. Toynbee and Ikeda, 233.

45. Toynbee and Ikeda, 231. For an informative account of Toynbee's life and writings in a different context, see William H. McNeill, *Arnold J. Toynbee: A Life* (New York: Oxford Univ. Press, 1989).

46. Yuan Zhiming, "*He shang* yu gaoji laosao" [*He shang* and the so-called sophisticated complaint], *Guangming ribao* 18 Aug. 1988:3.

47. Kenneth Winetrout, *Arnold Toynbee: The Ecumenical Vision* (Boston: Twayne, 1975), 35.

48. Winetrout, 36.

49. Gong Suyi, "Shoudu bufen zhuanjia xuezhe zuotan: cong *He Shang* xianxiang kan dianshi wenhua jianshe" [Experts and scholars in Beijing discussing *He shang*: From the *He shang* phenomenon to a construction of television culture], *Guangming ribao* 16 Aug. 1988:1. It is worth noting here that *He shang* also generated heated debates among audiences and scholars in Taiwan and Hong Kong. Taiwan scholars published a collection of critical essays, together with the *He shang* text, in Oct. 1988. An interesting response to *He shang* from Taiwan can be found in Jiang Xun, "He de lishi: zuihao de lishi jiaocai *He shang*" [A history of the river: the best history book *He shang*], in which he observed that it was hard to imagine that such an excellent television program as *He shang* could ever be produced by the three television stations in Taiwan, which, he hoped, would one day be able to depict "our own *Danshui he* [Danshui River] and *Zhuoshui xi* [Zhuoshui Stream] in Taiwan." For Jiang Xun's and others' essays from Taiwan and Hong Kong, see Su Xiaokang and Wu Luxiang, *He shang*, Weng Ningna, ed. (Taiwan: Jinfeng chubanshe and Fengyun shidai chubanshe, 1988), 226–28. See also Cui Wenhua, ed., *Haiwai He shang da taolun* [Great overseas debates on *He shang*] (Ha'erbin: Heilongjiang jiaoyu chubanshe, 1988).

50. Gong, 1.

51. Su Xiaokang, "Longnian," 284.

52. Su Xiaokang, "Longnian," 284.

53. Xiu Xinmin expressed her afterthoughts on *He shang* in a letter to the Director of Central Television Station, 19 June 1988, in Cui, *He shang lun*, 113–14.

54. Dong and Liu, 6.

55. Su Xiaokang, "Longnian," 276.

56. Deng Xiaoping, "Zai jiejian shoudu jieyan budui jun yishang ganbu shi de jianghua" [Speech at receiving army commanders of Beijing troops carrying out martial law], *Renmin ribao* 28 July 1989:1.

57. Cui Wenhua, "*He shang* dui Zhongguo dianshi de qishi hezai?" [What does *He shang* tell us about Chinese television?], in Cui, *He shang lun*, 133. For discussions on censorship in the PRC and its political system in literary production, see Perry Link, "Introduction: On the Mechanics of the Control of Literature in China," in Perry Link, ed., *Stubborn Weeds: Popular and Controversial Chinese Literature after the Cultural Revolution* (Bloomington: Indiana Univ. Press, 1983), 1–28, and his "Introduction" to Perry Link, ed., *Roses and Thorns: The Second Blooming of the Hundred Flowers in Chinese Fiction 1979–1980* (Berkeley: Univ. of California Press, 1984), 1–41.

58. Cui, "*He shang*," 134–35.

59. Cui, "*He shang*," 135.

60. Cui, "*He shang*," 134.

61. Jin Ren, "Zhao Ziyang tongzhi de 'jierushuo' he *He shang* de 'xinjiyuan'" [Comrade Zhao Ziyang's theory of "interference" and *He shang*'s "new epoch"], *Renmin ribao* 15 Aug. 1989:4.

62. Jin, 4. A similar article, entitled "Jielu *He shang* de fandong shizhi, suqing *He shang* de yingxiang liudu" [Exposing the counter-revolutionary nature of *He shang* in order to eliminate its pernicious influence], can be found in *Zhongguo jiaoyu bao* [Chinese education newspaper] 5 Aug. 1989:2.

63. T. D. Lee, "Du *He shang* yougan" [Afterthoughts on *He shang*], *Renmin ribao* 4 Nov. 1988:3.

64. "Nanjing," 3.

65. Wakeman, 21.

66. Benedict Anderson, *Imagined Communities: Reflections on the Origin and Spread of Nationalism* (New York: Verso, 1983), 14.

67. Anderson, 82.

68. Joseph R. Levenson, "The Past and Future of Nationalism in China," in his *Modern China: An Interpretative Anthology* (London: Macmillan, 1971), 9.

69. In a different context, Nasrin Rahimieh explores how the coming to terms with the Occident on the part of Egyptian, Palestinian, Iranian, Iraqi, North African, Turkish, and Indian writers "can be a means to self-definition." See Nasrin Rahimieh, "Responses to Orientalism in Modern Eastern Fiction and Scholarship," *Dissertation Abstracts International* 49 (1988): 05A. Univ. of Alberta.

70. John Timothy Wixted has studied one way in which Orientalist discourse has been exploited for power relationships and strategies of exclusion. Raising a cry of "reverse orientalism," Wixted challenges "a fundamental view" of ethnically Oriental scholars toward Western scholars—that only "we the Chinese" or "we the Japanese" can understand Chinese or Japanese culture and people. Wixted considers these attitudes expressions of "culturalism, nationalism, and a kind of 'ethnic racism'" (18–19). He argues that although Said "specifically

disclaims the view that only Blacks can talk with validity about Blacks, only women can talk with authority about women, etc.," he nevertheless "feels that what Palestinians have to say about Palestine, or Muslims about Islam, has a special, even privileged validity. I think there is an element of having-your-cake-and-eating-it-too in his [Said's] own praxis." See John Timothy Wixted, "Reverse Orientalism," *Sino-Japanese Studies* 2:1 (1989):23.

71. T. Minh-Ha Trinh, *Woman, Native, Other: Writing Postcoloniality and Feminism* (Bloomington: Indiana Univ. Press, 1989), 98.

CHAPTER 2

1. An earlier version of this chapter in essay form appeared in *Stanford Literature Review* 10:1, 2 (1993):143–65. I wish to thank David Palumbo-Liu, the co-editor, and Katarina Kirel, the managing editor of this journal, for their suggestions and help.

2. Jyotsna Singh, "Different Shakespeares: The Bard in Colonial/Postcolonial India," *Theater Journal* 41:4 (1989):446.

3. For a more thorough critique on the continuing presence and power of colonialism in postcolonial India, see essays collected in Carol A. Breckenridge and Peter van der Veer, eds., *Orientalism and the Postcolonial Predicament: Perspectives on South Asia* (Philadelphia: Univ. of Pennsylvania Press, 1993). In the words of the editors, this anthology, among other things, "poses the problem of knowledge and power from a historical perspective by showing the contradictory relations—intellectual, administrative, and cultural—between the (colonial) past and the (postcolonial) present," thus exploring what the editors called a "postcolonial predicament"—"we cannot escape from a history characterized by a particular discursive formation that can be called 'orientalism'" (2).

4. On May 4, 1919, citizens and students in Beijing protested in the streets against the Versailles treaty, which proposed to grant Japan the right to station police and to establish military garrisons in Jinan and Qingdao although China was among the winning countries after the war. The movement marked an important period of unparalleled intellectual exploration and debates among Chinese intellectuals on the future of China, especially on the values of new forms in language, education, and culture. For a comprehensive survey of the movement, see Chow Tse-tsung, *The May Fourth Movement: Intellectual Revolution in Modern China* (Cambridge: Harvard Univ. Press, 1960).

5. For important works that promoted postcolonial studies in modern Chinese literature and culture, see Rey Chow, *Woman and Chinese Modernity* (Minnesota: Univ. of Minnesota Press, 1991); *Writing Diaspora* (Bloomington: Indiana Univ. Press, 1993); Lydia H. Liu, *Translingual Practice* (Stanford, Calif.: Stanford Univ. Press, 1995) and Shu-mei Shih, *The Lure of the Modern* (Berkeley: Univ. of California Press, 2001).

6. See Pierre Bourdieu, *Distinction: A Social Critique of the Judgment of Taste*, trans. Richard Nice (Cambridge: Harvard Univ. Press, 1984); *The Logic of Practice*,

trans. Richard Nice (Cambridge: Polity Press, 1990); and John B. Thompson, ed., *Language and Symbolic Power*, trans. Gino Raymond and Matthew Adamson (Cambridge: Polity Press, 1991).

7. Wu Furong, ed., "*Makebaisi* yu Zhongguo wutai" [*Macbeth* and the Chinese stage], *Waiguo xiju* [Foreign drama] 2 (1981):92.

8. Wu Furong, 90.

9. Quoted from "Directors' Words," in the program notes of *Macbeth* produced by the graduates from the director training class for college drama teachers in the Central Drama College, directed by Xu Xiaozhong and Li Zibo, Beijing, 1980.

10. Xu Xiaozhong and Li Zibo, "Maren de beiju: tan beiju *Makebaisi* jiqi yanchu" [The tragedy of the horse-man: On *Macbeth* and its production], *Renmin xiju* [People's drama] 2 (1982):40–44.

11. Fang Ping, "Huanying ni, *Li'erwang*" [Welcome you, *King Lear*], *Shanghai xiju* [Shanghai drama] 5 (1982):19.

12. Fang, 19.

13. Fang, 20.

14. See Judith Shapiro, "22 Years as a Class Enemy," review of *A Single Tear*, by Wu Ningkun, *The New York Times Book Review* 28 Feb. 1993:12.

15. According to Chen Dingsha, *The Merchant of Venice* was first produced in China in 1913 by Xinmin She [New People Theater]. Throughout several different productions mounted around that time, the play's titles varied from *Yibangrou* [A pound of flesh], *Jiezhai gerou* [A pound of flesh as loan payment], to *Roujuan* [Meat coupon] and *Nülüshi* [Woman lawyer]. See Chen Dingsha, "Zhongguo zaoqi wutai shang de Shashibiya xiju" [Shakespearean productions on the early modern Chinese stage], *Xiju bao* [Drama journal] 12 (1983):56.

16. Zhang Qihong, "Zai shijian he tansuo zhong de jidian tihui" [A few words about my experience in directing *The Merchant of Venice*], *Renmin xiju* 1 (1981):17.

17. Zhang Qihong, 18.

18. Zhang Qihong, 18.

19. Zhou Peitong, "Jiyao dadan chuxin, yeyao zhongshi yuanzuo—ping Zhongguo Qingnian Yishu Juyuan yanchu de *Weinisi shangren*" [We need both daring innovations and faithful representations—on China Youth Art Theater's production of *The Merchant of Venice*], *Renmin xiju* 1 (1981):21.

20. Zhang Qihong, 17.

21. Yang Tianchun, "Kan *Weinisi shangren*" [Watching *The Merchant of Venice*], *Xiju yu dianying* [Drama and film] 7 (1981):29.

22. Hao Yin, "Yiqu dui xinsheng jinquzhe de zange: lun *Weinisi shangren* de zhenti" [A song of an enterprising spirit: on the true meaning of *The Merchant of Venice*], *Nanyang Shizhuan xuebao, shekeban* [Journal of Nanyang Normal College, social science ed.] 1 (1986):20–21.

23. Hao, 22.

24. Hao, 23.

25. Hao, 20. For a more detailed account of the reception of *The Merchant of Venice* in China since the beginning of the twentieth century, see Fan Shen, "Shakespeare in China: *The Merchant of Venice*," *Asian Theater Journal* 5:1 (1988):23–37.

26. Zhang Xiaoyang, "Shaju yanchu yu shidai shenmei yishi" [Shakespearean production and aesthetic consciousness of contemporary times], *Waiguo wenxue yanjiu* [Foreign literature studies] 3 (1988):68–74.

27. Zhang Xiaoyang, 68.

28. Zhang Xiaoyang, 72.

29. Zhang Xiaoyang, 72.

30. Peter Watts, "Introduction" to Henrik Ibsen's *Peer Gynt: A Dramatic Poem*, trans. and intro. Peter Watts (New York: Penguin, 1966), 15.

31. Watts, 16–17.

32. Xiao Qian's Chinese translation of *Peer Gynt* was published in *Waiguo xiju* 4 (1981):78–154. I thank Xiao Chi for sharing with me his and other audiences' responses to the play.

33. Henrik Ibsen, *Peer Gynt: A Dramatic Poem*, trans. and intro. Peter Watts (New York: Penguin, 1966), 222. Xu Xiaozhong, "Zaixian Yipusheng—daoyan *Pi'er jinte de sikao*" [Representing Ibsen: thoughts on directing *Peer Gynt*], *Xiju bao* 3 (1983):45. In this essay, Director Xu presented an interesting reading of this play: "not only is Peer Gynt an epitome of the nineteenth-century Norwegian petty bourgeoisie, but he also embodies the specific characteristics of the nineteenth-century adventurer in the capitalist world. Not only does he represent the negative traits of Norwegian citizens, he above all else stands for a stereotype of 'a citizen of the world.'" As for the play's "universal appeal," Xu observes that the symbolic and perhaps even grotesque style of the play ultimately expresses a philosophical concept of "how one should live his life." See Xu, 44, 45.

34. Isben, 222.

35. Isben, 222–23.

36. See Jan Kott, *Shakespeare, Our Contemporary*, trans. Boleslaw Taborski (Garden City, N.Y.: Doubleday, 1966).

37. Chen Yong, "The Beijing Production of *Life of Galileo*," in Antony Tatlow and Tak-Wai Wong, eds., *Brecht and East Asian Theatre: The Proceedings of a Conference on Brecht in East Asian Theatre* (Hong Kong: Hong Kong Univ. Press, 1982), 88–95.

38. Chen Yong, 90.

39. Lin Kehuan, "Bianzheng de xiju xingxiang: lun Jialilue xingxiang" [A dialectical dramatic image: on the characterization of Galileo], *Xiju yishu luncong* [Research series on dramatic art] 10 (1979):224.

40. Lin Kehuan, 223.

41. Lin Kehuan, 223.

42. For a detailed description in English of the Cultural Revolutionary theory of literature and art as promoted by Mao Zedong's wife Jiang Qing, see Ellen R. Judd, "Prescriptive Dramatic Theory of the Cultural Revolution," in Constantine Tung and Colin MacKerras, eds., *Drama in the People's Republic of China* (Albany: State Univ. of New York Press, 1987), 95–118.

43. Chen Yong, 94–95. Since my mother also played a role in the play, I had many opportunities to go backstage to talk to the cast members, who conveyed to me how scientists could relate to the play and its theme of persecution of the intellectuals, as they were so told by different members of the audience.

44. Zhou Peitong, "Shashibiya xiju zai Zhongguo" [Shakespearean plays in China], *Liaowang* [Observer] 15 (1986):39–41.

45. Kong Genghong, "Shashibiya: pinglun, yanchu jiqi 'Zhongguohua'" [Shakespeare: review, production, and Sinification], *Waiguo wenxue yanjiu* 4 (1986):92–95. For a more detailed account of Chinese operatic adaptations of Shakespearean plays, see Ruru Li's report, "Chinese Traditional Theater and Shakespeare," *Asian Theater Journal* 5:1 (1988):38–48.

46. Zhou Peitong, "Shashibiya," 39–41.

47. For studies in English on modern Chinese theater and its theatrical tradition, see the following works by Colin MacKerras, *The Chinese Theatre in Modern Times: From 1840 to the Present Day* (London: Thames and Hudson, 1975); *The Performing Arts in Contemporary China* (London: Routledge and Kegan Paul, 1981); *Chinese Drama: A Historical Survey* (Beijing: New World Press, 1990); and Colin MacKerras, ed., *Chinese Theater: From Its Origins to the Present Day* (Honolulu: Univ. of Hawaii Press, 1983).

CHAPTER 3

1. An earlier version of this chapter was delivered at the Annual Conference of American Comparative Literature Association, Boston, 1989, and was later published in *Representations* 35 (1991):143–63. I wish to thank two members of the Editorial Board, and Barrett Watten, the Associate Editor of *Representations*, for their helpful criticism of previous drafts of this study.

2. I use quotation marks for "misunderstanding" to suggest it as a sociological rather than epistemological concept. I eliminate quotation marks later in the chapter for the purpose of readability. The same is true for "misreading," "understanding," and "self-understanding." For an essay on Pound's Orientalism related to the critical issues addressed in this chapter, see Xiaomei Chen, "Rediscovering Ezra Pound: A Postcolonial 'Misreading' of a Western Legacy," *Paideuma* 23:2,3 (1994):81–105.

3. For Western scholarship on *menglong*, see Jeffrey C. Kinkley, "Introduction" and William Tay, "'Obscure Poetry': A Controversy in Post-Mao China," in Kinkley, 1–14, 133–57. See also John Minford, "Into the Mist," *Renditions* 19, 20 (1983):182–86; Leo Ou-fan Lee, "Beyond Realism: Thoughts on Modernist Experiments in Contemporary Chinese Writing," in Howard Goldblatt, ed., *Worlds Apart: Recent Chinese Writing and Its Audiences* (Armonk, N.Y.: M. E. Sharpe, 1990), 64–77; and Michelle Yeh, "Nature's Child and the Frustrated Urbanite: Expressions of the Self in Contemporary Chinese Poetry," *World Literature Today* (Summer 1991):405–9.

4. Harold Bloom, *The Anxiety of Influence* (New York: Oxford Univ. Press, 1973), 19.

5. In this regard, I am only talking about the *early menglong* poets who published in the underground journal *Jintian* [Today], including Jiang He, Yang Lian, Zhao Zhenkai, pseud. Bei Dao, and Shu Ting. Some of these *early Jintian* poets later wrote modernist poetry and were deliberately imitating Western styles. For a standard survey of Western influence on Chinese literature from the May Fourth era, see Bonnie S. McDougall, *The Introduction of Western Literary Theories*. For a study

on the cultural significance of modern/modernity/modernism/post-modernism in Chinese context influenced by Western figures since the May Fourth era, see Leo Ou-fan Lee, "In Search of Modernity: Some Reflections on a New Mode of Consciousness in Twentieth-Century Chinese History and Literature," in Cohen and Goldman, 109–35.

6. For an early account of *Today*, one of the most popular non-official literary journals after Mao's death between 1978 and 1980, and its relevance to the Democracy Wall movement, see Pan Yuan and Pan Jie, "The Non-Official Magazine *Today* and the Younger Generation's Ideals for a New Literature," in Kinkley, 193–220. For recent, informative materials on *menglong* poets and writers from the *Today* group, see Liao Yiwu, ed., *Chenlun de shengdian* [The fall of the sacred hall] (Wulumuqi: Xinjiang qingshaonian chubanshe, 1999), and Lydia H. Liu, ed., *Chideng de shizhe* [The lamp carriers] (Hong Kong: Oxford Univ. Press, 2001).

7. Liu Hongbin, "Bei Dao fangtan lu" [Interview with Bei Dao], in Liao Yiwu, ed., *Chenlun de shengdian* [The fall of the sacred hall] (Wulumuqi: Xinjiang qingshaonian chubanshe, 1999), 327–39, 333.

8. Liu Hongbin, "Bei Dao fangtan lu," 339.

9. Xu Xiao, "*Jintian* yu wo" [*Today* and I], in Liao Yiwu, ed., *Chenlun de shengdian*, 379–410, 387. Another version of Xu's essay can be found in Lydia H. Liu, ed., *Chideng de shizhe* [The lamp carriers] (Hong Kong: Oxford Univ. Press, 2001). Both Liao Yiwu and Lydia H. Liu's volumes are valuable works for studying the *Today* group.

10. For a study of Western influence on *menglong* poets, see Maghiel van Crevel, *Language Shattered: Contemporary Chinese Poetry and Duoduo* (Leiden: Centre of Non-Western Studies, Leiden University, 1996). For the influence of the Anglo-American "Imagist" school on Hu Shi and its implications for May Fourth movement poetry, see Michel Hockx, *A Snowy Morning: Eight Chinese Poets on the Road to Modernity* (Leiden: Centre of Non-Western Studies, Leiden University, 1994), 9–10. For a comparative study of the new poetic movement originated by Hu Shi and the American poetic movement, see Yoon Wah Wong's two chapters, "The 'New Tide' That Came from America" and "Imagism and Hu Shi's Programme for Literary Revolution of 1917" in his *Essays on Chinese Literature: A Comparative Approach* (Kent Ridge, Singapore: Singapore Univ. Press, 1988), 28–51. I thank Michel Hockx for bringing these sources to my attention.

11. Song Haiquan, "Baiyangdian suoyi" [Remembering Baiyangdian], in Liao Yiwu, ed., *Chenlun de shengdian*, 236–63, 250.

12. Shu Ting, "Shenghuo, shuji yu shi" [Life, books, and poetry], in Liao Yiwu, ed., *Chenlun de shengdian*, 297–308, 300–301.

13. Leo Ou-fan Lee, *The Romantic Generation*, 37.

14. The original Chinese text, under the pseudonym Hong Huang, appeared in the third pamphlet published by *Today*'s Literary Research Society in 1980. Translations are from "The New Poetry—A Turning Point? (A Misty Manifesto)," *Renditions* 19, 20 (1983):191–94. The actual author is Xiao Chi, then a graduate student in the Program of Classical Chinese Literature and Theory at People's University of Beijing.

15. As opposed to the Chinese view, which sees the *menglong* movement as Western modernist, scholars who live outside the People's Republic read it, together with some other post-Mao texts, as belonging to the "New Realism of 1979–1981," which depicted "a political system caught up in corruption, oppor-

tunism, and bureaucratism." See Helen F. Siu and Zelda Stern, "Introduction," in their *Mao's Harvest: Voices from China's New Generation* (New York: Oxford Univ. Press, 1983), xiii. Michael S. Duke sees the *menglong* poetry as part of "the tradition of critical realism" in May Fourth literature that "did not die" after 1949. See his "Introduction" to his *Contemporary Chinese Literature: An Anthology of Post-Mao Fiction and Poetry* (Armonk, N.Y.: M. E. Sharpe, 1985), 3. William Tay reads *menglong* as "political allegory" to the Cultural Revolution. *Menglong* poems did not elicit for Tay—or for other Western readers familiar with imagist poetry—the "defamiliarizing effect" that their experimentation seemed to stimulate in China, and, "with it, all kinds of negative criticism." See Tay, "Obscure Poetry," 135, 137. Leo Ou-fan Lee considers "the poetic world" of *menglong* "transparent rather than dense, impressionistically mimetic rather than abstrusely mythic." See his "Beyond Realism," 67.

16. Miao Deyu, "Weishenme xie rangren dubudong de shi?" [Why would one write incomprehensible poems?], *Shikan* [Poetry monthly], Oct. 1980:53.

17. Leo Ou-fan Lee, "Beyond Realism," 65.

18. Yuan Kejia, Dong Hengxun, and Zheng Kelu, eds., *Waiguo xiandaipai zuopin xuan* [Selected works of foreign modernist literature], 2 vols. (Shanghai: Shanghai wenyi chubanshe, 1981), Vol. 1, Part 1:5.

19. Yuan, Dong, and Zheng, 9.

20. Xie Mian, "Shiqule pingjing yihuo" [After the peace was gone], *Shikan* Dec. 1980:9–10.

21. Xie Mian, "Zai xin de jueqi mianqian" [Confronting the new aesthetic principle], *Guangming ribao* 7 May 1980:4, 7.

22. Sun Shaozhen, "Xin de meixue yuanze zai jueqi" [A new aesthetic principle is emerging], *Shikan* Mar. 1981:56. For a more detailed account of Sun's article, see Tay, "Obscure Poetry," 146–47.

23. Sun Shaozhen, 56–58.

24. Cheng Daixi, "Ping 'xin de meixue yuanze zai jueqi'" [A review on "a new aesthetic principle is emerging"], *Shikan* Apr. 1981:5.

25. Xu Jingya, "Jueqi de shiqun—ping woguo shige de xiandai qingxiang" [The emergence of new groups of poetry—on the modernist tendency in contemporary poetry in our country], *Dangdai wenyi sichao* [Contemporary trends in literature and art] 1 (1983):14–55, 24. Xu's essay was an abridged version of an earlier article first published in *Xinye* [New leaves], a university student journal in Liaoning Province.

26. Xu Jingya, 24.

27. Xia Zhongyi, "Tan xiandaipai yishu xingshi he jiqiao de jiejian" [On borrowing modernist artistic forms and techniques], *Wenyi bao* [Literary gazette] 4 (1984):58–61.

28. David Perkins, *A History of Modern Poetry: From the 1890s to the High Modernist Mode*, 2 vols. (Cambridge: Harvard Univ. Press, 1976, 1987), Vol. 1, 456.

29. Perkins, Vol. 2, 229.

30. Perkins, Vol. 2, 216–17.

31. Laszlo Gefin, *Ideogram: History of a Poetic Method* (Austin: Univ. of Texas Press, 1982), 4.

32. T. S. Eliot, "Tradition and Individual Talent," in his *Selected Essays: 1917–1932* (New York: Harcourt, Brace and Company, 1932), 4.

33. Peter Bürger, *Theory of the Avant-Garde*, trans. Michael Shaw (Minneapolis: Univ. of Minnesota Press, 1984), xxxvi.

34. Peter Bürger, 53–54.

35. Matei Calinescu, *Five Faces of Modernity: Modernism, Avant-Garde, Decadence, Kitsch, Postmodernism* (Durham, N.C.: Duke Univ. Press, 1987), 140.

36. Calinescu, 140.

37. English translations by Alisa Joyce, Ginger Li, and Yip Wai-lim in *Renditions* 19, 20 (1983):221–26. The poem first appeared in *Jintian* 5 (1979):18–21 and was later collected in Lao Mu, ed., *Xin shichao shiji* [Selected works of new poetic movement], Vol. 1, Weiminghu Series (Beijing: Beijing Daxue Wusi Wenxueshe, 1985), 121–25.

38. English translations by Hsin-sheng C. Kao, in Kai-yu Hsu, ed., *Literature of the People's Republic of China* (Bloomington: Indiana Univ. Press, 1980), 672. For examples of poems composed by the same generation available in English, see Eugene C. Eoyang, ed., *Selected Poems of Ai Qing*, trans. Eugene C. Eoyang, Peng Wenlan, and Marilyn Chin (Bloomington: Indiana Univ. Press, 1982).

39. The poem was written in May 1979, first appeared in *Jintian* 4 (1979):1–5, and was later collected in Lao, Vol. 1, 106–11. The English translations are mine.

40. This poem was written on Mar. 27, 1977, first published in *Jintian* 1 (1978):25, and was later collected in Lao, Vol. 1, 63–64. I thank Irving Lo for letting me cite his unpublished English translation. For other translations of Shu Ting's poems, see "Shu Ting: Selected Poems," trans. Eva Hung, intro. Tao Tao Liu in *Renditions* 27, 28 (1987):253–69.

41. Irving Singer, *Courtly and Romantic*, Vol. 2 of *The Nature of Love*, 3 vols. (Chicago: Univ. of Chicago Press, 1984), 377. This is, of course, a replica of the May Fourth romantic generation's passionate search for a romantic love and freedom that sets itself against traditional Chinese culture as characterized by Leo Ou-fan Lee. See Lee, *The Romantic Generation*, 156–57.

42. George Gordon Byron, "When a Man Hath No Freedom to Fight for at Home," in M. H. Abrams et al., eds., *The Norton Anthology of English Literature*, 3rd ed. (New York: Norton, 1975), 1709.

43. *The Song of Youth* by Yang Mo was published in 1958. A summary of the plot and a sample translation in English can be found in Kai-yu Hsu, *Literature of the People's Republic*, 328–38.

44. I would like to thank Eugene C. Eoyang, who helped me clarify certain issues on *menglong* poetry.

45. Gu Gong's "The Two Generations" was published in *Shikan* Oct. 1980:49–51. The English translations are from Siu and Stern, 9–15, 10.

46. The English translations are Bonnie S. McDougall's. See Bei Dao, *The August Sleepwalker*, trans. and intro. Bonnie S. McDougall (New York: New Directions, 1990), 78. Bei Dao was the chief editor of *Jintian*.

47. Bei, "Cruel Hope," 25.

48. Bei, "Cruel Hope," 26.

49. Miao Yushi et al., "Jinnianlai shige pinglun siren tan" [Four critics' views on poetic criticism in recent years], *Shi tansuo* [Poetic experiment] 3 (1982): 84.

50. Gu Cheng, "Xinshihua" [On new poetry], *Wenyi bao* 24 Apr. 1988:2.

51. For a view of generic changes as dependent on the literary expectations of readers, see Hans Robert Jauss, *Toward an Aesthetic of Reception*, trans. Timothy Bahti, intro. Paul de Man (Minneapolis: Univ. of Minnesota Press, 1982), 3–79.

52. Zhou Qiwan, "Yuanyu dangdai shenghuo de shi" [Poems rooted in contemporary times], *Shi tansuo* 3 (1982):48–49.

53. Zhou Qiwan, 50.

54. Shi Tianhe, "Zhongguo zuigu de yishou yixiang shi" [The earliest imagist poem in China], *Shi tansuo* 11 (1984):21–22.

55. Huang Ziping, "Daolu: shanxing di zhankai" [Road: Spreading in a fanshape], *Shi tansuo* 4 (1982):54.

56. Xiao Chi, "Zhongguo gudai shuqing shi de ziran yixiang" [The natural images of expressive poetry in classical Chinese tradition], *Shi tansuo* 2 (1982):149.

57. For a detailed analysis of Yang Lian's poetry in English, see Sean Golden and John Minford, "Yang Lian and the Chinese Tradition," in Goldblatt, 119–37. They noted "one of the most interesting aspects of Yang Lian's work from the point of view of a Western critic: what may at first glance seem to be a perfect case of a young poet trying to use Western modernist techniques in a Chinese setting turns out to be a young poet well acquainted with Western modernist techniques trying to rediscover what is essential in his own culture" (123).

58. Xiao Chi, *Zhongguo shige meixue* [The aesthetics of Chinese poetics] (Beijing: Beijing Daxue chubanshe, 1986), 265.

59. Jiang He's "Chasing the Sun" was collected as one of the twelve poems under the title of "Taiyang he ta de fanguang" [The sun and its reflection], in Lao, Vol. 1, 154–72.

60. Jiang He, "Taiyang," in Lao, Vol. 1, 156–60. The English translation of this poem is mine.

61. Liu Xiaobo, "Yizhong xin de shenmei sichao—cong Xu Xing, Chen Cun, Liu Suola de sanbu zuopin tanqi" [A new aesthetic trend—on three recent works of Xu Xing, Chen Cun, and Liu Suola], *Wenxue pinglun* [Literary review] 3 (1986):41.

62. Leo Ou-fan Lee has pointed out that Liu Suola's story is "a rather ordinary story in conventional realistic language. Liu Suola's daring 'modernism' lies apparently more in her new subject matter, as in her subsequent stories." See Lee, "Beyond Realism," 70.

63. For an English translation, see *Half of Man Is Woman*, trans. Martha Avery (New York: Norton, 1988).

64. For an elaborated discussion on the role of "misunderstanding" in the making of intra- and inter-cultural literary history, see Xiaomei Chen: "The Poetics of 'Misunderstanding': An Ahistorical Model of Cross-Cultural Literary History," *Canadian Review of Comparative Literature* 19:4 (1992):485–506.

65. Barbara Johnson, *The Critical Difference* (Baltimore: Johns Hopkins Univ. Press, 1980), 5.

66. See Michel Foucault, *The Archaeology of Knowledge,* trans. A. M. Sheridan Smith (New York: Pantheon Books, 1972).

CHAPTER 4

1. I wish to thank Marvin Carlson, whose exhilarating teaching of European and comparative drama at Indiana University inspired the writing of an early

version of this chapter, which was published in *Comparative Literature Studies* 29:4 (1992):397–416.

2. For a debate on the paradoxical and problematic relationship between Western literary theory and the study of modern Chinese literature in the West, see a group of contending essays published in *Modern China* 19:1 (1993): Perry Link, "Ideology and Theory in the Study of Modern Chinese Literature: An Introduction," 4–12; Liu Kang, "Politics, Critical Paradigms: Reflections on Modern Chinese Literary Studies," 13–40; Zhang Longxi, "Out of the Cultural Ghetto: Theory, Politics, and the Study of Chinese Literature," 71–101. For attempts to discuss modern Chinese literature in the context of Western theory and practice, see Liu Kang and Xiaobing Tang, eds., *Politics, Ideology, and Literary Discourse in Modern China: Theoretical Interventions and Cultural Critique* (Durham, N.C.: Duke Univ. Press, 1993).

3. King-kok Cheung, "'Don't Tell': Imposed Silence in *The Color Purple* and *The Woman Warrior*," *PMLA* 103 (1988):162.

4. In addition to a number of popular works written by other Chinese American writers such as Amy Tan, Frank Chin, David Henry Hwang, and many others, several scholarly studies on Asian American literature have also been adapted for course materials in university classrooms, such as Elaine H. Kim's *Asian American Literature: An Introduction to the Writings and Their Social Context* (Philadelphia, Pa.: Temple Univ. Press, 1982), and Sauling Cynthia Wong's *Reading Asian American Literature: From Necessity to Extravagance* (Princeton: Princeton Univ. Press, 1993).

5. For an English translation of *Wildman*, see Gao Xingjian, *Wild Man, Asian Theater Journal* 7:2 (1990):195–249, trans., intro. and annot. Bruno Roubicek.

6. For a brief survey of the Western influence on Gao Xingjian and in his plays, see Geremie Barmé, "A Touch of the Absurd—Introducing Gao Xingjian, and His Play *The Bus Stop*," *Renditions* 19, 20 (1983):373–77. For an early account of Gao Xingjian's indebtedness to Antonin Artaud, Jerzy Grotowski, V. E. Meyerhold, and Mei Lanfang, see William Tay, "Avant-garde Theater in Post-Mao China: *The Busstop* by Gao Xingjian," in Goldblatt, 111–18.

7. Barmé, 373.

8. Wang Xining, "An Unconventional Blend," *China Daily* 21 May 1985:5.

9. Wang Xining.

10. For an informative study of the main features of traditional Chinese theater available in English, see Tao-Ching Hsü, *The Chinese Conception of the Theatre* (Seattle: Univ. of Washington Press, 1985). Hsü's work is especially helpful in the context of this essay for its comparative perspective, which treats as well other theatrical conventions such as the Greek, the Elizabethan, and the Japanese.

11. Gao Xingjian, "Guanyu yanshu de jianyi yu shuoming" [Suggestion and explanation for the production of *Wildman*], *Shiyue* [October] 2 (1985):169.

12. Gao Xingjian, "Guanyu."

13. Gao Xingjian, "Guanyu."

14. The quotations of the Chinese text are from Gao Xingjian, *Yeren* [Wildman], *Shiyue* 2 (1985):142–68, 168. The translations are mine unless otherwise indicated.

15. Julian Baum, "Peking's *Wildman* Jolts Theater Goers," *The Christian Science Monitor* 24 June 1985:9–10.

16. Antonin Artaud, *The Theater and Its Double*, trans. Mary Caroline Richards (New York: Grove Press, 1958), 48.

17. Artaud, 58.
18. Artaud, 36.
19. Artaud, 90.
20. Artaud, 90.
21. The quotation is from Bruno Roubicek's English translation of *Wild Man,* 245.
22. Artaud, 91.
23. Leonard Cabell Pronko, *Theater East and West: Perspectives toward a Total Theater* (Berkeley: Univ. of California Press, 1967), 16.
24. Artaud, 83.
25. Artaud, 70.
26. Artaud, 70.
27. For a study in English on the primitive Chinese theater as religious ritual, see Yu Qiuyu, "Some Observations on the Aesthetics of Primitive Chinese Theater," trans. Hu Dongsheng, Elizabeth Wichmann, and Gregg Richardson, *Asian Theater Journal* 6:1 (1989):12–30. Drawing examples from various types of exorcistic performance (*nuo xi*), which are still more popular than film and television programs in the Guangxi Zhuang Autonomous Region, Yu argues that in primitive Chinese performance, the aesthetic and ritual experience are very difficult to separate and that "ancient Chinese ritual performance to a great degree reflected the principal aspects of ancient Chinese society—ritual performance actually had become a rich social ceremony" (15).
28. Gao Xingjian, "*Yeren* yu wo" [*Wildman* and I], *Xiju dianying bao* [Drama and film newspaper] 12 May 1985:2.
29. For a study of Brecht's reception in China, see Adrian Hsia, "The Reception of Bertolt Brecht in China and Its Impact on Chinese Drama," in Tatlow and Wong, 46–64.
30. Ulrich Weisstein, *Comparative Literature and Literary Theory: Survey and Introduction* (Bloomington: Indiana Univ. Press, 1973), 29–30.
31. A number of important earlier essays on the notion of literary influence have been collected in Ronald Primeau, ed., *Influx: Essays on Literary Influence* (Port Washington, N.Y.: Kennikat Press, 1977). For some polemical observations that seek to defend the traditional claims of influence study, see Anna Balakian, "Literary Theory and Comparative Literature," in *Toward a Theory of Comparative Literature,* Vol. 3 of Proceedings of the XIth International Comparative Literature Congress, 20–24 Aug. 1985, ed. and intro. Mario J. Valdes (New York: Lang, 1990), 17–24. Balakian observes that

> the word "influence" has become a bad word, been confused with "imitation," and has even been viewed as a threat to ethnocentrism. It has been replaced by theoreticians with the concept of "intertextuality," which is random, idiosyncratic, resulting in a free play of inter-referentiality which displays the virtuosity of the critic-manipulator rather than the fruits of scholarly research in the form of deep-sea plunging into literary works. The current theoretical version of influence study has become a major feature of what could be called "aleatory criticism." (18)

32. For an informative survey of the scholarship in Chinese-Western comparative literature, see Cecile Chu-Chin Sun, "Problems of Perspective in Chinese-. Western Comparative Literature Studies," *Canadian Review of Comparative Literature*

13:4 (1986):531–48. For Sun, there are two common types of Chinese-Western comparative literature writings in the past twenty years that failed to recognize "(1) what comparative literature is about [and] (2) the unique role of Chinese-Western comparative literature in the field" (533). The *myopic* school of comparison, for example, is "characterized by an over-emphasis on surface and random aspects of the works compared. The cultural contexts and literary conventions are seldom taken into account, in order to render the similarities tenable. The main purpose of this type of comparison is to claim that, after all, Chinese literature is not all that different from Western literatures" (533). The *hypermetropic* school, according to Sun, primarily applies Western theories to Chinese literature, "often in a wholesale fashion" (533). Sun believes that the "danger of this kind of approach lies in its undue confidence about the universal applicability of Western theory at the expense of the distinctive (and frequently intractable) features of Chinese literature" (542). Informative and well-documented, Sun's article focuses on the lyric, and to a much lesser degree, the narrative, without touching on the issues of Chinese-Western dramatic studies, which in many ways remains the stepchild of comparative studies of Chinese and Western culture.

33. In his essay "On Dramatic Theories," Gao Xingjian surveyed the major dramatic traditions in the West, including those of Brecht and Artaud. Exploring the reasons why in recent years Chinese audiences have increasingly lost their interest in modern Chinese drama, Gao pointed out that the predominant Ibsenique tradition of social plays on the present Chinese stage has given too much emphasis to dramatic dialogues. For him, the Ibsenique tradition should be enhanced, if not replaced, by other dramatic traditions such as those of Brecht, Artaud, Chekhov, Gorky, and especially the classical Chinese theater, which employed singing, acting, dancing, and speaking in order to provide its audiences with theatrical experiences rather than mere concepts and ideas. See Gao Xingjian, "Lun xijuguan" [On dramatic theories], *Xiju jie* [The dramatic circle] 1 (1983):27–34.

34. Pronko, 35.

35. See Bloom, *The Anxiety of Influence*. Sensitive to feminist issues, I have changed Bloom's terms such as "father tradition" to "parental tradition" in my use of his concepts.

36. For a study in Western scholarship, see, for example, A. Owen Aldridge's chapter "Voltaire and the Mirage of China" in his *The Reemergence of World Literature: A Study of Asia and the West* (Newark: Univ. of Delaware Press, 1986), 141–66. Aldridge's conclusions are telling in light of the present study:

> Voltaire's source was a translation of 1731 by a French Jesuit, Joseph Henri Prémare, which was later included in a famous compilation by another Jesuit, Jean Baptiste Du Halde, under the title *Description géographique, historique, chronologue, politique, et physique de l'empire de la Chine et de la tartarie chinoise* (1735). Among the essential ingredients of the original Chinese work were song and music, but these were completely eliminated from Prémare's translation and from Voltaire's adaptation as well. Since Voltaire's neoclassical drama departed from both the form and the substance of his Chinese source, one would be justified in asking whether his work should really be considered as an example of the penetration of Chinese culture. Should it instead be dismissed as mere Chinoiserie? The answer is that Voltaire himself understood a great deal more about Chinese civilization than his play reveals, but that he was prevented by the prevailing taste of the times from closely following his model. (145)

See also Basil Guy, *The French Image of China before and after Voltaire,* Vol. 21 of *Studies on Voltaire and the Eighteenth Century* (Geneva: Institut et musée Voltaire, 1963).

37. Fan Xiheng, "Chong *Zhaoshi gu'er* dao *Zhongguo gu'er*—shang" [From *The Orphan of Zhao* to *Orphelin de la Chine* (Part I)], *Zhongguo bijiao wenxue* [Chinese comparative literature] 4 (1987):164–66.

38. Pronko, 37.

39. Ding Yangzhong, "Brecht's Theatre and Chinese Drama," in Tatlow and Wong, 29.

40. Pronko, 56.

41. Pronko, 57. For more information on the paradoxical relationship between Brecht's and Mei Lanfang's theories of theater, see William Huizu Sun, "Mei Lanfang, Stanislavsky and Brecht on China's Stage and Their Aesthetic Significance," in Tung and MacKerras, 137–50. For a more general article on the reception of Mei Lanfang's performance in the Soviet Union in 1935 on the part of European theater artists such as Stanislavksy, Meyerhold, Craig, Brecht, Eisenstein, Piscator, Tairov, and Tretiakov, see Georges Banu, "Mei Lanfang: A Case against and a Model for the Occidental Stage," trans. Ella L. Wiswell and June V. Gibson, *Asian Theater Journal* 3:2 (1986):153–78. See also Huang Zuolin, "A Supplement to Brecht's 'Alienation Effects in Chinese Acting,'" in Tatlow and Wong, 96–110.

CHAPTER 5

1. Gao Xingjian, "Guanyu," 169.

2. Thornton Wilder, *Our Town: A Play in Three Acts* (New York: Coward McCann, 1938), 10.

3. Donald Haberman, *The Plays of Thornton Wilder: A Critical Study* (Middletown, Conn.: Wesleyan Univ. Press, 1967), 8.

4. Haberman, 57.

5. Wilder, 13.

6. Haberman, 57–58.

7. Richard H. Goldstone, *Thornton Wilder: An Intimate Portrait* (New York: Saturday Review Press, 1975), 138.

8. Goldstone, 138.

9. Goldstone, 141.

10. Claus Clüver, *Thornton Wilder und André Obey: Untersuchungen zum modernen epischen Theater* (Bonn: Bouvier, 1978), 373.

11. David Castronovo, *Thornton Wilder* (New York: F. Ungar, 1986), 86.

12. Rex J. Burbank, *Thornton Wilder,* 2nd ed. (Boston: Twayne, 1978), 74.

13. Haberman, 85.

14. Haberman, 87.

15. Haberman, 85.

16. Haberman, 85.

17. Wilder, 57.

18. Wilder, 13.

19. Wilder, 13, 58.

20. Wilder, 71.

21. Haberman, 85.

22. Peter Szondi, *Theory of the Modern Drama,* ed. and trans. Michael Hays (Minneapolis: Univ. of Minnesota Press, 1987), 83–87.

23. Ma Chih-yüan (Ma Zhiyuan), *Autumn in Han Palace,* in *Six Yüan Plays,* trans. Liu Jung-en (London: Penguin, 1972), 193.

24. Wilder, 9–10.

25. Wilder, 12.

26. Wilder, 26–27.

27. Wilder, 69, 82.

28. Wilder, 114.

29. Goldstone, 119–200.

30. Wilder, 54.

31. For more information, see Mei Shaowu, "Mei Lanfang as Seen by his Foreign Audiences and Critics," in Wu Zuguang, Huang Zuolin, and Mei Shaowu, *Peking Opera and Mei Lanfang* (Beijing: New World Press, 1981), 46–65.

32. Stark Young, "Mei Lanfang," *The New Republic* 5 Mar. 1930:74. See also his "Ambassador in Art," *The New Republic* 6 Apr. 1932:206–8.

33. Mei, 54.

34. Tao-Ching Hsü, *The Chinese Conception of the Theatre* (Seattle: Univ. of Washington Press, 1985), 6–7.

35. Banu, "Mei Lanfang," 154.

36. Earl Miner, *The Japanese Tradition in British and American Literature* (Princeton: Princeton Univ. Press, 1958), 228.

37. Miner, 228.

38. Miner, 228.

39. Miner, 228. According to Earl Miner, Thornton Wilder acknowledged the influence of nō theater and Elizabethan theater in his reply to Miner's letter of inquiry. See Miner, 298.

40. J. Dyer Ball, *Things Chinese, or, Notes Connected with China,* 5th and rev. ed. (Shanghai: Kelly and Walsh, 1925), 659.

41. Young, "Mei Lanfang," 75.

42. "Xieyi xiju" was translated by Huang as "essentialist theater," which may confuse Western readers with the familiar implication of essentialism. I substitute for this term "suggestive theater," even when I paraphrase Huang's explanation of his concept in his English essay. I thank an anonymous reader for Oxford Univ. Press for suggesting this change.

43. Huang Zuolin's theory was first outlined in a speech delivered at the National Conference of Modern Spoken Drama and Opera held in Guangzhou in 1962, and was first published in *Renmin ribao* [People's daily] 25 Apr. 1962. For an English version, see Huang Zuolin, "Mei Lanfang, Stanislavsky, Brecht—A Study in Contrasts," in Wu, Huang, and Mei, 14–29.

44. Huang Zuolin, "Mei Lanfang, Stanislavsky, Brecht—A Study in Contrasts," in Wu, Huang, and Mei, 19.

45. Huang Zuolin, "Mei Lanfang," 28–29.

46. Huang Zuolin, "Mei Lanfang," 20.

47. Huang Zuolin, "Mei Lanfang," 20.
48. Huang Zuolin, "Mei Lanfang," 21.
49. Huang Zuolin, "Mei Lanfang," 21.
50. Huang Zuolin, "Mei Lanfang," 29.
51. Huang Zuolin, "Mei Lanfang," 15–16.
52. Huang Zuolin, "Mei Lanfang," 27.
53. For more information in English on the reception of Stanislavsky in China, see William Huizhu Sun, "Mei Lanfang, Stanislavsky and Brecht on China's Stage and Their Aesthetic Significance," in Tung and MacKerras, 137–50.
54. Huang Zuolin, "A Supplement," 96.
55. Huang Zuolin, "A Supplement," 96.
56. Huang Zuolin, "A Supplement," 96–97.
57. Huang Zuolin, "A Supplement," 97.
58. Adrian Hsia, "The Reception," 46.
59. Chen Yong, "The Beijing Production," 90.
60. See Han Tongsheng, "*Xiaozhen fengqing* pailian shiling" [Sidelights on the rehearsal of *Our Town*], *Xiju bao* [Drama journal] 8 (1987):363.
61. See *Xiju bao* 11 (1987):366.
62. I thank an anonymous reader for reminding me of this point.

CHAPTER 6

1. Juliet Mitchell, *Women: The Longest Revolution: Essays on Feminism, Literature, and Psychoanalysis* (London: Virago, 1984), 289. A different version of this chapter was published in Marilyn Robinson Waldman, Artemis Leontis, and Müge Galin, eds., *Understanding Women: The Challenge of Cross-Cultural Perspectives. Papers in Comparative Studies* 7 (1991–1992):205–22.
2. See Rosemary Jackson, *Fantasy: The Literature of Subversion* (London: Methuen, 1981), and Carol Farley Kessler, comp., ed. and intro., *Daring to Dream: Utopian Fiction by United States Women, 1836–1919* (Boston: Pandora Press, 1984).
3. For the accounts of woman and theater, see Michelene Wandor, *Understudies: Theatre and Sexual Politics* (London: Methuen, 1981); Jill Dolan, *The Feminist Spectator as Critic* (Ann Arbor: UMI Research Press, 1988); and Sue-Ellen Case, ed., *Performing Feminisms: Feminist Critical Theory and Theatre* (Baltimore: Johns Hopkins Univ. Press, 1990).
4. See Terry Lovell, "Writing like a Woman: A Question of Politics," in Mary Eagleton, ed., *Feminist Literary Theory: A Reader* (Oxford: Basil Blackwell, 1986), 83–85.
5. Ching-kiu Stephen Chan, "The Language of Despair: Ideological Representations of the 'New Women' by May Fourth Writers," *Modern Chinese Literature* 4 (1988):19.
6. Chan, 20.
7. See Peter Szondi, *Theory of the Modern Drama*.
8. Elisabeth Eide, *China's Ibsen: From Ibsen to Ibsenism* (London: Curzon Press), 1987, 75.

9. Yue Ming-Bao, "Gendering the Origins of Modern Chinese Fiction," in Lu, 48.

10. Yue, 54.

11. For an account of feminist issues in the May Fourth period and Hu Shi's role in introducing "Ibsenism" to the Chinese intellectuals and its lasting influence on the development of modern Chinese fiction, see Eide, *China's Ibsen*, Part One: "Individualism and Liberalism" and Part Two: "Feminism." Eide mentions in her "Introduction" that her study does not deal with the considerable influence of Ibsen on the development of modern Chinese drama. See also Vera Schwarcz, "Ibsen's Nora: The Promise and the Trap," *Bulletin of Concerned Asian Scholars* 7:1 (1975):3–5; Kwon-kan Tam, "Ibsen and Modern Chinese Dramatists: Influences and Parallels," *Modern Chinese Literature* 2:1 (1986):45–62; and Constantine Tung, "T'ien Han and the Romantic Ibsen," *Modern Drama* 9:4 (1967):389–95. For a groundbreaking and exemplary work from feminist perspectives on the May Fourth women writers, see Meng Yue and Dai Jinhua, *Fuchu lishi dibao* [Emerging from the surface of history] (Zhengzhou: Henan renmin chubanshi, 1989).

12. The above information is cited by Hong Shen in his "Daoyan" [Introduction] in Hong Shen, ed., *Zhongguo xin wenxue daxi—xiju ji* [The selected works of modern Chinese literature—the dramatic genre], Vol. 9 (Shanghai: Liangyou tushu yinshua gongsi, 1935), 16–19. For the original sources, see Qian Xuantong, "Suigan lu" [Random thought], *Xin qingnian* [New youth] 5:1 (1918): 85; Zhou Zuoren, "Ren de wenxue" [Humanistic literature], *Xin qingnian* 5:6 (1918):609–18; and Hu Shi, "Jianshe de wenxue geming lun" [On the constructive theory of literary revolution], in *Hu Shi wencun* [The selective works of Hu Shi], Vol. 1 (Shanghai: Yadong tushuguan, 1921), 71–96.

13. Hu Shi's *The Greatest Event in Life* was first published in *Xin qingnian* 6:3 (1919). Directed by Hong Shen, it was performed in Sept. 1923 by Xiju Xieshe [Drama association]. For an English translation and a brief introduction to this play and its cultural background, see Edward Gunn, *Twentieth-Century Chinese Drama*, vii–xxiii, 1–10.

14. By calling this play a "feminist" text, I evoke Toril Moi's definition that views feminist criticism as "a specific kind of political discourse: a cultural and theoretical practice committed to the struggle against patriarchy and sexism, not simply a concern for gender in literature." See Moi's "Feminist, Female, Feminine," in Ann Jefferson and David Robey, eds., *Modern Literary Theory: A Comparative Introduction*, 2nd ed. (London: Batsford, 1986), 204–21.

15. For a representative Western feminist view of women's position in the patriarchal family structure, see Kate Millett, *Sexual Politics* (Garden City, N.Y.: Doubleday, 1970).

16. Hong Shen noted in his "Daoyan" that according to Hu Shi, *The Greatest Event in Life* was originally written in English for Chinese students studying in America and was later translated into Chinese upon the request of several Chinese female students who wanted to perform the play. The returned script here refers to the Chinese translation of the play, not the one sent to *Xin qingnian* where it was first published in 1919. This situation obviously changed at a later time: the success of the 1923 Shanghai production of the play was credited to director Hong Shen's daring experiment with the use of actresses to end the conventional rule of

male acting for woman characters, as Yan Xiwu and Sun Qingwen noted in their "Zan Hong Shen zai yishu shang de shouchuang jingshen" [On the innovative artistic spirit of Hong Shen], in Sun Qingwen, ed., *Hong Shen yanjiu zhuanji* [Selected essays on Hong Shen] (Hangzhou: Zhejiang wenyi chubanshe, 1986), 134.

17. Hong Shen, "Daoyan," 23.

18. The theory of the gaze was first developed in film theory and later applied to performing art in general. In her pioneering essay "Visual Pleasure and Narrative Cinema" (*Screen* 16:3, 1975, 6–19), Laura Mulvey argues that there are three ways of male stereotyping of women in cinema that create men as active subjects and women as passive "others": the voyeuristic gaze of the camera from the male perspective, women as objects of the male gaze in film narrative, and the gaze of male spectators in the cinema. For an informative study related to the male gaze and its implications for feminist performing art and popular culture, see Jill Dolan, "Ideology in Performance: Looking through the Male Gaze," in her *The Feminist Spectator as Critic* (41–58), and Lorraine Gamman and Margaret Marshment, eds., *The Female Gaze: Women as Viewers of Popular Culture* (London: The Women's Press, 1988).

19. Randy Kaplan, "Images of Subjugation and Defiance: Female Characters in the Early Dramas of Tian Han," *Modern Chinese Literature* 4 (1988):87–97, 89.

20. Kaplan, 89.

21. Guo Moruo, "Xiezai *Sange panni de nüxing* houmian" [Epilogue on *A Trilogy of Three Revolutionary Women*], in Zhongguo xiju chubanshe, ed., *Guo Moruo juzuo quanji* [The complete works of drama by Guo Moruo] (Beijing: Zhongguo xiju chubanshe, 1982), 189–203, Vol. 1, 194. Guo Moruo's *Zhuo Wenjun* was first published in *Chuangzao yuekan* [Creation monthly] 2:1 (1923) and was later collected in *Sange panni de nüxing* [A trilogy of three revolutionary women] (Shanghai: Guanghua shuju, 1926).

22. Guo, 196. Guo Moruo's *Wang Zhaojun* was first published in *Chuangzao yuekan* 2:2 (1924) and was later collected in *Sange panni de nüxing*.

23. Guo, 200. Guo Moruo's *Nie Ying* was written in 1925, first published by Guanghua shuju as a separate play, and was later collected in *Sange panni de nüxing*.

24. Guo, 189.

25. Guo, 189. English translations are mine.

26. Su Hsueh-lin, "Present Day Fiction and Drama in China," in Joseph Schyns et al., eds., *1500 Modern Chinese Novels and Plays* (Peking: Verbiest Academy, 1948; Hong Kong: Lung Men Bookstore, 1966), xxxvii.

27. Mary Eagleton, ed., *Feminist Literary Theory*, 45.

28. Chen Dabei is one of the most important early dramatists of the May Fourth period. In 1920, together with Pu Boying, Chen initiated Zhonghua Xiju Xieshe [China drama association] in Beijing to promote what Chen called *aimei ju* [amateur theater], by which he meant to evoke the French etymology "amare" [to love], to engage in dramatic activities for aesthetic experiment rather than for commercial purposes. Together with Shen Yanbing, Zheng Zhenduo, Ouyang Yuqian, Wang Zhongxian, Xu Banmei, Zhang Yuguang, Ke Yicen, Lu Bingxin, Shen Bingxue, Teng Ruoqu, Xiong Foxi, Zhang Jinglu, Chen organized Minzhong Xijushe [People's theater] in Beijing in May 1921. In the same year, they published

Xiju [Drama], the first journal on modern Chinese drama in the May Fourth period. Chen Dabei also played an important part in founding Renyi Xiju Zhuanmen Xue-xiao [People's art drama school] in Beijing, the first of its kind in modern China. It is shocking, however, to see how Chen Dabei has been unjustifiably neglected in the contemporary Chinese scholarship. One cannot even find, for instance, his name entry in the PRC reference works such as *Zhongguo mingren dacidian* [Who is who in China] or *Zhongguo yishujia cidian* [The dictionary of Chinese artists].

29. According to Teng Sui-ming, *Miss Youlan* was performed by the China Drama Association after its founding in 1920. Different sources refer to it as an early May Fourth play without identifying when it was first written. It was later collected in Chen Dabei's *Miss Youlan*, published by Xiandai shuju in 1928. The quotations from this play are taken from Hong Shen, *Zhongguo xin wenxue daxi— xiju ji*, 27–67.

30. Chen Dabei, *Youlan nüshi*, 36.

31. Su Hsueh-lin, xxxvi.

32. Chen Dabei, 54.

33. For distinctions between liberal feminism, cultural (radical) feminism, and material feminism where theater is concerned, see Dolan, *The Feminist Spectator*, 1–18.

34. Alison Jaggar, *Feminist Politics and Human Nature* (Totowa, N.J.: Rowman and Allanheld, 1983), 366.

35. Chen Dabei, 60.

36. Dolan, 10.

37. Chen Dabei, 46.

38. Tani E. Barlow, "Theorizing Woman: *Funu, Guojia, Jiating* [Chinese Women, Chinese State, Chinese Family]," *Genders* 10 (1991):137–38.

39. Bing Xin is the pen name of Xie Wanying. Her short story "Two Families" was first published in installments in *Chenbao* [Morning newspaper] from Sept. 18 to 22, 1919.

40. Shoshana Felman, "Women and Madness: The Critical Phallacy," *Diacritics* 5 (1975):4.

41. Betty Friedan, *The Feminine Mystique*, 20th Anniversary ed. (New York: Norton, 1983), 22.

42. Friedan, 18.

43. *Homecoming* was written in 1922 and published in *Dongfang zazhi* [Eastern miscellany]. It was later collected in *Juben huikan* [The selected works of drama], Vol. 1, published by Shangwu yinshuguan in 1928. Directed by Hong Shen, it was first performed by Shanghai Drama Association in 1923. According to Su Guanxin, Ouyang Yuqian himself directed the play in 1925, performed by a group of young actors and actresses, in Shenyang. See Su Guanxin, "Chronicle of Ouyang Yuqian: 1889–1962 (1)," *Guangxi Shifan Xueyuan xuebao* [Guangxi Normal College journal] 4 (1982):34–50.

44. Hong Shen, "Daoyan," 70.

45. For a theory of "the dialogic imagination," see Mikhail Mikhaïlovich Bakhtin, *The Dialogic Imagination: Four Essays by M. M. Bakhtin*, ed. Michael Holquist, trans. Caryl Emerson and Michael Holquist (Austin: Univ. of Texas Press, 1981).

CHAPTER 7

1. *Wild Swans* by Jung Chang has been widely adopted as a textbook to teach American students about modern Chinese history, culture, politics, and women's history. It depicts the lives of three generations of women: a warlord's concubine, a Communist woman warrior, and a little girl growing up in the chaotic Cultural Revolution. For a study of similar texts, see Peter Zarrow, "Meanings of China's Cultural Revolution: Memoirs of Exile," *Positions* 7:1 (1999):165–91, and Xiaomei Chen, *Acting the Right Part: Political Theater and Popular Drama in Contemporary China* (Honolulu: Univ. of Hawaii Press, 2002), 26–32.

2. Aihwa Ong and Donald Nonini, eds., *Ungrounded Empires: The Cultural Politics of Modern Chinese Transnationalsim* (New York: Routledge, 1997), 4.

3. Ong and Nonini, 9. Italics in original.

4. Ong and Nonini, 12.

5. Ong and Nonini, 14.

6. Michelle Yeh, "International Theory and the Transnational Critic: China in the Age of Multiculturalism," in Rey Chow, ed., *Modern Chinese Literary and Cultural Studies in the Age of Theory: Reimagining a Field* (Durham, N.C.: Duke Univ. Press, 2000), 251–80, 262.

7. Due to space limitations, this chapter cannot address the issue of what Rey Chow called "volatile realities of ethnicity," which argued for the inclusion of other Chinese experiences outside the PRC and in non-Mandarin-speaking ethnic and linguistic groups. A full-length study would naturally take up these matters. Rey Chow, "Introduction," in Ray Chow, ed., *Modern Chinese Literary and Cultural Studies in the Age of Theory*, 1–25, 5.

8. Kirk A. Denton, "The Distant Shore: Nationalism in Yu Dafu's 'Sinking,'" *Chinese Literature: Essays, Articles, Reviews* 14 (1992):107–23.

9. Denton, 110.

10. Denton, 112. C. T. Hsia, in his classic history, characterized Yu's story as an autobiographical "portrayal of a lonely and patriotic youth bent on self-destruction." It descended from "the Japanese and European decadent writers as well as those Chinese poets and essayists who have habitually bewailed their loneliness and poverty as outcasts from philistine officialdom." See C. T. Hsia, *A History of Modern Chinese Fiction*, 3rd ed., with an introduction by David Der-wei Wang (Bloomington: Indiana Univ. Press, 1999), 105, 103.

In his trailblazing study, Leo Ou-fan Lee placed Yu's "Sinking" in the intersection of sex, racism, and nationalism. Although sex is part of a process of reaching maturity, Lee argues that what made "Yu's case interesting was that his sexual awakening should have taken place in a foreign land with foreign women." The political and ideological reading in nationalist terms, therefore, must be also understood in the context of psychological and personal factors. See Leo Ou-fan Lee, *The Romantic Generation of Modern Chinese Writers* (Cambridge: Harvard Univ. Press, 1973), 91, 89.

11. Denton, 122.

12. Shu-mei Shih claimed that "in every one of the Japan stories written during 1921 and 1922, Yu's Chinese protagonists were victims of Japanese imperialism's subjugation of China." See Shu-mei Shih, *The Lure of the Modern* (Berkeley: Univ. of California Press, 2001), 120.

13. See Denton's "The Distant Shore" for an insightful analysis in this regard.

14. Niu Daifeng, *Lu Xun zhuan* [Biography of Lu Xun] (Beijing: Zhongguo wen-lian chuban gongsi, 1999), 82. Niu also pointed out that Lu Xun was the first Chinese student to study in Sendai, a small town that gave Lu Xun a friendly welcome. In contrast to racial discrimination elsewhere against the Chinese, residents of Sendai treated him warmly, fearing even to lose him to other cities. See Niu, *Lu Xun zhuan*, 79–80.

15. In "Professor Fujino," the protagonist scored "above 60 points" in his exam. Niu Diafeng recorded in his *Lu Xun zhuan* that among the 142 students in his class, Lu Xun was ranked 66th after the final examination. See Niu, 84.

16. Lu Xun, "Tengye xiansheng [Professor Fujino]," in his *Lu Xun quanji* [Complete works of Lu Xun] (Beijing: Renmin chubanshe, 1981), 2:302–9, 305–6. For an English translation, see his "Mr. Fujino," in his *Selected Works of Lu Hsun* (Beijing: Foreign Languages Press, 1956), 4:402–9.

17. Rey Chow, *Primitive Passions* (New York: Columbia Univ. Press, 1995), 5.

18. Lydia Liu, *Translingual Practice* (Stanford, Calif.: Stanford Univ. Press, 1995), 64–65, 61.

19. Lu Xun, "Tengye xiansheng," 307.

20. Li Jieren, "Tongqing" [Sympathy], cited from a reprint in *Zhongguo liuxuesheng wenxue daxi* [A compendium of Chinese overseas student literature] *Jinxiandai xiaoshuo juan* [Modern fiction volume] (Shanghai: Shanghai wenyi chubanshe, 2000), 481–556, 481–82. Li Jieren (1891–1962) was a writer and translator in the May Fourth period. In 1919, he started *Xingqiri zhoukan* [Sunday weekly] and went to study French literature and literary criticism in France. He returned to China in 1926. "Sympathy" was written in 1923 in France and was first published in *Young China* [Shaonian Zhongguo] 4:4–6 (June–August 1923).

21. Li Jieren, 521.

22. Denton, 117.

23. Li Jieren, 516–17.

24. Li Jieren, 515–16.

25. Li Jieren, 552.

26. Peng Ming, *Wusi yundong shi* [A history of the May Fourth movement]. Revised ed. (Beijing: Renmin chubanshe, 1998), 139–44.

27. Peng Ming, 548.

28. Peng Ming, 548–54. Peng Ming cited Chen Yi and Wang Ruofei, early leaders of the CCP, as saying that their experience in French factories was so oppressive that it made them realize the cruelty of capitalist exploitation (549). The work-study program in France is a complicated issue that cannot be fully addressed here. For those interested in the topic, see Marilyn A. Levine, *The Found Generation: Chinese Communists in Europe during the Twenties* (Seattle: Univ. of Washington Press, 1993). In comparison with America as a destination for Chinese students, Levine noted: "During the postwar period, when the exclusion laws were still in effect in the United States, France was the destination for the refugees of the world. At the same time that over one hundred Chinese students were accepted into the scholastic community at Montargis, hundreds of Chinese were employed at the nearby Langlee factory, as were some twelve hundred Russian refugees. The French were very generous toward the Chinese who reached their shores. The

government encouraged the placing of Chinese in educational institutions and factories and provided personnel and economic support" (91–92). Levine also presented a Chinese view of France as inspirational: "As the 'oldest' civilization in Europe, French civilization was deemed to be the most advanced in Europe with respect to its intellectual, philosophical, and moral development. The elegance of the French language and the expressiveness of the French personality were also much admired" (91).

29. The Chinese imagining of the French warrants a book-length study. One can point out at least three important strands in this period: (1) the May Fourth discourse of seeing France as part of the West where Chinese intellectuals looked for science and democracy; (2) the early Chinese Communist movement to work and study in France to "seek for the truth for the Chinese revolution"; and (3) the PRC depiction of France as one of the oldest imperialist countries. Its relationship to China differed from that of Britain, Japan, and Russia, however, which were viewed as the major imperialist powers craving Chinese territorial rights and special privileges at the beginning of the twentieth century. With its imposition of the 1844 Sino-French Treaty of Whampoa, France "attached special importance to the privilege of propagating Christianity in China." As a result, the Manchu government recognized Catholic and Protestant faiths as lawful, and Western missionaries "began to infiltrate into China." See Hu Sheng, *Imperialism and Chinese Politics* (Beijing: Foreign Languages Press, 1955), 15. France also played a part in the eight allied countries that suppressed the Boxer Uprising in 1900, which resulted in an indemnity that specified 70,878,240 taels for the French share. See Immanuel C. Y. Hsu, "Late Ch'ing Foreign Relations, 1866–1905," in Denis Twitchett and John K. Fairbank, eds., *The Cambridge History of China*, Vol. 11: *Late Ch'ing, 1800–1911*, Part 2 (Cambridge: Cambridge Univ. Press, 1980), 70–141, 127.

30. Jiang Guangci (1901–1931) went to study in Moscow with Liu Shaoqi and Ren Bishi in 1921 and returned to China in 1924. "On the Yalu River" first appeared in his collection of writings titled *Yalujiang shang* [On the Yalu River] published by Shanghai yadong tushuguan in 1927. A reprint of the story can be found in *Zhongguo liuxuesheng wenxue daxi* [A compendium of Chinese overseas student literature], *Jinxiandai xiaoshuo juan* [Modern fiction volume] (Shanghai: Shanghai wenyi chubanshe, 2000), 576–96.

31. Ying Hu, *Tales of Translation: Composing the New Women in China, 1899–1918* (Stanford, Calif.: Stanford Univ. Press, 2000), 10, 5.

32. Cheng Zhongyuan noted that Zhang Wentian left San Francisco near the end of 1923. He arrived in Shanghai around January 20, 1924. See his *Zhang Wentian zhuan* [Biography of Zhang Wentian] (Beijing: Dangdai Zhonguo chubanshe, 1993), 60, 70, n. 46.

33. During the crucial moment of the Long March (1934–35) at Zunyi, Zhang Wentian (1900–1976) was the only member of the Secretariat to oppose the unsuccessful military strategy of Otto Braun, the Comintern representative, and Bo Gu, the Chinese party chief, and later assisted Mao Zedong's rise to power. Despite his important role as the party chief in the latter part of the Long March and his many later achievements, Zhang's leadership was marginalized in CCP history until recently. Zhang's major contributions, such as his support for Mao's policies in Zunyi conference, consequently remain relatively unknown. Rarely mentioned is

his crucial role at the Wayaobao conference in December 1935, in which the CCP decided to promote a united front with the KMT to fight against Japanese aggression. From 1951 to 1955, Zhang served as Chinese ambassador to the Soviet Union. After Zhang supported Peng Dehui's criticism of Mao and the Great Leap Forward at the 1959 Lushan conference, he lost his position as the deputy minister of foreign affairs. He was persecuted during the Cultural Revolution and died in Wuxi in 1975 under a false name. He never fulfilled his last wish, which he had expressed several times in his letter to Mao Zedong, to return to Beijing to see, once again with his own eyes, the "new look" of his socialist motherland, after a lifelong devotion to it. In post-Mao China, a few scholarly works have attempted to present a more complete biography of Zhang. They see him as one of the most important CCP leaders wrongly neglected in party history. See Cheng Zhongyuan, *Zhang Wentian zhuan*. See also, Shi Songhan, *Zhang Wentian sixiang yanjiu* [On Zhang Wentian thought] (Beijing: Zhongguo dangshi chubanshe, 1993). Shi's work focuses on Zhang's achievement as a party chief in the Northeast (Manchuria) from 1945 to 1949, another episode erased in party history. For a study in English of Zhang's diplomatic career, see Xiaohong Liu, "A Revolutionary Institution-Builder: Zhang Wentian," in her *Chinese Ambassadors: The Rise of Diplomatic Professionalism since 1949* (Seattle: Univ. of Washington Press, 2001), 31–52.

34. Cheng Zhongyuan, 23.

35. Since literary histories have hardly mentioned Zhang Wentian's career as a May Fourth writer (and a very talented one at that), a brief account of his literary career is in order. His interest in literature matured only after he returned from Japan, where he had studied from July 1920 to January 1921. As a member of the Young China Study Association, he befriended fellow members such as the dramatist Tian Han and the new poet Kang Baiqing, then also residing in Japan. His first scholarly essay, titled "*Tuo'ersitai de yishu guan*" [On Tolstoy's concept of art, 1921], was published in a special issue of *Xiaoshuo yuebao* (The short story monthly) on Russian literature. This issue marked the first systematic introduction of Russian literature to Chinese readers, with contributions from major writers such as Lu Xun, Shen Yanbing, and Zheng Zhenduo. Zhang also coauthored an essay that introduced Oscar Wilde and co-translated his *The Ballad of Reading Gaol*. Countering the attack on Wilde's "art for art's sake" concept, Zhang believed that Wilde's individualism was not self-serving but sought to tap fully the individual's potential talents; he urged the Chinese people to change their way of thinking in order to give real meaning to their lives. By the same token, in his essay introducing Goethe's *Faust*, he urged conservative and fearful Chinese to learn from Faust's spirit and fully participate in life's journey, despite the obstacles encountered in a suffocating Confucian society. See Cheng Zhongyuan, *Zhang Wentian zhuan*, 38–43.

36. Cheng Zhongyuan, 46.

37. Cheng Zhongyuan, 47, 44–50.

38. Zhang Wentian's *Lütu* [Journey] was first published in installments in *Xiaoshuo yuebao* [Short story monthly] 15:5, 6, 7, 9, 10, 11, 12 (1924), and later as a separate volume by Shangwu yinshuguan (1925). A reprint of the story can be found in *Zhongguo liuxuesheng wenxue daxi, Jinxiandai xiaoshuo juan*, 597–729, 607.

39. Zhang Wentian, 632.

40. Zhang Wentian, 651.

41. David Henry Hwang, *M. Butterfly* (New York: Penguin Books, 1989), 95.

42. David Henry Hwang, 17.

43. David Henry Hwang, 99.

44. Zhang Wentian, 613.

45. Hu Ping and Zhang Shengyou, *Shijie da chuanlian* [Exchanging revolutionary experience in the world], in Ke Ling et al., eds., *Ci'an yu bi'an* [This shore and that shore] (Shanghai: Wenhui chubanshe, 1999), 88–145, 89–90.

46. Based on Prosper Mérimée's novel, *Carmen* [*Kamen*] was adapted by Tian Han into a modern spoken-drama version in June 1930. It was performed by Tian's Southern Society [Nanguo She] to "borrow a foreign story to express the revolutionary sentiment to bring changes to Chinese reality," as Tian claimed in his postscript to *Carmen*, published in 1955 by Yishu chubanshe. After only three performances, *Carmen* was banned for advocating "class struggle"; so was the Southern Society. Zong Hui (Xie Weiqi), who played the male lead, was arrested and executed by the KMT government. *Carmen* has also occupied a central position in the Western-style opera in the PRC period. For an essay on its European contexts, see Robert L. A. Clark, "South of North: Carmen and French Nationalisms," in Claire Sponsler and Xiaomei Chen, eds., *East of West: Cross-Cultural Performance and the Staging of Difference* (New York: Palgrave, 2000), 187–216. What Clark describes as one of the reasons for the lack of success of the 1875 premiere of Georges Bizet's opera version, to some extent, applies to the success of the play with Chinese audiences: it is "a study in transgression." Every dimension of Carmen "is placed under the sign of the other: female; doubly foreign and radically other, as a gypsy in Andalusia; working class (she works in the tobacco factory at the beginning of the opera); sexually dissident in relation to the bourgeois mores of the day; and, finally, an outlaw (she and her friends run contraband). And so she remains, defiantly, to the end" (186).

47. Hu Ping and Zhang Shengyou, *Shijie da chuanlian*, 111.

48. Hu Ping and Zhang Shengyou, *Shijie da chuanlian*, 145.

49. The English title printed next to the Chinese title in the 1992 Beijing edition is *Manhattan's China Lady*. The change of the English title is mine.

50. Xiao Yin and Yi Ren, "*Manhadun de Zhongguo nüren zai zhengyi zhong*" [A debate on *A Chinese Woman in Manhattan*], in Xiao Yi and Yi Ren, eds., *Kuayue dayang de gong'an—Manhadun de Zhongguo nüren zhengyi shilu* [A lawsuit across the oceans: A factual account of the controversy on *A Chinese Woman in Manhattan*] (Beijing: Guangming ribao chubanshe, 1993), 1–2.

51. For readers' enthusiastic letters to Zhou Li in appreciation of her book, see Lin Feng, ed., *Cengjing canghai nan wei shui* [Difficult to be a drop of water after being the ocean] (Shanghai: Tongji Daxue chubanshe, 1993), 201–25. Lin's collection also includes other materials regarding the debate on the book.

52. See Xiong Yuanyi and Zhang Yulu, "Liuxuesheng wenxue yantaohui zongshu" [A seminar held on overseas student literature], *Renmin ribao* (overseas ed.) 4 Feb. 1993:8.

53. Xiao Yin and Yi Ren, "*Manhadun*," 1.

54. He Zhenbang, "Yiqu rensheng fendou zhige—du Zhou Li de *Manhadun de Zhongguo nüren*" [A song of dedication: Afterthoughts on Zhou Li's *A Chinese Woman in Manhattan*], Xiao Yin and Yi Ren, eds., *Kuayue dayang de gong'an*, 85.

55. He Zhenbang, 85.

56. Xiao Yin and Yi Ren, "*Manhadun*," 8–9.

57. You Zunming, et al., "Zhou Li qishu qiren" [Concerning Zhou Li's personality and her book], in Xiao Yin and Yi Ren, eds., *Kuayue dayang de gong'an*, 65.

58. Xiao Yin and Yi Ren, "*Manhadun*," 8.

59. Xiao Yin, "'Kuayang' caifang zhaji" [Overseas interviews], in Xiao Yin and Yi Ren, eds., *Kuayue dayang de gong'an*, 36.

60. Xiao Yin, "'Kuayang' caifang zhaji," 21.

61. Zhou Li, *Manhadun de Zhongguo nüren* [*A Chinese Woman in Manhattan*] (Beijing: Beijing chubanshe, 1992), 2. All citations from the book are from the sixth printing of this edition, which has a different pagination from an earlier one. The English translations are mine.

62. Zhou Li, 264.

63. Zhou Li, 1, 374, 334.

64. Homi K. Bhabha, "Introduction," in *Nation and Narration*, Homi K. Bhabha, ed. (London: Routledge, 1990), 4.

65. He Zhenbang, 88.

66. Zeng Zhennai, "*Manhadun de Zhongguo nüren* duhou" [Afterthoughts on *A Chinese Woman in Manhattan*], in Xiao Yin and Yi Ren, eds., *Kuayue dayang de gong'an*, 90–92.

67. Wu Liang, "Pipinde quexi" [An absence of criticism], in Xiao Yin and Yi Ren, eds., *Kuayue dayang de gong'an*, 99.

68. Yang Ping, "'Meiguo meng' de tuixiaoshang" [A saleswoman of the American dream], in Xiao Yin and Yi Ren, eds., *Kuayue dayang de gong'an*, 101–4.

69. Yang Ping, 103.

70. Xiao Li et al., "Zhongren fenshuo *Manhadun de Zhongguo nüren*" [Different opinions expressed on *A Chinese Woman in Manhattan*], in Xiao Yin and Yi Ren, eds., *Kuayue dayang de gong'an*, 105–6.

71. Xiao Yin, "'Kuayang' caifang zhaji," 18.

72. Li Shidong, "Qingting yidairen de shengyin" [Be aware of the voice of one generation], in Xiao Yin and Yi Ren, eds., *Kuayue dayang de gong'an*, 94–96.

73. Zhou Li, 490.

74. Zhou Li, 97–98.

75. Wang Jing, "*He shang* and the Paradoxes of Chinese Enlightenment," *Bulletin of Concerned Asian Scholars* 23:3 (1991): 23–32, 31.

76. Wang Jing, 25.

77. Zhou Li, 277.

78. Hu Ping claimed, as have other writers of reportage, that his stories were based on real people and real stories and that literary techniques were used when needed. For studies of Chinese reportage in English, see Perry Link, ed., James Feinerman, trans., with Perry Link, *People or Monsters? And Other Stories and Reportage from China after Mao* (Bloomington: Indiana Univ. Press, 1983); Yin-hwa

Chou, "Formal Features of Chinese Reportage and an Analysis of Liang Qichao's 'Memoirs of My Travels in the New World,'"*Modern Chinese Literature* 1:2 (Spring 1985):201–18; Xiaomei Chen, "Genre, Convention and Society: A Reception Study of Chinese Reportage," *Yearbook of Comparative and General Literature* 34 (1985):85–100; Rudolf Wagner, *Inside the Service Trade: Studies in Contemporary Chinese Prose* (Cambridge: Council on East Asian Studies, Harvard University, 1992); Zuyan Chen, "'River Elegy' as Reportage Literature: Generic Experimentation and Boundaries," *China Information* 7:4 (1993):20–32; Thomas Moran, "True Stories: Contemporary Chinese Reportage and Its Ideology and Aesthetic," Ph.D. diss., Cornell University, 1994; Charles A. Laughlin, "Narrating the Nation: The Aesthetics of Historical Experience in Chinese Reportage, 1919–1966," Ph.D. diss., Columbia University, 1996; and "Narrative Subjectivity and the Production of Social Space in Chinese Reportage," *Boundary* 2:25, 2 (Fall 1998):25–46.

79. Hu Ping, *Yimin Meiguo* [Immigrating to America] (Zhengzhou: Henan renmin chubanshe, 1997), 104, 106.

80. Hu Ping, *Yimin Meiguo*, 92.

81. Hu Ping, *Yimin Meiguo*, 94.

82. Hu Ping, *Yimin Meiguo*, 89.

83. Hu Ping, *Yimin Meiguo*, 107.

84. Mao Zedong, *Quotations from Chairman Mao Tsetung* (Beijing: Foreign Languages Press, 1972), 273. Hu Ping, *Yimin Meiguo*, 135.

85. Hu Ping, *Yimin Meiguo*, 136.

86. Hu Ping, *Yimin Meiguo*, 253.

87. Born in 1954, Yan Li went to the United States as a self-sponsored student in 1985 and founded the Yixing Poetry Club (Yixing Shishe) in 1987 while pursuing writing, painting, and photography. His "Xueye de xingwei" [The behavior of blood] was first published in the collection *The Best Funerals (Zuigao de zangli)*, published by Xianggang tianyuan shuwu in 1998. A reprint of the story can be found in *Zhongguo liuxuesheng wenxue daxi* [A compendium of Chinese overseas student literature], *Dangdai xiaoshuo Oumei juan* [Contemporary fiction volume, Europe and America], 506–35, 527.

88. Yan Li, "Wo ye he Baiyangdian zhan dian bianr" [I am also somewhat related to the Baiyangdian group of poets], in Liao Yiwu, ed., *Chenlun de shengdian* [The fall of the sacred hall] (Wulumuqi: Xinjiang qingshaonian chubanshe, 1999), 277–81, 277.

89. Huang Rui, "Xingxing jiuhua" [Old stories of the Star Exhibitions], in Liao Yiwu, ed., *Chenlun de shengdian*, 462–66, 466. Huang Rui listed Yan Li as one of the eighteen artists who had participated in both Star Exhibitions of 1979 and 1980 (466).

90. Ma Desheng, "The Age of Reflection" [Fanxing de shidai], in Liao Yiwu, ed., *Chenlun de shengdian*, 467–72, 468.

91. Xu Xiao, "Jintian yu wo" [*Today* and I], in Liao Yiwu, ed., *Chenlun de shengdian*, 379–410, 393.

92. In her informative study of the television series *Beijing Sojourners in New York*, based on Cao's fiction, Lydia H. Liu describes it as "a local product of the transnational co-authorship of the ideology of business entrepreneurship between

the post-socialist official discourse of China and that of the mainstream American media." See her "Beijing Sojourners in New York: Postsocialism and the Question of Ideology in Global Media Culture," *Positions* 7:3 (Winter 1999):763–97, 790.

93. In *Lüka* [Green card], published by Xinshijie chubanshe in Beijing in 1993, Cao Guilin depicts two girls from Beijing: Xiaoniu, who immigrated to America at the age of twelve with her parents, suffers from AIDS after working as a prostitute, and possibly commits suicide, though her body is never clearly identified. Chang Tiehua, while trying to help Xiaoniu, does everything possible to get a "green card," including becoming sexually involved with an "ugly" man who works in a Chinese restaurant. Although writing about life in America, Cao uses a typical Maoist discourse that depicts American society as if it were the "old society," China before 1949—a society full of exploitation and oppression for Chinese women. Chang Tiehua's story, indeed, might remind one of "The White-Haired Girl," the gist of the story being that the "old society" of post-1949 China had turned her from a woman to a ghost; the "new society" of the PRC eventually transforms her back into a human being. In Chang Tiehua's story, we see a parallel narrative of "her turning into a ghost in order to get a green card, and transform[ing] herself back into a human being again only after obtaining a green card." (See the blurb on the back cover of the Beijing edition.) Here we see an interesting case of Maoist discourse being used to depict post-Maoist society transplanted in America, a tendency shared by other stories of Chinese diaspora written by immigrants from the PRC.

94. Cao Guilin, *Niuyue shangkong de Zhongguo yeying* [A Chinese nightingale in the sky of New York] (Beijing: Xiandai chubanshe, 1994), 296.

95. Wang Hui listed these different kinds of nationalism as hitherto unstudied by Chinese intellectuals and believed that further differentiations and explorations of their various manifestations would ultimately free Chinese intellectuals from any uncritical expressions of Eurocentrism and Sinocentrism. See his "Yijiubajiu shehui yundong yu Zhongguo 'xin ziyouzhuyi' de lishi genyuan" [Social movements of 1989 and historical roots of Chinese neo-liberalism], *Zhongguo xiandai wenxue* [*Modern Chinese literature*] 19 (2000):451–501, 482–83.

96. Cao Guilin, *Niuyue shangkong de Zhongguo yeying*, 247.

97. Lydia H. Liu, 772. I agree with her conclusion to her study on *Beijing Sojourners in New York*, in which she states that "*postsocialism produces transnationalism just as much as transnationalism produces postsocialism*. These mutually embedded processes cannot but present a major challenge to the future study of ideology in transnational studies and cultural studies." Italics in the original.

98. For an informative study on the PRC counterculture in the past twenty years, see Geremie R. Barmé, *In the Red: On Contemporary Chinese Culture* (New York: Columbia Univ. Press, 1999).

Glossary

A Cheng (Ah Cheng)	阿城
A Chun	阿春
Ai Qing	艾青
aimei ju	爱美剧
An Yi	安怡
Baiyangdian	白洋淀
Bei Dao (Zhao Zhenkai)	北岛（赵振开）
Beijing Guangbo Xueyuan	北京广播学院
Beijing ren zai Niuyue	北京人在纽约
Beijing Renmin Yishu Juyuan	北京人民艺术剧院
bianyuan ren	边缘人
biaoxian ziwo	表现自我
Bing Xin	冰心
Bo Gu	博古
"Canchun"	残春
"Canku de xiwang"	残酷的希望
Cao Guilin (Glen Cao)	曹桂林
chang, nian, zuo, da	唱, 念, 做, 打
Chang Tiehua	常铁花
Chen Cun	陈村

Chen Dabei	陈大悲
Chen Dingsha	陈丁沙
Chen Duxiu	陈独秀
Chen Hanyuan	陈汉元
Chen Yi	陈毅
Chen Yong (Chen Rong)	陈颙
Chen Zhi'ang	陈志昂
Cheng Daixi	程代熙
Cheng Zhongyuan	程中原
"Chenlun"	沉沦
Chezhan	车站
chouxiang shi	抽象诗
chuangzuo zhuti	创作主体
Chuci-jiuge	楚辞 九歌
"Chushen lun"	出身论
Ci Jiwei	慈继伟
Ci'an yu bi'an	此岸与彼岸
Cihai	辞海
Cui Wenhua	崔文华
Da Zhongguo	大中国
Dai Jinhua	戴锦华
Danshui he	淡水河
Deng Xian	邓贤
di, te, pan	敌, 特, 叛
Ding Baolin	丁宝麟
Ding Yangzhong	丁杨忠
Ding Youlan	丁幽兰
Dong Yue	东月
dongya bingfu	东亚病夫
dongyang	东洋
duiwei	对位
duoshengbu jiegou	多声部结构

Faguo pinmin de zhen jingshen	法国贫民的真精神
"Falanxi ren yu jinshi wenming"	法兰西人与近世文明
Fan Xiheng	范希衡
Fang Lizhi	方励之
Fang Ping	方平
fansi wenxue	反思文学
feiren de wenxue	非人的文学
Feng Menglong	冯梦龙
fudiao	复调
gao, da, quan	高,大,全
Gao Wangling	高王凌
Gao Xingjian	高行健
Gong Suyi	宫苏艺
gongnongbing zhuyao yingxiong renwu	工农兵主要英雄人物
Gu Cheng	顾城
Gu Gong	顾工
Guangbo Dianying Dianshibu	广播电影电视部
Guo Moruo	郭沫若
"Guo shang"	国殇
Haizi wang	孩子王
Han Tongsheng	韩童生
Hangong qiu	汉宫秋
Hao Yin	郝寅
He Jingzhi	贺敬之
He Liwei	何立伟
"He ming"	鹤鸣
He Qifang	何其芳
He shang	河殇
He Zhenbang	何镇邦
Hei'an zhuan	黑暗传
Hong Huang	洪荒
Hong Shen	洪深

Hu Ping	胡平
Hu Sheng	胡绳
Hu Shi	胡适
Hu Yaobang	胡耀邦
huai fenzi	坏分子
huan yizhong huofar	换一种活法儿
Huang Rui	黄锐
Huang Ziping	黄子平
Huang Zuolin	黄佐临
Huanghe	黄河
"Huanghe dahechang"	黄河大合唱
huangmei xi	黄梅戏
huangpi shu	黄皮书
Huashuo Changjiang	话说长江
Huashuo Yunhe	话说运河
Huijia yihou	回家以后
huipi shu	灰皮书
Huo Xiangwen	霍湘文
Ji Junxiang	纪君祥
Ji Ren	吉人
Jiajing	嘉靖
Jialilue zhuan	伽里略传
Jiang Guangci	蒋光慈
Jiang He	江河
Jiang Qing	江青
Jiang Xun	蒋勋
Jiang Ying	姜英
Jiang Zengpei	江曾培
Jiang Zilong	蒋子龙
"Jiari, hupan, suixiang"	假日 湖畔 随想
Jiemo cangsang	芥末沧桑
jieshou zhuti	接受主体

Jiezhai gerou	借债割肉
Jin Ren	靳仁
jingchang	静场
"Jinianbei"	纪念碑
Jintian	今天
Juedui xinhao	绝对信号
Junkai	钧凯
Kamen	卡门
Kang Baiqing	康白清
Ke Ling	柯灵
Ke Yicen	柯一岑
Kong Genghong	孔耕蕻
Kuafu	夸父
Kuayue dayang de gong'an	跨越大洋的公案
kunqu	昆曲
Lao Mu	老木
Li Hangyu	李杭育
Li He	李贺
Li Jieren	李劼人
Li Menghan	李孟汉
Li Shidong	李师东
Li Xiaojiang	李小江
Li Xiong	李雄
Li Ying	李瑛
Li Zehou	李泽厚
Li Zibo	郦子柏
Liang Qichao	梁启超
"Liangge jiating"	两个家庭
Liangshi	粮食
Liao Yiwu	廖亦武
Li'erwang	李尔王
"Lihun"	离婚

Lin Biao (Lin Piao)	林彪
Lin Daiyu	林黛玉
Lin Kehuan	林克欢
Lin Zhaohua	林兆华
lishi de, shehui de, jituan de yishi	历史的, 社会的, 集团的意识
Liu Fenggang	刘凤冈
Liu Jun	刘军
Liu Ma	刘妈
Liu Mali	刘玛丽
Liu Shaoqi	刘少奇
Liu Suola	刘索拉
Liu Xiaobo	刘晓波
Liu Xinwu	刘心武
Liu Zaifu	刘再复
Lu Bingxin	陆冰心
Lu Jiachuan	卢嘉川
Lu Xinhua	卢新华
Lu Xun	鲁迅
Lu Zhiping	陆治平
Lüka	绿卡
Lütu	旅途
Ma Zhiyuan (Ma Chih-yüan)	马致远
Makebaisi	马克白斯
Manhadun de Zhongguo nüren	曼哈顿的中国女人
Mei Lanfang	梅兰芳
Mei Shaowu	梅绍武
"Meiyou xiewan de shi"	没有写完的诗
Meng Baige	孟白鸽
Meng Yue	孟悦
menglong	朦胧
Miao Deyu	苗得雨
Miao Yushi	苗雨时

minkan	民刊
Minzhong Xiju She	民众戏剧社
minzu shishi	民族史诗
Mo Zi	墨子
Mou Zhijing	牟志京
Nahan	呐喊
Nanren de yiban shi nüren	男人的一半是女人
neibu duwu	内部读物
Ni bie wu xuanze	你别无选择
Nie Ying	聂莹
Niu Daifeng	钮岱峰
Niuyue shangkong de Zhongguo yeying	纽約上空的中国夜莺
Nülüshi	女律师
nuo xi	傩戏
Nuola	娜拉
Ouyang Caiwei	欧阳采微
Ouyang Yuqian	欧阳予倩
Pan Gu	盘古
Pan Qun	潘群
Pei'er jinte	培尔 金特
Peng Ming	彭明
Pu Boying	蒲伯英
Qi wang	棋王
Qian Xuantong	钱玄同
Qiao Di	乔迪
Qingchun zhi ge	青春之歌
qishang congwen	弃商从文
"Qiu"	秋
Qu Yuan	屈原
Ren Bishi	任弼时
ren de wenxue	人的文学
"Renmin zhanzheng shengli wansui"	人民战争胜利万岁

Renyi Xiju Zhuanmen Xuexiao	人艺戏剧专门学校
Roujuan	肉卷
Sange panni de nüxing	三个叛逆的女性
shangdeng ren	上等人
Shanghai Xiju Xueyuan	上海戏剧学院
"Shanghen"	伤痕
shanghen wenxue	伤痕文学
"Shangshi"	伤逝
Shaonian Zhongguo Xuehui	少年中国学会
Shaoshan	韶山
Shi Songhan	施松寒
Shen Bingxue	沈冰血
Shen Yanbing	沈雁冰
Shi Tianhe	石天河
shidai shenmei yishi	时代审美意识
Shijie da chuanlian	世界大串联
Shijing	诗经
Shu Ting	舒婷
Shu wang	树王
sichou zhi lu	丝绸之路
Sima Xiangru	司马相如
Song Chunfang	宋春舫
Song Haiquan	宋海泉
Su Guanxin	苏官新
Su Shaozhi	苏绍智
Su Xiaokang	苏晓康
Subei ren	苏北人
Sun Qingwen	孙青纹
Sun Shaozhen	孙绍振
Tangfan gudao	唐蕃古道
Teng Ruoqu	藤若渠
"Tengye xiansheng"	藤野先生

Tian Han	田汉
Tian Jian	田间
"Tongqing"	同情
Wang Dan	王丹
Wang Feng	王枫
Wang Guangmei	王光美
Wang Hui	汪辉
Wang Huiqing	汪惠卿
Wang Luxiang	王鲁湘
Wang Qiming	王起明
Wang Ruofei	王若飞
Wang Xiaoni	王小妮
Wang Zhaojun	王昭君
Wang Zhen	王震
Wang Zhongxian	汪仲贤
wanquan de xiju	完全的戏剧
Wei Jingsheng	魏京生
Weinisi shangren	威尼斯商人
Weng Ningna	翁宁娜
wenhua yimin	文化移民
"Women weida de zuguo"	我们伟大的祖国
Wu Furong	吴福荣
Wu Liang	吴亮
Wu Xin	吴欣
Wu Zifang	吴自芳
Wu Zuguang	吴祖光
Wu Yuzhang	吴玉章
wuwei	无为
Wuyue wenxue	吴越文学
Xia Jun	夏骏
Xia Zhongyi	夏仲翼
xiadeng ren	下等人

Xian Xinghai	冼星海
Xiangxi wenxue	湘西文学
Xiao Chi	萧驰
Xiao Li	小黎
Xiao Qian	萧乾
Xiao Xiao	萧萧
Xiao Yin	萧音
Xiaoya	小雅
Xiaozhen fengqing	小镇风情
xibu wenxue	西部文学
Xidan	西单
Xie Mian	谢冕
Xie Wanying	谢婉莹
Xie Xuanjun	谢选骏
Xi'er	喜儿
xieyi xiju	写意戏剧
Xiju Xieshe	戏剧协社
Ximen	西门
xin wenxue	新文学
Xingshi hengyan	醒世恒言
Xingxing huazhan	星星画展
xinli kongjian	心理空间
Xinshichao shiji	新诗潮诗集
Xiong Foxi	熊佛西
Xiong Yuanyi	熊元义
Xiu Xinmin	修新民
xiyang	西洋
xiyu	西域
Xu Banmei	徐半梅
Xu Jingya	徐敬亚
Xu Xiao	徐晓
Xu Xiaozhong	徐晓钟

Xu Xing	徐星
"Xuexian"	雪线
"Xueye de xingwei"	血液的行为
xungen shi	寻根诗
xungen wenxue	寻根文学
"Yalujiang shang"	鸭绿江上
Yan Fu	严复
Yan Li	严力
Yan Tao	阎韬
Yan Xiwu	严西吾
Yan'an	延安
Yang Lian	杨炼
Yang Mo	杨沫
Yang Ping	杨平
Yang Tiancun	杨田村
yangji	洋妓
"Ye"	夜
Yeren	野人
Yi Ren	伊人
Yibangrou	一磅肉
Yimin Meiguo	移民美国
Yixing Shishe	一行诗社
Youlan nüshi	幽兰女士
Yu Dafu	郁达夫
Yu Luoke	遇罗克
Yu Qiuyu	余秋雨
Yuan Kejia	袁可嘉
Yuan Zhiming	远志明
yueju	越剧
Yungu	云姑
Yunqing	蕴青
yushi raodao zou	遇事绕道走

Zang Kejia	臧克家
"Zangli"	葬礼
Zeng Zhennan	曾镇南
Zhang Chengzhi	张承志
Zhang Gang	张刚
Zhang Jinglu	张静庐
Zhang Qihong	张奇虹
Zhang Ruogu	张若谷
Zhang Sheng	张升
Zhang Shengyou	张胜有
Zhang Wentian	张闻天
Zhang Xianliang	张贤亮
Zhang Xiaoyang	张晓阳
Zhang Xun	张寻
Zhang Yuanji	张元济
Zhang Yuguang	张聿光
Zhang Yulu	张玉鲁
Zhang Zhixin	张志新
Zhaojun	昭君
Zhao Xun	赵寻
Zhao Ziyang	赵紫阳
Zhaoshi gu'er da baochou	赵氏孤儿大报仇
Zhaoshi gu'er ji	赵氏孤儿记
Zhejiang Shaoxing Nüzi Shifan Xuexiao	浙江绍兴女子师范学校
zheli shi	哲理诗
zhen, shan, mei	真, 善, 美
Zhen'er	珍儿
Zheng He	郑和
Zheng Zhenduo	郑振铎
zhenxi	真戏
zhezi xi	折子戏
"Zhi xiangshu"	致橡树

Zhongguo Qingnian Yishu Juyuan 中国青年艺术剧院
Zhonghua minzu de renge 中华民族的人格
Zhonghua Xiju Xieshe 中华戏剧协社
Zhongshen dashi 终身大事
Zhongxue hongweibing bao 中学红卫兵报
Zhou Li 周励
Zhou Peitong 周培桐
Zhou Qiwan 周启万
Zhou Zuoren 周作人
Zhu De 朱德
Zhu Ziqing 朱自清
"Zhufu" 祝福
"Zhuiri" 追日
Zhuo Wenjun 卓文君
Zhuoshui xi 浊水溪
ziyou de renwen jingshen 自由的人文精神
ziwo 自我
Zong Hui 宗晖
"Zuguo a, zuguo" 祖国啊, 祖国
"Zuihou de anxi" 最后的安息

Selected Bibliography

Ah Cheng. *Three Kings: Three Stories from Today's China*. Trans. and intro. Bonnie S. McDougall. London: Collins-Harvill, 1990.

Ahmad, Eqbal. Review of *Culture and Imperialism*, by Edward Said. *Times Literary Supplement* 2 Apr. 1993:17.

Aldridge, A. Owen. *The Reemergence of World Literature: A Study of Asia and the West*. Newark: University of Delaware Press, 1986.

Amin, Samir. *Eurocentrism*. Trans. Russell Moore. New York: Monthly Review Press, 1989.

Anderson, Benedict. *Imagined Communities: Reflections on the Origin and Spread of Nationalism*. New York: Verso, 1983.

Appiah, Kwame Anthony. "Europe Upside Down: Fallacies of the New Afrocentrism." *Times Literary Supplement* 12 Feb. 1993:24.

Arkush, R. David and Leo O[u-fan] Lee, trans. and eds. *Land without Ghosts: Chinese Impressions of America from the Mid-Nineteenth Century to the Present*. Berkeley: University of California Press, 1989.

Artaud, Antonin. *The Theater and Its Double*. Trans. Mary Caroline Richards. New York: Grove Press, 1958.

Bakhtin, Mikhail Mikhaïlovich. *The Dialogic Imagination: Four Essays by M. M. Bakhtin*. Ed. Michael Holquist. Trans. Caryl Emerson and Michael Holquist. Austin: University of Texas Press, 1981.

Balakian, Anna. "Literary Theory and Comparative Literature." In *Toward a Theory of Comparative Literature*. Vol. 3 of Proceedings of the XIth International Comparative Literature Congress. 20–24 Aug. 1985. Ed. and intro. Mario J. Valdes. New York: Lang, 1990, 17–24.

Ball, J. Dyer. *Things Chinese; Or Notes Connected with China*. 5th and rev. ed. Shanghai: Kelly and Walsh, 1925.

Banu, Georges. "Mei Lanfang: A Case against and a Model for the Occidental Stage." Trans. Ella L. Wiswell and June V. Gibson. *Asian Theater Journal* 3:2 (1986):153–78.

Barlow, Tani E. "Colonialism's Career in Postwar China Studies." *Positions* 1:1 (1993):224–67.

———. "Theorizing Woman: *Funu, Guojia, Jiating* [Chinese Women, Chinese State, Chinese Family]." *Genders* 10 (1991):132–60.

———. "*Zhishifenzi* [Chinese intellectuals] and Power." *Dialectical Anthropology* 16 (1991):209–32.

Barmé, Geremie R. *In the Red: On Contemporary Chinese Culture*. New York: Columbia University Press, 1999.

———. "A Touch of the Absurd—Introducing Gao Xingjian, and His Play *The Bus Stop*." *Renditions* 19, 20 (1983):373–77.

———. "TV Requiem for the Myths of the Middle Kingdom." *Far Eastern Economic Review* 1 Sept. 1988:40–43.

———. and Bennett Lee, trans. and intro. *The Wounded: New Stories of the Cultural Revolution, 77–78*. Hong Kong: Joint Publishing, 1979.

Baum, Julian. "Peking's *Wildman* Jolts Theater Goers." *The Christian Science Monitor* 24 June 1985:9–10.

Bei Dao. "Cruel Hope." In his *The August Sleepwalker*. Trans. and intro. Bonnie S. McDougall. New York: New Directions, 1990, 24–28.

———. *The August Sleepwalker*. Trans. and intro. Bonnie S. McDougall. New York: New Directions, 1990.

———. "The Snowline." In his *The August Sleepwalker*. Trans. and intro. Bonnie S. McDougall. New York: New Directions, 1990, 78.

Bernal, Martin. *Black Athena: The Afroasiatic Roots of Classical Civilization*. Vol. 1 of *The Fabrication of Ancient Greece, 1785–1985*. New Brunswick, N.J.: Rutgers University Press, 1987.

Bernstein, Thomas. *Up to the Mountain and Down to the Villages: The Transfer of Youth from Urban to Rural China*. New Haven, Conn.: Yale University Press, 1977.

Bhabha, Homi K. "The Commitment of Theory." *New Formations* 5(1988):5–23.

———. "Introduction." In Homi K. Bhabha, ed., *Nation and Narration*. London: Routledge, 1990, 1–7.

Bloom, Harold. *The Anxiety of Influence*. New York: Oxford University Press, 1973.

Breckenridge, Carol A. and Peter van der Veer, eds. *Orientalism and the Postcolonial Predicament: Perspectives on South Asia*. Philadelphia: University of Pennsylvania Press, 1993.

Burbank, Rex J. *Thornton Wilder*. 2nd ed. Boston: Twayne, 1978.

Bürger, Peter. *Theory of the Avant-Garde*. Trans. Michael Shaw. Minneapolis: University of Minnesota Press, 1984.

Byron, George Gordon. "When a Man Hath No Freedom to Fight for at Home." In M. H. Abrams et al., eds., *The Norton Anthology of English Literature*. New York: Norton, 1975, 1709–10.

Calinescu, Matei. *Five Faces of Modernity: Modernism, Avant-Garde, Decadence, Kitsch, Postmodernism*. Durham, N.C.: Duke University Press, 1987.

Cao Guilin (Glen Cao). *Beijing ren zai Niuyue* [Beijing sojourners in New York]. Beijing: Zhongguo wenlian chubanshe, 1991.

———. *Niuyue shangkong de Zhongguo yeying* [A Chinese nightingale in the sky of New York]. Beijing: Xiandai chubanshe, 1994.

———. *Lüka: Beijing Girls in New York* [Green card: Beijing guniang zai Niuyue]. Beijing: Xinshijie chubanshe, 1993.

Case, Sue-Ellen, ed. *Performing Feminisms: Feminist Critical Theory and Theatre*. Baltimore: Johns Hopkins University Press, 1990.

Castronovo, David. *Thornton Wilder*. New York: F. Ungar, 1986.

Chan, Ching-kiu Stephen, "The Language of Despair: Ideological Representations of the 'New Women' by May Fourth Writers." *Modern Chinese Literature* 4 (1988):19–38.

Chang, Hao. *Chinese Intellectuals in Crisis: Search for Order and Meaning (1890–1911)*. Berkeley: University of California Press, 1987.

Chen Dabei. *Youlan nüshi* [Miss Youlan]. In Hong Shen, ed., *Zhongguo xin wenxue daxi—xijuji*. Shanghai: Liangyou tushu yinshua gongsi, 1935, 27–67.

Chen Dingsha. "Zhongguo zaoqi wutai shang de Shashibiya xiju" [Shakespearean productions on the early modern Chinese stage]. *Xiju bao* [Drama journal] 12 (1983):56.

Chen, Xiaomei. *Acting the Right Part: Political Theater and Popular Drama in Contemporary China*. Honolulu: University of Hawaii Press, 2002.

———. "Genre, Convention and Society: A Reception Study of Chinese Reportage." *Yearbook of Comparative and General Literature* 34 (1985):85–100.

———. "Rediscovering Ezra Pound: A Post-Postcolonial 'Misreading' of a Western Legacy." *Paideuma* 23:2,3 (1994):81–105.

———. "The Poetics of 'Misunderstanding': An Ahistorical Model of Cross-Cultural Literary History." *Canadian Review of Comparative Literature* 19:4 (1992):485–506.

Chen Yong. "The Beijing Production of *Life of Galileo*." In Antony Tatlow and Tak-Wai Wong, eds., *Brecht and East Asian Theatre: The Proceedings of a Conference on Brecht in East Asian Theatre*. Hong Kong: Hong Kong University Press, 1982, 88–95.

Chen Zhi'ang. "*He shang* zhi shang" [The elegy of *He shang*]. *Wenyi lilun yu piping* [Theory and criticism of literature and art] 1 (1989):54–60.

Chen, Zuyan. "'River Elegy' as Reportage Literature: Generic Experimentation and Boundaries." *China Information* 7:4 (1993):20–32.

Cheng Daixi. "Ping 'Xin de meixue yuanze zai jueqi'" [A review on 'A new aesthetic principle is emerging']. *Shikan* [Poetry monthly] Apr. 1981:3–8, 17.

Cheng Zhongyuan. *Zhang Wentian zhuan* [Biography of Zhang Wentian]. Beijing: Dangdai Zhonguo chubanshe, 1993.

Cheung, King-kok. "'Don't Tell': Imposed Silences in *The Color Purple* and *The Woman Warrior*." *PMLA* 103 (1988):162–74.

Choi, Chungmoo. "The Discourse of Decolonization and Popular Memory: South Korea." *Positions* 1:1 (1993):77–102.

Chou, Yin-hwa. "Formal Features of Chinese Reportage and an Analysis of Liang Qichao's 'Memoirs of My Travels in the New World.'" *Modern Chinese Literature* 1:2 (Spring 1985):201–18.

Chow, Rey. "Against the Lures of Diaspora: Minority Discourse, Chinese Women, and Intellectual Hegemony." In Tonglin Lu, ed., *Gender and Sexuality in Twentieth-Century Chinese Literature*. Albany: State University of New York Press, 1993, 23–45.

———. "Pedagogy, Trust, Chinese Intellectuals in the 1990s—Fragments of a Post-Catastrophic Discourse." *Dialectical Anthropology* 16 (1991):191–207.

————. *Primitive Passions*. New York: Columbia University Press, 1995.

————. *Woman and Chinese Modernity: The Politics of Reading between West and East*. Minnesota: University of Minnesota Press, 1991.

————. *Writing Diaspora: Tactics of Intervention in Contemporary Cultural Studies*. Bloomington: Indiana University Press, 1993.

Chow, Tse-tsung. *The May Fourth Movement: Intellectual Revolution in Modern China*. Cambridge: Harvard University Press, 1960.

Clark, Robert L. A. "South of North: Carmen and French Nationalisms." In Claire Sponsler and Xiaomei Chen, eds., *East of West: Cross-Cultural Performance and the Staging of Difference*. New York: Palgrave, 2000, 187–216.

Clüver, Claus. *Thornton Wilder und André Obey: Untersuchungen zum modernen epischen Theater*. Bonn: Bouvier, 1978.

Cohen, Paul A. *Discovering History in China: American Historical Writing on the Recent Chinese Past*. New York: Columbia University Press, 1984.

———— and Merle Goldman, eds. *Ideas across Cultures: Essays on Chinese Thought in Honor of Benjamin I. Schwartz*. Cambridge: Council on East Asian Studies, Harvard University, 1990, 1–13.

Comaroff, John L. "Images of Empire, Contests of Conscience: Models of Colonial Domination in South Africa." *American Ethnologist* 16:4 (1989):661–85.

"Controversial TV Series 'River Elegy.'" *China Reconstructs* 38 (Jan. 1989):47–49.

Cui Wenhua, ed. *He shang lun* [About *He shang*]. Beijing: Wenhua yishu chubanshe, 1988.

————, ed. *Haiwai He shang da taolun* [Great overseas debates on *He shang*]. Ha'erbin: Heilongjiang jiaoyu chubanshe, 1988.

————. "*He shang* dui Zhongguo dianshi de qishi hezai?" [What does *He shang* tell us about Chinese television?]. In Cui Wenhai, ed., *He shang lun*. Beijing: Wenhua yishu chubanshe, 1988, 123–42.

Dalby, Michael, "Nocturnal Labors in the Light of Day." *The Journal of Asian Studies* 39:3 (1980):485–93.

Dasgupta, Gautam. "*The Mahabharata*: Peter Brook's 'Orientalism.'" *Performing Arts Journal* 30:3 (1987):9–16.

Davies, David. Letter. *Times Literary Supplement* 19 Mar. 1993:15.

Deng Xian. *Zhongguo zhiqing meng* [The dream of Chinese educated youth]. Beijing: Renmin wenxue chubanshe, 1973.

Deng Xiaoping. "Zai jiejian shoudu jieyan budui jun yishang ganbu shi de jianghua" [Speech at receiving army commanders of Beijing troops carrying out martial law]. *Renmin ribao* [People's daily] 28 July 1989:1.

Denton, Kirk A. "The Distant Shore: Nationalism in Yu Dafu's 'Sinking.'" *Chinese Literature: Essays, Articles, Reviews* 14 (1992):107–23.

Dikötter, Frank. *The Discourse of Race in Modern China*. Stanford, Calif.: Stanford University Press, 1992.

Ding Yangzhong. "Bulaixite yu Zhongguo xiju xianzhuang" [Brechtian theater and the current development on the Chinese stage]. *Xiju* [Drama] 1 (1987):4–10.

————. "Brecht's Theatre and Chinese Drama." In Antony Tatlow and Tak-Wai Wong, eds., *Brecht and East Asian Theatre*. Hong Kong: Hong Kong University Press, 1982, 28–45.

Dirlik, Arif. "Marxism and Chinese History: The Globalization of Marxist Historical Discourse and the Problem of Hegemony in Marxism." *Journal of Third World Studies* 4:1 (1987):151–64.

———. *The Origins of Chinese Communism.* New York: Oxford University Press, 1989.

Dolan, Jill. *The Feminist Spectator as Critic.* Ann Arbor: UMI Research Press, 1988.

Dong Yue and Liu Jun, eds. "*He shang* weixin zhuyi lishiguan pouxi—shoudu bufen shixue gongzuozhe pipan *He shang* jiyao" [On a metaphysical view of history in *He shang*: Minutes on a critique of *He shang* by historians in Beijing]. *Renmin ribao* 23 Oct. 1989:6.

Duke, Michael S. "Introduction." In Michael S. Duke, ed., *Contemporary Chinese Literature: An Anthology of Post-Mao Fiction and Poetry.* Armonk, N.Y.: M. E. Sharpe, 1985, 3–6.

Eagleton, Mary, ed. *Feminist Literary Theory: A Reader.* Oxford: Basil Blackwell, 1986.

Eide, Elisabeth. *China's Ibsen: From Ibsen to Ibsenism.* London: Curzon Press, 1987.

———. "Performances of Ibsen in China after 1949." In Constantine Tung and Colin MacKerras, eds., *Drama in the People's Republic of China.* Albany: State University of New York Press, 1987, 306–25.

Eliot, T. S. "Tradition and Individual Talent." In his *Selected Essays 1917–1932.* New York: Harcourt, Brace and Company, 1932, 3–12.

Eoyang, Eugene C., ed. *Selected Poems of Ai Qing.* Trans. Eugene C. Eoyang, Peng Wenlan, and Marilyn Chin. Bloomington: Indiana University Press, 1982.

Fan Xiheng. "Chong *Zhaoshi Gu'er* dao *Zhongguo Gu'er*—shang" [From *The Orphan of Zhao* to *Orphelin de la Chine* (Part I)]. *Zhongguo bijiao wenxue* [Chinese comparative literature] 4 (1987):159–95.

Fang Ping. "Huanying ni, *Li'erwang*" [Welcome you, *King Lear.*] *Shanghai xiju* [Shanghai drama] 5 (1982):19–20.

Felman, Shoshana. "Women and Madness: The Critical Phallacy." *Diacritics* 5 (1975):2–10.

Field, Stephen. "*He shang* and the Plateau of Ultrastability." *Bulletin of Concerned Asian Scholars* 23:3 (1991):4–13.

Fokkema, Douwe. "Orientalism, Occidentalism and the Notion of Discourse: Arguments for a New Cosmopolitanism." *Comparative Criticism* 18 (1996):227–41.

Foucault, Michel. *The Archaeology of Knowledge.* Trans. A. M. Sheridan Smith. New York: Pantheon Books, 1972.

Friedan, Betty. *The Feminine Mystique.* 20th Anniversary ed. New York: Norton, 1984.

Fujii, James A. "Writing Out Asia: Modernity, Canon, and Natsume Soseki's *Kokoro.*" *Positions* 1:1 (1993):194–223.

Fuss, Diana. *Essentially Speaking: Feminism, Nature, and Difference.* New York: Routledge, 1989.

Gamman, Lorraine and Margaret Marshment, eds. *Female Gaze: Women as Viewers of Popular Culture.* London: The Women's Press, 1988.

Gao Wangling and Wu Xin. "*He shang* fanying le yizhong shiheng xintai" [*He shang* reflects an unbalanced mentality]. In Cui, *He shang lun.* Beijing: Wenhua yishu chubanshe, 1988, 180–86.

Gao Xingjian. *Gao Xingjian xijuji* [The collected plays of Gao Xingjian]. Beijing: Qunzhong chubanshe, 1985.

------. "Guanyu yanshu de jianyi yu shuoming" [Suggestion and explanation for the production of *Wildman*]. *Shiyue* [October] 2 (1985):169.

------. "Lun xijuguan" [On dramatic theories]. *Xiju jie* [The dramatic circle] 1 (1983):27–34.

------. *Wild Man.* Trans., intro. and annot. Bruno Roubicek. *Asian Theater Journal* 7:2 (1990):195–249.

------. *Yeren* [Wildman]. *Shiyue* 2 (1985):142–68.

------. "*Yeren* yu wo" [*Wildman* and I]. *Xiju dianying bao* [Drama and film newspaper] 12 May 1985:2.

Gefin, Laszlo. *Ideogram: History of a Poetic Method.* Austin: University of Texas Press, 1982.

Gellner, Ernest. Reply to letter of Edward Said. *Times Literary Supplement* 9 Apr. 1993:15.

------. "The Mightier Pen? Edward Said and the Double Standards of Inside-out Colonialism." Review of *Culture and Imperialism,* by Edward Said. *Times Literary Supplement* 19 Feb. 1993:3–4.

Goldblatt, Howard, ed. *Worlds Apart: Recent Chinese Writing and Its Audiences.* Armonk, N.Y.: M. E. Sharpe, 1990.

Golden, Sean and John Minford. "Yang Lian and the Chinese Tradition." In Howard Goldblatt, ed., *Worlds Apart: Recent Chinese Writing and Its Audience.* Armonk, N.Y.: M. E. Sharpe, 1990, 119–37.

Goldman, Merle with Timothy Cheek and Carol Lee Hamrin, eds. *China's Intellectuals and the State: In Search of a New Relationship.* Council on East Asian Studies, Harvard University, 1987.

Goldstone, Richard H. *Thornton Wilder: An Intimate Portrait.* New York: Saturday Review Press, 1975.

Gong Suyi. "Shoudu bufen zhuanjia xuezhe zuotan: cong *He shang* xianxiang kan dianshi wenhua jianshe" [Experts and scholars in Beijing discussing *He shang*: From the *He shang* phenomenon to a construction of television culture]. *Guangming ribao* [Guangming daily] 16 Aug. 1988:1.

Grieder, Jerome B. *Intellectuals and the State in Modern China: A Narrative History.* New York: Free Press, 1981.

Gu Cheng. "Xinshi hua" [On new poetry]. *Wenyi bao* [Literary gazette] 24 Apr. 1988:2.

Gu Gong. "The Two Generations." In Helen F. Siu and Zelda Stern, eds., *Mao's Harvest: Voices from China's New Generation.* New York: Oxford University Press, 1983, 9–15.

Gunn, Edward. *Twentieth-Century Chinese Drama: An Anthology.* Bloomington: Indiana University Press, 1983, vi–xxiii.

------. "The Rhetoric of *He shang*: From Cultural Criticism to Social Act." *Bulletin of Concerned Asian Scholars* 23:3 (1991):14–22.

Guo Moruo. *Sange panni de nüxing* [A trilogy of three revolutionary women]. Shanghai: Guanghua shuju, 1926.

------. "Xiezai *Sange panni de nüxing* houmian" [Epilogue on *A Trilogy of Three Revolutionary Women*]. In Zhongguo xiju chubanshe, ed., *Guo Moruo juzuo quanji*

[The complete works of drama by Guo Moruo]. Vol. 1. Beijing: Zhongguo xiju chubanshe, 1982, 189–203.

"Guo shang." *Cihai* [Chinese encyclopedia]. Shanghai: Shanghai cishu chubanshe, 1979.

Guy, Basil. *The French Image of China before and after Voltaire*. Vol. 21 of *Studies on Voltaire and the Eighteenth Century*. Geneva: Institut et musée Voltaire, 1963.

Haberman, Donald. *The Plays of Thornton Wilder: A Critical Study*. Middletown, Conn.: Wesleyan University Press, 1967.

Hamrin, Carol Lee and Timothy Cheek, eds. *China's Establishment Intellectuals*. Armonk, N.Y.: M. E. Sharpe, 1986.

Han Tongsheng. "*Xiaozhen fengqing* pailian shiling" [Sidelights on the rehearsal of *Our Town*]. *Xiju bao* 8 (1987):363.

Hao Yin. "Yiqu dui xinsheng jinquzhe de zange: lun *Weinisi shangren* de zhenti" [A song of an enterprising spirit: On the true meaning of *The Merchant of Venice*]. *Nanyang Shizhuan xuebao, shekeban* [Journal of Nanyang Normal College, social science ed.] 1 (1986):20–27.

He Jingzhi. "Our Great Motherland." Trans. Hsin-sheng C. Kao. In Kai-yu Hsu, ed., *Literature of the People's Republic of China*. Bloomington: Indiana University Press, 1980, 672.

He Zhenbang. "Yiqu rensheng fendou zhi ge—du Zhou Li de *Manhadun de Zhongguo nüren*" [A song of dedication: Afterthoughts on Zhou Li's *A Chinese Woman in Manhattan*]. In Xiao Yi and Yi Ren, eds., *Kuayue dayang de gong'an—Manhadun de Zhongguo nüren zhengyi shilu*. Beijing: Guangming ribao chubanshe, 1993, 94–96.

Hershatter, Gail. "The Subaltern Talks Back: Reflections on Subaltern Theory and Chinese History." *Positions* 1:1 (1993):103–30.

"Historians in the Capital Criticize *Heshang*: A Summary." In Su Xiaokang and Wang Luxiang, *Deathsong of the River: A Reader's Guide to the Chinese TV Series Heshang*. Ithaca: Cornell University East Asian Program, 1991, 311–27.

Hockx, Michel. *A Snowy Morning: Eight Chinese Poets on the Road to Modernity*. Leiden: Centre of Non-Western Studies, Leiden University, 1994.

Hong Huang. "The New Poetry—A Turning Point? (A Misty Manifesto)." Trans. Zhu Zhiyu with John Mitford. *Renditions* 19, 20 (1983):191–94.

Hong Shen. "Daoyan" [Introduction]. In Hong Shen, ed., *Zhongguo xin wenxue daxi—xiju ji*. Shanghai: Liangyou tushu yinshua gongsi, 1935, Vol. 9, 1–99.

———, ed. *Zhongguo xin wenxue daxi—xiju ji* [Compendium of modern Chinese literature—the dramatic genre]. Shanghai: Liangyou tushu yinshua gongsi, 1935. Vol. 9.

Honig, Emily and Gail Hershatter. *Personal Voices: Chinese Women in the 1980's*. Stanford, Calif.: Stanford University Press, 1988.

Hsia, Adrian. "Huang Zuoling[*sic*]'s Ideal of Drama and Bertolt Brecht." In Constantine Tung and Colin MacKerras, eds., *Drama in the People's Republic of China*. Albany: State University of New York Press, 1987, 151–62.

———. "The Reception of Bertolt Brecht in China and Its Impact on Chinese Drama." In Antony Tatlow and Tak-Wai Wong, eds., *Brecht and East Asian Theatre*. Hong Kong: Hong Kong University Press, 1982, 46–64.

Hsia, C. T. *A History of Modern Chinese Fiction*. 3rd ed., with an introduction by David Der-wei Wang. Bloomington: Indiana University Press, 1999.

Hsu, Immanuel C. Y. "Late Ch'ing Foreign Relations, 1866–1905." In Denis Twitchett and John K. Fairbank, eds., *The Cambridge History of China*, Vol. 11: *Late Ch'ing, 1800–1911*, Part 2. Cambridge: Cambridge University Press, 1980, 70–141.

Hsu, Kai-yu, ed. *Literature of the People's Republic of China*. Bloomington: Indiana University Press, 1980.

Hsü, Tao-Ching. *The Chinese Conception of the Theatre*. Seattle: University of Washington Press, 1985.

Hu Ping. *Yimin Meiguo* [Immigrating to America]. Zhengzhou: Henan renmin chubanshe, 1997.

—— and Zhang Shengyou. *Shijie da chuanlian* [Exchanging revolutionary experience in the world]. In Ke Ling et al., eds., *Ci'an yu bi'an* [This shore and that shore]. Shanghai: Wenhui chubanshe, 1999, 88–145.

Hu, Sheng. *Imperialism and Chinese Politics*. Trans. Foreign Languages Press. Beijing: Foreign Languages Press, 1955.

Hu Shi. "Jianshe de wenxue geming lun" [On the constructive theory of literary revolution]. In *Hu Shi wencun* [The selected works of Hu Shi]. Vol. 1. Shanghai: Yadong tushuguan, 1921, 71–96.

Hu, Ying. *Tales of Translation: Composing the New Women in China, 1899–1918*. Stanford, Calif.: Stanford University Press, 2000.

Huang Rui, "Xingxing jiuhua" [Old stories of the Star Exhibitions]. In Liao Yiwu, ed., *Chenlun de shengdian* [The fall of the sacred hall]. Wulumuqi: Xinjiang qingshaonian chubanshe, 1999, 462–66.

Huang Ziping. "Daolu: shanxing di zhankai" [Road: Spreading in a fan-shape]. *Shi tansuo* [Poetic experiment] 4 (1982):46–59.

Huang, Zuolin. "Mei Lanfang, Stanislavsky, Brecht—A Study in Contrasts." In Wu, Huang, and Mei, *Peking Opera and Mei Lanfang*. Beijing: New World Press, 1981, 14–29.

——. "A Supplement to Brecht's 'Alienation Effects in Chinese Acting.'" In Antony Tatlow and Tak-Wai Wong, eds., *Brecht and East Asian Theatre*. Hong Kong: Hong Kong University Press, 1982, 69–110.

"Huanghe dahechang" [The Yellow River chorus]. *Cihai* [Chinese encyclopedia]. Shanghai: Shanghai cishu chubanshe, 1979.

Huo Xiangwen. "Guanyu *He shang* timing dawen" [Reply to a reader's letter on the title of *He shang*]. *Renmin ribao* 26 Sept. 1988:8.

Hutchison, Alan. *China's African Revolution*. London: Hutchinson, 1975.

Hwang, David Henry. *M. Butterfly*. New York: Penguin Books, 1989.

Ibsen, Henrik. *Peer Gynt: A Dramatic Poem*. Trans. and intro. Peter Watts. New York: Penguin, 1966.

Inglis, Fred. "A Peregrine Spirit with an Eye for Eagles." Review of *Culture and Imperialism*, by Edward Said. *The Times Higher Education Supplement* 5 Mar. 1993:25, 27.

Jackson, Rosemary. *Fantasy: The Literature of Subversion*. London: Methuen, 1981.

Jaggar, Alison. *Feminist Politics and Human Nature*. Totowa, N.J.: Rowman and Allanheld, 1983.

Jauss, Hans Robert. *Toward an Aesthetic of Reception*. Trans. Timothy Bahti. Intro. Paul de Man. Minneapolis: University of Minnesota Press, 1982.

Ji Ren. "Wanli Changcheng shi fengbi de xiangzheng ma?" [Is the Great Wall a symbol of a closed-door policy?]. *Renmin ribao* 15 Aug. 1989:6.

Jiang Guangci. *Yalujiang shang* [On the Yalu River]. In Jiang Zengpei et al., eds., *Zhongguo liuxuesheng wenxue daxi* [A compendium of Chinese overseas student literature], *Jinxiandai xiaoshuo juan* [Modern fiction volume]. Shanghai: Shanghai wenyi chubanshe, 2000, 576–96.

Jiang He. "Jinianbei" [Monument]. In Lao Mu, ed., *Xin shichao shiji*. Vol. 1, Beijing: Beijing Daxue Wusu Wenxueshe, 1985, 112–14.

———. "Meiyou xiewan de shi" [Unfinished poem]. In Lao Mu, ed., *Xin shichao shiji*. Vol. 1, 121–25.

———. "Taiyang he ta de fanguang" [The sun and its reflection]. In Lao Mu, ed. *Xin shichao shiji*. Vol. 1, 154–72.

———. "Unfinished Poem." Trans. Alisa Joyce, Ginger Li, and Yip Wai-lim. *Renditions* 19, 20 (1983):221–26.

———. "Zangli" [Funeral]. In Lao Mu, ed., *Xin shichao shiji*. Vol. 1. Beijing: Beijing Daxue Wusu Wenxueshe, 1985, 118–21.

———. "Zuguo a, zuguo" [Oh, motherland]. In Lao Mu, ed., *Xin shichao shiji*. Vol. 1, 106–11.

Jiang Xun. "He de lishi: zuihao de lishi jiaocai *He sheng*" [A history of the river: The best history book *He shang*]. In Su Xiaokang and Wang Luxiang, *He shang*. Ed. Weng Ningna. Taiwan: Jinfeng chubanshe and Fengyun shidai chubanshe, 1988, 226–28.

"Jielu *He shang* de fandong shizhi suqing *He shang* de yingxiang liudu" [Exposing the counter-revolutionary nature of *He shang* in order to eliminate its pernicious influence]. *Zhongguo jiaoyu bao* [China education newspaper] 5 Aug. 1989:2.

Jin Ren. "Zhao Ziyang tongzhi de 'jierushuo' he *He shang* de 'xinjiyuan'" [Comrade Zhao Ziyang's theory of "interference" and *He shang*'s "new epoch"]. *Renmin ribao* 15 Aug. 1989:4.

Johnson, Barbara. *The Critical Difference*. Baltimore: Johns Hopkins University Press, 1980.

Judd, Ellen R. "Prescriptive Dramatic Theory of the Cultural Revolution." In Constantine Tung and Colin MacKerras, eds., *Drama in the People's Republic of China*. Albany: State University of New York Press, 1987, 95–118.

Kaplan, Randy. "Images of Subjugation and Defiance: Female Characters in the Early Dramas of Tian Han." *Modern Chinese Literature* 4 (1988):87–97.

Kapp, Robert A. "Edward Said's Orientalism: Introduction." *The Journal of Asian Studies* 39:3 (1980):481–84.

Kessler, Carol Farley. *Daring to Dream: Utopian Fiction by United States Women, 1836–1919*. Boston: Pandora Press, 1984.

Kim, Elaine H. *Asian American Literature: An Introduction to the Writings and Their Social Context*. Philadelphia, Pa.: Temple University Press, 1982.

Kinkley, Jeffrey C., ed. *After Mao: Chinese Literature and Society 1978–1981*. Cambridge: Harvard University Press, 1985.

Kong Genghong. "Shashibiya: pinglun, yanchu jiqi 'Zhongguohua'" [Shakespeare: review, production, and Sinification]. *Waiguo wenxue yanjiu* [Foreign literature studies] 4 (1986):92–95.

Kopf, David. "Hermeneutics versus History." *The Journal of Asian Studies* 39:3 (1980):495–506.

Kott, Jan. *Shakespeare, Our Contemporary.* Trans. Boleslaw Taborski. Garden City, N.Y.: Doubleday, 1966.

Lai, Pui-yee. "Intellectuals Alarmed by Film Series Clampdown." *Morning Post* 17 Oct. 1988:9.

Lao Mu, ed. *Xin shichao shiji* [Selected works of the new poetic movement]. Weiminghu Series. 2 vols. Beijing: Beijing Daxue Wusi Wenxueshe, 1985.

Laughlin, Charles A. "Narrative Subjectivity and the Production of Social Space in Chinese Reportage." *Boundary* 2:25, 2 (Fall 1998):25–46.

———. "Narrating the Nation: The Aesthetics of Historical Experience in Chinese Reportage, 1919–1966." Ph.D. diss., Columbia University, 1996.

Lee, Leo Ou-fan. "Beyond Realism: Thoughts on Modernist Experiments in Contemporary Chinese Writing." In Howard Goldblatt, ed., *Worlds Apart: Recent Chinese Writing and Its Audiences*. Armonk, N.Y.: M. E. Sharpe, 1990, 64–77.

———. "In Search of Modernity: Some Reflections on a New Mode of Consciousness in Twentieth-Century Chinese History and Literature." In Paul A. Cohen and Merle Goldman, eds., *Ideas across Cultures*. Cambridge: Council on East Asian Studies, Harvard University, 1990, 109–35.

———. "The Politics of Technique: Perspectives of Literary Dissidence in Contemporary Chinese Fiction." In Jeffrey C. Kinkley, ed., *After Mao: Chinese Literature and Society 1978–1981*. Cambridge: Council on East Asian Studies, Harvard University, 1985, 159–90.

———. *The Romantic Generation of Modern Chinese Writers*. Cambridge: Harvard University Press, 1973.

Lee, T. D. "Du He shang yougan" [Afterthoughts on *He shang*]. *Renmin ribao* 4 Nov. 1988:3.

Leung, Laifong. *Morning Sun: Interviews with Chinese Writers of the Lost Generation*. Armonk, N.Y.: M. E. Sharpe, 1994.

Levenson, Joseph R. *Liang Ch'i-ch'ao and the Mind of Modern China*. Cambridge: Harvard University Press, 1953.

———. "The Past and Future of Nationalism in China." In his *Modern China: An Interpretive Anthology*. London: Macmillan, 1971, 3–16.

Levine, Marilyn A. *The Found Generation: Chinese Communists in Europe during the Twenties*. Seattle: University of Washington Press, 1993.

Leys, Simon. *The Burning Forest*. New York: Holt, Rinehart and Winston, 1986.

Li Jieren. "Tongqing" [Sympathy]. In Jiang Zengpei et al., eds., *Zhongguo liuxuesheng wenxue daxi* [A compendium of Chinese overseas student literature]. *Jin xiandai xiaoshuo juan* [Modern fiction volume]. Shanghai: Shanghai wenyi chubanshe, 2000, 481–556.

Li, Ruru. "Chinese Traditional Theater and Shakespeare." *Asian Theater Journal* 5:1 (1988):38–48.

Li Shidong. "Qingting yidairen de shengyin" [Be aware of the voice of one generation]. In Xiao Yi and Yi Ren, eds., *Kuayue dayang de gong'an—Manhadun de Zhongguo nüren zhengyi shilu*. Beijing: Guangming ribao chubanshe, 1993, 94–96.

Li, Xiaojiang. "Open Letter to Su Shaozhi." Trans. Feng-ying Ming and Eric Karchmer. *Positions* 1:1 (1993):268–79.

Li, Zehou and Vera Schwarcz. "Six Generations of Modern Chinese Intellectuals." *Chinese Studies in History* 8:2 (1983–84):42–56.

Liao Yiwu, ed. *Chenlun de shengdian* [The fall of the sacred hall]. Wulumuqi: Xinjiang qingshaonian chubanshe, 1999.

Lin Kehuan. "Bianzheng de xiju xingxiang: lun Jialilue xingxiang" [A dialectical dramatic image: On the characterization of Galileo]. *Xiju yishu luncong* [Research series on dramatic art] 10 (1979):220–25.

Lin, Piao (Lin Biao). *Long Live the Victory of People's War! In Commemoration of the 20th Anniversary of Victory in the Chinese People's War of Resistance against Japan* [*Renmin zhanzheng shengli wansui*]. Beijing: Foreign Languages Press, 1965.

Link, Perry. "Ideology and Theory in the Study of Modern Chinese Literature: An Introduction." *Modern China* 19:1 (1993):4–12.

———. "Introduction." In Perry Link, ed., *Roses and Thorns: The Second Blooming of the Hundred Flowers in Chinese Fiction 1979–1980*. Berkeley: University of California Press, 1984, 1–41.

———. "Introduction: On the Mechanics of the Control of Literature in China." In Perry Link, ed., *Stubborn Weeds: Popular and Controversial Chinese Literature after the Cultural Revolution*. Bloomington: Indiana University Press, 1983, 1–28.

Link, Perry, ed., James Feinerman, trans., with Perry Link. *People or Monsters? And Other Stories and Reportage from China after Mao*. Bloomington: Indiana University Press, 1983.

Liu, Kang. "Politics, Critical Paradigms: Reflections on Modern Chinese Literary Studies." *Modern China* 19:1 (1993):13–40.

——— and Xiaobing Tang, eds. *Politics, Ideology, and Literary Discourse in Modern China: Theoretical Interventions and Cultural Critique*. Durham, N.C.: Duke University Press, 1993.

Liu, Lydia H. "*Beijing Sojourners in New York*: Postsocialism and the Question of Ideology in Global Media Culture." *Positions* 7:3 (Winter 1999):763–97.

———. *Translingual Practice*. Stanford, Calif.: Stanford University Press, 1995.

———, ed. *Chideng de shizhe* [The lamp carriers]. Hong Kong: Oxford University Press, 2001.

Liu, Tao Tao. Introduction. "Shu Ting: Selected Poems." Trans. Eva Hung. *Renditions* 27, 28 (1987):253–55.

Liu Xiaobo. "Yizhong xin de shenmei sichao—cong Xu Xing, Chen Cun, Liu Suola de sanbu zuopin tanqi" [A new aesthetic trend—on three recent works of Xu Xing, Chen Cun, and Liu Suola]. *Wenxue pinglun* [Literary review] 3 (1986):35–43.

Liu, Xiaohong. "A Revolutionary Institution-Builder: Zhang Wentian." In her *Chinese Ambassadors: The Rise of Diplomatic Professionalism since 1949*. Seattle: University of Washington Press, 2001, 31–52.

Lovell, Terry. "Writing like a Woman: A Question of Politics." In Mary Eagleton, ed., *Feminist Literary Theory: A Reader*. Oxford: Basil Blackwell, 1986, 83–85.

Lu, Tonglin, ed. *Gender and Sexuality in Twentieth-Century Chinese Literature and Society*. Albany: State University of New York Press, 1993.

Lu Xun. "Tengye xiansheng [Professor Fujino]." In his *Lu Xun quanji* [Complete works of Lu Xun]. 16 vols. Beijing: Renmin chubanshe, 1981. Vol. 2, 302–9.

———. "Mr. Fujino." In his *Selected Works of Lu Hsun*. 4 vols. Beijing: Foreign Languages Press, 1956. Vol. 1, 402–9.

Ma, Chih-yüan (Ma Zhiyuan). *Autumn in Han Palace.* In *Six Yüan Plays.* Trans. Liu Jung-en. London: Penguin, 1972, 189–224.

Ma Desheng. "The Age of Reflection" [Fanxing de shidai]. In Liao Yiwu, ed., *Chenlun de shengdian* [The fall of the sacred hall]. Wulumuqi: Xinjiang qingshaonian chubanshe, 1999, 467–72.

MacKerras, Colin. *Chinese Drama: A Historical Survey.* Beijing: New World Press, 1990.

———. *The Chinese Theater in Modern Times: From 1840 to the Present Day.* London: Thames and Hudson, 1975.

———. *The Performing Arts in Contemporary China.* London: Routledge and Kegan Paul, 1981.

———, ed. *Chinese Theater: From Its Origins to the Present Day.* Honolulu: University of Hawaii Press, 1983.

Mao, Zedong. *Mao Zedong's "Talks at the Yan'an Conference on Literature and Art": A Translation of the 1943 Text with Commentary.* Trans. Bonnie S. McDougall. Ann Arbor: Center for Chinese Studies, University of Michigan, 1980.

———. "Qingnian yundong de fangxiang" [The orientation of the youth movement]. In *Mao Zedong xuanji* [Selected works of Mao Zedong]. Beijing: Renmin chubanshe, 1964.

———. *Selected Works of Mao Tse-tung.* Vol. 2. Beijing: Foreign Languages Press, 1975.

McDougall, Bonnie S. *The Introduction of Western Literary Theories into Modern China, 1919–1925.* Tokyo: Center for East Asian Cultural Studies, 1971.

McNeill, William H. *Arnold J. Toynbee: A Life.* New York: Oxford University Press, 1989.

Mei, Shaowu. "Mei Lanfang as Seen by His Foreign Audiences and Critics." In Wu Zuguang, Huang Zuolin, and Mei Shaowu, *Peking Opera and Mei Lanfang.* Beijing: New World Press, 1981, 46–65.

Meisner, Maurice. *Marxism, Maoism, and Utopianism: Eight Essays.* Madison: University of Wisconsin Press, 1982.

Meng, Yue and Dai Jinhua. *Fuchu lishi dibao* [Emerging from the surface of history]. Zhengzhou: Henan renmin chubanshi, 1989.

Miao Deyu. "Weishenme xie rangren dubudong de shi?" [Why would one write incomprehensible poems?]. *Shikan* Oct. 1980:53.

Miao Yushi et al. "Jinnianlai shige pinglun siren tan" [Four critics' views on poetic criticism in recent years]. *Shi tansuo* [Poetic experiment] 3 (1982):82–93.

Millett, Kate. *Sexual Politics.* Garden City, N.Y.: Doubleday, 1970.

Minear, Richard H. "Orientalism and the Study of Japan." *The Journal of Asian Studies* 39:3 (1980):507–18.

Miner, Earl. *The Japanese Tradition in British and American Literature.* Princeton: Princeton University Press, 1958.

Minford, John. "Into the Mist." *Renditions* 19, 20 (1983):182–86.

Mitchell, Juliet. *Women: The Longest Revolution: Essays on Feminism, Literature, and Psychoanalysis.* London: Virago, 1984.

Miyoshi, Masao. *Off Center: Power and Culture Relations between Japan and the United States.* Cambridge: Harvard University Press, 1991.

Moi, Toril. "Feminist, Female, Feminine." In Ann Jefferson and David Robey, eds., *Modern Literary Theory: A Comparative Introduction.* 2nd ed. London: Batsford, 1986, 204–21.

Moran, Thomas. "True Stories: Contemporary Chinese Reportage and Its Ideology and Aesthetic." Ph.D. diss., Cornell University, 1994.

Mulvey, Laura. "Visual Pleasure and Narrative Cinema." *Screen* 16:3 (1975):6–19.

"Nanjing Daxue Zhongguo Sixiangjia Yanjiu Zhongxin juxing *He shang* zuotanhui" [Nanjing University Research Center for Chinese Thinkers held seminar on *He shang*]. *Guangming Ribao* 20 Nov. 1988:3.

Niu Daifeng. *Lu Xun zhuan* [Biography of Lu Xun]. Beijing: Zhongguo wenlian chuban gongsi, 1999.

O'Hanlon, Rosalind. "Recovering the Subject: *Subaltern Studies* and Histories of Resistance in Colonial South Asia." *Modern Asian Studies* 22:1 (1988):189–224.

Ong, Aihwa, and Donald Nonini, eds. *Ungrounded Empires: The Cultural Politics of Modern Chinese Transnationalism*. New York: Routledge, 1997.

Ouyang Yuqian. *Huijia yihou* [Homecoming]. In Hong Shen, ed., *Zhongguo xin wenxue daxi—xijuji*. Shanghai: Liangyou tushu yinshua gongsi, 1935. Vol. 9, 197–216.

Pan, Yuan and Pan Jie. "The Non-Official Magazine *Today* and the Younger Generation's Ideals for a New Literature." In Jeffrey C. Kinkley, ed., *After Mao*. Cambridge: Harvard University Press, 1985, 193–220.

Peng Ming. *Wusi yundong shi* [A history of the May Fourth movement]. Revised ed. Beijing: Renmin chubanshe, 1998.

Perkins, David. *A History of Modern Poetry: From the 1890s to the High Modernist Mode*. 2 vols. Cambridge: Harvard University Press, 1976, 1987.

Primeau, Ronald, ed. *Influx: Essays on Literary Influence*. Port Washington, N.Y.: Kennikat Press, 1977.

Pronko, Leonard Cabell. *Theater East and West: Perspectives toward a Total Theater*. Berkeley: University of California Press, 1967.

Qian Xuantong. "Random Thought" [Suigan lu]. *Xin qingnian* [New youth] 5:1 (1918):85.

Rahimieh, Nasrin. "Responses to Orientalism in Modern Eastern Fiction and Scholarship." *Dissertation Abstracts International* 49 (1988):05A. University of Alberta.

"Report Views Errors in 'River Elegy.'" *National Affairs* 26 Jan. 1990:25–31.

Said, Edward. *Culture and Imperialism*. New York: Alfred A. Knopf, 1993.

———. Letter. *Times Literary Supplement* 19 Mar. 1993:15.

———. *Orientalism*. New York: Vintage, 1979.

Schaub, Uta Liebmann. "Foucault's Oriental Subtext." *PMLA* 104:3 (1989): 306–15.

Schwarcz, Vera. "Ibsen's Nora: The Promise and the Trap." *Bulletin of Concerned Asian Scholars* 7:1 (1975):3–5.

———. *The Chinese Enlightenment: Intellectuals and the Legacy of the May Fourth Movement of 1919*. Berkeley: University of California Press, 1986.

Schwartz, Benjamin I. *In Search of Wealth and Power: Yen Fu and the West*. Cambridge: Harvard University Press, 1964.

Selden, Mark. "Introduction" to a Symposium on *He shang*. *Bulletin of Concerned Asian Scholars* 23:3 (1991):3.

Shapiro, Judith. "22 Years as a Class Enemy." Review of *A Single Tear*, by Wu Ningkun. *The New York Times Book Review* 28 Feb. 1993:12.

Shen, Fan. "Shakespeare in China: *The Merchant of Venice*." *Asian Theater Journal* 5:1 (1988):23–37.

Shi Songhan. *Zhang Wentian sixiang yanjiu* [On Zhang Wentian thought]. Beijing: Zhongguo dangshi chubanshe, 1993.

Shi Tianhe. "Zhongguo zuigu de yishou yixiang shi" [The earliest imagist poem in China]. *Shi tansuo* 11 (1984):21–25.

Shih, Shu-mei. *The Lure of the Modern: Writing Modernism in Semicolonial China.* Berkeley: University of California Press, 2001.

Shu, Ting. "Shu Ting: Selected Poems." Trans. Eva Hung. Intro. Tao Tao Liu. *Renditions* 27, 28 (1987):253–69.

———. "Zhi xiangshu" [To an oak tree]. In Lao Mu, ed., *Xin shichao shiji.* Beijing: Beijing Daxue Wusi Wenxueshe, 1985, Vol. 1, 63–64.

Silverberg, Miriam. "Remembering Pearl Harbor, Forgetting Charlie Chaplin, and the Case of the Disappearing Western Woman: A Picture Story." *Positions* 1:1 (1993):24–76.

Singer, Irving. *Courtly and Romantic.* Vol. 2 of *The Nature of Love.* 3 vols. Chicago: University of Chicago Press, 1984.

Singh, Jyotsna. "Different Shakespeares: The Bard in Colonial/Postcolonial India." *Theater Journal* 41:4 (1989), 445–58.

Siu, Helen F. comp., trans. and intro. *Furrows: Peasants, Intellectuals, and the State.* Stanford, Calif.: Stanford University Press, 1990.

——— and Zelda Stern. "Introduction." In Helen F. Siu and Zelda Stern, eds., *Mao's Harvest: Voices from China's New Generation.* New York: Oxford University Press, 1983, xiii–1.

Smith, Adam. *An Inquiry in the Nature and Causes of the Wealth of Nations.* London: Methuen, 1904.

Snow, Philip. *The Star Raft: China's Encounter with Africa.* London: Weidenfeld and Nicolson, 1988.

Spence, Jonathan D. *The Search for Modern China.* New York: Norton, 1990.

Spivak, Gayatri Chakravorty. "Can the Subaltern Speak?" In Cary Nelson and Lawrence Crossburg, eds., *Marxism and the Interpretation of Culture.* Urbana and Chicago: University of Illinois Press, 1988, 271–313.

———. "A Literary Representation of the Subaltern: A Woman's Text from the Third World." In her *In Other Worlds: Essays in Cultural Politics.* New York: Routledge, 1988, 241–68.

Stoler, Ann L. "Making Empire Respectable: The Politics of Race and Sexual Morality in 20th-Century Colonial Cultures." *American Ethnologist* 16:4 (1989):634–59.

Su, Hsueh-lin. "Present Day Fiction and Drama in China." In Joseph Schyns et al., eds., *1500 Modern Chinese Novels and Plays.* Beijing: Verbiest Academy, 1948. Reprint. Hong Kong: Lung Men Bookstore, 1966.

Su Xiaokang. "Huhuan quan minzu fanxing yishi" [Calling on the self-reflective consciousness of the Chinese nation]. In Cui Wenhua, ed., *He shang lun.* Beijing: Wenhua yishu chubanshe, 1988, 87–90.

———. "Longnian de beicang—guanyu *He shang* de zhaji" [The sorrow of the year of the dragon—sketches from *He shang* on location]. In his *Ziyou beiwang lu: Su Xiaokang baogao wenxue jingxuan* [Memoir on freedom: Selected works of Su Xiaokang's reportage]. Hong Kong: Sanlian shudian, 1989, 263–94.

―――― and Wang Luxiang et al. *Deathsong of the River: A Reader's Guide to the Chinese TV Series Heshang*. Intro., trans. and annot. Richard W. Bodman and Pin P. Wan. Ithaca: Cornell University East Asian Program, 1991.

――――. *He shang* [River elegy]. In Cui Wenhua, ed., *He shang lun* [About *He shang*]. Beijing: Wenhua yishu chubanshe, 1988, 1–80.

――――. *He shang* [River elegy]. Ed. Weng Ningna. Taiwan: Jinfeng chubanshe and fengyun shidai chubanshe, 1988.

Sun, Cecile Chu-Chin. "Problems of Perspective in Chinese-Western Comparative Literature Studies." *Canadian Review of Comparative Literature* 13:4 (1986): 531–48.

Sun Shaozhen. "Xin de meixue yuanze zai jueqi" [A new aesthetic principle is emerging]. *Shikan* Mar. 1981:55–58.

Sun, William Huizhu. "Mei Lanfang, Stanislavsky and Brecht on China's Stage and Their Aesthetic Significance." In Constantine Tung and Colin MacKerras, eds., *Drama in the People's Republic of China*. Albany: State University of New York Press, 1987, 137–50.

Szondi, Peter. *Theory of the Modern Drama*. Ed. and trans. Michael Hays. Minneapolis: University of Minnesota Press, 1987.

Tam, Kwok-kan. "Ibsen and Modern Chinese Dramatists: Influences and Parallels." *Modern Chinese Literature* 2:1 (1986):45–62.

Tandeciarz, Silvia. "Reading Gayatri Spivak's 'French Feminism in an International Frame': A Problem for Theory." *Genders* 10 (Spring 1991):75–90.

Tang, Xiaobing. "Orientalism and the Question of Universality: The Language of Contemporary Chinese Literary Theory." *Positions* 1:2 (1993):389–413.

Tatlow, Antony and Tak-Wai Wong, eds. *Brecht and East Asian Theatre: The Proceedings of a Conference on Brecht in East Asian Theatre*. Hong Kong: Hong Kong University Press, 1982.

Tay, William. "Avant-garde Theater in Post-Mao China: *The Bus-stop* by Gao Xingjian." In Howard Goldblatt, ed., *Worlds Apart: Recent Chinese Writing and Its Audiences*. Armork, N.Y.: M. E. Sharpe, 1990, 111–18.

――――. "'Obscure Poetry': A Controversy in Post-Mao China." In Jeffrey C. Kinkley, ed., *After Mao: Chinese Literature and Society*. Cambridge: Harvard University Press, 1985, 133–57.

"Television in China: Rolling River." *The Economist* 19 Nov. 1988:105.

Toynbee, Arnold J. and Daisaku Ikeda. *The Toynbee-Ikeda Dialogue: Man Himself Must Choose*. Tokyo: Kodansha International, 1976.

Trinh, T. Minh-Ha. *Woman, Native, Other: Writing Postcoloniality and Feminism*. Bloomington: Indiana University Press, 1989.

Tung, Constantine. "T'ien Han and the Romantic Ibsen." *Modern Drama* 9:4 (1967):389–95.

―――― and Colin MacKerras, eds. *Drama in the People's Republic of China*. Albany: State University of New York Press, 1987.

van Crevel, Maghiel. *Language Shattered: Contemporary Chinese Poetry and Duoduo*. Leiden: Centre of Non-Western Studies, Leiden University, 1996.

Wagner, Rudolf. *Inside the Service Trade: Studies in Contemporary Chinese Prose*. Cambridge: Council on East Asian Studies, Harvard University, 1992.

Wakeman, Frederic Jr. "All the Rage in China." Review of *River Dirge* by Xia Jun. *New York Review of Books* 2 Mar. 1989:19–21.

Walsh, Correa Moylan. *Feminism*. New York: Sturgois and Walton, 1917.

Wandor, Michelene. *Understudies: Theatre and Sexual Politics*. London: Methuen, 1981.

Wang Dan. "Biyao de bianhu" [A necessary defense]. In Cui Wenhui, ed., *He shang lun*. Beijing: Wenhua yishu chubanshe, 1988, 205–10.

Wang, Jing. "*He shang* and the Paradoxes of Chinese Enlightenment." *Bulletin of Concerned Asian Scholars* 23:3 (1991):27–32.

Wang Hui. "Yijiubajiu shehui yundong yu Zhongguo 'xin ziyouzhuyi' de lishi genyuan" [Social movements of 1989 and historical roots of Chinese neo-liberalism]. *Zhongguo xiandai wenxue* [Modern Chinese literature] 19 (2000):451–501.

Wang, Xining. "An Unconventional Blend." *China Daily* 21 May 1985:5.

Watts, Peter. "Introduction." *Peer Gynt: A Dramatic Poem* by Henrik Ibsen. Trans. and intro. Peter Watts. New York: Penguin, 1966.

Weisstein, Ulrich. *Comparative Literature and Literary Theory: Survey and Introduction*. Bloomington: Indiana University Press, 1973.

Wilder, Thornton. *Our Town: A Play in Three Acts*. New York: Coward McCann, 1938.

Winetrout, Kenneth. *Arnold Toynbee: The Ecumenical Vision*. Boston: Twayne, 1975.

Wixted, John Timothy. "Reverse Orientalism." *Sino-Japanese Studies* 2:1 (1989), 17–27.

Wong, Yoon Wah. "The 'New Tide' That Came from America" and "Imagism and Hu Shi's Programme for Literary Revolution of 1917." In his *Essays on Chinese Literature: A Comparative Approach*. Kent Ridge, Singapore: Singapore University Press, 1988, 28–51.

Wong, Sau-ling Cynthia. *Reading Asian American Literature: From Necessity to Extravagance*. Princeton: Princeton University Press, 1993.

Wu Furong, ed. "*Makebaisi* yu Zhongguo wutai" [*Macbeth* and the Chinese stage]. *Waiguo xiju* [Foreign drama] 2 (1982):90–92.

Wu Liang. "Pipin de quexi" [An absence of criticism]. In Xiao Yin and Yi Ren, eds., *Kuayue dayang de gong'an—Manhadun de Zhongguo nüren zhengyi shilu*. Beijing: Guangming ribao chubanshe, 1993, 97–100.

Wu, Zuguang, Huang Zuolin, and Mei Shaowu. *Peking Opera and Mei Lanfang*. Beijing: New World Press, 1981.

Xia Zhongyi. "Tan xiandaipai yishu xingshi he jiqiao de jiejian" [On borrowing modernist artistic forms and techniques]. *Wenyi bao* 4 (1984):58–61.

Xiao Chi. "Zhongguo gudai shuqing shi de ziran yixiang" [The natural images of expressive poetry in classical Chinese tradition]. *Shi tansuo* 2 (1982):134–49.

———. *Zhongguo shige meixue* [The aesthetics of Chinese poetics]. Beijing: Beijing Daxue chubanshe, 1986.

Xiao Li et al. "Zhongren fenshuo *Manhadun de Zhongguo nüren*" [Different opinions expressed on *A Chinese Woman in Manhattan*]. In Xiao Yin and Yi Ren, eds., *Kuayue dayang de gong'an—Manhadun de Zhonguo nüren zhengyi shilu*. Beijing: Guangming ribao chubanshe, 1993, 105–6.

Xiao Qian, trans. *Pi'er jinte* [*Peer Gynt*]. *Waiguo xiju* 4 (1981):78–154.

Xiao Yin. "'Kuayang' caifang zhaji" ["Overseas" interviews]. In Xiao Yin and Yi Ren, eds., *Kuayue dayang de gong'an—Manhadun de Zhongguo nüren zhengyi shilu.* Beijing: Guangming ribao chubanshe, 1993.

—— and Yi Ren. "*Manhadun de Zhongguo nüren* zai zhengyi zhong" [A debate on *A Chinese Woman in Manhattan*]. In Xiao Yin and Yi Ren, eds., *Kuayue dayang de gong'an—Manhadun de Zhongguo nüren zhengyi shilu.* Beijing: Guangming ribao chubanshe, 1993, 1–16.

——, eds. *Kuayue dayang de gong'an—Manhadun de Zhongguo nüren zhengyi shilu* [A lawsuit across the oceans: A factual account of controversy on *A Chinese Woman in Manhattan*]. Beijing: Guangming ribao chubanshe, 1993.

Xie Mian. "Shiqule pingjing yihuo" [After the peace was gone]. *Shikan* Dec. 1980:8–11.

——. "Zai xin de jueqi mianqian" [Confronting the emergence of a new aesthetic principle]. *Guangming ribao* 7 May 1980:4, 7.

Xiong Yuanyi and Zhang Yulu. "Liuxuesheng wenxue yantaohui zongshu" [A seminar held on overseas student literature]. *Renmin ribao* 4 Feb. 1993, overseas ed.:8.

Xu Jingya. "Jueji de shiqun—ping woguo shige de xiandai qingxiang" [The emergence of new groups of poetry—on the modernist tendency in contemporary poetry in our country]. *Dangdai wenyi sichao* [Current trends in literature and art] 1 (1983):14–15, 24.

Xu Xiao. "Jintian yu wo" [*Today* and I]. In Liao Yiwu, ed., *Chenlun de shengdian* [The fall of the sacred hall]. Wulumuqi: Xinjiang qingshaonian chubanshe, 1999, 379–410.

Xu Xiaozhong. "Zaixian Yipusheng—daoyan *Pi'er jinte* de sikao" [Representing Ibsen: Thoughts on directing *Peer Gynt*]. *Xiju bao* 3 (1983):44–49.

—— and Li Zibo. Dir. *Makebaisi* [*Macbeth*], by William Shakespeare. Zhongyang Xiju Xueyuan [Central Drama School], Beijing, China, 1980.

—— and Li Zibo. "Maren de beiju: tan beiju *Makebaisi* jiqi yanchu" [The tragedy of the horse-man: On *Macbeth* and its production]. *Renmin xiju* [People's drama] 2 (1982):40–42.

Yan Li. "Xueye de xingwei" [The behavior of blood]. In Jiang Zengpei et al., eds., *Zhongguo liuxuesheng wenxue daxi* [A compendium of Chinese overseas student literature], *Dangdai xiaoshuo Oumei juan* [Contemporary fiction: Europe and America]. Shanghai: Shanghai wenyi chubanshe, 2000, 506–35.

——. "Wo ye he Baiyangdian zhan dian bianr" [I am also somewhat related to the Baiyangdian group of poets]. In Liao Yiwu, ed., *Chenlun de shengdian* [The fall of the sacred hall]. Wulumuqi: Xinjiang qingshaonian chubanshe, 1999, 277–81.

Yan Xiwu and Sun Qingwen. "Zan Hong Shen zai yishu shang de shouchuang jingshen" [On the innovative artistic spirit of Hong Shen]. In Sun Qingwen, ed., *Hong Shen yanjiu zhuanji* [Selected essays on Hong Shen]. Hangzhou: Zhejiang wenyi chubanshe, 1986, 134.

Yang Ping. "'Meiguo meng' de tuixiaoshang" [A saleswoman of the American dream]. In Xiao Yin and Yi Ren, eds., *Kuayue dayang de gong'an—Manhadun de Zhongguo nüren zhengyi shilu.* Beijing: Guangming ribao chubanshe, 1993:101–4.

Yang Tianchun. "Kan *Weinisi shangren*" [Watching *The Merchant of Venice*]. *Xiju yu dianying* [Drama and film] 7 (1981):28–31.

Yeh, Michelle. "International Theory and the Transnational Critic: China in the Age of Multiculturalism." In Rey Chow, ed., *Modern Chinese Literary and Cultural Studies in the Age of Theory: Reimagining a Field*. Durham, N.C.: Duke University Press, 2000, 251–80.

———. "Nature's Child and the Frustrated Urbanite: Expressions of the Self in Contemporary Chinese Poetry." *World Literature Today* Summer (1991):405–9.

You Zunming et al. "Zhou Li qishu qiren" [Concerning Zhou Li's personality and her book]. In Xiao Yin and Yi Ren, eds., *Kuayue dayang de gong'an—Manhadun de Zhongguo nüren zhengyi shilu*. Beijing: Guangming ribao chubanshe, 1993, 61–73.

Young, Stark. "Ambassador in Art." *The New Republic* 6 Apr. 1932:206–8.

———. "Mei Lanfang." *The New Republic* 5 Mar. 1930:74–75.

Yu Dafu. "Chenlun." In his *Yu Dafu xiaoshuo ji* [Short stories of Yu Dafu]. Hangzhou: Zhejiang wenyi chubanshe, 1985, 16–50.

———. "Sinking." Joseph S. M. Lau and C. T. Hsia, trans. In Joseph S. M. Lau and Howard Goldblatt, eds., *The Columbia Anthology of Modern Chinese Literature*. New York: Columbia University Press, 1995, 44–69.

Yu, Qiuyu. "Some Observations on the Aesthetics of Primitive Chinese Theater." Trans. Hu Dongsheng, Elizabeth Wichmann, and Gregg Richardson. *Asian Theater Journal* 6:1 (1989):12–30.

Yuan Kejia, Dong Hengxun, and Zheng Kelu, eds. *Waiguo xiandaipai zuopin xuan* [Selected works of foreign modernist literature], 2 vols. Shanghai: Shanghai wenyi chubanshe, 1981. Vol. 1, Part 1.

Yuan Zhiming. "*He shang* yu gaoji laosao" [*He shang* and the so-called sophisticated complaint]. *Guangming ribao* 18 Aug. 1988:3.

Yue, Ming-Bao. "Gendering the Origins of Modern Chinese Fiction." In Tonglin Lu, ed., *Gender and Sexuality in Twentieth-Century Chinese Literature and Society*. Albany: State University of New York Press, 1993, 47–65.

Zarrow, Peter. "Meanings of China's Cultural Revolution: Memoirs of Exile." *Positions* 7:1 (1999):165–91.

Zeng Zhennan. "*Manhadun de Zhongguo nüren* duhou" [Afterthoughts on *A Chinese Woman in Manhattan*]. In Xiao Yin and Yi Ren, eds., *Kuayue dayang de gong'an—Manhadun de Zhongguo nüren zhengyi shilu*. Beijing: Guangming ribao chubanshe, 1993, 90–93.

Zhang, Longxi. "Out of the Cultural Ghetto: Theory, Politics, and the Study of Chinese Literature." *Modern China* 19:1 (1993):71–101.

———. "Western Theory and Chinese Reality." *Critical Inquiry* 19 (1992):105–30.

Zhang Qihong. "Zai shijian he tansuo zhong de jidian tihui" [A few words about my experience in directing *The Merchant of Venice*]. *Renmin xiju* 1 (1981):17–19.

Zhang Wentian. *Lütu* [Journey]. In Jiang Zengpei, et al., eds., *Zhongguo liuxuesheng wenxue daxi* [A compendium of Chinese overseas student literature], *Jinxiandai xiaoshuo juan* [Modern fiction volume]. Shanghai: Shanghai wenyi chubanshe, 2000, 597–729.

Zhang, Xianliang. *Half of Man Is Woman*. Trans. Martha Avery. New York: Norton, 1988.

Zhang Xiaoyang. "Shaju yanchu yu shidai shenmei yishi" [Shakespearean production and aesthetic consciousness of contemporary times]. *Waiguo wenxue yanjiu* 3 (1988):68–74.

Zhou Li. *Manhadun de Zhongguo nüren* [A Chinese woman in Manhattan]. Beijing: Beijing chubanshe, 1992.

Zhou Peitong. "Jiyao dadan chuxin, yeyao zhongshi yuanzuo—ping Zhongguo Qingnian Yishu Juyuan yanchu de *Weinisi shangren*" [We need both daring innovations and faithful representations—on China Youth Art Theater's production of *The Merchant of Venice*]. *Renmin xiju* 1 (1981):19–21.

———. "Shashibiya xiju zai Zhongguo" [Shakespearean plays in China]. *Liaowang* [Observer] 15 (1986):39–41.

Zhou Qiwan, "Yuanyu dangdai shenghuo de shi" [Poems rooted in contemporary times]. *Shi tansuo* 3 (1982):42–52.

Zhou Zuoren. "Ren de wenxue" [Humanistic literature]. *Xin qingnian* [New youth] 5:6 (1918):609–18.

Index

About the Author

Xiaomei Chen is associate professor of Chinese and comparative literature at Ohio State University. She is the author of *Acting the Right Part: Political Theater and Popular Drama in Contemporary China* (2002) and editor of *Reading the Right Text: An Anthology of Contemporary Chinese Drama with a Critical Introduction* (2003). She is coeditor, with Claire Sponsler, of *East of West: Cross-Cultural Performance and the Staging of Difference* (2000).